# ADDITIONAL PRAISE FOR

# ONCE IN A GREAT CITY

"Elegiac and richly detailed . . . [Maraniss] conjures those boom years of his former hometown with novelistic ardor. . . . He creates a mosaic-like picture of the city that has the sort of intimacy and tactile emotion that Larry McMurtry brought to his depictions of the Old West, and the gritty sweep of David Simon's HBO series *The Wire*. . . . [Maraniss] succeeds with authoritative, adrenaline-laced flair. . . . The result is a buoyant Frederick Lewis Allen–like social history that's animated by an infectious soundtrack and lots of tactile details, and injected with a keen understanding of larger historical forces at work—both in Detroit and America at large. . . . Maraniss's evocative book provides a wistful look back at an era when those cracks were only just beginning to show, and the city still seemed a place of 'uncommon possibility' and was creating 'wondrous and lasting things.' "

—Michiko Kakutani, *The New York Times*

"Captivating . . . Maraniss hears the joyous sound of a city suddenly, improbably filled with hope. . . . Maraniss asks himself what in the city has lasted, a question that often haunts former Detroiters. The songs, he decides. Not the reforms, not the dream of racial justice, not the promise of a Great Society, but the wonderfully exuberant songs that came pouring out of Berry Gordy's studio. That's the tragedy at the core of this gracious, generous book. All that remains of the hopeful moment Maraniss so effectively describes is a soundtrack. And that isn't nearly enough."

—*The Washington Post*

"*Once in a Great City* is incandescent. Through evocative writing and prodigious research, David Maraniss offers us an unforgettable portrait of 1963 Detroit, muscular and musical, during the early days of Motown and the Mustang. Bursting with larger than life figures from Henry Ford II, Walter Reuther, and Mayor Jerome Cavanagh, to Berry Gordy, Martin Luther King, and Reverend C. L. Franklin, Aretha's father, this book is at once the chronicle of a city during its last fine time and also a classic American story of promise and loss."

—Gay Talese

"The great virtue of Maraniss's bighearted book is that it casts a wide net, collecting and seeking to synthesize these seemingly disparate strands. . . . Even where material is familiar, the connections Maraniss makes among these figures feel fresh. He's even better on the lesser known. . . . Motown is clearly where Maraniss's heart is, and it is where his materials—music, race, civil rights—come together most naturally. . . . You finish *Once in a Great City* feeling mildly shattered, which is exactly as it should be."

—*The New York Times Book Review*

"Maraniss has written a book about the fall of Detroit, and done it, ingeniously, by writing about Detroit at its height, Humpty Dumpty's most poignant moment being just before he toppled over. . . . An encyclopedic account of Detroit in the early sixties, a kind of hymn to what really was a great city. . . . The display of municipal energies is so impressive that every page haunts us with the questions What went wrong? How could so much go so wrong so rapidly? How did a city of so many fruitful tensions and monuments and intermediary institutions turn into the ruins we see now, with scarcely a third of its 1950 population remaining and so many of the sites that Maraniss mentions ruined or destroyed?"

—*The New Yorker*

"David Maraniss is a journalist's journalist. . . . The book explores the optimism that existed in those days and the signs of major problems to come. It's a fascinating political, racial, economic and cultural tapestry."

—*Detroit Free Press*

"David Maraniss turns back the clock to paint the picture of an American metropolis in its prime, [however, one where] the seeds of the city's future fall were already starting to take root. . . . The simple breadth of the book is impressive, with Maraniss merging and wrangling disparate storylines about culture, politics, race, and the Ford Mustang into a single patchwork image of the Motor City."

—*Christian Science Monitor*

"A compelling portrait of one of America's most iconic cities. . . . Maraniss highlights the class and race frictions that demarcated and defined the city and gives readers a glimpse of the colorful life of mobsters and moguls, entertainers and entrepreneurs. Among the famous Detroiters he highlights are Henry Ford II, Lee Iacocca, Berry Gordy Jr., George Romney, and the Reverend C. L. Franklin. Maraniss captures Detroit just as it is both thriving and dying, at the peak of its vibrancy and on the verge of its downfall."

—*Booklist*, starred review

"A sprawling portrait of Detroit at a pivotal moment."

—*Publishers Weekly*

"A colorful, detailed history of the rise and ultimate decline of Detroit."

—*Library Journal*

"Fast-paced, sprawling, copiously detailed look at 18 months—from 1962 to 1964—in the city's past. . . . Maraniss's brawny narrative evokes a city still 'vibrantly alive' and striving for a renaissance. An illuminating history of a golden era in a city desperately seeking to reclaim the glory."

—*Kirkus Reviews*

"[A] glimmering portrait of Detroit . . . that will leave the reader thoroughly haunted. . . . *Once in a Great City* has it all: significant scenes, tremendously charismatic figures, even a starry soundtrack. . . . Reading about the city in its heyday is like falling backward in time and running into someone whose youthful blush you'd completely forgotten. Detroit is that someone. She is bright and laughing, flickering before you like a specter from the past. I doubt I'll forget her anytime soon."

—*Bookpage*

"A sobering portrait of a city that felt itself to be at the peak of its power and influence. . . . The principal strength of Maraniss's book lies in his skill at marshaling copious research to serve his sophisticated account of a complex, vibrant city balanced on its tipping point. . . . Sadly, one can't avoid the conclusion that never again will it be the city David Maraniss portrays with empathy and candor in this impressive book."

—*Shelf Awareness*

"The book bustles with vivid characters. . . . This is a beautifully written tribute to that lost, great city."

—*The Boston Globe*

"Combining hindsight and insight with deep-dive research, Maraniss provides a clear-eyed flashback to a once-powerful manufacturing metropolis intoxicated by cheap gasoline, swaggering hubris and blue-sky confidence. . . . Maraniss examines modern history in the dogged manner of David Halberstam and Robert Caro. Between the lines, he leaves an unwritten thought for both today's optimists and pessimists. If things could go change so much in just fifty years, what might the next half-century bring?"

—*The Detroit News*

"One of America's finest non-fiction writers, a son of Detroit, offers a lively and meticulously researched account of how the city, once the engine room of America, began sputtering."

—*The Economist*

"Maraniss's well-written and researched book well remembers the city of Detroit in the early 1960s as a place where factories hummed, Motown rocked and the present gave little warning that Detroit would become a 'city of decay.' "

—*Seattle Times*

## ALSO BY **DAVID MARANISS**

*Barack Obama:*
*The Story*

*Into the Story:*
*A Writer's Journey through Life, Politics, Sports and Loss*

*Rome 1960:*
*The Summer Olympics That Stirred the World*

*Clemente:*
*The Passion and Grace of Baseball's Last Hero*

*They Marched into Sunlight:*
*War and Peace, Vietnam and America, October 1967*

*When Pride Still Mattered:*
*The Life of Vince Lombardi*

*The Clinton Enigma:*
*A Four and a Half Minute Speech Reveals This President's Entire Life*

*First in His Class:*
*A Biography of Bill Clinton*

*The Prince of Tennessee:*
*Al Gore Meets His Fate* (with Ellen Nakashima)

*"Tell Newt to Shut Up!"* (with Michael Weisskopf)

# A DETROIT STORY

# ONCE IN A GREAT CITY

DAVID MARANISS

SIMON & SCHUSTER PAPERBACKS

New York London Toronto Sydney New Delhi

**To the people of Detroit**

Simon & Schuster Paperbacks
An Imprint of Simon & Schuster, Inc.
1230 Avenue of the Americas
New York, NY 10020



First Simon & Schuster trade paperback edition September 2016

SIMON & SCHUSTER PAPERBACKS and colophon are registered trademarks of Simon & Schuster, Inc.

For information about special discounts for bulk purchases, please contact Simon & Schuster Special Sales at 1-866-506-1949 or business@simonandschuster.com

The Simon & Schuster Speakers Bureau can bring authors to your live event. For more information or to book an event contact the Simon & Schuster Speakers Bureau at 1-866-248-3049 or visit our website at www.simonspeakers.com.

*Interior design by Joy O'Meara*
*Maps by Gene Thorp*

Manufactured in the United States of America

10 9 8 7

The Library of Congress has cataloged the hardcover edition as follows:

Maraniss, David.
Once in a great city : a Detroit story / David Maraniss.
pages cm
Includes bibliographical references and index.
1. Detroit (Mich.)—History—20th century. I. Title.
F574.D457M35 2015
977.4'34—dc23

ISBN 978-1-4767-4838-2
ISBN 978-1-4767-4839-9 (pbk)
ISBN 978-1-4767-4840-5 (ebook)

Photo insert credits can be found on page 443.

# CONTENTS

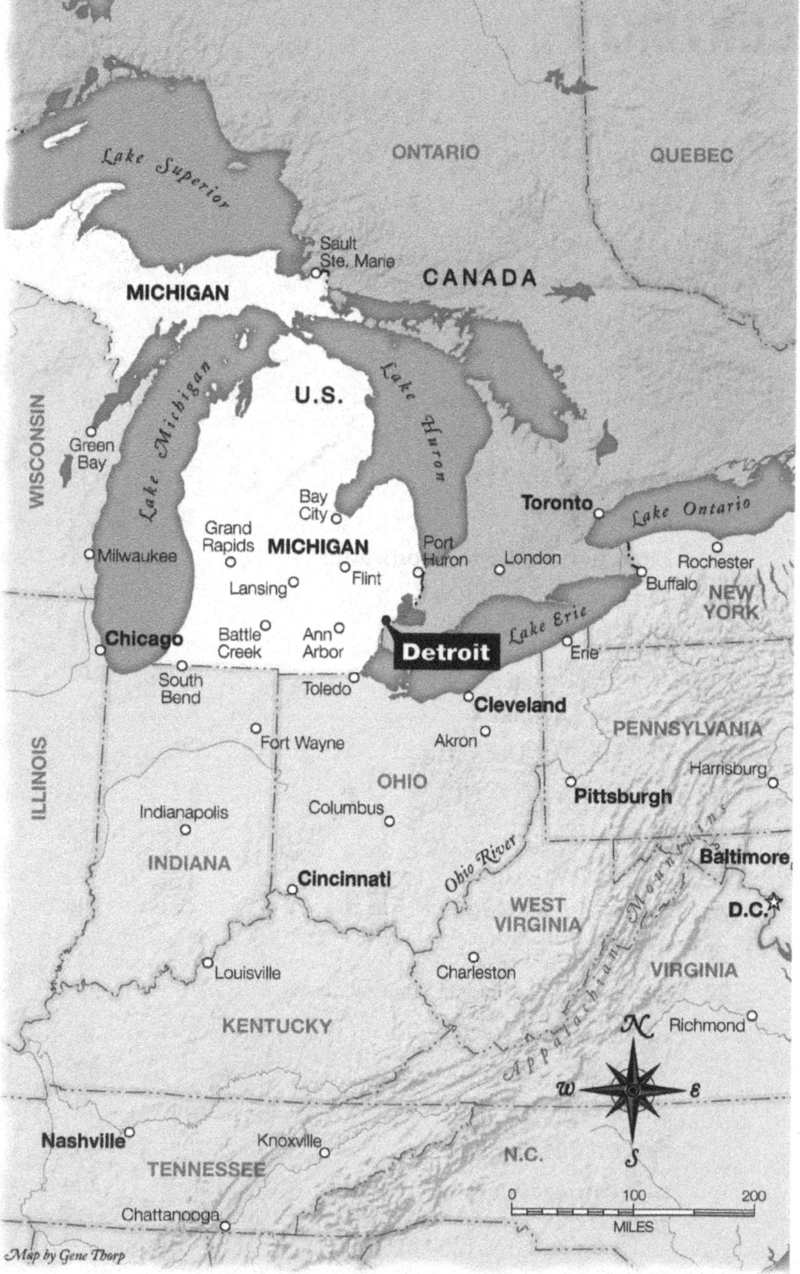

Lake Superior
ONTARIO
QUEBEC
Sault Ste. Marie
CANADA
MICHIGAN
U.S.
Lake Michigan
Lake Huron
WISCONSIN
Green Bay
Bay City
Toronto
Lake Ontario
Grand Rapids
MICHIGAN
Port Huron
London
Rochester
Milwaukee
Flint
Lansing
Buffalo
NEW YORK
Battle Creek
Ann Arbor
Lake Erie
Chicago
Detroit
Erie
South Bend
Toledo
Cleveland
Fort Wayne
Akron
PENNSYLVANIA
ILLINOIS
OHIO
Harrisburg
Pittsburgh
Indianapolis
Columbus
INDIANA
Ohio River
Baltimore
Cincinnati
Appalachian Mountains
WEST VIRGINIA
D.C.
Louisville
Charleston
VIRGINIA
KENTUCKY
Richmond
N
W
E
S
Nashville
Knoxville
TENNESSEE
N.C.
0
100
200
MILES
Chattanooga
Map by Gene Thorp

# AUTHOR'S NOTE

In a sense this book had been in the works since the summer of 1949, when I was born at Women's Hospital in Detroit, but the inspiration came on Super Bowl Sunday in early February 2011 as I watched the title game at a bar in midtown Manhattan. At halftime, with the Green Bay Packers on their way to victory, I was caught in the swirl of emotions of an anxious fan and barely paying attention to the studio commentary and commercials. Then I looked up at the screen to see a green freeway sign that said DETROIT. A series of images flashed by in rhythm to a pulsing sound track. Wintry landscape. Smokestacks. Abandoned factories. World-class architecture. The Joe Louis Fist. The Diego Rivera murals *Detroit Industry*. Ice skaters gliding, runners in hooded sweatshirts pounding onward, determined to keep going. The giant sculpture *The Spirit of Detroit*. A narrator, his voice confidently embracing the scene: *Now we're from America. But this isn't New York City, or the Windy City, or Sin City, and it certainly isn't the Emerald City.*

The camera swooped inside a Chrysler 200, leathered warm and black, and there was Marshall Mathers, the rapper known as Eminem, cruising down Woodward Avenue in his hometown, city of my birth, the back beat hypnotic as he approached the Fox Theater and stepped from the sedan and past the golden marquee and walked down the aisle toward a black gospel choir, robed in red and black, their voices rising high and hopeful into the darkness from the floodlit stage. Then silence, and Eminem pointing at the camera: *This is the Motor City. This is what we do.*

By the time it was over, I was choked up. It took my wife to point out the obvious: this was a commercial, playing on emotion, selling something, image more than reality, and Detroit was a mess, its people struggling. All inarguably true, yet I also realized that my response was real and had been triggered by something deeper than propaganda. I had lived in Detroit for the first six and a half years of my life. My earliest memories were there, in our flat on Dexter Avenue and house near Winterhalter School, where I learned to read and write in an integrated classroom. Hudson's department store, the Boblo boat, Belle Isle, Briggs Stadium, Vernors ginger ale, the Rouge pool, the Fisher Y, the Ford Rotunda out by the highway on the way to our grandparents' house in Ann Arbor—these were the primordial places and things of my early consciousness. I've spent the rest of my life elsewhere, most of it in the college towns of Madison and Austin and in Washington, D.C., so I'd never thought of myself as a Detroiter. But Detroit came first, and the Chrysler commercial, whatever its intent, got me thinking in another direction.

I had no interest in buying the car; I wanted to write about the city. Detroit's decay was already in the news, and its eventual bankruptcy was predictable, but its vulnerable condition was something others could analyze. If the Detroit of today had become a symbol of urban deterioration, it seemed important not to forget its history and a legacy that offered so many reasons to pull for its recovery. The story of Detroit was not just about the life and times of one city. The automobile, music, labor, civil rights, the middle class—so much of what defines our society and culture can be traced to Detroit, either made there or tested there or strengthened there. I wanted to illuminate a moment in time when Detroit seemed to be glowing with promise, and to appreciate its vital contributions to American life. To tell the story, I chose to go back not to the fifties, when my family lived there, but once again to the sixties, a decade I've explored in various ways in many of my books. It was not intentional, but as I was finishing, I came to think of *Once in a Great City* as the middle text in a sixties trilogy, filling the gap in time and theme between *Rome 1960,* about the sports and politics of the Summer Olympics, and *They Marched into Sunlight,* dealing with the Vietnam war and the antiwar movement in 1967.

The city itself is the main character in this urban biography, though its populace includes many larger-than-life figures—from car guy Henry Ford II to labor leader Walter Reuther; from music mogul Berry Gordy Jr. to the Reverend C. L. Franklin, the spectacular Aretha's father—who take Detroit's stage one after another and eventually fill it.

The chronology here covers eighteen months, from the fall of 1962 to the spring of 1964. Cars were selling at a record pace. Motown was rocking. Labor was strong. People were marching for freedom. The president was calling Detroit a "herald of hope." It was a time of uncommon possibility and freedom when Detroit created wondrous and lasting things. But life can be luminescent when it is most vulnerable. There was a precarious balance during those crucial months between composition and decomposition, what the world gained and what a great city lost. Even then, some part of Detroit was dying, and that is where the story begins.

# ONCE IN A GREAT CITY

## Chapter 1

# GONE

**THE NINTH OF NOVEMBER** 1962 was unseasonably pleasant in the Detroit area. It was an accommodating day for holiday activity at the Ford Rotunda, where a company of workmen were installing exhibits for the *Christmas Fantasy* scheduled to open just after Thanksgiving. Not far from a main lobby display of glistening next-model Ford Thunderbirds and Galaxies and Fairlanes and one-of-a-kind custom dream cars, craftsmen were constructing a life-size Nativity scene and a Santa's North Pole workshop surrounded by looping tracks of miniature trains and bountiful bundles of toys. This quintessentially American harmonic convergence of religiosity and consumerism was expected to attract more than three-quarters of a million visitors before the season was out, and for a generation of children it would provide a lifetime memory—walking past the live reindeer Donner and Blitzen, up the long incline toward a merry band of hardworking elves, and finally reaching Santa Claus and his commodious lap.

The Ford Rotunda was circular in an automotive manufacturing kind of way. It was shaped like an enormous set of grooved transmission gears, one fitting neatly inside the next, rising first 80 then 90 then 100 then 110 feet, to the equivalent of ten stories. Virtually windowless, with its steel frame and exterior sheath of Indiana limestone, this unusual structure was the creation of Albert Kahn, the prolific architect of Detroit's industrial age. Kahn had designed it for the Century of Progress exposition in Chicago, where Ford's 1934 exhibit hall chronicled the history of transportation from the horse-drawn carriage to the latest Ford V-8. When that Depression-era fair shuttered, workers dismantled the Rotunda and moved it from the south side shore of Lake Michigan to Dearborn, on the southwest rim of Detroit, where it was reconstructed to serve as a showroom and visitors center across from what was then Ford Motor Company's world headquarters. Later two wings were added, one to hold Ford's archives and the other for a theater.

In the fullness of the postwar fifties, with the rise of suburbs and two-car garages and urban freeways and the long-distance federal interstate system, millions of Americans paid homage to Detroit's grand motor palace. For a time, the top five tourist attractions in the United States were Niagara Falls, the Great Smokey Mountains National Park, the Smithsonian Institution, the Lincoln Memorial, and the Ford Rotunda. The Rotunda drew more visitors than Yellowstone, Mount Vernon, the Statue of Liberty, or the Washington Monument. Or so the Ford publicists claimed. Chances are you have not heard of it.

To appreciate what the Rotunda and its environs signified then to Detroiters, a guide would be useful, and for this occasion Robert C. Ankony fills the role. Ankony (who went on to become an army paratrooper and narcotics squad officer, eventually earning a PhD in sociology from Wayne

State University) was fourteen in November 1962, a chronic juvenile delinquent who specialized in torching garages. Desperate to avoid drudgery and boredom, he knew the Rotunda the way a disaffected boy might know it. Along with the Penobscot Building, the tallest skyscraper downtown, the Rotunda was among his favorite places to hang out when he played hooky, something he did as often as possible, including on that late fall Friday morning.

"The Highway" is what Ankony and his friends called the area where they lived in the southwest corner of Detroit. The highway was West Vernor, a thoroughfare that ran east through the neighborhood toward Michigan Central Station, the grand old beaux arts train depot, and west into adjacent Dearborn toward Ford's massive River Rouge Complex, another Albert Kahn creation and the epicenter of Ford's manufacturing might. In *Detroit Industry,* the legendary twenty-seven-panel murals at the Detroit Institute of Arts painted by Diego Rivera and commissioned by Edsel Ford, the founder's son, among the few distinguishable portraits within the scenes of muscular Ford machines and workers is that of Kahn, wearing wire-rim glasses and work overalls. Ankony experienced Detroit industry with all of his senses: the smoke and dust and smells drifted downwind in the direction of his family's house two miles away on Woodmere at the edge of Patton Park. His mother, Ruth, who could see the smokestacks from her rear window, hosed the factory soot off her front porch every day. What others considered a noxious odor the Ankonys and their neighbors would describe as the smell of home.

On the morning of November 9, young Bob reported to Wilson Junior High, found another boy who was his frequent collaborator in truancy, and hatched plans for the day. After homeroom, they pushed through the double doors with the horizontal brass panic bars, ran across the school grounds and over a two-foot metal fence, scooted down the back alley, and were free, making their way to West Vernor and out toward Ford country.

It was a survival course on the streets, enlivened by the thrill of avoiding the cops. Slater's bakery for day-old doughnuts, claw-shaped with date fillings, three cents apiece. Scrounging curbs and garbage cans for empty soda bottles and turning them in for two cents each. If they had enough pennies, maybe go for a dog at the Coney Island on Vernor. Rounding the curve where Vernor turned to Dix, past the Dearborn Mosque and the Arab storefronts of east Dearborn. (Ankony's parents were Lebanese and French; he grew up being called a camel jockey and "little A-rab.") Fooling around at the massive slag piles near Eagle Pass. Dipping down into the tunnel leading toward the Rouge, leaning over a walkway railing and urinating on cars passing below, then up past the factory bars, Salamie's and Johnny's, and filching lunches in white cardboard boxes from the ledge of a sandwich shop catering to autoworkers on shift change. Skirting the historic overpass at Miller Road near Rouge's Gate 4, where on an afternoon in late May 1937 Walter Reuther and his fellow union organizers were beaten by Ford security goons, a violent encounter that Ankony's father, who grew up only blocks away, told his family he had witnessed. Gazing in awe at the Rouge plant's fearsomely majestic industrial landscape from the bridge at Rotunda Road, then on to the Rotunda itself, where workmen were everywhere, not only inside installing the Christmas displays but also outside repairing the roof.

To Ankony, the Rotunda was a wonderland. No worries about truant officers; every day brought school groups, so few would take notice of two stray boys. With other visitors, including on that day a school group from South Bend, they took in the new car displays and a movie about Henry Ford, then blended in with the crowd for a factory tour that left by bus from the side of the Rotunda over to the Rouge plant, then the largest industrial complex in the United States. Ankony had toured the Rouge often, yet the flow of molten metal, the intricacies of the engine plant, the mechanized perfection of the assembly, all the different-colored car parts coming down the line and matching up, the wonder of raw material going in and a finished product coming out, the reality of scenes depicted in Rivera's murals, thrilled him anew every time. The Rouge itself energized him even as Rivera's famed murals frightened him. The art, more than the place itself, reminded him of the gray, mechanized life of a factory worker "in those dark dungeons" that seemed expected of a working-class Detroit boy and that he so much yearned to avoid.

When the Rouge tour ended in early afternoon, Ankony and his pal had had enough of Ford for the day and left for a shoplifting spree at the nearby Montgomery Ward store at the corner of Schaefer Road and Michigan Avenue, across the street from Dearborn's city hall. They were in the basement sporting goods department, checking out ammo and firearms, when they heard a siren outside, then another, a cacophony of wailing fire trucks and screeching police cars. The boys scrambled up and out and saw smoke billowing in the distance. Fire!—and they didn't start it. Fire in the direction of the Rotunda. They raced toward it.

Roof repairmen since midmorning had been taking advantage of the fifty-degree weather to waterproof the Rotunda's geodesic dome panels. Using propane heaters, they had been warming a transparent sealant so that it would spray more easily. At around 1 p.m., a heater ignited sealant vapors, sparking a small fire, and though workmen tried to douse the flames with extinguishers they could not keep pace and the fire spread. The South Bend school group had just left the building. Another tour for thirty-five visitors was soon to begin. There was a skeleton staff of eighteen office workers inside; many Rotunda employees were at lunch. A parking lot guard noticed the flames and radioed inside. Alarm bells were sounded, the building was evacuated, the roof repairmen crab-walked to a hatch and scrambled down an inside stairwell, and the Dearborn and Ford fire departments were summoned, their sirens piercing the autumn air, alerting, among others, two truant boys in the Monkey Ward's basement.

By the time firefighters reached the Rotunda, the entire roof, made of highly combustible plastic and fiberglass, was ablaze. Two aerial trucks circled around to the rear driveway. From the other side, firefighters and volunteers stretched hoses from Schaefer Road and moved forward cautiously. It was too hot, and the water pressure too limited, to douse the fire with sprays up and over the 110 feet to the roof. The structure's steel frame began to buckle. At 1:56, fire captains ordered their men away from the building, just in time. Robert Dawson, who worked in the Lincoln-Mercury building

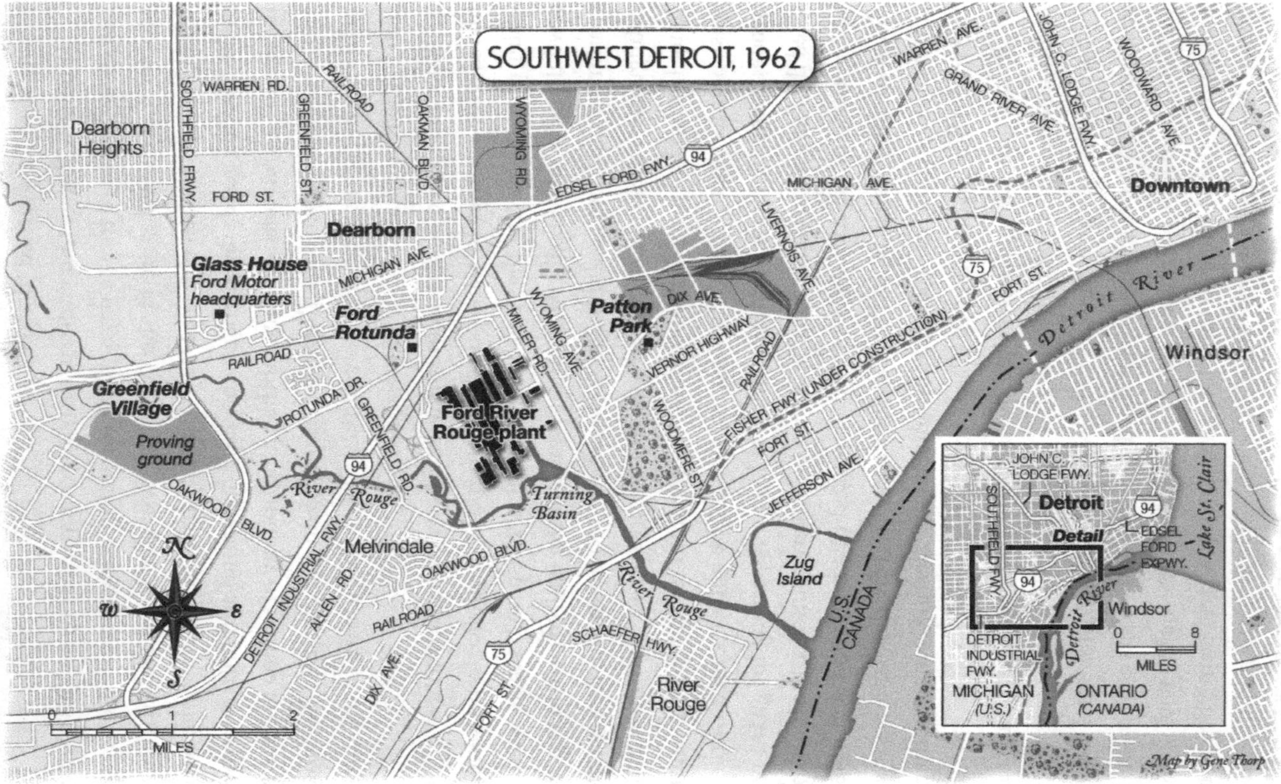
SOUTHWEST DETROIT, 1962
Dearborn Heights
WARREN RD.
SOUTHFIELD FRWY.
GREENFIELD ST.
RAILROAD
OAKMAN BLVD.
WYOMING RD.
FORD ST.
EDSEL FORD FWY.
94
MICHIGAN AVE.
WARREN AVE.
GRAND RIVER AVE.
JOHN C. LODGE FWY.
WOODWARD AVE.
75
Downtown
Dearborn
Glass House
Ford Motor headquarters
Ford Rotunda
MICHIGAN AVE.
RAILROAD
Greenfield Village
Proving ground
ROTUNDA DR.
GREENFIELD RD.
MILLER RD.
WYOMING AVE.
Patton Park
DIX AVE.
LIVERNOIS AVE.
VERNOR HIGHWAY
RAILROAD
FISHER FWY. (UNDER CONSTRUCTION)
FORT ST.
Ford River Rouge plant
River Rouge
Turning Basin
WOODMERE ST.
FORT ST.
JEFFERSON AVE.
Detroit River
Windsor
OAKWOOD BLVD.
Melvindale
OAKWOOD BLVD.
DETROIT INDUSTRIAL FWY.
ALLEN RD.
RAILROAD
DIX AVE.
FORT ST.
SCHAEFER HWY.
River Rouge
Zug Island
U.S.
CANADA
N
W
E
S
0
1
2
MILES
JOHN C. LODGE FWY.
SOUTHFIELD FWY.
Detroit
Detail
EDSEL FORD EXPWY.
Lake St. Clair
Detroit River
Windsor
DETROIT INDUSTRIAL FWY.
MICHIGAN (U.S.)
ONTARIO (CANADA)
0
8
MILES
Map by Gene Thorp

across the street, looked over and saw a "ball of fire" on the roof but at first no flames below. "Suddenly the roof crashed through. Everything inside turned to flame. Smoke began sifting through the limestone walls. Then, starting at the north corner, the walls crumbled. It was as though you had stacked dominoes and pushed them over." The fire had reached the Christmas displays, fresh and potent kindling, and raged out of control, bright flames now shooting fifty feet into the sky. The entire building collapsed in a shuddering roar, a whirlwind of hurtling limestone and concrete and dust.

Fire officials, aided by a prevailing northeast wind, concentrated on saving the north wing, where the Ford archives were stored. The south wing was already gone, its 388-seat theater a crisped shell. At the perimeter, Bob Ankony and his buddy angled for a closer look. "There were a bunch of security guys there trying to keep us back. One guy, we were pushing him to get past. We wanted to get right up to the fire," Ankony recalled. "I was into burning garages. We had torched garages with cars in them. Now we just wanted to see cars on fire. We were youths and stupid." The security guard held them back. The boys picked up chunks of rock and dirt and started throwing them at the guard. This attracted the attention of some nearby Dearborn cops, who took the teenagers into custody and hauled them to the police station.

For days thereafter, Ankony and his pal held exalted status among the Cabot Street Boys, the gang of young delinquents in his southwest Detroit neighborhood. Word spread that they had taken their petty arson up several notches and burned down the great Rotunda. The more they denied it, the more they were disbelieved.

The rest of Detroit was mourning the loss. In his "Town Crier" column, Mark Beltaire of the *Free Press,* who as a teenager had visited the original Rotunda pavilion at the fair in Chicago, wrote, "Tears for a building? Of course, and many when such as the Ford Rotunda dies. Over the years the Rotunda acquired a special personality all its own. It was known and recognized by people who had never been inside. They were aware of the Rotunda especially by night, even while driving many miles away." Another columnist wrote that the Rotunda "had stood for more than a quarter century as testimony to Detroit's industrial eminence. Its history was wrapped inextricably with that of the modern automotive industry." The Rotunda's manager, John G. Mullaly, who had been on leave to organize Ford Motor Company pavilions at the Seattle and New York World's Fairs, returned to tour the charred remains with the manager of the Christmas program. Fifteen million dollars up in smoke, a holiday tradition ruined, and a symbol of the Motor City's might in ashes, the visitor count permanently capped at 13,189,694. Mullaly and his boss, Henry Ford II, would not say so pub-

licly yet, but it was obvious that the Ford Rotunda could not and would not be rebuilt. Something was forever gone.

Late that same afternoon, as firefighters hosed down the remains of the Rotunda, George Edwards, commissioner of the Detroit Police Department, sat twelve miles away at 1300 Beaubien, waiting anxiously for his desk phone to ring. The address was literal and figurative: 1300 Beaubien was police headquarters and also shorthand for cop brass. The ten-story building was yet another Albert Kahn creation, hulking on a city block between Clinton and Macomb. Edwards had been at his job less than a year. He had stepped down from the Michigan Supreme Court and taken the top cop job at the behest of Detroit's new mayor, Jerome Cavanagh, a liberal Catholic acolyte of President Kennedy, and was tasked with reforming the force, making it more citizen-friendly, improving its relationship with the city's black population, or "Negro community," as it was called then. "It may well be that in the next several years the greatest contribution that I can make lies in seeking to resolve the dangerous tensions which threaten Detroit, and in seeking to make the Constitution a living document in one of our great cities," Edwards wrote to a close friend in a letter explaining the "improbable sequence of events" that led him to take the position. But even with that idealistic vision, his primary job as commissioner, always, was to fight crime, and the word he now so anxiously awaited dealt with the complicated nexus of those two missions.

The phone call finally came three and a half hours later, at 8:30 that night. Senior Inspector Art Sage, head of the vice squad, was on the other end of the line. "Boss, we got it," Sage reported triumphantly. "We got the whole schmozzle."

The whole schmozzle in this case was the gambling operation run out of the Gotham Hotel, long known to local cops and feds as the iron fortress of the numbers racket in Detroit. In the late afternoon dimness, two Department of Street Railways buses had pulled up to the establishment off John R Street at 111 Orchestra Place. The doors whooshed open, and out stormed 112 men wielding fire axes, crowbars, and sledgehammers from a joint task force of Detroit police, Michigan state police, and the intelligence unit of the Internal Revenue Service. The first officers off the bus also carried a warrant to search the entire hotel. Never before had they been able to obtain such a sweeping search warrant; for previous raids, of a more modest scale, they had had to ask for legal authority to search one room, two or three at most, and had been foiled by the gamblers, who protected their fortress with a sophisticated system of internal security monitors, alarms, and spies working inside the hotel and circling the nearby streets with two-way radios.

This time a federal undercover agent was planted inside for the single purpose of beating the desk clerk to the alarm buzzer, which he succeeded in doing. With a plan, an expansive warrant, and a full raiding company eager to go, the odds seemed better that the law would find what it was after. "They broke in here like members of the Notre Dame football team," John J. White, the Gotham's proprietor, told a sympathetic reporter from the *Michigan Chronicle.* In its headline of the raid, Detroit's leading black newspaper inserted the word "raging" before "football team."

The Gotham was not just any hotel. In its day, it was the cultural and social epicenter of black Detroit. John White was a capitalist success story, a small-town kid from Gallipolis, Ohio, who came to the big city with his siblings after his mother died, hovered around the gamblers and off-books financiers of Hastings Street, and eventually acquired enough money to buy the hotel in 1943. At a time when that section of town—not far from Wayne State University, one block from Woodward Avenue, and a short walk from Orchestra Hall—was mostly white, he extended the perimeter of the historically black district known as Paradise Valley. The Gotham, two solid brick towers connected in the middle with a penthouse on top, had once been the grand personal residence of Albert D. Hartz, who made his millions selling medical supplies. It was built for him by—who else?—architect Albert Kahn.

To walk into the Gotham on any day for most of the two decades after White took over was to enter a hall of fame of black culture. Everyone had stayed there. On the wall behind the front desk were signed photographs of Jackie Robinson, Joe Louis, Adam Clayton Powell, and the Ink Spots. The Brown Bomber, who had grown up in Detroit from age twelve, became a breakfast regular in the Gotham's Ebony Room, ordering five scrambled eggs with ketchup and a bone-in steak. The hotel's front counter had been built by Berry Gordy Sr., a jack-of-all-trades and father of the namesake president of Motown Records. Berry Gordy Jr.'s four older sisters—and soon enough all of Motown's women singers—were taught etiquette, posture, and social graces by Maxine Powell, who stayed at the Gotham for many years and held classes there. On a wall behind the thickly cushioned leather chairs in the lobby were color portraits of Sugar Ray Robinson, Judge Wade McCree, Congressman Charles Diggs Jr., and other black notables. John Conyers Jr., a young lawyer who would go on to join Diggs in Congress, made his way through Wayne State University Law School by selling Filter Queen vacuum cleaners; his biggest sale was to John White and the Gotham housekeeping staff. The Gotham deal was of such note, Conyers recalled, that it was reported in the following Wednesday's edition of the *Michigan Chronicle.* The leading black businessmen in Detroit gathered regularly at the hotel in formal-wear for events of the Gotham Club, distinguished fellows who were also lifetime members of the Detroit branch of the NAACP.

Employees at the Gotham were instructed to follow John White's courtesy code, which was printed and posted on every floor: *Never argue with a guest. It is never enough to be pleasant only with our guests. Spread it around among your fellow workers also. Guests judge our hotel by the three C's: courtesy, cheerfulness, and cordiality. Make it obvious you like people. Try to be tolerant toward the grouch and tactful with the impatient guest. A cheerful "Glad to see you, sir," or "It's nice to have you back with us madam," has made many a hotel cash register ring with repeat business.* (The Gordy family was connected to the courtesy code as well: the posters were printed by the Gordy Printing Company run by Fuller Gordy, Berry Jr.'s oldest brother.)

The poet Langston Hughes took note of the courtesies and other refinements at the Gotham in a 1949 column published in the *Chicago De-*

*fender*. "There is a kind of miracle taking place in Detroit," he wrote. "For this miracle good Catholics would thank Saint Christopher, the patron saint of travelers. I, as a good race man, thank whatever gods there be for the wonder of it all. This miracle I speak of is the Hotel Gotham, owned, managed and staffed by Negroes. The Hotel Gotham is one of the few Negro hotels in America where the dresser drawers open without a struggle, and where when you get them open they are not filled with the debris of all the guests who have occupied the room before you got there—hairpiece, spilled powder, comic books, cigarette butts, waste paper. It is one of the few Negro hotels where the closet shelves are neatly dusted and clean, and there are no beer bottles in odd corners that the maids have forgotten to remove, and no discarded bed springs leaning against the walls in the halls."

Who knew that the great bard could also be a combination of city health inspector and Leona Helmsley? In any case, the attributes of the Gotham that he so admired were shared by many other notables. Sammy Davis Jr. rented the entire fifth and sixth floors during stays in Detroit. B. B. King got married in room 609. Goose Tatum of the Harlem Globetrotters stayed in room 603. Louis Armstrong's valet would wash fifty handkerchiefs a night in the hotel's laundry. Duke Ellington, Billy Eckstine, Dizzy Gillespie, Billie Holiday, Josephine Baker, Ella Fitzgerald, Count Basie, Carmen McRae, Cab Calloway, Dinah Washington, and Nat King Cole enjoyed the luxury of the Gotham when they were performing at the Paradise Theater down the street or at the Flame Show Bar on John R. Many of them were chauffeured to the Gotham and around town in the back of a black Chrysler limousine driven by Papa Dee, a pint-size escort with long black-and-silver hair who dressed like Wyatt Earp. The Reverend C. L. Franklin, Detroit's flashiest and most entertaining preacher over at New Bethel Baptist, once kept an office at the Gotham, and he and his daughters, Erma, Carolyn, and Aretha, often took meals in the Ebony Room, whose world-class chef, Arthur Madison, was revered for, among other reasons, his delicious cheesecake and pastries known as Gotham rolls.

Martin Luther King Jr. stayed at the Gotham in the late summer of 1959 and wrote a thank-you letter dated September 25 after returning from a vacation in Hawaii: "Dear Mr. White, This is just a note to say how delighted I was to have the opportunity of meeting you on my recent visit to Detroit and being in your beautiful hotel. I certainly appreciate all of the courtesies that you extended, and I was greatly impressed by your concern for, and dedication to the ideas that we must all work to realize."

During his meeting with King, White broached the idea of placing a copy of one of the civil rights leader's books in every room to go along with the traditional top-drawer Bible. In a follow-up letter to King's thank-you note, White reported that the deed had been accomplished: "Dear Rev. King, We finally received our order for the books and have placed them in the rooms. They have been well received and we have received many compliments from our guests regarding the selection of *Stride Toward Freedom*. I enjoyed your philosophy so much that I felt the book must be passed on. I have sent a copy to the Police Department to be placed in their library."

And now here came those police barging into the Gotham with fire axes and crowbars and sledgehammers. Inspector Sage and Anthony Getto of the IRS had worked out the plan the night before at the federal building. They calculated that more than $15 million in illegal operations flowed through the hotel each year, most of it in numbers, and they were finally going to crack what was described as "one of America's largest non-taxpaying enterprises." Extra federal officers were flown to Detroit overnight to supplement the local cops. They divided into squads, each squad assigned a floor of the hotel. Although the agent stationed in the lobby beforehand managed to outrace a gambling spy to the alarm buzzer, a quick-thinking Gotham regular cut off power to the elevators soon after the first officers bum-rushed the front door. One squad raced to the tenth-floor penthouse, where a private club was operating, and interrupted a dice game with at least $5,000 in cash on the felt table. But when a club member demanded to see a search warrant, two officers had to clamber all the way down the stairs to the first floor to retrieve it, then huff and puff back to the top.

The proprietor was detained in his office. White, who had been honored with a Man of Distinction award in 1956 for advancing race relations and providing jobs in Detroit's black community, knew many of the officers and was on cordial terms with the department, but the exchange of pleasantries now covered a high-stakes confrontation. He later claimed that he would have given the police a pass key to every room had they asked for one, but instead they were "smashing everything in sight," floor by floor, axing their way into all 171 rooms. A reporter who had been tipped to the raid described how officers "started breaking down every door. Hallways were littered with splintered doors hanging from hinges."

Along with the penthouse, Sage and Getto and their men were interested in the corner suites, where their intelligence indicated that numbers runners would be counting the daily take. The suites were mostly empty, no runners caught in the act, but abundant clues remained. Commissioner Edwards had been fixated on the Gotham all year, since he had received an anonymous letter the previous January documenting the hotel's sophisticated gambling operation. He came to believe, he said later, that "stopping gambling at the Gotham was mandatory for the reputation of the city, the reputation of the police department, and for the reputation of the police commissioner." Now, on his first visit after the raid, he saw the evidence, including fifteen pairs of loaded dice and several decks of marked cards. "In the largest room of [each] suite, a number of tables had been pulled together and covered with felt to make them a large working area for processing 'the business'—the bet slips and the tabulations. In each there were adding or calculating machines to automate the process. The windows were carefully blanketed to exclude any shred of daylight. Liquid refreshments [were evident] for lightening the labors. Impressive evidence of the volume of business done was provided by the linen closets. In place of blankets, sheets, and pillow cases, these contained boxes of coin wrappers—more coin wrappers than I have ever seen in a bank."

Forty-one people were arrested. John White and eight associates who were believed to run the numbers operation were charged with failing to buy federal gambling stamps, while the others faced lesser state gambling charges. A professional safecracker was brought in to drill open several safes and after a few dry holes hit a jackpot of $49,222. The neat stacks of betting slips and other documents they recovered reaffirmed the contention of vice experts that among the bettors were thousands of Detroit factory workers playing ten to fifteen dollars a week on the numbers.

After being released on a $10,000 bond, White returned to the Gotham and drew up a list of damages and grievances. To a *Chronicle* reporter he described the raid as "a needless and uncalled for binge" that produced little. He took photographs of the damages and accused the officers of consuming his whiskey, soda, milk, and food. He canvassed employees and residents and charged that many personal items were missing, including six transistor radios, two binoculars, and a motion picture projector. The chef, Arthur Madison, said that his room was destroyed by the raid, the door axed, his dressers ransacked, and clothes strewn on the floor. Maybelle Moore, the hotel manicurist, reported seven dollars missing from her cash box.

White also claimed that adding machines and accounting slips found in one room were items a friend and hotel tenant had brought to the Gotham after his gasoline station at the corner of Brady and John R had been leveled in the name of urban renewal. The excuse would not hold, but the role of urban renewal in the raid was undeniable. Over the previous several years, in the name of progress, the city powers that be—politicians, planners, developers, construction magnates, and financiers—had overseen the demolition of large swaths of old black Detroit. Hastings Street, its vibrant, seedy heart, had been obliterated, making way for the Chrysler Freeway. The word on the street for what was going on was not urban renewal but "Negro removal."

Now the Gotham was designated for demolition to make way for a hospital parking garage. A federal judge had granted the sweeping search warrant precisely because the hotel's fate was assumed and the place was being emptied. When White complained to the law-enforcement raiders that they were destroying the Gotham, they responded by telling him not to worry, that the medical center was going to take his property anyway. The hotel that Langston Hughes had declared a miracle, that fed Joe Louis his eggs and steak, that displayed Martin Luther King's civil rights book in every room was giving way to change, for better and worse. Some part of Detroit was dying at the Gotham with every swing of the ax and blow from a sledgehammer, as surely as it was dying twelve miles away, where young Bob Ankony watched an inferno render the Ford Rotunda into smoldering ruins on that same November day.

## Chapter 2

# ASK NOT

**ONE MONTH EARLIER**, at 10:55 on the morning of October 7, Raymond Murray was stationed at the west entrance of the Sheraton Cadillac hotel when the president of the United States walked out toward a rippling sea of people stretching two blocks down Washington Boulevard. Murray was a rookie cop, sprung from the army and just a month out of the police academy, still living with his mother on Mansfield Street on Detroit's west side. He had finished first in his academy class on the scholastic tests, but it was his lack of seniority rather than apparent potential that got him assigned to the presidential detail when he reported for roll call that morning at 1300 Beaubien. He did not have a squad car and walked the mile from headquarters to the hotel. Sheraton Cadillac was the official name—it had been part of the chain for a decade by then—but Book Cadillac is what many people in Detroit called it, ever since the Book brothers opened it in the twenties as the largest hotel in America.

With its 1,200 rooms, four restaurants, capacious ballrooms, and dark, plush gentlemen's bar, the Book Cadillac was to establishment Detroit what the Gotham Hotel had been to black Detroit, a fulcrum of culture, sports, society, and political power, the place to stay and be seen. Spencer Tracy and Katharine Hepburn lodged there when filming Frank Capra's *State of the Union*. American League teams booked the Book when they came to play the Tigers. It was at the Book on May 2, 1939, that Lou Gehrig, the Iron Horse, feeling the incipient effects of his as-yet-undiagnosed amyotrophic lateral sclerosis, went up to the room of his manager and asked to be scratched from the Yankees lineup after playing in 2,130 straight games. Elvis and Sinatra and Presidents Hoover, FDR, and Truman made it their Detroit hotel of choice, and now President John F. Kennedy was staying there.

He had arrived the night before on the second stop of a political swing through the Midwest. This was JFK's first visit as president, but Detroit and nearby Ann Arbor held special meaning in his rise as places where he formulated some of the rhetoric and promise of his New Frontier. He had launched his 1960 general election campaign with a Labor Day speech to sixty thousand Detroiters who filled Cadillac Square and heard him recite an early and less poetic variation of what would become the immortal "ask not" line of his inaugural address: "The new frontier is not what I promise I am going to do for you. The new frontier is what I ask you to do for our country." Six weeks later, at two in the morning, after landing in Detroit, Kennedy made his way to Ann Arbor and greeted ten thousand students waiting for him outside the University of Michigan Union. There, in an impromptu speech, he first broached the notion of what would become the Peace Corps. "How many of you, who are going to be doctors, are willing to spend your days in Ghana?" he asked. "Technicians or engineers, how many of you are willing to work in the foreign service and spend your lives traveling around the world?" The answer came back with resounding affirmation when thousands of Michigan students signed a petition saying they were ready to serve their country peacefully abroad.

No unforgettable rhetoric or grand ideas were planned for this return trip. Upon arrival at Detroit Metropolitan Airport the night before, JFK declared that Michigan had "its best years ahead," then spent a few hours in the hotel's presidential suite granting audiences to local officials, including Mayor Cavanagh, a promising JFK disciple, and Police Commissioner Edwards, who was in the running for appointment to the federal bench. The suite was open for visitors again in the morning. First came Michigan's governor, John Burley Swainson, who shared a story of World War II bravery with the naval hero president; Swainson had earned France's Croix de Guerre at age nineteen after losing both legs in a land-mine explosion while fighting near Metz with the 95th Infantry, part of Patton's army. He had won the statehouse on the ticket with JFK in 1960, but now his brief two-year term was in jeopardy as he trailed in polls against the Rambler man, George Romney, who had entered politics after making his name as president of American Motors Corporation, Detroit's upstart car company.

Soon a more intriguing guest carrying a bouquet of roses was ushered into the room, a lithe twenty-year-old dancer named Emese Szklenkay. The president took the young woman's hand. "Glad to meet you. I've read about you in the papers," he said. "How do you do?" Emese responded softly, in Hungarian. She had been with her Hungarian dance troupe performing in Paris two weeks earlier when she slipped away from her communist handlers, into freedom, an act of derring-do arranged by Michigan relatives and witnessed by a reporter from the *Free Press*. Detroit had an established Hungarian population centered in Delray, an industrialized section of the city's southwest corner, not far from Bob Ankony's neighborhood, that grew with a second wave of immigrants after the failed 1956 revolution. Emese asked the president to accept her roses as "a token of hope of the Hungarian people for freedom." He took them and suggested that they pose for pictures. As she left the room, she turned back and wished Kennedy good luck, in English.

A few minutes later, the president was striding out the Washington Boulevard entrance, smiling as he passed Raymond Murray, the rookie cop. Murray's instructions had been to stand guard outside the hotel along with other officers assigned to the presidential detail and look for unusual activity in the area. He did not have a mobile radio. If anything came up, he would have to pass it along by word of mouth. There were no incidents, but one impression from that day stayed with him. As Murray scanned the cityscape from the hotel entrance, he kept thinking that "someone could easily shoot from one of the many tall buildings in the downtown area and kill the president."

The Cass Tech band, from the most illustrious public high school music program in a city of music, played the march song "Harvardiana" as Kennedy made his way to the speakers stand. Police Commissioner Edwards stood nearby. JFK seemed in a buoyant mood, noted Tom Wicker, who covered the White House for the *New York Times* and was on the press bus for the Midwest swing. Congress had just passed the Trade Expansion Act, sweeping legislation—to that point the administration's most significant achievement—that started to break down long-standing tariff walls at home and abroad. The bill was on its way to the president for a signing ceremony in the Fish Room soon after JFK returned to Washington. He had made a point of calling it bipartisan, and in Detroit it had the support of two nationally powerful figures who were more often adversaries, Walter Reuther of the UAW and Henry Ford II of Ford Motor Company. Reuther was more sympathetic to free trade than many labor leaders. He called opponents of the Kennedy measure shortsighted, unable to see that it would lead to greater efficiencies of production and economic growth. But many Republicans had opposed it, and in his speech outside the Sheraton Cadillac, for the first time, Kennedy wielded the trade issue as a partisan weapon, saying, "A majority of the Republicans from this state, a majority of the Republican leadership, opposed our bill to make it possible for Detroit to sell cars in Europe."

The president chose a different angle of attack against Romney, who, like other car guys, as they called themselves, supported the trade expansion bill, believing it would be good for their industry. Armed with background memos from his political advisers, JFK understood that Romney was favored to defeat Swainson and that he would do so in a Democratic state by appealing heavily to independent voters. "One of the most interesting political phenomena of our times is to see Republican candidates in various states who run for office and say, 'Elect the man,'" Kennedy told his Detroit audience. "You can't find the word Republican on their literature, and I don't blame them. But we write the word 'Democrat' in large letters because the Democratic party stands for progress."

It was a sun-splashed autumn morning, and Kennedy basked in the glow after his speech, at one point rising from the back of the parked presidential limousine, a 1963 white Lincoln Continental provided by Ford, and waving to the multitudes before he and Governor Swainson embarked on a twelve-mile zigzag through the Democratic heart of the city, mostly black and East European ethnic precincts. They rode up Cass and across to Woodward near the Fox Theater, then northward on Woodward past Wayne State University and the noble bookend edifices of the Detroit Institute of Arts and Detroit Public Library, all the way to the block-wide fortress of General Motors, topped with its Corinthian colonnade, another Albert Kahn legacy, turning right at East Grand and taking the boulevard across toward the Polish Catholic enclave of Hamtramck and up through the northeast side. Police officials estimated that as many as a hundred thousand people lined the route. Commissioner Edwards, who rode in a backup car, later described Kennedy's reception in a letter to a friend in Washington, exclaiming that "the crowds which greeted him on the streets were the largest and most enthusiastic which I have ever seen since I first came to Detroit in 1936." They seemed most effusive along Joseph Campau Street in Hamtramck, with another cluster awaiting the president's arrival at City Airport, the small municipally owned field where JFK and his party would depart by helicopter for Flint and Muskegon.

Raymond Brennan, an engineer in the trim department at Chrysler Corporation, was in the airport swarm along with his two boys, Terry and James. Twenty minutes earlier, they had watched the motorcade glide by on Woodward, then drove directly to the airport for another glimpse. When the caravan approached, they scrambled for a better view, climbing atop a narrow pipe that ran horizontally three feet aboveground next to a five-foot iron fence with ornamental spikes. They were leaning over the fence when the pipe buckled and broke under their weight, sending Brennan and one of his sons directly into the spikes, which pierced their ribs. With the crowd's focus on JFK, no one noticed their predicament or heard their screams for about thirty seconds, a seeming eternity. Finally some spectators saw them and extricated them from the fence. Ambulances were arriving to take them to the hospital when the president's helicopter disappeared on the horizon. By the time Kennedy got word of the incident, the

Brennans were out of the hospital, recuperating at home. He sent them a note and autographed photos for the sons.

Kennedy was much in demand in Detroit that fall. The plan was for him to return on November 1, five days before the election, for more campaigning. Henry Ford II had tried to lure him back before that for the opening of the Detroit Auto Show, but three visits to the city within a month were deemed too many by the White House political and scheduling staffs. They chose the campaign trips over the car show and offered Vice President Johnson to the auto group instead. This was a close call, since Ford, a lifelong Republican, seemed on the verge of coming over to the Kennedy side.

Henry Ford II and JFK were the same age, both born in 1917. Ford was at Hotchkiss when Kennedy was at Choate; Ford was at Yale when Kennedy was at Harvard. The Manhattan upper-crust Catholic parents of Ford's wife, Anne McDonnell, were friends of the Kennedys. Kathleen Kennedy, Jack's closest sister, known as Kick, had been a bridesmaid at Henry and Anne's wedding in 1940 (eight years before she died in a plane crash in France), and JFK once courted Anne's sister, Charlotte McDonnell. Ford told an oral historian later that he knew Kennedy so well that once, during a visit to the Oval Office, the president took him in a back room and showed him secret U-2 reconnaissance photos. So far during his presidency, Kennedy had called on Ford several times. Along with Reuther, he served on the president's twenty-one-member labor-management advisory committee "to promote collective bargaining, industrial peace, sound wage and price policies and higher living standards." During the summer of 1962, Kennedy had asked Lem Billings, his prep school roommate and first friend, to persuade Ford to lead a business committee to help fund a national cultural center in Washington, what later became the John F. Kennedy Center for the Performing Arts. Ford was already providing the White House with limousines on terms the president described in a thank-you letter as "a very favorable lease system" and now assigned the company's top Washington lobbyist, Rod Markley, to do whatever the administration asked concerning the cultural center plans.

Could Kennedy pry the best-known business executive in the country away from the Republicans? Ford had endorsed Romney, his industry rival, for governor, arguing that "after fourteen years of Democratic rule, with the UAW calling the shots, it's about time we had a change." But the presidency might be different. In a telegram earlier that year to Henry and Anne's debutante daughter, Charlotte, who was celebrating her twenty-first birthday at the 21 Club in Manhattan, Kennedy noted wryly, "I hope you will count this an appropriate time to reconsider whatever political advice you may so far have received. Happy twenty-first birthday, John F. Kennedy." Whether Kennedy knew it when he climbed into the helicopter at City Airport and whirled away from Detroit that noonday in October, the family advice Charlotte was receiving might have been more to his liking. Her father was thinking that he had "made a mistake with Jack" by not supporting him more openly. Not only did he enjoy Kennedy personally, but he was feeling optimistic about the country's economic condition. After a downward turn from the midfifties, life seemed flush again in Detroit. At least the auto industry was back and booming.

## Chapter 3

# THE SHOW

**THERE WAS THE** show, but first there was the show before the show. First the car guys showed off to one another; then they showed their new cars to the public. The mood of the car guys depended on the excitement level of the public for their cars, and when their show before the show began on October 18, a Thursday evening, the prospects for the larger event, the 1962 Detroit Auto Show, seemed unparalleled.

Nineteen sixty-two was rounding out as the second-best car year ever, and in October so far sales were moving at a faster pace than in any single month in history. The outlook for the next year was only better. Earlier that day, Ford boasted that it was increasing production over the next two months by twenty-eight thousand cars based on the record early sales of new models. General Motors sounded equally bullish, its factories in full gear. Chrysler was bringing back six hundred idled workers to boost output, and American Motors plants were humming six days a week, two shifts.

The Motor City had an intoxicating buzz. The *Today* show was in town broadcasting live each morning with Hugh Downs and Jack Lescoulie, and *NBC News* was also preparing a prime-time Sunday special narrated by Chet Huntley. *Look* magazine, just reaching newsstands, had devoted its cover to the gleaming, wide-mouthed grilles of 1963 cars. Goodyear's pug-nosed blimp was puttering overhead, a blinking billboard encouraging the local populace to make plans to see the show. Even the U.S. State Department was into boosterism, its chief of protocol encouraging foreign visitors to put Detroit on their itineraries. And here, at Ford Auditorium, the royal court of the automobile empire and related industry barons were gathering for a gala invitational concert featuring the Detroit Symphony Orchestra. Detroit wanted to think of itself as a city of national and international stature, the center of the modern industrial world, and this was the celebration of its importance, the auto-culture variation of Hollywood's Academy Awards, New York's Fashion Week, and Washington's White House Correspondents Dinner.

The modernist Ford Auditorium, rising on the riverfront downtown off Jefferson Avenue, had been home to the orchestra since it opened in 1956. The name reflected its genesis: it was built in honor of the original Henry Ford and his wife, Clara, and funded by Ford Motor Company and its dealerships. Critics often panned the symphony hall's acoustics, saying the room could not compare to the old Orchestra Hall on Woodward, out near the Gotham Hotel, in its heyday, although that opinion was not unanimous; some singers (including, later, Martha Reeves of Motown) raved about the Ford's vibrant sound. But acoustics were not at the top of the agenda for this concert. Being there was.

The orchestra itself had to make special plans to appear. The musicians, in the midst of an East Coast tour, were flown back that morning from Boston on round-trip tickets that would return them to perform in Worcester the next evening. Their noted resident conductor, the Parisian Paul Paray, had departed the previous night from New York after a concert in Stamford, Connecticut, taking an overnight train to Toledo, where he was met by a driver and chauffeured north to Detroit to set the stage. The "big wheels" of Detroit, as a local society writer called them, appeared at the Ford Auditorium's semicircular front drive in midnight-black limos and emerged in dark tuxedos and dark business suits. It was a warm night, but that did not curtail the number of women wearing mink stoles over short, bright-colored dresses with matching satin shoes.

Henry Ford II arrived with his wife, Anne, from their mansion in Grosse

Pointe Farms, ten miles east and northeast on Jefferson following the Detroit River and around the curve to the gilded shore of Lake St. Clair. In Detroit's sociogeographic strata of that era, of rich and richer, nouveau riche and old money, the delineations were clear, the lines seldom crossed: Bloomfield Hills and Birmingham were for company presidents and managers; parts of the other Grosse Pointes were for bankers and doctors and a few mobsters. But Grosse Pointe Farms was for owners. Henry and Anne, the quintessence of the owner class, were destined for separation—he had spiced up his life with a wildcard jet-setting Italian, Maria Cristina Vettore Austin—but divorce was more than a year away, and the Fords could put up appearances in social settings as important as this. Charlotte Ford later called her parents' relationship "a marriage without laughter. It seems to me in retrospect the last old-fashioned marriage. It was second nature not to ask questions, not to be emotionally involved. If we [the children] were distant from them, they were formal with each other. Each of them had a function, the emotions seemed very limited, it was all very proper." This sensibility, Charlotte noted, was passed down from the first generation of Fords. She thought of her grandmother Clara as "sort of like the queen of England." Growing up in the mansion in Grosse Point Farms, she recalled, there were fifteen servants. Dinner was served by butlers in tails. With the Christmas season approaching, there was no expectation that the Fords might trim their own tree; that was done by the Ford Motor Company art department. "If we cried there were always nurses there. . . . I went to boarding school for four years and was miserable. Cried almost every day. No one asked, 'Are you happy?' Instead it was, 'This is what you are going to do.' It was a very severe home with a lot of rules in that sense."

Now, in their final year together, with Ford hosting the automobile society, Henry and Anne were playing their proper roles. Anne was a patron of the arts, a force behind the auditorium and major benefactor of the symphony and other cultural institutions. Earlier that year, Mr. and Mrs. Henry Ford II—in this case meaning Mrs. Ford, even though he too had a sharp eye for art—had donated a priceless masterwork, Picasso's *Portrait of Manuel Pallares,* to the Detroit Institute of Arts.

The concert began with a bright rendition of the overture from Mozart's *Marriage of Figaro*, which was sufficient for many of the car guys, who jollied downstairs to the social hall at intermission, where champagne was flowing, and never returned to their seats. There were preperformance parties and postperformance parties and more coming the next night and the next: a lavish dinner sponsored by Pontiac at the Detroit Athletic Club on Madison Street (another Albert Kahn building), a dinner-dance in the Statler Hilton ballroom across from Grand Circus Park, cocktails from American Motors in the Sheraton Cadillac ballroom. All for the show before the show.

Friday noon at Cobo Hall, the Automobile Manufacturers Association held a press luncheon in a ballroom near the seven-acre exposition hall where the show was being staged. The president of the association and main speaker was Ford's Mr. Ford, known in the trade press by several nicknames: the shorthand HF2, Hank the Deuce, or just the Deuce. He was not always friendly with the press, but he was always good copy. Sometimes he would brush off reporters; at other times he would call them to spill industry beans. He had some traits of his grandfather, especially a killer-cold ability to fire people without compunction, yet there was enough of the irrepressible rogue in him to make him compelling, if never endearing. Hotchkiss and Yale did not stain him with the patina of eastern sophistication. He displayed some of the wit of JFK, his contemporary, but none of the president's intellectual cool, and in many ways was more like the Texan vice president, LBJ, scheduled to address the auto show in a few days. He sounded just like LBJ once when he disdainfully asked a subordinate, Cal Beauregard, "Are you a sock puller-upper like McNamara?" Robert McNamara had left Ford's presidency to become Kennedy's secretary of defense. When Beauregard asked what that meant, Ford replied, "Well, whenever McNamara gets nervous he pulls up his socks." Not something the Deuce would do. Impeccably dressed yet with a touch of the peasant, with his manicured nails and beer gut and carefree proclivities, his frat-boy party demeanor and head full of secrets, the Deuce was at once the "symbol of the American capitalist," as noted labor writer William Serrin once described him, and the antithesis of the parade of bland General Motors bosses who came and went during his long reign. Most of all, he knew his trade.

As he took the podium to speak to the auto press, Ford had more than the newest car models on his mind. Even with the family history coursing through his blood, he was as much a market guy as a car guy, and he was thinking about new markets. Social demographics were aligning for a period of tremendous growth in the automobile industry, HF2 said. There were then 76 million motor vehicles in the United States and 87 million drivers, but the inexorable trend was toward two-car families, exponentially increasing sales with the rise of incomes, the increase in women drivers (up 56 percent just since 1956), and the arrival of the largest generation of potential young drivers in history, the teenagers of the postwar baby boom, the first of whom were now turning sixteen and getting behind the wheel.

Beyond the American market, there was a more promising world stage, despite the perils of the cold war. No country was as car-obsessed and economically sound as America, Ford said, but others would catch up someday, and not just the common market of Europe. He saw the world inevitably growing smaller and more connected: "We will re-live in Asia, Africa, and Latin America something very much like our own experience of a half-century ago, when we too were an agrarian people, isolated and parochial. The automobile will do for many other lands and peoples what it has done for us." For the automakers of Detroit to survive and thrive, Ford said, they had to take advantage of that global transformation with trade and investment throughout the world. That much seemed clear. "I only wish," he added, "that we could have an equally clear picture of what is going to happen in the next half century, if man is left free to pursue progress."

Ask not what the world can do to us, ask what we can do in the world—that was the essence of HF2's sensibility. Even though, for the first time, half the vehicles being made in the free world were manufactured outside the United States, the battle for sales seemed to be on overseas turf, not at home. Import sales had dropped in the past two years just as domestic car sales exploded. If there was concern about the impact of foreign imports on the American car market, it was focused mostly on one country and one brand: the German Volkswagen. VW's sales worldwide outpaced Chrysler and American Motors and trailed only GM and Ford, and its beetle-bodied little cars had been infiltrating the U.S. market slowly but surely throughout the previous decade, with a few hundred dealerships and a new plant in New Jersey. Volkswagen's impact in America was still modest, but nonetheless significant enough that the company's chief, Heinz Heinrich Nordhoff, had been flown in from Wolfsburg to address the Detroit Economic Club that weekend of the auto show launch. Only seventeen years had passed since Nordhoff ran the Opelwerk Brandenburg, making trucks for the Nazis. Described with understatement as a conservative, he would devote much of his speech to his distaste for government interference.

There was no sign of Japan, the other former Axis power, in Detroit that October. Only a decade earlier, Japan's auto industry had been dying, but it received life support when the United States turned to the Japanese for a ready supply of military vehicles during the Korean War. By 1957 Nissan and Toyota had begun importing a small number of cars into the United States. They displayed their models at an international auto show in Los Angeles the following year, then withdrew after poor road tests, and only now were inching back to America. Six months before this gathering in Detroit, there had been an international auto show in New York, and Japanese companies were there, but not talking much and providing no sales figures for their various compacts. Not that the American companies cared much about compacts now. They were back to believing that big was better. As K. T. Keller, one of the old-time car guys celebrated at the auto show that year, was fond of saying, he didn't like any car so small he could piss over it.

Ford asserted at his press luncheon speech that 1963 cars were far superior to the models five years earlier, and consumers were getting better value for the dollar. What they were getting is what the automakers thought they wanted: more power, more luxury, more room, even more aluminum—70 pounds on average for the 1963 cars compared with

66.5 pounds the year before. Starting in the late fifties, there had been a trend toward compacts, but that seemed over now. It was not the start of a revolution, one auto writer noted, but more a passing fancy. American Motors staked its existence on smaller and less expensive cars, but the Big Three—GM, Ford, and Chrysler—were all seeing compact sales diminish even as overall sales boomed. The only models *not* selling more than previous years were compacts—the Ford Falcon, Mercury Comet, Chevy Corvair, and Studebaker Lark—while the Plymouth Valiant was lagging behind expectations. Only months earlier, Ford had abandoned a subcompact car concept code-named Cardinal that had been the brainchild of Robert McNamara, the sock puller-upper, before he left the company in late 1960 for Washington. Lee Iacocca, head of the Ford Division, never liked the Cardinal and managed to get it killed. He had his own concept for the car of the sixties decade and its rising baby-boom generation, but that was still more than a year away.

Saturday it rained in Detroit, and there were several hundred people huddling up near the doors of Cobo Hall, the first wave of nearly seventy thousand opening-day visitors, so officials let them in an hour early, at ten instead of eleven. The press and two thousand invited guests had had their run of the auto show on Friday evening, but this was the first glimpse for the general public; a ticket cost one dollar for adults, thirty-five cents for children. Ticket sales were only part of how the AMA would recoup the millions it spent on what its managing director, Harry A. Williams, called "the most beautiful automobile show ever presented." The rest would come from the sale of floor space to the auto companies at five dollars per square foot. With 300,000 square feet in play, that seemed sufficient.

From the lobby off Washington Boulevard, the auto show was organized like spokes on a wheel. At the hub was a revolving tower, thirty feet high, called a Spectro-form, a term more exotic than the tower itself, meant to convey something new. The American sensibility always leaned toward the fresh and new, but especially now: New Frontier, new president and first lady, new generation, new appliances, new communities, new houses, new cars. The Spectro-form was white, with an hourglass figure, and had an electronic sign at its waist flashing the theme of the show: *America Drives Ahead.*

Displays on the spokes circling the tower—prime real estate—had been drawn by lot. Rambler took one spoke, Ford and Mercury two, and General Motors five. Chrysler and Studebaker got relegated to side areas, though Chrysler had achieved enough publicity earlier that week when Mayor Cavanagh boarded the steamship *T. J. McCarthy* as it plowed down the Detroit River to deliver its auto show cargo of Imperials and Valiants to Cobo, the latest shipment in the total of 2.5 million cars it had hauled to interior ports since World War II. Each exhibit space offered a different experience beyond cars. You were supposed to feel that you were in a country club, ski chalet, fraternity house, or at a country picnic. That was mere backdrop; the visitors crowded around the flashiest of the 320 vehicles on display, especially the new Buick Riviera and Corvette Stingray. This would be the tenth year for the Corvette, with its futuristic fiberglass body and compact wheel base, and Chevy was producing more of them than ever before. The Riviera, the creation of Bill Mitchell, the flamboyant GM designer, had a bit of the Rolls-Royce look. It was a stylish full-size luxury sedan that did not seem overly trendy, and over time some would place it among the most beautiful cars ever built.

The newly crowned Miss America, Jacquelyn Jeanne Mayer of Ohio, was there for Oldsmobile, showing off the F-85 Cutlass convertible. Auto shows always had beautiful young women around, the oldest trick in advertising, but there was a twist this year, reflecting the modest hint of a new attitude, inside and out. The rise in women drivers had influenced these new cars. The seats were smoother, the steering wheels more flexible, the floors padded with vinyl mats to prevent damage from high heels. Studies showed that women now spent more time driving than preparing food. They wanted radios, whitewall tires, automatic transmission, power brakes and steering, and the safety of padded dashboards. (Seat belts were not yet mandatory nationwide. Only three states—Wisconsin, New York, and Rhode Island—required them in new cars, and only two high-performance sports cars, the Corvette and Studebaker Avanti, included them as standard equipment.)

The sociological progression of women employed at auto shows went like this: in the early fifties they were blond bathing beauties who posed in swimsuits and high heels; in the late fifties they modeled in gowns matching the car interiors; now they were called narrators and were there to describe the cars and answer questions. Eleanor Breitmeyer, club editor of the *Detroit News* society page, noted that many narrators were following a fashion trend dictated not by New York but by one woman in Washington: "As a result of the First Lady's fashion leadership, many models [were] wearing versions of Mrs. Kennedy's bouffant hairdo and her favorite ensembles, the pillbox hat with two-piece sleeveless over blouse dress or empire-waisted evening gown."

The crowds at the auto show were predominantly white, but not exclusively so. African Americans in Detroit were as attached to the auto industry, and to cars, as any other group, and were enjoying car ownership at record levels. That week of the show the *Michigan Chronicle* claimed that "four of every five Negro urban families own a car" and that black families "spend more than a billion dollars a year on auto travel." The statistics were loose. In the racism of that era, overt or subtle, urban blacks faced inordinate obstacles getting car loans from banks. But the point was nonetheless well taken. Black customers were a seldom mentioned but strategic market for the auto companies, even though, as the *Chronicle* pointed out, "there has been a bare minimum of black salesmen in show rooms and very little advertising to reach the negro car buyer." At that time there was not a single car dealership in the United States with black ownership. Perhaps the most successful black car man in the country was Detroit's own Ed Davis, and his struggles were symptomatic of the larger problem.

Born in Shreveport, Louisiana, Davis arrived in Detroit at age fifteen in 1926 to live with an aunt. He came north alone to receive a better education and enrolled at Cass Tech downtown. In high school he earned transportation money by working in a car repair shop. After that he set up his own car wash at a service station, then was employed at the Dodge Main foundry in Hamtramck, and eventually reached the sales floor part time at Lampkins Chrysler, out on Woodward Avenue in Highland Park. As Davis described it, his fellow salesmen, all white, would have nothing to do with him; he was allotted a lonely office on the second floor far from the main showroom. At lunchtime he had to drive six miles toward downtown to eat at the Lucy Thurman YWCA because no restaurants nearby would serve him. By 1938 he had saved enough money to open Davis Motor Sales, a used-car lot in Paradise Valley. After a few years, Studebaker, in an effort to sell more cars in Detroit, offered him a franchise at the same location. That lasted until 1956, when he dropped Studebaker because so few people were interested in it. Davis Motor Sales was still highly successful selling used cars when urban renewal swept through Paradise Valley and Black Bottom and properties around his lot were condemned for the construction of the Fisher Expressway. Early in 1962 he gave in to the inevitable and closed his business there, hoping for a better opportunity elsewhere in the city. He spent the days of the auto show lobbying car executives to crack the Big Three race barrier and make him the nation's first black owner of one of their franchises. It would happen, but not yet.

The black population in Detroit had its own automobile preferences. Among the population at large, Ford trailed Chevy by a significant margin, but among black car-buyers the two were nearly even. This reflected Ford's history. Old man Henry Ford had been a notorious anti-Semite, but his company's standing in the black community remained strong. Ford was the first of the major auto companies to actively recruit black workers, its five-dollars-a-day motto fueling the first great migration from the South decades earlier. James Price, the first black employed at Ford, started as a tailor and eventually became general superintendent in charge of abrasives at the Rouge plant. His rise was not the norm; most blacks held down the least desirable jobs, in the foundry, where nearly 80 percent of workers were black. (Most of the other 20 percent were East Europeans known on the job as "bohunks.") Don Marshall, who came out of the Detroit Police Department, led a personnel group in charge of recruiting black employees. They developed a symbiotic relationship with African American ministers at many of the city's largest Baptist churches that became Ford pipelines. At the huge Second Baptist Church downtown, the oldest African American church in the Midwest, founded by a handful of former slaves and by the early sixties bursting with a membership of 4,500, a recommendation from A. A. Banks, the minister, was all it took to get a job at Ford. That connection went back to the twenties, when the church's powerful leader, Rev. Robert Bradby, would recommend "very high-type fellows" to Ford and sermonize against attempts to unionize the auto plants and in return received money from the company. While the church's position on unions changed over the decades as black organizers assumed key roles in the UAW, the Ford conduit persisted. Deacons at Second Baptist wore Ford pins on their suits as badges of honor. In the vernacular of the working class, black and white, there was always a possessive in the company name: you didn't work at Ford, you worked at *Ford's.* The linguistic origins evoked the direct connection between the old man and the place of business. Chrysler also enjoyed a special niche with black customers, who bought them at a far higher percentage than whites did. When Ed Davis finally broke through and got his dealership on the west side out at the corner of Dexter and Elmhurst, it was for Chrysler.

Early Sunday evening, the Deuce and the big wheels gathered again, this time at the Reynolds Metals building across the city line beyond Eight Mile Road in Southfield. Mayor Cavanagh was there, surrounded by the car guys and their spouses: the Roy Abernathys from American Motors, the Bunkie Knudsens and Ed Coles from General Motors, the C. E. Briggses from Chrysler, and the Eugene Bordinats from Ford. Four hundred guests enjoyed champagne and chateaubriand in a room dominated by twenty-one color television sets, all tuned to NBC.

Detroit and its auto show were going prime time. A network crew of fifty had been in and around Cobo Hall starting the previous Saturday, when trucks began pulling in from New York with cameras, six miles of cable, and the equipment for taping and remotes. The last filming had been done before dawn, at four Saturday morning, when the exhibition hall was empty and Huntley and the *Today* hosts could perform their minute-and-a-half spiels on fifteen different cars without crowd interference. Late that night the finished product was hand-carried back to New York on two separate flights, and now here it was, filling up the screens at Reynolds Metals. Ford gave a cameo interview, as did Cavanagh, but aside from the cars the stars of the show were some make-believe characters called Muppets, still seven years away from *Sesame Street* fame. The auto show special two years earlier had been critiqued for being too dry; this one went to the other extreme. They were "clever little puppets," noted one reviewer, "but there must be another way to add entertainment . . . with more auto-related features."

A sense of anxiety had started to seep in by then. The Detroit newspapers had published special sections on the auto show that morning, but the news on the front page unavoidably distracted attention from the local celebration, and by Sunday evening out at Reynolds Metals there was more talk about that news than about cars.

"President Has Cold, Halts Trip" was the headline in the *Washington Post* that morning, with variations on the theme in the local papers. The stories reported that JFK had been in his hotel room at the Sheraton Blackstone Hotel in Chicago on Saturday morning, in the middle of a campaign swing, when the White House physician traveling with him recommended that he cut short his trip and return to Washington to recuperate. Pierre Salinger, the White House press secretary, told the traveling press that the doctor had noticed the night before that Kennedy's voice sounded "husky." A larger, five-column headline dominating the page more clearly explained the "cold": "Marine Moves in South Linked to Cuban Crisis." Security in Washington was unusually tight. Rumors were sweeping the country about a high-stakes cold war confrontation.

Did this mean LBJ would not make it to Detroit? A trivial question, perhaps, but one that auto show officials could not help asking. In public they insisted that Johnson was still coming, and plans remained in place. The vice president would arrive at Detroit Metropolitan at 4:30 Monday, where Henry Ford II would greet him, and the entourage would then move by car to Cobo Hall for a half-hour tour of the exhibition hall, then on to the presidential suite at the Book Cadillac to rest and clean up, and back to Cobo for the dinner speech to an audience of 2,300. But all the Deuce had to do was read the banner headline in Monday morning's paper to understand how slim were the odds of any of that happening: "Capital Tense: Big Action on Cuba May Be Imminent."

After campaigning in St. Louis, Lady Bird Johnson arrived at midday on Monday. It was her first visit to Detroit. A delegation of Democratic women waited at the Willow Run terminal to meet her, but before greeting them she slipped into an office for a phone call. She emerged without betraying the call's purpose. Anything to do with events in Washington? No clues forthcoming. "It's not my nature to be fearful," she said, when someone asked whether she was alarmed. She was escorted to the Kingsley Inn near suburban Birmingham for a tea party. That evening, when she and her husband were scheduled to be at Cobo Hall, she remained at the Book Cadillac, attending a reception in the ballroom hosted by Governor Swainson and then holing up in the presidential suite, where she talked to a small group of Detroit women active in labor and politics. The vice president never made it to Detroit. President Kennedy, Henry Ford II's first choice for the speech, ended up on national television before the banquet began, explaining to the American public that reconnaissance photos of Cuba clearly showed the construction of missile sites and that the United States would force the Soviets to stand down.

Once the big wheels of Detroit understood the gravity of the situation, they rallied around the president. HF2, writing on behalf of his colleagues, dispatched a telegram to Kennedy that night: "At a meeting of the board of directors of the Automobile Manufacturers Association held immediately following your address to the nation tonight and just before the banquet of the 44th National Automobile Show, there was a spontaneous and unanimous expression of confidence and support in the action you have just taken to ensure that peace and justice shall be maintained in this hemisphere and elsewhere in the world. My associates and I—the principal officers of the companies comprising the automotive industry—pledge to you aid and assistance in full measure in the critical days now beginning." Walter Reuther, who had been invited to the auto banquet for the first time and sat on the dais near Ford, offered his own words of support. Reuther was JFK's most frequent Detroit correspondent, flooding the White House with telegrams and long letters, never hesitant to provide counsel and moral guidance. "Your decision in the Cuban crisis rests upon a sound moral basis," he now wrote. "During the past month when less calm and less responsible voices in America were urging premature and ill-advised action against Cuba, you demonstrated restraint and mature judgment. You acted decisively and determinedly after there was undisputed evidence to provide the moral basis for the commitment of American power.... You met the test of moral leadership which demands the delicate balance between your dedication to work for peace and your determination to defend our security."

Mayor Cavanagh had prepared a brief speech for the evening, as a warm-up act for LBJ, but it turned out he had to fill in as the main speaker. "Ladies and gentlemen, I regret that the pressure of public events has prevented the scheduled speaker, Vice President Lyndon Johnson, from attending this distinguished gathering," Cavanagh began. This was the first national auto show held during his administration, he noted, and it revealed Detroit at its finest, reflecting the deep connection between the city and its main industry. "Detroit is proud to be called the Motor City.... If the automobile has had a profound effect upon the nation and the world, it has had an even greater effect upon the fortunes of the city of Detroit. Detroit was an old city long before the automobile, but it owes its present position as one of the world's great industrial centers to the growth of the automobile industry. Fifty years ago, at the beginning of the auto age, our city covered only about forty square miles and had a population of less than six hundred thousand. Today it covers three times the area and has more than twice the population. In terms of the metropolitan area, of course, the growth has been substantially higher. I am confident that the automobile industry will continue to grow and that the state of Michigan and the city of Detroit will continue to share in that growth."

But for Detroit to fulfill its potential, Cavanagh said, it had to look beyond automobiles to electronics and aerospace, the technologies of defense. Only two decades earlier, as America geared up for World War II, Detroit was invaluable, its auto industry transformed into the Arsenal of Democracy, the factories turning out bullets, casings, torpedoes, incendiary bombs, radios, radar units, air-raid sirens, B-24 bombers, airplane parts, tanks, trucks, landing craft, jeeps, gun barrels, machine guns, gas masks, helmets, tires, propellers, submarine nets, binoculars, smoke screens, searchlights, and tents. Now, Cavanagh said, "Detroit and Michigan are prepared to carry out the full demands of our country, whether in peace or crisis." With Soviet missiles in Cuba and President Kennedy insisting that the Soviets stand down, the nation faced a crisis, and the arsenal could be ready again. No other region of the country had so much manufacturing capacity and technological skill for the asking, if only the government would ask. As matters now stood, the entire state of Michigan was receiving only 2.7 percent of the nation's defense dollars.

In peace, the mayor said, Detroit was undergoing a renaissance, "on the threshold of the greatest development culturally and commercially that she has ever enjoyed."

It was not yet on Cavanagh's mind, and wholly beyond the sphere of the car guys in the Cobo Hall ballroom, but a vital part of Detroit's cultural development was taking place outside a few modest houses five miles away on West Grand Boulevard, where two busloads of black musicians and singers, homegrown and stunningly talented, were preparing to leave the next morning on their first national tour.

## Chapter 4

# WEST GRAND BOULEVARD

**MOTOWN. IN LINGUISTICS,** that is known as a portmanteau, the conjoining of two words to create a new word with its own meaning. Motor and town. Cars and Detroit. The derivation came organically out of the language of the city. Long before Motown, the record company, there was Jacktown, the street name for the Michigan state prison in Jackson. There were also the ethnic neighborhoods in Detroit: Greektown, Corktown, Poletown, Bricktown, Mexicantown. Motown began as a place, but more than that it was a sound.

To get to Motown from downtown in 1962 required one turn. Drive straight up Woodward Avenue, the city's dividing line east and west, and hang a left at West Grand Boulevard, moving past General Motors on the left and the Fisher Building on the right and farther along to the 2600 block and its row of solid two-story homes, ending with the white one at 2648 that had the large *Hitsville USA* sign in script above the front picture window. The boulevard was at its broadest there, a half football field across to the far curb, with the flat, wide-open feel of much of Detroit's vast west side, a landscape that could evoke a sense of quotidian drowsiness if not for the jolts of creativity crackling out of that stretch of houses.

On the morning of Tuesday, October 23, the scene was even more frenzied than usual, apart from the deliberate demeanor of Esther Gordy Edwards, oldest sister of Motown's founder, Berry Gordy Jr.

Mrs. Edwards, her younger charges usually called her, though sometimes they slipped into the informal "Shug," short for "sugar." Her seven siblings had another name for her, "Sua" (pronounced *soo-uh*), for "big sister." Compact, organized, keenly intelligent, always immaculately dressed, her hair perfectly coiffed, with the Gordy family's signature apple cheeks and twinkling eyes, she was at age forty-two twice as old as many of the artists and more than three times older than the youngest of them, the blind kid wonder. Only a few weeks earlier, she had left her job as chairman of the Recorder's Court Jury Commission, where she had been the first African American to hold that prestigious position overseeing the selection of jurors for Detroit's municipal courtrooms. Roberta Wright, her close friend and former college classmate at Howard University, had tried desperately to talk her out of resigning from the commission to work full time in the music business her younger brother had been running for three years. "That's not going to work," Wright told her. "Your brother is just playing around with those tapes. You have to have a good job." Esther, the wife of a state representative and stepmother of a future federal judge, was not one for excess frivolity. But this would be fun, she said. And with a son at Western Michigan in Kalamazoo and a stepson at law school in Ann Arbor, she also needed the earning potential Motown offered. "I'll work with you," she told her brother. "You go up, I will. You go down, I will." And now here she was, standing on the sidewalk, trying to bring order to the chaos before the Motown troupe left on its first long road show.

Two old buses idled outside on the street as the passengers, their luggage packed for a fifty-six-day tour, climbed aboard and found seats. Forty-five people in all: a posse of bodyguards and roadies, the musicians from Choker Campbell's Show of Stars twelve-piece band, the comedian-emcee Bill Murry, and a vibrant collection of Motown's solo and group singing acts, including the Miracles, Mary Wells, Marvin Gaye, Little Stevie Wonder, the Marvelettes, the Vandellas, the Contours, the Supremes, the Temptations, Marv Johnson, and Singin' Sammy Ward.

An ensemble busting with talent, but there was a certain pecking order. Mary Wells was the reigning queen, with a new release, "Two Lovers." The

Marvelettes remained the top women's group two years after their huge crossover hit, "Please, Mr. Postman." The Contours exuded the most explosive energy, rocking with their contagious "Do You Love Me (Now That I Can Dance)," a tune Berry Gordy wrote from experience after his early teenage years had been scarred by rejection on the dance floor. The Vandellas provided a similarly joyous sound, with Martha Reeves's southern gospel intonations punching their rhythm and blues. Marvin Gaye brought the coolest voice with the sultriest appeal. Little Stevie, only twelve, was somewhere between novelty and genius, a legally blind wunderkind who could play any instrument but was at that stage to the later Stevie Wonder what Cassius Clay as a teenage Olympian was to the later Muhammad Ali: a young man with uncommon skill and brash charm but not yet much meaning behind it. The Temptations, still largely unknown beyond the West Grand studio walls, not long past the time when they lip-synched at sock hops as the Primes, went along for parts of the journey to sing backup, and the Supremes, who started as the Primettes, tag-along little sisters to the Primes, had to cajole just to be a warm-up act. Top billing went to the Miracles, led by William Robinson, who could do it all—sing, write, and produce—and also happened to be Berry Gordy's best buddy and closest musical associate. That status placed Smokey and his miraculous crew, including his wife, Claudette, off the old buses and into their own Cadillac accompanying the caravan.

Their day of departure was not a typical Tuesday morning. Detroit awoke to a banner headline, "Cuba Blockaded," with an even more alarming subhead: "U.S. Set to Sink Red Ships to Back Ban." Motown was riding off to the future on a day when, as much as any other in the twentieth century, it seemed there might be no future, the world on the precarious brink of a nuclear confrontation between the United States and the USSR. And the first stop on the tour was only two miles from the White House. Ads were already purchased in the *Washington Post* and *Afro-American. Nothing But Stars!* The Motown troupe would open at the Howard Theater on October 26, a day after the jazzmen Les McCann and Miles Davis closed.

Esther Edwards had organized the logistics of the tour with Thomas

(Beans) Bowles, the trip director, a baritone saxophonist, flute player, and arranger who had come to Motown out of the Detroit jazz world. Many of the venues on the tour, especially those in the South, were strung together for them by Henry Wynne of Supersonic Attractions, a black impresario based in Atlanta who had a knack for maneuvering around race restrictions and was practiced at squeezing advance money out of local promoters. Motown artists had been on the road before; they had played at the Regal in Chicago, the Apollo in Harlem, the Uptown in Philly, and other great venues of that era. All-star revues were an established part of the American music scene. Edwards had studied the mechanics of Dick Clark's *Caravan of Stars* to figure out how it was done. But this first *Motortown Revue*, as it was called, was the essence of the business model formulated by her little brother Berry—the complete sales package, all things Motown, vertical and horizontal, everything and everyone together, imported from Detroit, all in the family.

Motown eventually became synonymous with Berry Gordy Jr., but it was more the product of the entire Gordy family, especially his older sisters. He had four of them, starting with Esther, then Anna, Loucye, and Gwen. He also had three brothers. Fuller and George were older. As a boy, Berry Jr. thought his junior appellation meant that he was the chosen one—until he learned that his mother agreed to make him a namesake at his birth on November 28, 1929, a month after the stock market crash, in hopes that he would be the last Gordy kid. Even that did not work; Robert arrived last. (Fortunately, as it turned out; it was Robert who saved Berry from drowning during a boyhood swimming adventure across the border in Windsor, Ontario.) If Berry Jr. was special, his sisters made him so. Gwen and Anna smothered him with unconditional love and confidence. Loucye provided housing and math skills. And Esther was the organizer and mother hen, "the keeper of the castle," as Berry Jr. said a half-century later in an interview for this book. She ran the family's entrepreneurial fund and wrote the $800 family check that helped underwrite the launch of his own record company in 1959. When he doubted his manhood, comparing himself unfavorably to his father, she was the one who gave him a copy of Rudyard Kipling's "If" and had him memorize the lines.

The Gordys may not have been a representative black family in Detroit, but their rise illuminated many aspects of the African American experience there and benefited from the particular attributes of the city. Berry Gordy Sr. and Bertha Ida Fuller Gordy—Pops and Mom to the artists of Motown—arrived in Detroit from rural Georgia in 1922 during the first Great Migration northward. Although they left the South to escape racial oppression and search for opportunity, they were by no means starting from nothing. Berry had inherited property and a financial cushion from his father, who had died young in a lightning storm as one of the largest black landholders south of Athens in Oconee County. He and Bertha had been inculcated in the self-help business philosophy of Booker T. Washington, an African American variation of the individualist capitalism strain that courses through American history and myth. Soon after arriving in Detroit, Berry Sr. established his own Booker T. Washington grocery on the east side at the corner of St. Antoine (pronounced An-twine) and Farnsworth, a loud shout from the hustle of Hastings Street, and became an active member of the Booker T. Washington Trade Association, an essential network promoting the city's black businesses. The grocery was one of many enterprises Pops and Mom undertook over the following decades, including plastering and construction for him, real estate and insurance for her. Their children were always part of the operation; the girls worked the grocery cash register when they were so small they had to stand on a box to reach it.

Berry Gordy Jr. had neither the manual strength of his father nor the educated grace of his mother. In describing what he considered the trinity of his old man's attributes—"He worked from sunup to sundown, he had muscles of steel, and he killed rats"—the son was being worshipful and self-deprecating, but also elevating himself from a life that he did not want to repeat. The rats part was real. In the kitchen of their east side home, rats came out at night, and Pops "would be stepping on them and banging them and the kids would be going 'That's great.'" They were all cheering except Junior, who would jump on a chair and shudder in fear, turning away from the sight. Years later, when he stood at the top of the family hierarchy at Motown and his siblings called him Chairman, the inside joke was that the name derived from the days when he jumped on the kitchen chairs to avoid the rats, the little chair man.

Bertha, who had been a schoolteacher in Georgia and later graduated from the Detroit Institute of Commerce, stressed the importance of education to her children, but Berry Jr. was more consumed by trying to overcome his insecurities than applying himself as a student. His mind worked in unconventional patterns. As a boy he had trouble with the alphabet from A to Z but could recite it backward flawlessly. He felt intimidated by the faster-talking kids on Detroit's east side and considered himself a square who could never get the girls, so he tried to impress his classmates by being a comedian and troublemaker. At these he was successful enough to get booted out of music, the one class he cared about, after one year. His first mentor in music was unlikely: a maternal uncle, Burton Fuller, who was even more haughty than his mother, so much so that no one else in the family could tolerate his disapproving nature. Burton played classical piano. "I asked if he would give me lessons," Gordy recalled. "Yes, he would be glad to and was thrilled that I asked him because he had no good connections with the kids in the family because they were always talking among themselves about how he didn't like anybody and what was he going to do with his money when he died?"

The one who liked the snooty uncle was Berry Jr., if only because of music. During his early teens, he rode the bus across town to the west side to learn how to play piano. "He lived in a fancier part of town, a nice neighborhood, and I would go to his house and play. And he had me working on the scales," Gordy said. Quick but impatient, the nephew wanted to get on with it and play Bach and Haydn, but Uncle Burton insisted that he play the scales, hour after hour, week after week, before moving on to chords. Berry was also a daydreamer, ruminating about girls and songs about girls, and as he built his chords during practice he would linger on them and improvise simple progressions that could form the rudiments of a love song like "Paper Doll" by the Mills Brothers or "We Three" by the Ink Spots—songs about young men who were as lonely and insecure as he. "I would be playing for my uncle and he would say, 'Yes, come on, come on,' and I would have an idea in my head and I would not want to lose my idea so kind of hold it a little longer and play it again and he would say, 'No.' So at the end of that he said, 'I cannot teach you any more. You've got your own ideas'—because when I hit those chords I would get these little melodies and I was thinking about girls, my mind was off the lesson. And doing the repetitious arpeggios and scales for a whole lesson just drove me crazy." The uncle, frustrated, eventually told him, "Go out and find someone else who can help you."

That someone turned out to be the radio—and the family piano. After listening to performers like Hazel Scott (wife of Harlem's evocative congressman Adam Clayton Powell) play boogie-woogie on the radio, he would sit down at the baby grand in the living room and try to repeat what he had heard. He became good enough at it that later he would reach the semifinals of bandleader Frankie Carle's Boogie-Woogie contest at the Michigan Theater.

The family piano's role in the music that flowed out of the residential streets of Detroit cannot be overstated. The piano, and its availability to children of the black working class and middle class, is essential to understanding what happened in that time and place, and why it happened, not just with Berry Gordy Jr. but with so many other young black musicians who came of age there from the late forties to the early sixties. What was special then about pianos and Detroit? First, because of the auto plants and related industries, most Detroiters had steady salaries and families enjoyed a measure of disposable income they could use to listen to music in clubs and at home. Second, the economic geography of the city meant that the vast majority of residents lived in single-family houses, not high-rise apartments, making it easier to deliver pianos and find room for them. And third, Detroit had the egalitarian advantage of a remarkable piano enterprise, the Grinnell Brothers Music House.

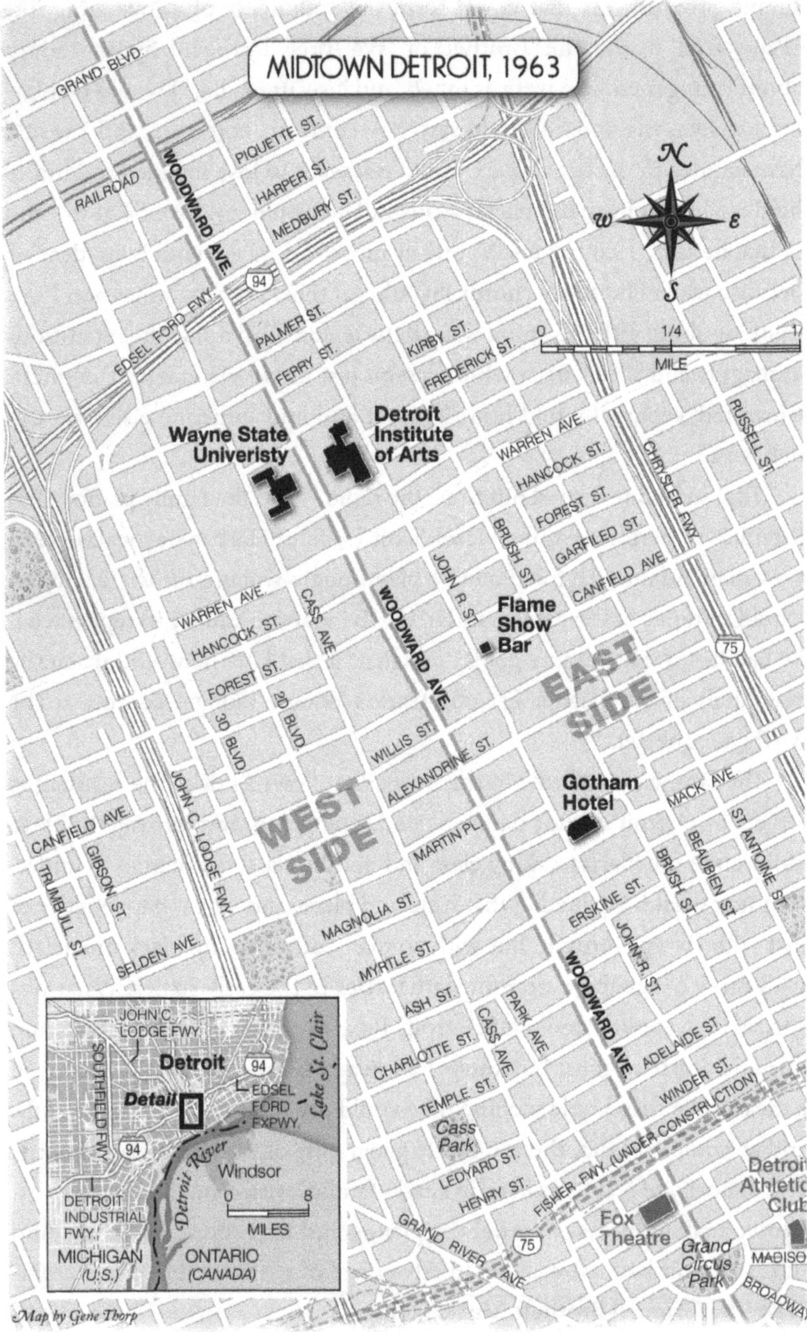
MIDTOWN DETROIT, 1963
GRAND BLVD.
PIQUETTE ST.
HARPER ST.
MEDBURY ST.
RAILROAD
WOODWARD AVE.
94
EDSEL FORD FWY.
PALMER ST.
FERRY ST.
KIRBY ST.
FREDERICK ST.
N
W
E
S
0
1/4
MILE
Wayne State Univeristy
Detroit Institute of Arts
WARREN AVE.
HANCOCK ST.
FOREST ST.
GARFILED ST.
CANFIELD AVE.
BRUSH ST.
JOHN R. ST.
CHRYSLER FWY.
RUSSELL ST.
Flame Show Bar
75
EAST SIDE
WARREN AVE.
HANCOCK ST.
FOREST ST.
CASS AVE.
2D BLVD.
3D BLVD.
WILLIS ST.
ALEXANDRINE ST.
WEST SIDE
Gotham Hotel
MACK AVE.
MARTIN PL.
CANFIELD AVE.
GIBSON ST.
TRUMBULL ST.
JOHN C. LODGE FWY.
ST. ANTOINE ST.
BEAUBIEN ST.
BRUSH ST.
ERSKINE ST.
JOHN R. ST.
MAGNOLIA ST.
SELDEN AVE.
MYRTLE ST.
ASH ST.
PARK AVE.
CASS AVE.
CHARLOTTE ST.
ADELAIDE ST.
WINDER ST.
TEMPLE ST.
Cass Park
LEDYARD ST.
HENRY ST.
FISHER FWY. (UNDER CONSTRUCTION)
GRAND RIVER AVE.
Fox Theatre
Grand Circus Park
Detroit Athletic Club
MADISON
BROADWAY
JOHN C. LODGE FWY.
SOUTHFIELD FWY.
Detroit
Detail
EDSEL FORD EXPWY.
Lake St. Clair
Detroit River
Windsor
0
8
MILES
DETROIT INDUSTRIAL FWY.
MICHIGAN (U.S.)
ONTARIO (CANADA)
Map by Gene Thorp

Founded in Ann Arbor nearly a hundred years earlier by the brothers Ira, Clayton, and Herbert, Grinnell's was not just the dominant music store in Detroit but the largest retail music emporium in the nation, as well as a prolific manufacturer of pianos. Its headquarters (designed, to be sure, by Albert Kahn) was down the block on Woodward from the J. L. Hudson Company, Detroit's largest department store, and in its own realm it had the same bountiful feel as Hudson's, evoking the good times of the city—customers and sales staff everywhere, floor after floor of glistening merchandise. By late 1962 Grinnell's was so popular that it was finalizing plans to extend into five floors in the Saunders Building next door. The expansion denoted the confluence of art and finance, where Detroit's love of music met a powerful belief in the downtown's economic viability.

If you were a youngster interested in music in Detroit, you knew Grinnell's and probably spent time there. David Williams, whose uncle Randolph Wallace operated the Garfield Lounge and Randora Hotel on the John R strip, famous for its Monday night twenty-nine-cent chicken-in-a-basket dinners, spent the Saturday mornings of his youth catching the city bus outside his family house on West Grand and riding it down to Grinnell's for a forty-five-minute clarinet lesson. Looking back on Grinnell's fifty years later from his office in another music city, Nashville, as Vanderbilt's vice chancellor for university affairs and athletics, Williams remembered a full floor of rehearsal rooms, all soundproofed, with music stands and encouraging teachers offering individual lessons in clarinet, trumpet, trombone, saxophone, flute, guitar, and most of all piano. Music was the soul of the city, Williams recalled, and "the pride of a family was to have a piano."

What defined Grinnell's was its connection to the community, another Detroit trademark. Hudson's was a mixed bag in that regard. It was known for its uncommonly generous returns policy and for making quality goods affordable to the working class, but it was also segregated in the sense that it had no blacks on its sales staff. Grinnell's, which hired some black musicians and piano tuners, provided pianos and other instruments to people of all races and incomes, offering a variety of flexible rental and purchase plans. It also supplied instruments to the city schools (in Detroit elementary schools alone, more than twelve thousand students were in instrumental music classes), hosted recitals at its downtown store, and sponsored piano music festivals in the city and state. "Grinnell's had this thing where you could take lessons down at the store on Woodward, but the other thing you could do is buy a piano on time, on layaway," noted Dan Aldridge, a historian of Detroit's black culture. "So you have all these working-class families in Detroit who had their own piano. It was because of Grinnell's."

The Gordy family was among Detroit's piano multitudes. In 1949, when Berry Jr. was twenty, *Color* magazine published a feature story titled "America's Most Amazing Family" that showed the entire Gordy clan—Pops and Mom, all eight siblings, and a few grandchildren by then—gathered around a baby grand piano at the family residence at 5139 St. Antoine. "If there were a national contest to select the most gifted family in America, the editors of *Color* would nominate the Gordy family," the article asserted. The story extolled the family's entrepreneurial genius and diverse talents, including a prizewinning bowling team composed of the four brothers (led by Fuller, who was perhaps the city's best kegler), and an equestrian Bit and Spur Riding Club involving the sisters and founded by Loucye, who among other skills was a riding instructor. Berry Jr. was described as "the musician in the family . . . who provides the music for frequent family song sessions in the Gordy home."

Berry was so obsessed with music that he could play a piano in his mind if need be, or some version of one. In his late twenties he found himself working on an assembly line out at Ford. In the decade since he had dropped out of Northeastern High, he had married and become a father; he had tried to emulate his childhood hero, Joe Louis, as a boxer (although far down in skill and class, a 113-pound featherweight instead of a heavyweight); he had served in Korea as a draftee driving a chaplain's jeep; and he had failed in his first efforts as a businessman. Esther's only half-joking refrain hit home: "Well, if you're so smart, why ain't you rich?" Now he just needed a steady income, and his mother-in-law, with her union connections, landed him the auto job. It had taken him only one day laboring in the foundry to reinforce the notion that he was not like his father. "I was taking hot metals as they came out of the thing and it was burning my hand even though I had asbestos gloves and all that stuff, so I figured with my piano playing and my music, you know I just couldn't. After one day of work I . . . went home and told my wife [Thelma Coleman Gordy], 'I can't do this.' There were such loud noises I couldn't hear anything. And of course she was very upset with me. I couldn't lose a job. Her mother got the job for me." Rather than allow him to quit altogether, his mother-in-law found another job for him three weeks later at the Lincoln-Mercury assembly line, and that is where he developed the piano of his imagination.

His sequence on the line involved upholstery: snapping a metal clamp into place. Once he mastered it, he realized that he could gain four or five free minutes for every minute of work by moving his way up the assembly rather than waiting for the line to reach his station. It was unorthodox and against union and floor procedures, but he went about it with such enthusiasm that his fellow workers seldom complained. "They didn't really like it but I was overly nice. Overly nice," he said. "I would do my job . . . and I was overly fast. When somebody was working on the back of the car I would jump in that car, and then go up to the next person, 'Excuse me.' I was not supposed to be up there. Then I would go back and as the cars moved up the line I had three or four already done. Then I would go to my tunes." As the tunes popped out of his head he wrote them down in a notebook he stashed in his back pocket, using the most basic method of musical notation, simpler than anything he had learned from Uncle Burton. As melodic lines came to him, he remembered them by giving each note a number, like an eight-year-old following the numbers on a toy piano or xylophone. His baseline was "Mary Had a Little Lamb"—3212333—and he went from there, composing one love song after another.

Later much would be made of the idea that the music-making process at Motown was inspired by Gordy's experience on the automobile assembly line, a notion he himself promoted, despite the possibly negative connotations of mass-producing art. In many ways the parallels were obvious; the Motown operation on West Grand did in fact have a bit of the Rouge plant concept to it, taking raw materials and turning them into finished commercial products one sequence at a time, evoking a brand through a sound as identifiable if not as repetitious as a fleet of Ford Galaxies. But the less noted and more important point about Gordy's transference of his auto plant experience to his later success at the music studio involved not the rote of it all but the opposite: the improvisational freedom he developed on the assembly line and repeated at Motown. It was while snapping clasps on Mercury upholstery that he figured out some essential components of creative work: how to shape time and circumstances to his advantage rather than be a slave to them and how to accomplish what was needed while also doing what he wanted.

His first job making money from music, or trying to, came before the auto job, when he ran a record store, the 3-D Record Mart, specializing in jazz. Detroit had been a noted jazz town, black and white, since the twenties, when Jean Goldkette's famed orchestra brought the Dorsey brothers and Bix Beiderbecke to town. After the war, the jazz clubs, led by the Blue Bird Inn, with its bright indigo blue exterior, featured homegrown Milt Jackson on vibes and the Jones brothers: Hank, the pianist, Thad, the trumpeter, and the sublime Elvin, who later played drums in the John Coltrane quartet. Paul Chambers and Ron Carter, two of the premier double-bass men in modern jazz, both got their musical training at Cass Tech. The drummer Louis Hayes, pianists Barry Harris and Tommy Flanagan, trumpeter Howard McGhee, saxophonists Lucky Thompson and Yusef Lateef, guitarist Kenny Burrell—all came out of Detroit. To love jazz was to be cool in the world of Gordy and his east side contemporaries, but soon enough he confronted the reality that jazz was too cool for business; not enough customers were buying records at his shop. "I was trying to force jazz on these people, telling them how talented Duke Ellington was, and Dizzy Gillespie, Stan Kenton, Sonny Stitt, all these people, the jazz and bebop. I wanted to educate my people. And they all wanted the blues. 'You got anything by Muddy Waters? You got any of this blues, that blues?' And I would say, 'Look, I don't sell that stuff.'" His refusal to "sell that stuff" led to the shuttering of the store in bankruptcy.

Like his parents and siblings, Gordy had an entrepreneur's sensibility. Failure was not an end but a lesson. Music was his passion, and so was selling, but trying to sell something that people didn't want was not just futile; it was restricting. "Music was in my soul. I heard gospel, I loved gospel. The blues was in my soul, but I never had permission to love it because it was not what the young hip people were doing. None of the young hip people I knew were into the blues. Blues was for old people. And they have their whiskey and their stuff like that. But after going out of business because people wanted the blues, I wanted to find out why. After that happened, I started to realize, wait a minute, blues is not a lower class of music than jazz, it's just a different kind. And these people in Detroit, which was kind of like a southern town, they were home folk. They worked all week and they wanted to talk about their joys and their pain. Especially the pain. And so they would listen to the real music that told them about their pain, and how they felt." The songs Gordy wrote and championed, starting with the tunes he composed on the assembly line, followed that idea: clear story lines, basic and universal, music for all people, focusing on love and heartbreak, work and play, joy and pain.

The transition from anonymous assembly-line balladeer to Motown impresario was accomplished with crucial assistance from his sisters. The first boost came from Gwen and Anna, who, in keeping with the family's enterprising nature, ran the cigarette and photo concession at the Flame Show Bar, Detroit's top black nightclub, at the corner of John R and Canfield down from the Gotham Hotel, along a stretch known alternately as "the strip" and "Little Vegas" and "the street of music." From his days as a boxer, little Berry had stood tall in Anna's and Gwen's eyes. They attended his bouts, nurtured his dreams, believed in him "one hundred percent," and shared his love of music and ambition to achieve something special.

In the fire song of Detroit—with the Chesterfield Lounge, the Garfield Lounge, the 20 Grand and its Driftwood Lounge, the Grand Bar, the Blue Bird Inn, Club El Sino, the Music Bar, and the Frolic Bar, among others—the Flame Show Bar burned brightest through the fifties. Its owner, Morris Wasserman, was Jewish. (The connective roots between Jews and blacks went deep in the city, intertwining music, shopkeeping, education, housing, civil rights, even the mob, going back to the Prohibition days of the Purple Gang of Jewish mobsters and their black policy or numbers men.) The Flame's clientele was a mix of hip blacks and whites. Billie Holiday, Della Reese, Dinah Washington, Ruth Brown, Etta James, Sarah Vaughan, Betty Carter, Sam Cooke, B. B. King, T-Bone Walker, Solomon Burke—blues stars were booked there one after another. One of Gordy's prized lifetime possessions was a photograph his sisters had taken of him posing at the Flame with Billie Holiday during a break in her performance there in May 1957, two years before she died in a Manhattan hospital bed at age forty-four, drug-addled, diseased, and lonely. At the Flame that night, Gordy recalled, "she was sitting over there, and I said 'I gotta meet Billie Holiday 'cause I love her.' And they [his sisters] said, 'Go over there, she is really nice.' She said, 'Come on baby, come on over here, baby.' And I wanted a photo taken and I had some friends with me, 'Can they be in it, too?' 'Sure, baby, whatever you want.' And she was so sweet to me. So sweet."

Inside the Flame, the night scene was bathed in mirrored reflections of emerald and gold, ruby red and deep satin blue, splendor dark and smoky, everything exotic, hypnotizing, enthralling to Gordy. John White and the gamblers from the Gotham were regulars on weeknights, along with high-end pimps and prostitutes. The stage was at shoulder level, behind a flickering bar that stretched thirty yards. Lawyers, doctors, writers, other musicians, visiting athletes, and businessmen waited on weekend nights to land some of the 250 choice seats. The women, including Berry's sisters, invariably were sharply dressed in well-fitted gowns. "The Flame Show Bar, that was a beautiful thing," Gordy recalled. "To see women dressed in beautiful clothes and stuff like that, and I was in awe of the people that came in there. The men were dapper, and by then I was dapper too." He entered that world with his hair processed and threads that Gwen and Anna said made him look like a five-foot-five-and-a-half-inch pimp.

The sisters introduced him around. Here was Maurice King, leader of the club's house band, the Wolverines. There was Roquel Billy Davis, a songwriter. Up onstage was Ziggy Johnson, the master of ceremonies, a short and spry dance maestro who concocted the steps for the Chick-a-Boom, the Satin, and the Soft. Ziggy knew everyone. You had arrived when he put your name in bold print in his club scene gossip column, "Zagging with Ziggy," in the *Michigan Chronicle*. Here was Al Green, manager of Jackie Wilson and operator of a local music publishing company. There was Mr. Excitement himself, performing two nights on the same bill with Lady Day. And over there was young Nat Tarnopol, who worked with Green. Some of the makings of Gordy's future right there. King would become director of artistic development at Motown. Davis would write some early songs with him. Ziggy would publicize Motown at every stage. And Green and then Tarnopol (after Green died prematurely) would pave the way for Gordy to write big hits for the electric, sweet-singing, pompadoured Wilson, including "Reet Petite," "To Be Loved," and "Lonely Teardrops."

The loan that helped fund Motown was not an informal oral agreement, not in the entrepreneurial Gordy family. It was a written document, signed on June 12, 1959, with a payback date of June 12, 1961. The loan note form came from the Home Federal Savings and Loan Association of Detroit, but that institution was crossed out and Ber-Berry Co-op was inked over it in neat block lettering. That is where the $800 came from; Ber-Berry was the family fund, a money pool into which all blood relatives and their spouses contributed ten dollars a month. Ber for Bertha, Berry for Senior—matriarch and patriarch. The parents and all eight brothers and sisters had a vote on when and how loans could be distributed. Anna and Gwen were always supportive of their little brother, but Esther's vote was most important. Sua, big sister, was president of the co-op. She was the hardest to persuade, but finally relented. The interest rate was 6 percent.

The fourth sister, Loucye, also played an essential role in Motown's evolution. The Gordy sisters as a quartet were undervalued by history, and Loucye most keenly, perhaps because she died first, of brain cancer at age forty-one in 1965, when the record company was at its zenith. Years earlier, before West Grand Boulevard, she offered her brother lodging and logistics. The genesis of what became Motown began in the basement of her house on Hague Street, where Berry was staying after his divorce from Thelma. It was there that the original team operated. The First Five, they called themselves: Smokey Robinson, Brian Holland, Robert Bateman, Janie Bradford, and Raymona (Ray) Liles (who would become Gordy's second wife). They had coalesced around Gordy between 1957 and 1959, a period when he broke off from Jackie Wilson and his management group and decided that he had to have his own record company and publishing arm to avoid being shortchanged on royalties. The First Five was there at the creation and there when the move was made to West Grand. Loucye took on the role of publisher, heading up Jobete Music. Smokey, Bateman, and Holland wrote and sang. Janie Bradford was the first secretary, and more.

Bradford had arrived in Detroit from St. Louis as a teenager to live with her older sister, Clea, a singer recording with Chess Records and a close friend of Jackie Wilson. She considered herself a writer, a spoken-word poet long before that became a genre, and was not intimidated by Gordy. Her first words to him were "If you can write a song, I can write a better song than you any day." Not quite true, but reflective of her self-confidence and desire. When she showed him a notebook of poems she had written, he taught her the difference between verse and lyrics. *You need the hook and the song structure,* he told her, *with a beginning, a middle, and an end. You gotta do it like a story.* The lesson was made clear when he incorporated lines from two of her poems in the lyrics of songs on Jackie Wilson's *Lonely Teardrops* album, "The Joke (Is Not on Me)" and "We Have Love," though Bradford's name inadvertently was left off the credits for "We Have Love," a not infrequent occurrence in those early days.

During the first year of Motown, 1959, when Gordy was recording the Miracles and a handful of other artists under the Tamla label (a name he concocted from an unlikely inspiration, his adoration of the 1957 Debbie Reynolds song "Tammy"), Bradford contributed a key stanza to "Money (That's What I Want)," one of the company's first hits, sung by Barrett

Strong. "Mr. Gordy was at the piano, getting the rhythm going, and that was one of the few days I did not go home early," Bradford recalled. Going home early was one of her tricks. She would set the clock at West Grand an hour ahead, say it was quitting time, and then when she got to her place on Calvert Street call back and tell someone to reset it. "I was still there that day, and he got the track going, and said the title was something everybody wanted—money. And I think within fifteen minutes we had the song finished." Her money line: "Your love give me such a thrill/But your love don't pay my bills."

Three years into the enterprise, the bills were being paid, Tamla had morphed into Motown, and the studio, teeming with singers, band members, producers, arrangers, writers, technical engineers, and recording engineers, was pumping out music twenty-two hours a day, closing only for cleanup from eight to ten each morning. The all-night hours caught the eye of Anthony Fierimonte, a young cop who walked a beat in the 12th Precinct, whose territory stopped directly across the boulevard from Motown. "I get to the corner and see all these cars. . . . And make a note in my book. Blind Pig," Fierimonte recalled. That meant he thought it was an illegal off-hours drinking establishment. "What I should have done is quit my job and asked for a job at Motown. How stupid can you get?" Motown had expanded down the street, with a closed-in passageway connecting two of the three houses. Most of the action was in Studio A, a retrofitted garage with a hole in the ceiling that produced a unique sound and was nicknamed "the snakepit." The label on 45s and albums, originally pink with black lettering, had been changed—after some reluctance on Gordy's part—to what would become an American icon: a dark blue band, below a map with Detroit denoted by a red star, and MOTOWN in rainbow lettering. West Grand was the place to be, where everyone was young and free. It felt like a cross between a college dormitory and an experimental laboratory. "We loved that house, until we'd spend more time there than home," Smokey Robinson wrote later. "The house was our hangout. It was also our studio and recreation center. It had to be the most energetic spot on the planet." Smokey, who had his own shortcut out of the place, driving from the back alley across the ridge of an open lot down from Mott's Funeral Parlor, wrote a happy ditty that he and the Motown crew would sing:

*Oh, we have a very swinging company*
*Working hard from day to day*
*Nowhere will you find more unity*
*Than at Hitsville, USA.*

The artists were underpaid and overworked, the operation violated the work standards of the local musicians' union, the boss was a perfectionist and hypercritical, yet the overriding sense was that here anything was possible. Fame, money, and success had not yet redefined all the relationships.

Lily Hart, a woman who lived across the boulevard, was brought in to cook lunch for the employees, who craved her special chili. Berry and his wife, Ray, lived above the studio. Pops Gordy had quit his plastering business to become Motown's handyman. The four sisters were all part of the operation, their musical careers interwoven with their personal lives. Anna was with Marvin Gaye, the cool crooner who walked softly (corns and bunions on his feet) and talked softer. He had arrived at Motown as a five-dollar-a-session drummer and piano player but was now bursting into stardom with "Stubborn Kind of Fellow" and was soon to write "Pride and Joy," a song about Anna, whom he would marry the following year, a notable event for many reasons, including their age difference (she was seventeen years older). Gwen was with Harvey Fuqua, the singer and songwriter who came to Motown after serving as Anna's business partner at Anna Records and mentoring Gaye when he was a member of Harvey and the New Moonglows. Loucye was with Ron Wakefield, a saxophone player, and was taking care of Motown's accounts. Esther's husband, George H. Edwards (the black state representative, not to be confused with the white police commissioner of the same name but different middle initial), also helped out occasionally with the books. His son, Harry T. Edwards (Esther's stepson), arrived that year to attend the University of Michigan Law School and spent the summer and spare moments thereafter trying to install a personnel system at Motown based on what he had learned as an undergraduate majoring in industrial relations at Cornell. He was only twenty-two, but there was a freedom at Motown that allowed people to use and develop their various talents with less emphasis on age and experience. Gordy told young Edwards that he could do what he wanted as long as he stayed away from the artistic side of the operation.

When Harry was not in Ann Arbor studying, he lived with his father and stepmother in their big house at 87 Woodland, up near the border with Highland Park. He had grown up with his mother in New York and had not known much about his father's life, or his father's second wife, before reaching Michigan, but quickly came to realize there was much going on beneath her deliberate demeanor. "She was just very, very savvy about how to hold together operations and she was very shrewd with people," he recalled five decades later during an interview in his Washington office, where he served as senior circuit judge for the U.S. Court of Appeals for the D.C. Circuit. "She fooled people a lot because she wouldn't say a lot. She talked very slowly. And I knew after a while what she was doing. She was gathering information. So she was giving some people the impression that she didn't know anything, because she wasn't shooting her mouth off. She talked slowly and she ate slowly. She drove me crazy because the meal would be on the table for three hours after she served. She would come back and nibble. But she was always a multitasker, always doing several things. She took what she did very seriously and she usually did it quite well. She was a no-nonsense person."

The decision to send Motown artists on the road together in the final months of 1962 seemed obvious to Berry Gordy after he analyzed what he had seen at the Regal Theater in Chicago earlier that year: a packed house, a night overflowing with music, and every performer except one belonging to his company. Why not make it all Motown all the time, reinforcing the brand, taking it places it had never gone before, selling records along the way, and have his no-nonsense big sister make sure things did not get out of control? Easier said than done, that last part. Even with

Esther and other chaperones nearby, there was no effective way to tamp down the free-for-all, fun-seeking, competitive, sexually charged sensibility of this fleet of young men and women traveling together across the country for so long, if that had ever been a priority. Card games, drinking, ribald joking, heaters breaking, toilets overflowing, the sweet scent of pot, frequent hookups of various Contours and Marvelettes and Temptations and Supremes; Diana Ross, the most ambitious Supreme, alternately playing that game, squealing on others, and squabbling jealously with the lead singer of the Marvelettes—all part of the scene. "I remember sitting on that cramped up bus," recalled Martha Reeves, who was twenty-one that fall. "Every seat filled. I slept mostly at the window when I could get a window seat. Everyone on the same bus. The band members and male groups talked too bad so they were in the back and we were in the front. Esther Gordy said they were talking too bad and she was trying to teach us to be proper ladies."

Little Stevie Wonder sat nearby, annoying Reeves and anyone around him by drumming, humming, improvising on his harmonica, constantly making a racket no matter the time of night, which he said meant nothing to him because he was blind and could not see daylight anyway. Stevland Morris—born two months prematurely in Saginaw, instructed in Braille at Detroit's Fitzgerald School for the Blind, brought to Motown by Ronnie White, one of the Miracles, and looked after now by Esther and his musical arranger, Clarence Paul—was so talented and effervescent that no one could stay mad at him long. His colleagues often joked that he did not seem nearly as blind as he claimed to be. How was it that Little Stevie could always find the spare dimes people left on top of the candy machine in the front office at West Grand and use them to buy his favorite Baby Ruth bars? And how could he steal the pennies Janie Bradford saved on her desk for her baby son back home and run away from her so deftly? "He would be outside before I could catch him," Bradford recalled. "So he claims to be blind but can really see. I think he knew where the furniture was in the office so he knew how to navigate his way out of there better than we could seeing. I would chase him and eventually catch him and his response would be, 'Oh, taking money from a poor blind boy!'" Where was the line between blind innocence and wide-eyed lechery when he entered the office of publicist Al Abrams and stumbled around feeling the walls until, as Abrams later remembered it, "somehow his groping always brought him straight to Rosie [Abrams's secretary] and her breasts. He'd stand there copping a feel with his hands on her breasts with a grin on his face and say, 'Now I know I'm in the right office.'" On the other hand, as *Billboard*'s Nelson George, a leading expert on black music, pointed out, Stevie was blind enough to break several tape recorders and ruin recording sessions now and then by barging into the studio, unaware that the red light was on.

This precocious kid, not even in his teens, who wanted to be just like the rest of them, from songs to sex to stage, a place that if he had his way he would never leave. At least once before, Clarence Paul had had to drag Little Stevie and his harmonica and electric piano off the stage, and it would happen again on this tour. Fans thought it was part of the act. Not really. Stage time was too competitive for that.

The bus was no place for the Chairman, so Berry Gordy caught a flight from Detroit to Washington to attend opening night at the Howard Theater. Three days earlier, standing on the sidewalk next to his big sister, he had delivered a final pep talk, saying that they were representing not only Motown but all of Detroit, and now he wanted to see his troops in action. He had a complicated relationship with the opening act, the Supremes, and their lead singer, Diana Ross. She was only eighteen, a recent graduate of Cass Tech, where her classmates knew her as Diane. Gordy had suggested changing the final *e* to an *a* to give her name another syllable and more style. The Primettes became the Supremes for the same reason. Gordy was protective of Diana, if not obsessed with her. She and her singing companions had been hanging out at West Grand Boulevard for eighteen months already, pushing to get their chance, and Gordy, who had a keen sense of talent, could now see something special in this skinny girl. In his notion of Motown as an assembly line, he saw her as raw material that could be transformed into a top-of-the-line vehicle for his musical dreams, sleek and sophisticated. She was at that point a vast distance from perfection, but that was his vision for her, and he sometimes afforded her special treatment. Just to relent to her pleas and let the Supremes go on this first tour was a rare instance where his bottom-line business instincts were overtaken by sentiment. He did not think they were ready. Before the *Revue* buses had motored away from Detroit, he had spent several hours fiddling with mixes of "Let Me Go the Right Way," a single he hoped would earn Diana, Mary Wilson, and Florence Ballard some measure of recognition and erase the nickname they still carried in Motown: the No-Hit Supremes.

But as Gordy watched in dismay at the Howard, their one song went badly—no energy, little sex appeal, the crowd eager to move on to the flamboyant Contours, the vibrant Martha Reeves and the Vandellas, the hometown fellow, Marvin Gaye (whose last name was Gay when he left Washington five years earlier), and Mary Wells, who was winning them over with "Two Lovers," a Smokey-written hit released nationally on the third day in D.C. that climbed the charts for the rest of the tour. If the Supremes did not improve, Gordy said, they would be sent home. To that degree, the *Revue* was a meritocracy. The Miracles had earned their way to top billing through record sales and national renown, but beyond that the marquee could be rearranged depending on who was getting the hottest response from audiences along the way.

During their five days in Washington, the troupe stayed at a boardinghouse near the theater. Smokey Robinson started off feeling ill and got sicker day by day, his temperature rising dangerously over 103 degrees. Late at night, after the performances, Claudette took him to Howard University Hospital, where he was iced down in a device that he said "looked like a laundry basket." Doctors determined that he was suffering from the Asian flu, the third virulent strain to ricochet through America since 1957. Now the billing on marquees would change, at least for a time. Smokey was sent back to Detroit to recover.

Just in time, perhaps, for the tour from then on became a physical and mental endurance test. Sixteen cities in sixteen days before a one-day break on November 19, then another fifteen cities in fifteen days until a second day off. First a northern swing to the Franklin Park Theater in Boston, the old New Haven Arena, and the Aud in downtown Buffalo, then a long stretch below the Mason-Dixon line, starting in Raleigh and on through the heart of the old Confederacy, zigzagging from North Carolina to South Carolina, Georgia, and Alabama, and back for a return gig in Washington, then down again to Florida, the Carolinas, Kentucky, Tennessee, and Virginia before a final turn north for a pre-Christmas ten-day climax at the famed Apollo in Harlem. Two busloads of young black men and women rambling through segregated territory in the fall of 1962, with the civil rights movement fully engaged, did not go unnoticed or without incident. This was a time when there were challenges to Jim Crow in state after state, from the Congress of Racial Equality systematically seeking to integrate Howard Johnson's restaurants in North Carolina to James Meredith breaking the color line at Ole Miss in Oxford, a breakthrough earlier that fall that precipitated a white riot and required the protection of three thousand federal troops.

Some Motown performers had not experienced such overt segregation before, though Detroit was hardly devoid of racial barriers and frictions. Esther Gordy Edwards was among the handful of people on the trip old enough to remember what happened in Detroit during three violent days in June 1943, when the city, extolled as the Arsenal of Democracy for its crucial role in the war effort, exploded in a race riot that left thirty-four dead and hundreds injured, most of them black citizens. The riots were sparked by a confrontation between white sailors and black youths on the bridge leading out to Belle Isle, the jewel of the city's park system, but the causes ran much deeper: a combustible mix of whites from Appalachia and blacks from the Deep South who had migrated to Detroit since the start of World War II; the competition among those newcomers for jobs in the auto and defense industries and for government housing; a series of muggings by young black men; the race-based actions of a white police force; and racial fearmongering among white laborers. ("I'd rather see Hitler and Hirohito win than work next to a nigger!" one white spokesman shouted over a loudspeaker at a Packard plant where the assembly line for aircraft engines had been recently integrated.)

Twenty years later these points of tension were far from resolved. Mayor Cavanagh, who was swept into office in 1961 with overwhelming black support, had been pushing racial progress, implementing an affirmative action plan in city government, appointing a black accountant, Alfred Pelham, as the city's first black comptroller, and, with the selection of Commissioner Edwards, trying to change the police culture. But there remained in the black community a deep distrust of the cops and a countervailing sensibility on the overwhelmingly white force that tended to associate blacks with trouble. There were fewer confrontations in the workplace, but more in schools and neighborhoods, as widespread urban renewal and the blockbusting tactics of unscrupulous real estate operators dramatically reshaped Detroit's social geography.

"Negro Home Terrorized in Northwest Community," blared a headline in the *Michigan Chronicle* days before the *Motortown Revue* left Detroit. The article detailed the plight of Mr. and Mrs. Leroy Church, a black couple who moved into a previously all-white block on Tuller Street between Livernois and Wyoming and were greeted by a mob of white youths "believed urged on by adult agitators working behind the scenes," who "yelled insults, broke out several windows, and started a rubbish fire." This was not an isolated incident. In *The Origins of the Urban Crisis*, a classic study of the decline of postwar Detroit, social historian Thomas J. Sugrue calculated that white Detroiters, usually affiliated with or inspired by neighborhood community associations, "instigated over two hundred incidents against blacks moving into formerly all-white neighborhoods, including harassment, vandalism, and physical attacks" in the postwar era. There were notable spikes in such violence during two periods, first during an economic slump in the midfifties and again during the early sixties, the period of this book. These clashes, according to Sugrue, who was born in Detroit, were "political acts, the consequence of perceptions of homeownership, community, gender, and race deeply held by white Detroiters."

What the troubadours of Motown experienced during their swing through the South differed mostly in the ubiquity of racism. The theaters where they performed were segregated, either all of one race or the races separated by partitions. So were the hotels, swimming pools, restaurants, and gas stations. There are no documents confirming their most trying moments, but oral histories and recollections of various artists center around a few commonly told incidents in which the versions depart from one another only in minor details, including a time when bullets were sprayed into the *Motortown Revue* banner on the side of a bus. Martha Reeves, whose family came to Detroit from Eufaula, Alabama, and often returned to the South during the summers of her childhood, was accustomed to the affronts she and her colleagues faced. She noted that the buses had Michigan plates, and the troupe was often mistaken for a band of Freedom Riders. "I knew about what was to be expected," Reeves recalled. "Once we stopped at a gas station in a remote area [near Macon, Georgia]. Dust everywhere. Two guys went ahead to see if we could use the restroom. 'Hey, man, can we use your bathroom?' And the gentleman behind the counter was frightened. 'What y'all niggers want? Where you come from?' He thought we might be Freedom Riders. 'Get out of here!' And they said, 'Man, you don't know who we are? We are the Contours and Miracles.' We had ridden maybe five or six hours without stopping. I got off and a double-barreled shotgun was pointed in my face. We got back on the bus and I went later in the bush, I am not ashamed to say."

The tour was traumatic but had some saving graces. For the most part, the audiences, black and white, were young, large, energized, and ready to dance and sing along. "It was not horrible. If it was, we would not have stayed out there," Claudette Robinson, who lived in New Orleans until she was eight and married Smokey when she was seventeen, recalled in an oral history compiled by Susan Whitall, the Motown expert at the *Detroit News*. One of the more memorable moments came in Birmingham while Smokey was still incapacitated by the flu. It was the night of November 9, the day back in Detroit that the Ford Rotunda burned down and police raided the Gotham Hotel. At first it seemed the timing of Smokey's illness could not have been worse. That very day Motown released "You've Really Got a Hold on Me," a soulful song he had written and produced and planned to introduce to the crowd at Birmingham's municipal auditorium. But Claudette saved the evening by taking the lead herself, and as she recalled it, most could not tell the difference since they had never seen the Miracles before. Shouts from the audience. *You treat me badly / I love you madly / You've really got a hold on me.* More shouts and swoons: "Oooh, Smokey."

Eleven days later, the tour suffered a severe blow that had nothing to do with race. Eddie McFarland, a twenty-four-year-old roadie and driver, and Beans Bowles, the trip manager, had left Greenville, South Carolina, ahead of the *Revue* buses to prepare for the next stop, in Tampa. McFarland was at the wheel, Bowles in the cramped backseat, surrounded by instruments, including his flute, and a pouch holding $12,000 in receipts. They were exhausted from after-hours partying and drinking with the crew the night before. McFarland, who had stayed up all night, apparently dozed off as they were slicing across Florida near Gainesville on U.S. Rte. 301, and their station wagon veered into a truck. Bowles was found trapped in the backseat with serious injuries to his arms and legs and a gruesome puncture wound—the force of the crash dispatched his flute like a torpedo into his body under and through a shoulder until it protruded from his neck. He lived. McFarland was taken to the University of Florida Teaching Hospital, but died there. Janie Bradford, back at West Grand, took the call reporting the accident and spread the word through Motown. The rest of the traveling troupe did not know what had happened until they reached Tampa. "I remember Mrs. Edwards telling us at a meeting before the next show," Martha Reeves said. " 'Brace yourself,' she said. 'Be strong. We had an accident,' and then we had to swallow it up and perform." Katherine Anderson Schaffner of the Marvelettes, the group McFarland drove for most often, recalled, "It was devastating when we were told that Eddie had died. We were all so young. You never think about death, and then . . ." Detroit's major newspapers did not report the accident, but news spread swiftly in black Detroit. Esther Gordy returned home with her brother and McFarland's mother, who had flown down to Gainesville the morning after the accident. Would the tour go on? Gordy was conflicted, but he had contracts to fulfill and could not turn away from the big reward waiting at the end: those ten days in New York City.

McFarland was buried in Detroit the following Thursday after a wake the night before at the headquarters on West Grand. He left behind a young wife, Juanita, and two toddlers at their home on Melbourne Street on the east side.

Smokey returned to the *Revue* in time for the Apollo, a musical polestar he had heard about since he was six or seven and living on Belmont Street. He already had his nickname by that early age, coined by an uncle, Claude, who first called him "Smokey Joe," then shortened it. The name would be a reminder, Claude said, that despite his nephew's light complexion "you won't ever forget that you are black." No more chance of that than of Smokey not liking music. Two older sisters and his mother, before she died when he was ten, flooded their home with music of all kinds, "from gospel to classical to gut-bucket blues, to my sisters playing music they called bebop, which included Charlie Parker. The first voice I ever remember hearing in my life is Sarah Vaughan, because my sisters loved Sarah Vaughan and Billy Eckstine." They had an upright piano from Grinnell's that he experimented on just as young Berry Gordy had over on St. Antoine, figuring out simple chord combinations. Then there was the music at the big house on Oakland Avenue where his childhood buddy Cecil lived. That was Cecil Franklin, son of the singing reverend, C. L. Franklin, brother of the singing sisters, including Aretha. Everything at the Franklin home was polished and ornate, including the baby grand that Smokey first saw Aretha play when she was only three. He was smitten from then on. "Not only was she a cutie pie, but her musical talent was phenomenal. . . . As a child, she played nearly as good as she plays now—that's how advanced she was."

Smokey's advancement was more measured. He sang with the Five Chimes at Northern High, then formed a group called the Matadors and caught the attention of Gordy, who changed their name to the Miracles and taught Smokey how to transform poetry into winning lyrics. Now he had top billing at the Apollo, and as the *Revue* caravan reached Harlem, memories of his first appearance at the legendary theater washed over him. It was four years earlier, in 1958. He was eighteen. Gordy was his manager.

The Miracles had cut one record for Gordy so far, "Bad Girl." Everything about the trip to New York seemed intimidating. "First of all, we grew up in Detroit, and I don't think any of us had ever been out of Detroit, you know, other than going to Ypsilanti or Ann Arbor or somewhere like that in Michigan that's very close by," he recalled in an interview about the Apollo conducted for the Columbia University Libraries Center for Oral Histories. "But we were on our way to New York City, which in itself was . . . oooh, man! Not only were we going to New York City, we were going to play at the Apollo Theater, which was oooh, man, because you know we'd heard about the Apollo Theater and we thought there was this guy waiting backstage with a hook, and if you weren't good enough he'd pull you offstage. Because we'd heard about the amateur shows and blah blah all that. And not only that, one of my singing idols was the headliner, Ray Charles."

Wednesday morning, seven o'clock, they appeared onstage for rehearsal. They would go on the Ray Charles show following the one-legged tap dancer Peg Leg Bates. Charles (Honi) Coles, a noted tap dancer, ran the theater then. The Miracles knew nothing about how to rehearse for a professional show. They arrived only with what were called onionskins—chord sheets of their records but no arrangements for the band. "Comes our time to go over our music with the band. We've only got these onionskins. Honi Coles hit the ceiling," Robinson recalled. "'What do you mean by coming here with these? What are you doing? How dare Berry Gordy send you here!' And on and on, he's just raising hell. So for some reason or other, which he didn't have to be there, Ray comes in that morning. Ray came in and Honi's raising hell because we don't have arrangements.

"So Ray said, 'What's going on, Honi?'

"'These kids come in from Detroit, Berry Gordy sent them here, and they don't have arrangements.'

"Ray says, 'That's okay, man. Don't worry about it.' And I'm in awe because I'm looking at Ray Charles, man! So he says, 'Any of you kids know how to play your music?'

"So I said, 'Yes, Mr. Charles, I can play it on the piano.'

"He said, 'Okay.' He said, 'Come over here and sit down beside me and play it.' So I sat down and I started to play it and I started singing 'She's not a bad girl,' and after I'd sung about one verse of the song, Ray said, 'Okay, baby, I got it,' and he started playing it like he wrote it. I mean he just started playing it like he knew it already and he had written it and I was singing what he had written, you know, and I'm singing and he's playing.

"He says, 'Okay, saxophones, write this down. I want you to play [this]. Write that down.' So they wrote it down. 'Trumpets, I want you to play [this]. Write that down.' So they wrote that down. 'Bass player, play [this].' And he sat there and he did an arrangement to both of our songs that morning right there, and they wrote it down and he did it. From that moment on, I could have been in Timbuktu and they called me and said, 'Okay, Smoke, you got one day off, but we're giving something for Ray Charles in New York, we want you to come,' I would have come. Because not only was he a musical idol to me, I'm in awe of Ray Charles, but he was that kind of man that he would sit down and do something like that for us, and we're just teenagers. We're standing there scared to death, and he sat there and did that. So that was one of the greatest musical gestures in the history of music, so far as I'm concerned."

In the making of Motown, then, there is a place for the grace of Ray Charles. And a few things more. Ray's full name was Ray Charles Robinson. Smokey's father ran away from home in Alabama when he was twelve and knew nothing about his relatives. He looked like Ray Charles. Smokey used to joke with Ray, "I think you're my uncle." And it turned out that Honi Coles had a connection to Motown as well. For many years, his tap dance partner was Charles Sylvan Atkinson, who went by the stage name Cholly Atkins. Atkins & Coles was their team. By 1962 Cholly Atkins was a noted rhythm and blues choreographer who was working with Smokey and the Miracles on their dance moves when they came to the Apollo in December with the *Motortown Revue*. Berry Gordy and Harvey Fuqua were so impressed that they later brought Atkins in to become Motown's chief choreographer. The Temptations, the Miracles, the Four Tops, Gladys Knight and the Pips—the joyous moves that helped define Motown came mostly from Cholly Atkins. His old partner, Honi Coles, who had been so hard on the greenhorn Miracles that first rehearsal, decades later became Smokey's good golfing pal.

The temperatures in New York City were in the teens for most of the ten days of the Apollo run that December. The troupe stayed at the Hotel Theresa in Harlem, New York's version of Detroit's Gotham. Ron Brown, who later became commerce secretary under President Clinton, had grown up in the Theresa, where his father was the manager. Fidel Castro had stayed there when he visited the United Nations in 1960. Like the Gotham, the Theresa had once earned the praise of Langston Hughes, but now appeared past its prime. The nearby Apollo also seemed in decline; the dressing rooms were cold, scattered, and rat-infested. The famed marquee had the Miracles and Mary Wells on the top row, the Marvelettes and Marvin Gaye in the next row, then "The Motor-town Revue" in red on the third row with the Contours, and Stevie Wonder and the Supremes on the bottom. Berry Gordy had recorded live performances before, but never a full album of his signature stars. This was the first: *Recorded Live at the Apollo in New York*. The program was oriented toward the latest hits, featuring "Two Lovers" and "You've Really Got a Hold on Me." But what stood out on the recording was the raw energy and youthfulness of the audience members, especially the girls, who could be heard singing and chanting and shouting all the way through.

In his last *Michigan Chronicle* column of the year, Ziggy Johnson took note of Motown's success in 1962 and made predictions for 1963: "There will be more live shows hitting the road. Sepias will be cast in better roles in the movie industry. Television will open its doors to an all-Negro weekly show. Detroit will attract more tourists and the big buildings will continue to go up. The Temptations will move up as one of the leading singing groups. Aretha Franklin will come into her own." The Temptations were indeed moving up. They had just landed their first weeklong gig at the 20 Grand's Driftwood Lounge, joined by the comedian Billy Murry and an exotic dancer named Roxanne. The rest of Motown's artists had one final performance that year. It was on New Year's Eve and represented their only ensemble show in Detroit, a reprieve of their journey but in familiar territory. The *Motortown Revue* had taken Detroit to the nation and served as a powerful booster rocket in Motown's rise. Now they would entertain the home crowd. The concert was at the coliseum out at the Michigan State Fairgrounds at Woodward and Eight Mile. Esther Edwards made the arrangements. Mary Wells, the Miracles, Little Stevie, Marvin Gaye, the Marvelettes, all there, along with the singer who got Berry Gordy started, Jackie Wilson. Advance tickets were available at one outlet downtown. You could buy them at Grinnell's.

Chapter 5

# PARTY BUS

**HERE WAS THE LINDELL** Cocktail Bar in the first days of 1963. The joint was on the edge of Detroit's skid row, at the corner of Cass and Bagley, attached to the seedy, four-story Lindell Hotel. Like all of skid row, the building was soon to be a goner, slated for demolition in the name of urban renewal. Jimmy and John Butsicaris were about to move their establishment down a few blocks to a spot at Cass and Michigan. At the suggestion of Doc Greene, a sports columnist at the *Detroit News,* they would bless their relocated bar with a revised name, calling it the Lindell A.C., the letters standing for—or mocking the idea of—Athletic Club. There was a noted A.C. in Detroit already, the Detroit Athletic Club, which could not have been less like the Lindell. One was the exclusive redoubt of the city's ruling class; the other the after-hours hangout of pro athletes and scribes and hangers-on of various sorts, including gamblers.

The old Lindell had a brick front with masonry gone awry like a bad set of teeth, some bricks protruding, others crumbling. A grimy picture window faced the downtown street, but patrons were cloaked behind drawn venetian blinds. Neon lettering was attached to the window, and in front of the blinds the owners had arranged a display window of a basketball and autographed photos of Detroit athletes. Inside, the bar's counter ran thirty feet down one wall. In the back, in dim light, stood two pool tables. Word was that Ron Kline, a journeyman right-handed pitcher for the Tigers, had lost his shirt in a pool game the previous year and paid off on the spot. The side walls met a high ceiling and were splotched with bar grime, at least where the wall could be seen amid athletic mementoes: baseball bats sliced lengthwise, helmets, gloves, balls, and rows of photographs of Lions, Tigers, Red Wings, Pistons, and favorite players from other cities. In the fifties it had been a nightlife home away from home for fabled Yankees Mickey Mantle, Whitey Ford, and Billy Martin, the bad boy credited with inspiring the sports decor. If you were in Detroit to play ball, you likely found your way to the Lindell. But on this first week of January 1963, the bar was attracting agents from the Federal Bureau of Investigation and the National Football League as well, all sniffing for information about the clientele and the Detroit Lions lineman who had invested $50,000 as a part owner.

That was Alex Karras, the talented all-pro defensive tackle, twenty-six years old, six-foot-two, 260 pounds of irascibility, son of a Greek doctor, hammy, intelligent, sarcastic, freewheeling, hard-drinking, and beloved by Detroit sports fans, who placed him in their modern-day pantheon with baseball's Al Kaline, hockey's Gordie Howe, and football's Night Train Lane. Karras was a born grappler and actor whose mayhem inspired one of the Lindell's famous brawls, when he and William Fritz Afflis, aka Dick the Bruiser, a pro wrestler and former NFL lineman for the Green Bay Packers, commenced demolition on one another and the establishment. A Lion of such talents eventually found his way to Hollywood, where his many roles included that of the imbecilic brute Mongo in Mel Brooks's *Blazing Saddles*. The Lindell was his kind of place.

Bars, jocks, mobsters, gambling—those were the four corners of a Detroit story that broke on January 5 but had been in the works since the previous August. The Lindell became part of the story mostly because of Karras's connection to it. Karras became part of the story mostly because of his connection to the Party Bus, which was a story in itself.

The Party Bus was the movable feast of the local mob. It was an erstwhile Department of Street Railways coach registered under the name of Odus Tincher, a convicted gambler with the look of a milquetoast bank teller who fronted an illegal barbut game (a Turkish variation of craps) out of the private Lesod Club. Lesod was an acronym for Lower East Side of Detroit, although the operation had long since moved downtown, brazenly situated on West Columbia across the street from the Detroit Women's Club. Tincher worked for the Giacalone brothers, Anthony and Vito, familiarly known as Tony Jack and Billy Jack, who were rising powers in the Detroit mob and used the Party Bus as their occasional means of good-times transportation. The bus was painted blue and silver, the colors of the football Lions, and had garish yellow curtains and upholstery inside, along with a well-stocked bar and bunk beds. On nights when the Party Bus was rolling through Detroit and over to the Grosse Pointes and back, it was usually followed by the vice squad. The police knew all about it. In off-hours at their own favorite hangout, Sindbad's, down by the Detroit River, cops would talk about the time the Party Bus cozied up to a strip joint with Billy Jack at the wheel, captured the barmen and all the entertainers inside along with a supply of liquor, and rumbled off into the night.

The link between the Party Bus and football players began in the drowsy early Saturday morning darkness of the previous August 18, when officers from the Criminal Investigations Bureau entered another hangout, the Grecian Gardens on Monroe Street in Greektown, only one block south of police headquarters. Inside they happened to see Wayne Walker, a Lions linebacker, sitting with the Giacalone brothers at a table in the back. Also visible was Jimmy Butsicaris, Alex Karras's pal who had brought him into part ownership of the Lindell Cocktail Bar. The officers had entered the restaurant based on a complaint of illegal liquor sales, but now they had something more to interest them, so they left and staked out the scene from their car. The Grecian Gardens, as it happened, was a familiar Lions lair, much like the Lindell. The players often held what they called Loyalty Parties there, a night of male bonding, team building, and prodigious drinking without management, coaches, and wives. But this was not the cleanest crowd for Walker to be seen with, not with Tony Jack and Billy Jack at the table and so many other underworld characters connected to the place. The bar operator, Gus Colacasides, considered the kingpin of Greektown gambling, kept secret black books of gamblers and bribable lawmen. The building was owned by the widow of the late Pete Corrado, known as "the Enforcer" during his heyday in the rum-running Prohibition era, when the Detroit River, with Canadian booze on the other side, swarmed with smugglers. Two modern-day enforcers, Sammy Giordano and Pete Vitale, worked at the Gardens now, and a Corrado son, Anthony, provided muscle for the Giacalones.

The police officers watched the mobsters and Walker leave from the back door and part ways. They saw the Giacalones and barkeep Butsicaris board the Party Bus along with Odus Tincher and Anthony Thomas. The cops knew Thomas, who possessed a string of convictions and the nickname Screechy. He was on the mob chart they kept at the precinct office and looked the part, dressed in black shirt and white tie, driving a big red Cadillac. One of the Detroit Police Department rookies, David Wright, who worked Woodward Avenue up near Wayne State, had recently stopped Thomas in his Caddy and was standing outside his car when another sedan pulled up snug to his side and trapped him between the two vehicles. "This nice young officer here was not going to give me a ticket," Screechy scratched, which precipitated an exchange of fuck-you pleasantries before Wright walked back to his squad car with his hand on his gun. Now the vice officers were tailing Screechy, Tony Jack, Billy Jack, and their pals on the Party Bus for 170 miles to Cleveland, where the Lions were playing a preseason game later that day against the Dallas Cowboys, part of an unusual NFL doubleheader, with the hometown Browns hosting the Pittsburgh Steelers in the second matchup. After the game, the mobsters returned to the Party Bus, but this time the surveillance crew noticed Alex Karras and a teammate climbing aboard for the three-hour ride back to Detroit. The most prominent Lion was in the mob's rolling den.

On Monday, at his office at 1300 Beaubien, George Clifton Edwards Jr., the police commissioner, received an oral report on the weekend episode from John O'Neill, one of his trusted lieutenants. Edwards, the son of a civil liberties lawyer from Dallas and educated at Southern Methodist and Harvard, was now forty-seven, lean and bespectacled, with the Wilsonian look of a Presbyterian minister or college president. He had arrived in Detroit in 1936 with fifty dollars, his life's possessions in a single suitcase, and his hopes resting in the dream that he could write a novel on the industrial urban condition, a Detroit auto plant variation of *The Jungle*, Upton Sinclair's turn-of-the-century muckraking novel on the meatpacking industry in Chicago. After landing a job at an auto plant, he was tutored in the rough-and-tumble of the Detroit labor movement by the Reuther brothers of the UAW and rose through city politics and law to the bench and then the police commissioner's job, far to the left of the force he was asked to lead but no one's patsy. When the *Free Press* broke the story that he was taking the job, the article called him "a liberal with a capital L." Along with advancing civil rights in the city and attempting to weed out corruption on the force, he had made gambling and the mob a priority since taking the top cop job the previous January. His distaste for the Detroit underworld went back to his earliest days with Walter Reuther, when the unsavory connections between legal and illicit power centers in the city emerged in the most harrowing way.

Late on an April night in 1938, Edwards and his wife, Peg, were at Reuther's apartment at 13233 LaSalle, along with six other couples invited to an intimate birthday party for Victor Reuther's wife, Sophie. They had ordered chop suey dinners from a nearby Chinese restaurant, and when the doorbell rang, Walter quickly opened the door, expecting the delivery man. Instead two thugs bulled their way in, brandishing revolvers. While one intruder held the guests at bay with his gun ("Stay back or I'll plug you!" he said), the other went after "the redheaded guy" with a blackjack, and when Walter Reuther pried that away, he and the assailant struggled over a floor lamp. Edwards told the gunmen that if they shot Walter they would have to shoot them all. The men fled after one guest escaped out a back window and called the police. Not long after, the two thugs were caught; it turned out that one had mob connections, going back to a four-month sentence for bootlegging in the twenties, and had until two weeks earlier worked as an investigator for Ford Motor Company. Was it merely coincidence that at the time of the home invasion Walter Reuther was preparing to testify at the trial of six Ford goons who had attacked him and his labor comrades a year earlier in the battle of the overpass at the Rouge plant? Not likely. Yet when the assailants, Eddie Percelli and Bud Holt, were put on trial, they came up with the novel defense that Reuther had hired them to stage the incident and then double-crossed them. The jury bought their story and found them innocent. In the courtroom after he was cleared, Bud Holt, who had charmed the jury, was surrounded by six women jurors eager to shake his hand.

Edwards had been in Detroit less than two years then, but from that moment on he never looked at the place the same way again. "I never wrote the novel," he once explained. "But I think perhaps I lived it." By the time he took over the Detroit Police Department he carried with him a dark understanding of the many ways the mob moved in the city. He kept a three-ring notebook in his office titled *MAFIA: Members-Relatives, Associates-Suspects.* It listed and described every thug suspected of being in the Detroit mob, sometimes called the partnership or the outfit. He wanted his men to follow leads wherever they went. He had pushed for the raid on the Gotham Hotel in November as a means of cutting into organized crime's numbers treasury and concluded that the publicity resulting from that raid had a dampening effect on gambling across the city. The more sunlight, the more publicity, the better, he thought, as long as it was based on solid legwork. Sometimes publicity was his best weapon, and easier than prosecution. But the connection to the Lions was worrisome. He enjoyed football. He was not looking to bust the athletes, but it infuriated him that "the crumbs of the underworld would try to force themselves on Lions players."

The day after receiving the report, Edwards dispatched O'Neill and another aide to the suburbs to meet with George Wilson, the Lions coach. At the Fox & Hounds, an old English Tudor restaurant on Woodward Avenue out near the team's training camp at the Cranbrook Schools in Bloomfield Hills, O'Neill detailed to the coach what they knew about Karras and the Party Bus and the downtown bars and mobsters. No big deal, Wilson essentially responded. His boys were responsible and popular and dealt with all sorts of people and would not get involved in gambling.

Over the fall and early winter, as the 1962 season played out with the Lions finishing 12 and 3, second in the Western Division to the Packers, several lines of investigation converged. Word spread that the office of NFL commissioner Pete Rozelle was probing various reports of other players on other teams associating with gamblers. In late December, Edwards passed along the information his inspectors had gathered to the principal owner of the Lions, William Clay Ford, a grandson of Henry Ford and younger brother of the Deuce, and then sent a report to Rozelle. Along with information about the Party Bus and the Grecian Gardens, Edwards informed the NFL that Karras had become a part owner of the Lindell Cocktail Bar, which did not seem as mobbed as the Gardens but had some connections to gamblers and prostitution. The FBI, meanwhile, was conducting a separate investigation of Detroit mobsters, whose telephones they had been tapping for more than a year. Everything popped into the open again in early January, when the Lions traveled to Miami to play the Steelers in the Playoff Bowl, a dreary postseason game involving the second-place finisher in each division.

On the day before the game, Rozelle met with reporters in nearby Hollywood Beach. The big news from this session was the commissioner's declaration that some players had been "associating with undesirable types." His investigators, mostly former FBI agents, had been following scores of leads. So far, Rozelle said, there was "smoke but no fire" in terms of proving anything beyond imprudent associations by the players, but there was reason for concern. The first publicized leads were to Chicago. "Bears Fullback Reveals Lie Tests in 'Fix' Quiz," ran a banner headline. The fullback in question, Rick Casares, said that he had taken and passed two lie detector tests administered by the NFL to determine if he had shaved points for gamblers in any games. The concerns arose because Casares was seen with an underworld bookie, Zaza Yitkavitz, and he and other Bears were known to frequent two nightclubs connected to Chicago's mob, a strip joint on North Clark and a club out by O'Hare International Airport.

After Rozelle talked to the press, a reporter for the *Detroit News* interviewed Edwin J. Anderson, the Lions general manager. Anderson could not have sounded more out of the loop. "In my twelve years with the Lions, not a single Detroit player has been under suspicion in any way of association with gamblers or unsavory characters of any kind," he said. He was also quoted as scoffing at "the idea that any young man in [his] right mind would vary a hair's breadth from the accepted line of conduct." Given the training camp meeting at the Fox & Hounds with Detroit officers, one could not say that Coach Wilson too was out of the loop, yet he commented to the press that same day that he "had not heard of any investigation involving the Lions." With a game at hand, Wilson was left alone after that, but Anderson's comments precipitated a meeting hours before kickoff with Rozelle and William Clay Ford. He emerged with a slightly different attitude, saying he was now unhappy that Karras was part owner of the Lindell bar and wished the player would sell his interest.

The cast of characters at the Orange Bowl included Alex Karras and Wayne Walker on the field, George Wilson on the sideline, William Clay Ford and Pete Rozelle in the stands. Also in the stands were Vito Giacalone, Mike (another enforcer) Rubino, and two sons of old-time Prohibition-era Detroit mobsters, Anthony J. Zerilli and young Corrado. Zerilli had a linen supply company and Corrado was in the vending machine trade. Rozelle knew they were in Miami, as did Edwards and leaders of his vice squad in Detroit, who had called their Miami counterparts beforehand, provided descriptions and flight information, and asked for surveillance from arrival to departure. Billy Jack and his boys rented a Cadillac at the airport and checked into a hotel under assumed names. A few hours before the game, they met with Joe Masset, an old Detroit booze smuggler who had long ago resettled in Miami. Then they headed for the stadium. An undercover Miami policewoman sat nearby, and one of her colleagues snapped photographs from a middle distance. By then Rozelle's comments and the Casares story were out there. According to the Miami police report, Giacalone and his men sat stoically, showing "little interest in the game but looked at the player benches through binoculars." They left town without any contact with players.

The story caught fire in the Detroit press over the next four days. Rozelle told reporters that whatever he knew about Lions associating with unsavory figures came from the police commissioner in Detroit. That led to reporting about the Party Bus and Grecian Gardens and Karras and the Lindell bar and the Miami surveillance. Wayne Walker acknowledged being at the Gardens but said he had not gambled and had done nothing wrong. Karras responded to Anderson's belated call to give up his interest in the Lindell by saying that he would sooner quit football. The Butsicaris boys were like brothers to him, he said. He said he knew the Giacalones enough to say hello. Then he went after Rozelle, appearing on national television to acknowledge that he had gambled on games but that that was his right as long as he did not bet on games involving his team. At the cop shop at 1300 Beaubien, Edwards went into full publicity mode. He held a press conference the following Wednesday, January 9, detailing the chronology of his department's investigation. From then on, he said, he would use public exposure as a weapon: "It is going to be our policy to expose organized crime to public view when we can legitimately do so with established fact. We want to cut down the trade these people have; we want to cut down their tolerance in the community. . . . If people feel we are serious about this they will give us more information which we can investigate."

Rozelle was focused on the football players and eventually would suspend Karras for a year and Paul Hornung of the Packers indefinitely (also a year, as it turned out), both for betting on games. He also levied fines against Wayne Walker and five other Lions. But Edwards concentrated on mobsters, and they, as it happened, were also concentrating on him. FBI wiretaps indicated that all the publicity about gambling and the Lions was bothering them. Tony and Vito Giacalone were heard complaining during a conversation on January 21 that they were unable to "get to" Edwards. The normal means were not working, so they thought about embarrassing him with their embrace. "I'm going to haul my fucking bus out," Vito said. "I'm going to get a great big picture of Edwards and put it on there and say we—every hoodlum—we love him. This will knock his fucking wheels off. Hoodlums love Edwards and we are voting for him." How they might be voting for him was another matter; he was not running for office then. But the point was clear.

According to Edwards's unpublished biography, later archived at the Walter P. Reuther Library at Wayne State University, and a book drawn largely from his earlier text by a family friend, author Mary M. Stolberg, his next moves involved the press. Late in January he had lunch at the Detroit Athletic Club with Harvey W. Patton, managing editor of the *Detroit News*, and the paper's ace reporter, John M. Carlisle. Patton offered the paper's Washington bureau as a conduit for Edwards to pass information along to the Permanent Committee on Investigations, the Senate panel investigating organized crime led by Democrat John L. McClellan of Arkansas. Edwards agreed, and also allowed Carlisle a behind-the-scenes look at what Detroit police were finding. His next lunch at the Detroit Athletic Club was with the editor of the *News*, Martin S. Hayden, a second-generation newsman who was a pillar of the city establishment, though with a reputation for holding tough against critics of his newspaper, from politicians and advertisers to mobsters. So it was not surprising that Edwards would turn to Hayden as a confidant. Was his life endangered by the Giacalones? Edwards did not believe so, but he was not naïve about violence in Detroit. "I don't want you to think I've developed a cops-and-robbers mentality," Edwards said, according to Hayden's later recollection. "What I'm going to tell you is serious. It is also brief and I'm not going to be able to give you supporting details. For reasons I can't tell you, I've decided to write you a letter. It is written and I have turned it over to a close friend with instructions to deliver it to you if anything should happen to me. If you ever publish it, which I hope you won't, I guarantee you'll have the damndest newspaper story you have ever seen."

Edwards had placed the letter in the hands of John Herling, a labor journalist and liberal activist in Washington who had been his close friend for more than twenty-five years, back to the days when they were both followers of the socialist Norman Thomas. A year earlier Herling had invited Edwards to the White House Correspondents Dinner and introduced him to the attorney general, Robert F. Kennedy. During that conversation, they had talked about the Detroit mob and how organized crime in Michigan swelled during the Prohibition-era rum-running between Detroit and Canada. Now, on the manila envelope Edwards gave Herling, he wrote, "For Robert Kennedy, to be opened only in the event of my death by violent means or by unnatural causes where certainty of death cannot be determined." The contents of the letter have been lost to history, except for a cover note that read, "Enclosed is an envelope which represents a little bit of extra life insurance. I have taken care that the Mafia here in Detroit knows this is placed somewhere—but you may be certain that they do not know where." This was the publicity gambit again, with higher stakes. Edwards had already asked his trusted lieutenants to make sure that word got back to the Giacalones about his letter.

What the Giacalones did not yet know is that Edwards and his Criminal Investigations Bureau were in the process of setting up a sting to ensnare them. Nonstop surveillance with cameras, tape recorders, and miniature radio transmitters were all part of the scheme, but the key to the sting was a "bought cop" who was not really bought, and for that role they recruited a police sergeant who as a Marine corporal during the war had "crawled on his belly in the volcanic ash of Iwo Jima."

## Chapter 6

# GLOW

**WHEN IT CAME TO HIS WARDROBE,** Jerome Cavanagh, the mayor of Detroit, considered himself a top-drawer gentleman. The dress shirts for his six-foot, 200-pound frame were custom made at J. M. Citron, a haberdashery on Washington Boulevard, and his silk ties were imported from New York. "This tie costs more than your entire outfit," he liked to say, his blue eyes twinkling, only sort of joking, if someone happened to catch him admiring his apparel in the mirror. In a cozy study adjoining his spacious eleventh-floor office downtown, he kept four extra suits, thirteen striped ties, and a cabinet of fresh shirts, ready for a change of clothes at a moment's notice. The finery clothed a natural-born entertainer. If three pals accompanied Mayor Cavanagh to the London Chop House on West Congress after work and were escorted to his usual spot, Table No. 1, their favorite drinks waiting on the red-checkered tablecloth, there would be eight or ten people pulling up chairs by the end of the night listening to him spin stories. The blarney came with his Irish heritage, but he had more taste for the good life, and public life, than his father, Sylvester, who spent four decades cleaning boilers at Ford's Rouge plant. The son, at age thirty-four, thrived on being in the know on all things gossipy and political, and though trained at the University of Detroit School of Law and partial to the New Frontier politics of JFK, he had the sensibility of an old-style newspaper guy. Many of his aides came from that ink-stained world, former newspapermen at the *De-*

*troit News* and *Free Press* and *Times*, an evening Hearst paper that went belly-up a year before his election.

Jim Trainor, his press secretary, marveled at how the mayor could "charm birds out of trees" and was perhaps himself living proof. He had been recruited to work for Cavanagh after being a tough old crow at the *Times*, a city editor straight out Ben Hecht's *The Front Page*, chewing cigars and chewing out reporters with equal vigor, his ornery cynicism covering a soft heart. Another aide, Bob Toohey, had been taken by Cavanagh's charisma since they both worked as guides at Henry Ford's Greenfield Village back in their college days. Whenever an important delegation arrived, Toohey recalled, Cavanagh invariably was assigned their tour. "He was charming. Once I had a group behind Jerry's and we were going into the Menlo Park area, where his group already was, and I was able to listen to his speech. He slipped under the ropes and was at Edison's desk and goes into this spiel—*That chair right there is the chair Thomas Edison sat in*—and he had this ability to mesmerize. People followed him like a school of fish."

Now, in the early months of 1963, after one year as mayor, Cavanagh had a whole city following him. His tour guide spiel had risen to another realm, the ultimate urban sales pitch. Detroit was a city on the move, he said repeatedly during speeches that winter. It was a city with "a tremendously interesting and dramatic story to tell . . . a city which will continue in the future to be as it has been in the past—the envy of every other metropolitan area." Mayors are expected to say such things—hyperbolic boosterism is a job requirement—but Cavanagh had reason to believe some of his own rhetoric.

It was in that frame of mind that he rode the elevator in the City-County Building from his office to a large hearing room a few floors below on February 15, a frozen Friday afternoon. Rising twenty stories above the bottom end of Woodward Avenue, the City-County Building was part of the new Detroit. It was built around the same time as the nearby Ford Auditorium, in the midfifties, a few years before Cobo Hall, and had a similar modern Internationalist design, its gleaming white marble exterior echoing the United Nations Building in New York. That worldly touch was what Detroit was now trying to sell; it was the crux of conversation at the meeting Cavanagh was about to attend: the first gathering of the Detroit Olympic Committee.

The city was going for it all then, striving in its underdog middle-American way to be the center of the modern world, bidding to be the site for the Republican and Democratic national conventions in 1964 and the 1968 Summer Olympics. The political conventions seemed out of reach and would soon go to San Francisco and Atlantic City, though just being in the running gave Detroit a publicity boost (and, for mayoral aide Jack Casey, the consolation gift of a baseball signed by Ted Williams courtesy of a GOP committeewoman from Maine he had escorted to a Tigers game during a site visit). But the Olympics was another matter. At a meeting in Chicago four months earlier, the U.S. Olympic Committee had endorsed Detroit as its candidate in the competition to become the host city. The final selection from major cities around the world would be decided in October by a vote of the International Olympic Committee, and Detroit seemed to have much going for it.

Avery Brundage, longtime president of the IOC, had made his fortune in Chicago, but he was born in Detroit. Douglas Roby, one of two other Americans on the IOC executive committee, was a full-blooded Detroiter, a former football player at Michigan, who spent his career at American Metal Products Company, which manufactured automobile parts. Roby's job connected him to Fred Matthaei Sr., founder of American Metal, who happened to be chairman of the Detroit Olympic Committee and mastermind of its effort. Matthaei (pronounced math-eye) not only knew Roby and other key Olympic decision makers; he possessed a keen understanding of the peculiarities of the IOC. For a quarter century he had doggedly pursued his dream of making Detroit the summer venue and had accumulated as much inside dope on the politics of the organization as anyone except President Brundage. Almost alone during that span, Matthaei had carried Detroit to the final selection round five times, an extraordinary feat in itself, but he had never closed the deal. He had traveled to IOC conventions in London in 1939, Lausanne in 1946, Paris in 1949, Rome in 1955, and Munich in 1959, promoting Detroit every time and coming up short every time. He was seventy now, his hair gone white, and this was the city's best chance ever, he thought, and perhaps its last.

By 2:30 that afternoon, the assemblage of Olympic boosters at the City-County Building totaled more than three hundred, including a coterie of Detroit's ruling class. Benson and William Clay Ford, the Deuce's two younger brothers, both vice presidents of Ford Motor Company, were there, along with Richard Cross, chairman of American Motors, Louis Goad, executive vice president of General Motors, Lynn Townsend, president of Chrysler Corporation, and a suited executive flock from Detroit's leading banks, utilities, tire companies, airlines, newspapers, and public relations firms. As honorary cochairman, Cavanagh called the meeting to order, followed by his honorary partner, George Romney, who had been sworn in as Michigan's governor only six weeks earlier. Romney's inauguration at the Michigan State Capitol in Lansing had been marked by its bipartisan nature, an ambience that puzzled his fellow Republicans and discombobulated some Democrats, but now, in pushing for the 1968 Summer Games, bipartisanship was at least temporarily in order.

There was, as it turned out, more to it than trying to sell Detroit to the world. As Roby and Matthaei explained when called on by Cavanagh, Detroit was now under attack again from its sun-soaked American nemesis, Los Angeles, whose civic and Olympic leaders had refused to accept the USOC's earlier choice of Detroit and demanded—and somehow won—a reopening of bids. The word from L.A., delivered by messengers ranging from Governor Edmund G. Brown to Hollywood crooner Bing Crosby, was condescending toward the midwestern competitor. Detroit was dismissed as second rate, economically troubled, not big enough for the occasion. Los Angeles had the experience, having staged the 1932 Summer Games, and boasted superior facilities, finances, hotel rooms, attractions, and weather. Cavanagh bemoaned the reopening of bidding as "unwarranted and unsportsmanlike." Romney complained that L.A. was "trying to rob Michigan of its Olympic birthright." Roby surmised that the West Coast gambit could only wound Detroit and was nervous about the second vote, which would be held in New York on March 18. The Detroit newspapers railed against Los Angeles, though Martin Hayden, editor of the *News*, argued that the attempt at subversion had a unifying effect: "Our governor, our mayor, the business community, legislators from both parties and aroused citizenry suddenly find themselves marching in step toward a common objective. Here is the unforeseen and happy miracle wrought by the assault of a rival."

So that was Detroit, anxious but as cohesive as the Rouge assembly line, with all parts snapping into place. Or so it seemed.

The following week, as city leaders mobilized to protect their Olympic standing, Wayne State University's Institute for Regional and Urban Studies, led by sociologist Albert J. Mayer, issued a report titled "The Population Revolution in Detroit." The report became a one-day story, relegated to a second section of the *Free Press*, but in retrospect, the findings and projections were of startling importance and haunting prescience.

The 1960 U.S. Census placed Detroit's population at 1,670,144. By Wayne State's calculations, if current trends continued the city's population in 1970 would decline to about 1,259,515—a loss of about a quarter of the population in one decade. That was disturbing enough, but even more troublesome, the report said, was who was leaving Detroit and who was being left behind. "Productive persons who pay taxes are moving out of the city, leaving behind the non-productive," the report noted. "Non-productive" was not used as a pejorative but as a statistical calculation. For the purposes of the study, "productive" was defined by measurements of economics and age. The most productive were people who held jobs and were between ages twenty-five and forty-four, while moderately productive included those who worked and were between ages fifteen and sixty-four. The rest fell into the nonproductive category. According to the sociologists, the city encompassed not only Detroit but two small municipalities, Hamtramck and Highland Park, that were in whole or in part geographically within the city. The metropolitan complex, meaning the suburbs to which most people were fleeing, included Wayne County past the city limits plus Oakland and Macomb Counties.

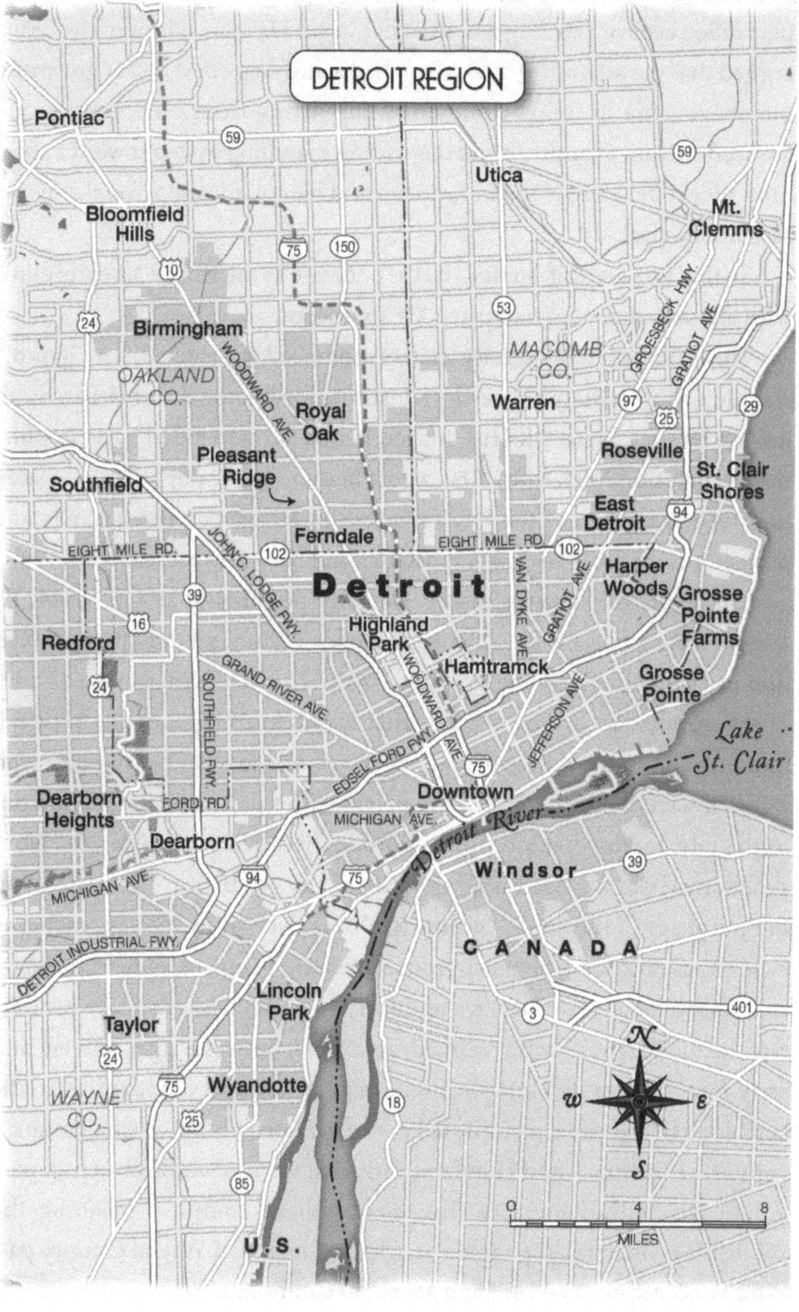
DETROIT REGION
Pontiac
59
Utica
59
Mt. Clemms
Bloomfield Hills
75
150
10
53
24
Birmingham
MACOMB CO.
GROESBECK HWY
GRATIOT AVE
OAKLAND CO.
WOODWARD AVE.
Royal Oak
Warren
97
25
29
Pleasant Ridge
Roseville
St. Clair Shores
Southfield
East Detroit
94
Ferndale
EIGHT MILE RD.
102
EIGHT MILE RD.
102
JOHN C. LODGE FWY.
Harper Woods
Detroit
39
VAN DYKE AVE
GRATIOT AVE
Grosse Pointe Farms
16
Highland Park
Redford
Hamtramck
GRAND RIVER AVE
WOODWARD AVE.
Grosse Pointe
24
SOUTHFIELD FWY
JEFFERSON AVE
Lake St. Clair
EDSEL FORD FWY
75
Downtown
Dearborn Heights
FORD RD
MICHIGAN AVE.
Detroit River
Dearborn
Windsor
39
94
75
MICHIGAN AVE
DETROIT INDUSTRIAL FWY
CANADA
Lincoln Park
3
401
Taylor
N
24
75
Wyandotte
W
E
18
WAYNE CO.
25
S
85
0
4
8
MILES
U.S.

There was a racial component to the study that the authors did not want to be misconstrued or distorted. In the 1960 Census, Detroit's population was 28.9 percent black. By 1970, according to their estimate, the city would be 44.35 percent black. But African Americans who had the resources to move and could find housing in the suburbs would do so with the same urgency as whites: "Present population trends clearly demonstrate that the city is, by and large, being abandoned by all except those who suffer from relatively great housing, educational and general economic deprivations." Cavanagh, who inherited a municipal debt when he took office, had tried to deal with the city's financial difficulties by pushing through an income tax that also applied to commuters who worked in the city. But the report suggested that the commuter tax would at best be of short-term benefit. With the suburbs growing not only from new housing but from shopping centers, offices, and industrial facilities, more people would not only live but also shop and work out there, turning the commuter tax into "a hollow mockery." The authors were also skeptical of any beneficial effects coming from Detroit's urban renewal, which, they said, despite all the money poured into it, produced very little housing, only about a thousand units to that point, with "only a few thousand more contemplated." The inadequacy of public housing resulting from urban renewal had been a subject sociologist Mayer had been lamenting for years. As he once described it, "The elephantine efforts have brought forth a mouse."

Step out of chronology for a moment to consider this. The Wayne State report was issued four years before Detroit was rocked by rebellion and riot in the summer of 1967, an event considered pivotal in the city's decline and transformation. The report was written fifty years before Detroit declared bankruptcy in 2013, its population down to 688,000, the shriveled tax base incapable of supporting financial obligations. The report predicted a dire future long before it became popular to attribute Detroit's fall to a grab bag of Rust Belt infirmities, from high labor costs to harsh weather, and before the city staggered from more blows of municipal corruption and incompetence. Before any of that, the forces of deterioration were already set in motion.

Detroit was being threatened by its own design of concrete and metal and fuel and movement, and also by the American dilemma of race. The Motor City's proud grid of urban freeways had made it easier for people to live in the suburbs and work in the city. Years of urban renewal had uprooted traditional neighborhoods, many of them predominantly black, and set in motion the rippling effect of white ethnic enclaves washing farther outward beyond Eight Mile Road, the city boundary. The giant suburban shopping malls of Eastland and Northland (surrounded by a vast concrete plain holding 9,984 parking spaces), with Westland coming and Southland on the decade's far horizon, were gradually tightening the noose around the city's downtown hub. The auto companies themselves, while still identified symbolically as being in and of Detroit, had been relying more on plants and suppliers located outside the city and around the country. When Cavanagh and others thought Detroit's future was to be envied, when they were striving to land the Olympics and earn the imprimatur of a world-class city, the sociologists at Wayne State were analyzing data and trends and noticed something troubling. They saw the shadows forming.

Composition and decomposition. Detroit dying and thriving at the same time. Seven weeks earlier, Cavanagh had christened the year 1963 with the mayor's traditional New Year's Day greeting to Detroiters. The *Free Press* ran it on the January 1 front page: "1962 has been a good year for most of us in Detroit. Fewer people are out of work, business in general is on the upturn, and our auto plants are busy turning out quality cars that have made Detroit famous throughout the world. The improved economic picture is only a part of the renaissance which has marked 1962 as the year of Detroit's rebirth. Our city is striking out at blight and other stifling factors of urban life. Detroit is becoming a better place to live—not only through dramatic improvements in neighborhoods, expressways, and physical surroundings—but better also in a spiritual way. Gradually, we are learning how to live together, with understanding as human beings. . . . Now we must see to it that our progress, our momentum, is carried into 1963."

Cavanagh's own momentum came to a sudden stop that very first day of the year. He was traveling back to Detroit after attending Romney's inauguration in Lansing when he started feeling a heavy, dull ache in his left side. After examining him, his doctor called in a chest specialist, who determined that he had pneumonia and sent him to Providence Hospital. His police aide, Sgt. Henry Wood, said the mayor seemed unperturbed about his condition but worried that he would miss watching the second half of the Rose Bowl between Wisconsin and Southern Cal. The doctors said he had worked and played himself to exhaustion, with his twenty-hour days and late nights at various restaurants around town. No more of that for now, nothing but treatment and bed rest for ten days. A daily hospital diet restricted to no more than a thousand calories. A few books at his bedside, including a biography of Fiorello La Guardia, the little flower of New York, and *A Nation of Sheep* by William Lederer. When he was released from Providence and spirited off to a weekend retreat by his wife, who was seven months pregnant, expecting their seventh child, his doctor instructed him to slow down and "have dinner at home more than once or twice a week."

That same day, January 11, *Life* magazine hit the newsstands. The cover was dominated by actress Ann-Margret posed in pink, leg up, arms out, hair swirling, but the left side of the page announced a story and photo spread inside of an altogether different sort: "Glow from Detroit Spreads Everywhere."

The celebration of Detroit started on page 26 with a two-page photograph of a beefy middle-aged car dealer in a swirl of miniature cars. "Boom . . . in Detroit," the caption read. This was Arnold Klett's moment of glory, representing his city and the car industry. Business was flush. He sold Cadillacs, at the top of the General Motors line, and people were buying them. GM was trying to keep up but lagged weeks behind on delivery. Klett alone had thirty-five customers waiting for Caddys, and until the real cars rolled in he was handing out toy models and posing happily for *Life*.

The photos were shot by Burk Uzzle, who months earlier had joined the Chicago bureau as *Life*'s youngest contract photographer, only twenty-three. Uzzle was at the start of a memorable career capturing indelible American moments through the lens of his Pentax and Leica, from the somber daze of Martin Luther King Jr.'s funeral in Atlanta to the psychedelic drizzle-dazzle of the nation's tribal counterculture at the Woodstock music festival in New York State. Detroit was one of his first assignments. He visited Ford, Chrysler, GM, and American Motors, day and night, inside and out, from the boiler rooms to the executive suites and the design rooms, and even ventured up to Lansing to capture the inaugural ball for car guy Romney. Dozens of contact sheets from the Detroit assignment later found their way to a photojournalism archive at the Library of Congress, supplementing the array of photographs printed in *Life*. He photographed workers, white and black, on the assembly line, snapping parts into chassis frames, adjusting steering wheels, soldering doors, eating in the cafeteria, cashing paychecks, drinking and playing cards in nearby bars, and row after row of finished automobiles, gleaming in the winter snow, stacked high on triple-decker rail transport cars, ready to roll to St. Louis. Uzzle composed the most evocative shot, inspiring the cover headline, in the pitch darkness of the late shift outside the east side Chrysler plant: shadowy outlines of the factory and its smokestacks lit by the glowing neon Chrysler sign, heavy dark smoke billowing into the cold midnight sky. The caption: "Signaling the prosperity of the industry, a Chrysler Corp. plant in Detroit blasts on into the night." "That was back in the days when smoke was viewed as a sign of progress and prosperity," Uzzle recalled. "People in Detroit were delighted to have us photograph it. It meant that things were booming."

The main story was written by Keith Wheeler, a go-to writer in the stable of *Life* scribblers at Manhattan headquarters. The optimism that first became apparent at the Detroit Auto Show the previous October had intensified into cocky confidence. The car consumer had drifted away for years, Wheeler wrote, "but now he's back, panting like the exhaust of a 325 horsepower Cadillac for the same old sweetheart, the American automobile. Well, perhaps not quite the same girl: she has been to the beauty parlor and the masseuse, and you'd hardly know her by the new contours."

What brought people flocking to new cars? Wheeler offered several theories: the prospect of a federal tax cut; a surge of public confidence after surviving the Cuban Missile Crisis; a drift away from the foreign car lure "of littleness for the sake of littleness," a Madison Avenue–driven thirst for the best and fanciest. "'In every make, with every model, it's the top of the line that goes,' said a gleeful industry man."

Sixty years after the mass production of the first Fords, human and automotive trend lines were crossing. In 1963 far more cars than people were being born in the United States—about 7.3 million new cars, an all-time high, compared to about 4.1 million new people. But cars turned to scrap faster than humans to dust. By 1963 some five million old cars were hauled off to junkyards, while not quite two million dead were laid in their graves. Here was the flip side of the old derogatory acronym for low-performing Fords: Found on Road Dead. Obsolescence made auto industry hearts grow fonder. *Life*'s photos were making the case: shiny new 1963 cars rolling out of town on triple-decker rail transport cars signaled the industry was alive and the Motor City was on the move.

People tend to see what they wish to see, comforted by facts that support their vision. How could Detroit be troubled when cars were selling at record levels, and not only that, but when so many key economic indicators appeared strong? Experts who tracked the supply line to automakers from the tool-and-die trade noted robust signs month by month. Orders were coming in nearly a third higher than the year before. When car companies added tool orders, they placed a bet on the near future, and when the tool industry cranked into a higher gear, the positive effects reverberated down the line to the steel and chemical industries, adding to an overall sense of momentum. Could the boom strengthen the tax base in Detroit itself, slowing the trend of suppliers scattering far and wide? That dispersion was irreversible, but promising news came in February, when the Budd Company, a large independent supplier to the car industry—making wheels, rims, chassis frames, brakes, and jigs—announced a $15 million modernization of its plant on Detroit's east side, the sector of the city that had suffered a debilitating decline in jobs and housing during the fifties. Budd's plans were hailed as "the first major industrial improvement on the city's east side since World War II."

Detroit aglow and modern. At the corner of Jefferson and Washington, a new hotel was rising downtown for the first time since the 1920s. It was to be called the Pontchartrain, "the Pontch" for short, borrowing its name from a long-gone Detroit establishment over by Cadillac Square that during the early days of the twentieth century had served as the "mother of motors," a hangout for gossipy first-generation automakers. Minoru Yamasaki, a world-class architect who had moved to Michigan during World War II, when an architectural firm there helped him avoid internment, had made a profound mark on Detroit with a softer style of modernism, most notably the McGregor Memorial Conference Center at Wayne State. He was adding to his defining work with a new thirty-two-story Michigan Consolidated Gas Company Building over on Woodward Avenue. His downtown design included the first-ever lobby requiring the installation of three-story-high sheets of glass. (Soon after Michigan Gas, "Yama" would start drafting the World Trade Center in lower Manhattan.) Up Woodward several blocks, the skeleton of what would become the First Federal Bank Building was starting to kiss the sky with its sheath of sleek black granite.

Compose and decay. All along Michigan Avenue, the remnants of skid row, including the Lindell Cocktail Bar, were seeing the wrecking ball, and over in Paradise Valley, the Gotham Hotel, months after the law enforcement raid on the numbers operation, now faced its death sentence: a condemnation lawsuit filed by city lawyers. The lone question remaining before its demolition to make way for a medical center parking lot was whether the city had to pay for the property or could seize it since owner John White and his confederates had gambling-related income tax liabilities.

Not all was sleek modernism in this makeover of Detroit, and not all of it was confined to the traditional white establishment. Over on East Grand, the House of Diggs, the city's leading black mortuary run by Congressman Charles C. Diggs Jr. and his family, accentuated the year's boom with the grand opening of its nouveau classic Boulevard Chapel, "conveniently located on Detroit's growing east side." The Diggs family had been in the undertaker business for more than four decades. Charles Diggs Sr. had started it all in a first-floor funeral parlor on Russell Street near the local headquarters of the United Negro Improvement Association, founded by Marcus Garvey, the pan-African redeemer whose teachings the mortician once followed. The elder Diggs eventually expanded his business into a vast enterprise that included burial insurance and diversified the family's interests into politics, gaining election to the Michigan State Senate and paving the way for Junior's rise to Congress, as well as setting a father-son pattern of stellar civil rights activism intermingled with problematic political ethics. The Diggs name was among the most prominent in black Detroit. More than seven thousand visitors toured the new funeral chapel one Sunday afternoon, lured by door prizes (silver tea set, AM-FM radios, and ladies' wristwatches) and a live broadcast of the *House of Diggs Radio Hour* featuring the congressman and the Voices of Tabernacle choir. Myrtle Gaskill, a face in the crowd as the women's editor of the *Michigan Chronicle*, reported that she and other visitors were "awed by [the chapel's] magnificence," with its accents of Moorish and Mediterranean detail, its oriental decor, and its lush carpet of lavender, turquoise, aqua, lilac, emerald, and absinthe green.

In the months since Berry Gordy Jr. had set his artists on the American road for the first *Motortown Revue*, the music entrepreneur and his recording studio had earned more local and national acclaim, adding to the glow from Detroit. At the annual awards dinner of BMI (Broadcast Music Inc.), the agency that collected and distributed royalties for most rhythm and blues companies during that era, Gordy and Motown came home with five separate awards for hit songs, more than any other studio. One of the songs was written by Gordy himself ("Do You Love Me?") and two ("You Beat Me to the Punch" and "The One Who Really Loves You") by his pal Smokey Robinson, who at age twenty-three was about to be promoted to vice president of Motown. The Detroit branch of the NAACP, the largest local chapter of the civil rights organization, also honored Gordy at its fifty-fourth birthday dinner that February. On the dais sharing recognition with Gordy were Dr. Thomas M. Bachelor, a distinguished African American physician, and the Right Reverend Richard S. Emrich, the Episcopal bishop of the Michigan diocese, who had taken a leading role in fighting for housing equality in Detroit. Gordy's special citation came "in recognition of his spectacular rise in a very competitive field," one that had very few blacks in positions of control. The studio at West Grand Boulevard now employed more than fifty people, most of them black. Gordy's rise had lifted Detroit as well, the award stated, giving it recognition "as the center of the rhythm and blues recording industry."

Motown was in full assembly-line mode now, manufacturing shiny new hits all in a row. Gordy talked about his music as "the sound of young America." But how to define that sound? What were the components? On February 22 Motown released a record titled "Come and Get These Memories" that seemed to provide some answers. It was written by Holland-Dozier-Holland (Brian Holland, Lamont Dozier, and Eddie Holland), who were emerging then as the company's most reliable and identifiable songwriters along with Smokey. The origins of the song reached down into country music. Years earlier Dozier had tried to write something with Loretta Lynn in mind. He came up with the rudiments of a melody and some lyrics about a woman moving on, "Here's your old Teddy Bear," but could not finish it until he joined the Holland brothers and "decided to embellish it." They took Martha and the Vandellas into the West Grand studio in late January, and when they emerged, Esther Gordy recalled her brother exclaiming, "That's the sound I've been looking for!" It was deceptively simple and catchy, with elements of country, gospel, jazz, and pop. Just enough downbeat syncopation to keep it snapping, just enough female independence in the message to keep the innocent lyrics from descending too far into schmaltz, a good dose of pure joy to the feeling, and more of the gospel force of Martha Reeves, setting her on the path toward stardom.

The rise of Martha Reeves reflected the soul of Detroit and the magic of its music. The forces that shaped her in many ways shaped the city. Her family, like so many black families there, came up from the rural South at the start of World War II, drawn by the Arsenal of Democracy and its abundant factory jobs. She grew up in the church, singing. She was tutored by committed public school music teachers with sophisticated methods and strong expectations in an education system that honored music. And she came out of the rough-and-tumble of the east side. That last part is more important than outsiders might realize. The citizens of Detroit had many ways to define themselves—by ethnic heritage, by Catholic parish, by Baptist church, by auto company, by highway, by southern state of origin—but the first thing anyone would tell you in describing their Detroit background was east side or west side.

Martha Reeves was east side, and the name she gave her singing group was her way of saying so. "Vandellas" sounds like some feminization of "Vandals," but it has no connection to the ancient east European tribe or its modern-day ransacking connotations. It was another portmanteau like Motown, and Reeves coined it herself. The *della* came from Della Reese, the black gospel and jazz singer from Detroit's Black Bottom neighborhood on the east side. Reeves idolized her. In an interview for this book, she recalled when she was seventeen and first heard Della sing: "I was in New Liberty Baptist Church, sitting there with a friend, and the pastor said, 'Della's in the house. Della, give us a song.' And after the applause, the most beautiful black woman I had ever seen, so pretty and tall and she had her hair in a French roll and I had never seen a black woman with hair in a French roll, just like a queen, and she stood up and sang 'Amazing Grace' and her voice shook the rafters. And I knew it was a gift from God. She was blessed. And the next morning I am ironing my blouse to get ready to go to work at Citywide Cleaners and I turn on the little TV and there is Della singing 'Don't You Know' and I said, 'That's Della Reese. I saw her in church!'" If *della* marked Martha's sense of musical majesty, *van* denoted her sense of place. It came from Van Dyke Street, the artery that ran through her childhood neighborhood. To say Van Dyke in Detroit was to say east side. *Van* and *dellas*. And so, Martha and the Vandellas.

The Reeves family migrated north from Eufaula, Alabama, in 1942, when Martha was eleven months old. She was the third of twelve children, a Reeves dozen that comprised the heart of the choir at the little storefront church of Rev. Elijah Joshua Reeves Sr., their grandfather. When she was three, Martha performed so well singing "Surely God Is Able" that she won a box of chocolate-covered cherries, and she never stopped singing after that, at home, at church, and at school.

Here we find another significant factor in explaining the musical luminescence of Detroit, with its rich history of jazz and rhythm and blues musicians. Why Detroit? What gave this city its unmatched creative melody? One part of the answer is the availability of pianos to working-class families in the city, a result of steady auto jobs, disposable income, single-family housing, and the reach of Grinnell's, the remarkable music store and piano maker with its central multistory headquarters on Woodward Avenue overflowing with affordable instruments. Another part is the city's gospel and blues heritage, with so many Detroiters migrating from the rural South and bringing with them an oral, life-singing tradition they continued in the city's church pews on Sundays and on weekend nights spent at music clubs or in home music parties held in living rooms and basements. Then there was the vitality of a black-owned radio station, WCHB. (The call letters were the initials of the owners, Wendell Cox, a Detroit dentist, and his partner, Haley Bell.) The deejays Martha Jean (The Queen) Steinberg and Frantic Ernie nourished local talent and gave the artists valuable airtime. Add to that the inimitable skill and imagination of a single ambitious person, Berry Gordy Jr., in assessing talent and figuring out how to make it shine. And also the luck of creative proximity, the random crucible of talents like Aretha Franklin and Smokey Robinson and Diana Ross living so close to one another during their childhood. But connecting these was the least appreciated and perhaps most important factor of all: the music teachers and programs in the Detroit schools.

Talk to musicians in Detroit and odds are they will recall—vividly and fondly—the teachers who pushed them along. Paul Riser came to Motown in 1962 as a trombone player straight out of Cass Tech, a social naïf among the older cool-cat jazzmen of the Funk Brothers house band, but also a musical prodigy with skills at reading, writing, and arranging scores that he had learned in the public schools. Harold Arnoldi, the music teacher at Keating Elementary, plucked him out of the crowd at age seven and became a mentor and father figure to Riser, helping him get instruments at a discount and encouraging his development. Then, at Cass Tech, Riser rose under the guidance of Dr. Harry Begian, who inculcated in his music students the classics and fundamentals. "He was like a military drill sergeant, but he did it from his heart," Riser recalled. "I didn't understand what he was doing until I graduated years later and got a degree. I was able to laugh about it, his discipline. Harry Begian treated us as ladies and gentlemen and got us ready for the marketplace, attitude-wise, discipline-wise. I sat first chair trombone at Cass Tech, and he saw something in me, again, just as Arnoldi did. That got me ready for Motown."

For Martha Reeves, the public school influence traced back to her music teacher at Russell Elementary School. "Emily Wagstaff, a beautiful little German lady whose accent was so thick I could barely understand what she was saying," Reeves later recalled. "She pulled me from class five minutes before tick-tock and chose me to be a soloist. My public school teachers had the biggest hearts and they were patient, and they could choose. They could pick out the stars and know they can instruct them and fill out their greatness." At Northeastern High her music teacher was Abraham Silver, who, much like Begian at Cass Tech, had a capacity to teach music theory as well as direct a choir and infused his students with an appreciation for the classics and the fundamentals. Freedom through discipline: once they learned the fundamentals they could move freely into the genres of jazz, pop, and rhythm and blues.

Reeves later remembered how Silver singled her out and then nurtured her. "He went through the whole choir section to see who could sing Bach arias. My name being Reeves, I was near the end. Some others did pretty good but no one really nailed it. So I stood up with my knees knocking. I nailed it. I had never heard of Bach. Or I had maybe heard it on the radio. One of my favorite pastimes as a teenager was listening to symphonic music and trying to hit some of those high notes." Decades later, recalling the scene, Reeves hit those soprano notes beautifully. "So I did learn a lot listening to symphonic music. But Bach was a new name to me. Hallelujah! We were the first choir at Northeastern to be recorded. And the first choir from Northeastern to sing at Ford Auditorium. The first time I appeared before four thousand, four hundred people. I was seventeen, about to graduate. And that was one of the biggest thrills I can remember in my teenage life, to hear that applause. It was not just for me but for the entire choir, but I was the soloist. No microphones. You had to throw your voice. Abraham Silver. He taught us not only how to sing but how to read it. That made a big difference. That we learned how to read notes. That we did it correctly."

The route from Abraham Silver and Northeastern High to Berry Gordy Jr. and Motown records took only a year, but it was an unorthodox route, or might seem so except for the fact that many artists reached Motown by unusual paths. Reeves tried several jobs in high school and the year after: waiting tables at her uncle's restaurant near Dubois Street, conducting door-to-door sales for Stanley Home Products and the Fuller Brush Company, and working the counter and keeping the books at a branch of Citywide Cleaners. But she never stopped singing, and through a friend she joined a girl group called the Delphis, for whom she sang second soprano, not lead. After the group disbanded, she won a singing contest at a local recreation club, and her prize was the opportunity to perform in the Gold Room, a section of the 20 Grand nightclub reserved for teenagers. Three nights, fifteen dollars. On the third night, she was singing "Canadian Sunset" and "Fly Me to the Moon." In the audience was William Stevenson, better known as Mickey, one of Motown's talent scouts, an A and R man (artists and repertoire). He gave Reeves his card. That was a Sunday night. The next morning she took the bus across East Grand Boulevard to the west side, foreign territory, got off at the stop between Woodrow Wilson and Churchill, and walked across the wide boulevard to the house with the *Hitsville USA* sign. As Reeves recalled, there was a line outside, but she moved right past it to the front desk. The rest of her story of that day as she later told it is part legend but deeply infused with the sensibility of that time and place, accurately evoking the creativity, chaos, and freedom that made Motown possible.

"I walked up to the lobby, to the glass enclosure, and [receptionist] Juana Royster, with this high voice, said 'May I help you?' and I said 'I am here to see Mr. William Stevenson,' and she said, 'Oh, you mean Mickey?' She said, 'Close the door.' And I walked across the threshold to where the A and R was then, and there was Mr. Stevenson standing there in the doorway. He had taken off his jacket and rolled up his sleeves and he had been up all night writing a song with the drummer, Marvin Gaye. When I saw him he said to me, 'What are you doing here?' I said, 'Don't you remember giving me a card? You said I had talent.' 'Yeah,' he said, 'but you were supposed to take that card and ask for an audition. We have auditions every third Thursday.' So instead of fainting or crying I looked kind of dismayed, and the phones were ringing repeatedly and he said, 'Answer this phone. I'll be right back.' So I did. He went off and for three or four hours I was answering phones. So I got clever, got a little notepad and tore it into sections and was taking down messages. There were seventeen men there, all of whom had two or three women calling them on a regular basis."

At some point she was confronted by James Jamerson, a bass player, and Benny Benjamin, a drummer, two members of the house band that came to be known as the Funk Brothers. "They were there banging on the door and saying 'Where in the em in em is Mickey? Who are you?' 'My name is Martha Reeves. I don't know, he said he would be right back.' And they said they were not going to cut the session across the hall until they got the five dollars they were due for the session they cut yesterday. Five dollars. Before the union came. So I got to meet them. I called the sales department and said, 'Two gentlemen are here who would like to be compensated for the session they did yesterday.' 'Well, we don't pay until Friday.' So I put them directly on the phone with her. When they finished, all this foul language and demands, she said to them, 'Put the A and R secretary back on the phone.' She made me official on that first day. And I was there three months or so before Berry Gordy even knew I was there."

Like so many women before her, Reeves started as a secretary, but soon enough she was helping rhyme lyrics, then providing backup when the female studio singers, the Andantes, were not available. Then she was bringing in some of her old group to help, and then recording a demo of a Mary Wells tune and impressing the Chairman, and finally getting her own shot and picking the name Vandellas and heading out on the road with that first *Motortown Revue*. And now here she was recording a song that compelled Gordy to exclaim "That's the sound!"—an assessment with which one of its creators concurred. "I always thought the Motown sound started with 'Come and Get These Memories,'" Lamont Dozier said. On West Grand Boulevard in those first months of 1963, it was a sound that added to the glow from Detroit.

The song's live premiere that spring was at the 20 Grand down at West Warren and 14th, on the stage of the Driftwood Lounge, upstairs above the bowling alley. It was a benefit for Beans Bowles, recovering slowly from injuries he had suffered in the early morning crash during the first *Motortown Revue* that took Eddie McFarland's life. An overflow crowd at the nightclub included Beans's wife, Agnes, his mother, Mrs. Molly Bowles, and his two brothers, John Bowles Jr. and Calvin Bowles. The *Hitsville Platter*, Motown's in-house newsletter ("It's What's in the Grooves That Counts"), noted that Martha and the Vandellas "did a wonderful rendition of *Come and Get These Memories*, which proved to be quite a fast-moving, Number One rated tune." The Supremes, Little Stevie, and Marvin Gaye also performed, along with the irrepressible Contours, who ended their frenetic version of "Do You Love Me" with each member of the group "doing an acrobatic flip off the stage onto the dance floor."

Los Angeles was the common enemy. When the *Free Press* ran clip-out petitions for readers to send to the U.S. Olympic Committee in support of Detroit's 1968 bid, more than 400,000 people signed and sent them. When WXYZ radio and WJBK-TV delivered editorials urging listeners and viewers to write to the USOC in New York, the Olympic House on Park Avenue was flooded with mail postmarked Detroit. When Mayor Cavanagh turned for help to the Economic Club of Detroit, it immediately dispatched a telegram of support to every member of the USOC. When Governor Romney told the legislature it needed to act with uncommon speed in figuring out a way to pay for and build a 110,000-seat Olympic stadium out at the Michigan Fairgrounds for $25 million, the lawmakers moved the bill to his desk within two weeks. The University of Michigan's Bureau of Business Research boosted the local effort by releasing a report that estimated the Olympics would offer the tangible result of $224 million in consumption, construction, and stimulated expenditures over the next five years, along with the intangible promise of "a more favorable impression of Michigan." Could L.A. possibly steal the bid away from Detroit? The gossip changed day by day inside the walnut-wainscoted walls of the Detroit Athletic Club, hangout of the city's business elite. Some concern arose eleven days before the vote, when Fred Matthaei received an ambiguous letter from President Brundage. "The imbroglio in which the USOC finds itself is most unfortunate, and the resulting publicity is bound to be harmful to all concerned," Brundage wrote of the Midwest versus West Coast dispute. "It is not my place to interfere and I have kept strictly out [of] the squabble. I have not forgotten that, while I did vote for Detroit on a previous occasion, I was bitterly and unreasonably assailed by that city's newspapers. Such is life!"

Out in Los Angeles that March, the newspapers steered clear of Brundage criticism and ran stories day after day about hapless Detroit. "Financial Woes Hurt Detroit's Olympic Bid," ran a headline in the *Los Angeles Times* on March 10. The story raised questions about Detroit's ability to pay off the debts it would incur building the stadium. It pointed out that the state of Michigan carried a debt and the city of Detroit had just enacted an income tax to get out of the red itself. Los Angeles had the hotel rooms, the stadium, the weather, all waiting, and offered the Olympic movement a guaranteed payoff of $2 million to $5 million to boot. "On the basis of these facts," the piece concluded, "who would you vote for between Los Angeles and Detroit if you were a member of the USOC board of directors, seeking to bring the 1968 Olympics to the best city in the United States?"

The Michigan delegation arrived in New York on Sunday morning, March 18. Mayor Cavanagh hosted a cocktail party at four that afternoon at his suite in the Hotel Commodore and then continued the festivities later that night at Toots Shor's. If he could charm birds out of trees, how might he do with stuffy old Olympic owls? The vote came on Monday, after a long day of proposals and pictures and promises and pleas. Detroit's four most prominent public relations firms had packaged the city's presentation under the title "The Detroit You've Never Met." Matthaei opened, Cavanagh and Romney closed. Whatever questions had been raised in the past were irrelevant now, Cavanagh said. "We are now financially and spiritually ready." The final decision was a blowout: Detroit 32, Los Angeles 4.

Paul Zimmerman, sports editor of the *Los Angeles Times,* avoided any pretense of objectivity with his lead: "The United States Olympic Committee 'bought a pig in a poke' Monday."

Romney, the car guy, toasted the Detroit public relations and ad men who helped make it possible. "Now I know why Chevrolet sells so many cars," he told Tom Adams, president of the Campbell-Ewald agency. Cavanagh suggested the new stadium be named in honor of the industrialist and sportsman who had carried the dream through the decades: Matthaei Olympic Stadium. Since that January day when she escorted her husband out of Providence Hospital, Mary Helen Cavanagh had not had much luck tamping down his frenetic schedule. He remained, for her and their brood, a challenging man. But now she offered him a personal victory present: their seventh child, another son.

Aides suggested the boy's middle name be Olympic.

Chapter 7

# MOTOR CITY MAD MEN

**FOUR AGENCY MEN FROM J. WALTER THOMPSON** slipped into Dearborn early that spring to meet secretly with Lee Iacocca and his Ford Division design team for a first look at what would become Ford's 1964 lineup of new cars. J. Walter Thompson was the largest advertising agency in the world, and Ford was its most important client. It had been that way since old man Henry Ford decided during World War II that he needed outside help to promote the cars he would start making when the war ended and auto plants returned to business as usual after turning out tanks and trucks and matériel in the Arsenal of Democracy. J. Walter Thompson was the answer, Ford's aides told him, and starting back then with the *There's a Ford in Your Future* campaign, the car company and the ad agency had developed a symbiotic bond through the years. The top people at Ford, especially Iacocca, a natural-born salesman, were always thinking about marketing, and the top people at JWT needed to have more than a passing understanding of the automobile business. The relationship was fluid and sensitive, and although disputes inevitably arose over costs and results, both sides realized that success depended on shared planning and inherent trust.

J. Walter Thompson was one year short of its hundredth anniversary in 1963. It was the leading agency of Madison Avenue during the advertising heyday of the early sixties, so recognized in a *Time* magazine cover story a year earlier, although its headquarters was not precisely on Madison Avenue, the street that came to emblematize the industry, but several blocks away on Lexington near Grand Central Station. The top corporate and creative work was done there in Manhattan, because that is where corporate heads and creative people wanted to be, but the day-to-day handling of the crucial Ford account was the responsibility of the field office in Detroit. It could be said of J. Walter Thompson—as of so much else in America—that Detroit was the economic engine. In a client list that included Eastman Kodak, Seven-Up, Pan Am, Singer, Lever Bros., Kraft Foods, Scott Papers, Liggett & Myers, and Chesebrough-Pond's, the Ford account stood apart, bringing in by far the most money and requiring the largest staff. It was no accident that JWT's chairman, Norman Strouse, rose to his eleventh-floor corner suite on West Wing South at 420 Lex after managing the Detroit office for a decade.

Strouse brought vast experience dealing with Ford to his meeting with Iacocca. A self-taught farm boy from rural Washington State who began his advertising career at nineteen by answering a want ad in the *Seattle Post-Intelligencer* seeking an assistant ad director, he eventually landed with J. Walter Thompson's San Francisco office and was transferred to Detroit in the final days of 1945, after service in the navy. His arrival there coincided with the transformation of Ford Motor Company under Henry Ford II and his stable of Whiz Kids, the young managers including Robert McNamara, JFK's secretary of defense, who applied statistical analysis they had learned as military officers to the operation of a manufacturing company. "I observed from the sidelines one of the great management case histories of all time: the conversion of Ford from an antiquated organization to a modern one," Strouse said later. The mission for Ford then was one it would face repeatedly: to overcome an image of being old-fashioned, behind the times, unhip, and colorless, a perception that began with the late-life Model T and Henry Ford's belief that consumers could have whatever color car they wanted so long as it was black. The *There's a Ford in Your Future* theme had about run its course when Strouse arrived, since Ford cars were being made and sold again, and his first campaign launched with a new motto: *Ford's Out Front*. Just as HF2 and the Whiz Kids were changing management on the inside, Strouse and JWT tried to do something similar on the outside. "We were trying to take the Ford name, the Ford image that had existed as an old conservative company, and bring it into modern times."

Over the ensuing years, Strouse worked from the notion that there were four basic appeals in selling cars, and only two of the four were "subject to statistical or factual measurement, the other two were subjective in the mind of the buyer." The first two he labeled *Transportation* and *Investment. Transportation* was mileage, speed, dependability, pickup, capacity, and freedom from annoyance. *Investment* was price, cost of operation, and resale or trade value. The subjective aspects he called *Enjoyment* and *Applause. Enjoyment* included driving ease, comfort, beauty, gadgets, and feel. *Applause* involved "approval of experts, envy of neighbors, opinion of best girl, the thing to do etc." In a repetitive cycle, whatever gains Ford made in *Transportation* and *Investment* were minimized over the years by its lagging behind in the subjective areas of *Enjoyment* and *Applause*. Even when it came out with a breakthrough car exuding excitement, like the Thunderbird, it was seen as trying to copy or catch up with Chevrolet and its Corvette. What was true in the late 1940s was true again in 1963.

In developing its advertising plan for Ford that year, Strouse's team at JWT conducted an exhaustive study of research data from its own shop to determine how Ford was viewed by the public, what it called "not just Ford's share of market but Ford's share of mind in the market place." According to an internal memo, the study determined that Ford retained its traditional image of low-cost transportation, "but as valuable as that image may be, it is becoming something of an albatross. Ford is strong among the low income, blue collar groups, but when we move into the areas of young people, people on the way up, the performance minded, the college educated, the professional groups, people in prestige occupations, the Ford image has faded."

That conclusion, the JWT team understood, coincided with the long-term plans Iacocca had for change. His stated goal over the sixties was to build Ford Division cars that were both fun to drive and free of maintenance problems, with an emphasis on imagination, flair, performance, reliability, and sound engineering. The new models were already moving in that direction. But how could Ford's marketing and JWT's advertising persuade the public of this reality? "It is one of the obvious but often not really understood facts of life that there can be no share of market without share of mind—and moving minds to Ford is the life blood of continuing success and profits," the JWT memo stated. "The things people believe in are as real to them as facts."

As the secret meeting in Dearborn with Ford's design team neared an end, Iacocca motioned to Strouse and his three companions to follow him. They were Dan Seymour, second in command as JWT president in New York, and the two leaders of the Detroit office, Bill Laurie and Franklyn R. Thomas. "When Iacocca signaled us away, we were understandably a bit puzzled," Thomas wrote later in a document housed at the J. Walter Thompson archive at Duke University's John W. Hartman Center for Sales, Advertising and Marketing History. "There's more than one reason why an important client wants to talk with you privately. We were ushered along strange corridors, through bulky fire doors, past innumerable security guards. At one point, we were asked to exchange our ordinary security badges for extraordinary ones."

When they reached their destination, "somewhere deep in the bowels of Ford styling studios," Thomas recalled, "we saw against the far wall a vague outline of a car under a stained canvas shroud." Soon the cover was stripped away, and there in front of the ad men stood a full-scale clay mockup of a top-secret car that was then known only by its code name, T-5. It was a white beauty, the JWT men agreed, jaunty and sleek with a stub tail and long hood, unlike any automobile they had seen before. "Iacocca and the other Ford people explained the car, pointed out features and objectives, and watched our enthusiasm catch fire," Thomas wrote. "We now had our official assignment plus an unforgettable taste of the exciting thing this car would be." The T-5 was not in the lineup of 1964 cars, which, in the normal industry way of doing business, were to reach the public in fall 1963, but instead was to be unveiled on its own in spring 1964, the target date coinciding with the opening of the 1964 New York World's Fair. The ad men left Dearborn with three goals: first, find a way to convey the excitement they felt when they saw the mockup; second, come up with a name for the car; and third, figure out how to position it in the market. Here might be the answer Ford and its ad agency had been desperately seeking: a car that merged appearance and reality, fantasy and fact—a car that could move minds. *Transportation*, *Investment*, *Enjoyment*, and *Applause* all in one package.

The Detroit offices of J. Walter Thompson were on floors 21 and 22 of the Buhl Building at 535 Griswold Street downtown, across the street from the Penobscot tower. When Strouse first showed up for work there after the war, he was one of fewer than thirty JWT employees in Detroit. By the time he left to take charge in New York not quite a decade later, the Ford account was bringing in nearly 25 percent of the agency's domestic revenue, and the Detroit staff grew proportionately, eventually reaching 285 in 1963, with another 29 in satellite offices to handle a companion account representing Ford dealers across the country. During his first months there after the war, Strouse had discovered that few in Detroit knew JWT was in the city and that it was essential for him to learn the ground rules. Campbell-Ewald, the Detroit agency that kept the massive Chevy account, was known as a solid corporate citizen; JWT, not so much. The ground rules were simple: engage in Detroit socially and understand the rhythms of a company town. Detroit, Strouse came to realize, was "intensely an automotive community—everybody lives, breathes, and sleeps automobiles. It's like a feudal city." He liked it, thought it was interesting, "but it was narrow, there's no doubt about it. And you had to *work* at getting out of the narrow confinement of the automobile business, into other things that had no relation to it."

Strouse did this as best he could. He became a collector, specializing in esoteric printings of folios and rare books, anything to do with Robert Louis Stevenson, and an accumulation of owl effigies, the owl being the trademark of J. Walter Thompson. He escaped to a summer home in Harbor Springs on Little Traverse Bay in the northern tip of lower Michigan, where he could lose himself in a wild blackberry patch and tool around in a Falcon station wagon supplied by Ford. And he plotted a retirement in the Napa Valley wine country of Northern California. Anything to ease the stress of the ad business, a notorious killer. All you had to do was read the obituaries in *Advertising Age,* the bible of the industry, to see that ad men were dying at an average age of sixty-one, compared to sixty-eight for other related professions. The mortality rate was one reason Strouse habitually studied his workforce for the next man up, instituting a system where he could watch people who might succeed him. "You see people dropping dead of a heart attack at 46 or 35 for that matter," he once wrote. "So this is a fact of life you have to recognize and be prepared for."

The Strouse-picked man running JWT's Detroit office in 1963 not only understood the ground rules of the community; he was part of the rule-making elite. This was William D. Laurie, who came to the agency with a life history that neatly connected cars, advertising, and Detroit society. Laurie grew up in Grosse Pointe, graduated from the University of Michigan, married Thayer Hutchinson, the elegant debutante daughter of B. E. Hutchinson, once treasurer of the Chrysler Corporation, and settled the family in a modernist house on a double lot his father-in-law procured for them in Grosse Pointe Farms, the toniest of the Grosse Pointe enclaves. Unlike Strouse, who was physically unprepossessing, Laurie looked the part of the quintessential Mad Men account executive, charming and handsome with his slick-combed hair and Brooks Brothers suits. He was a sophisticated aesthete and power player in Detroit who began his career as an apprentice copywriter in a local agency, Maxon Inc., where his first auto client was the old Reo automobile, and rose to vice president with accounts including Packard, Hotpoint, Pfeiffer Beer, Mohawk Carpets, and Hiram Walker & Sons Distillery. Hiram Walker was a nineteenth-century Detroiter who made his fortune distilling whisky across the river in Windsor (the Canadians spelled the liquor without an *e*) and was the grandfather of Arthur Buhl, the Detroit businessman who built the Buhl Building, where J. Walter Thompson made its Detroit offices. Laurie came to work in the

Buhl Building in 1957, lured to JWT from Maxon after a breakfast at Strouse's penthouse apartment on Beekman Place overlooking the United Nations Plaza and the East River in Manhattan. Upon meeting Laurie, Strouse proclaimed him "the kind of man one can like almost on sight . . . what the English used to call so charmingly 'a man of parts.'"

Some of Laurie's parts were defined by the many professional and social clubs to which he belonged: Adcraft Club, Country Club of Detroit (situated in Grosse Pointe), Detroit Club, Detroit Athletic Club, Little Club of Grosse Pointe, Witenagemot Club, and Yondotega Club. The range here was from exclusive to more exclusive to most exclusive. Yondotega was in that last category, a hideaway for the Fords, Fishers, Briggses, and Buhls, affectionately known, in a vernacular peculiar to the rich, as "just an old dump" on East Jefferson along the Detroit River. "Yondotega" was said to be Algonquin for "happy spot on the river." The dump was limited to a hundred members, and the only way you could get in was if someone died. The happy hundred living white men could play cards and eat elegant meals together on Wednesday nights, Bill Laurie frequently among them. He loved the exclusive clubs, all of them.

The only black people who entered this elite life were servants. In its upper reaches, Detroit was not all that different in those relationships from Montgomery, Alabama, where Laurie's namesake father had made his start in the ad business before moving the family to Grosse Pointe. The younger of Laurie's two sons, David, who was ten in 1963, later said he knew only two African Americans growing up. One was Julia Newton, their live-in maid and nanny, who had previously served a Brahmin family in Boston. "She basically brought me up. Her room was right next door to mine. She would get me up in the morning. I loved Julia to death," he recalled. The other was a woman named Cynthia who performed the same tasks for his Hutchinson grandparents. By the late sixties, when as a teenager he had long hair and was protesting the war in Vietnam, David Laurie thought more about "the racial underpinnings of living in Detroit." He asked his parents, "How come we don't know any black people?" It was, he said, "a weird place."

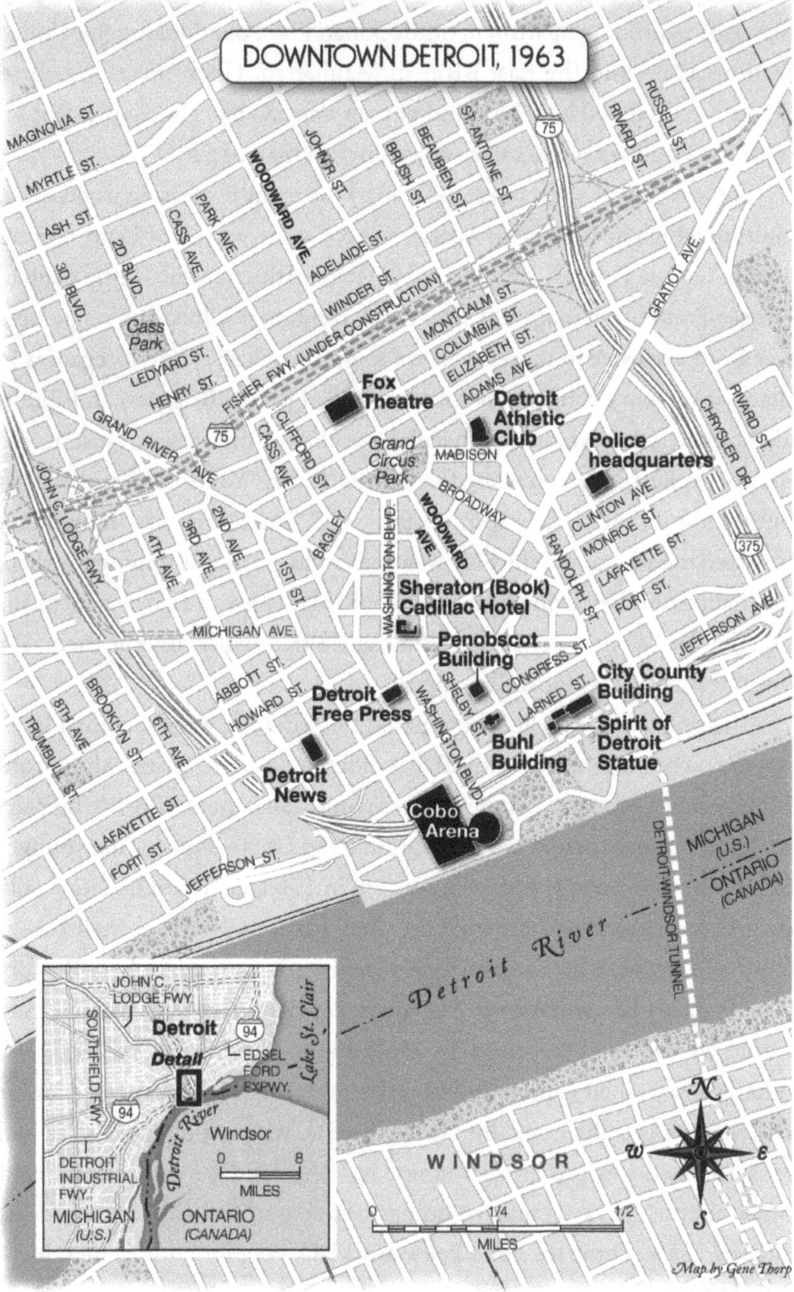
DOWNTOWN DETROIT, 1963
MAGNOLIA ST.
MYRTLE ST.
ASH ST.
3D BLVD.
2D BLVD.
CASS AVE.
PARK AVE.
WOODWARD AVE.
JOHN R. ST.
BRUSH ST.
BEAUBIEN ST.
ST. ANTOINE ST.
75
RIVARD ST.
RUSSELL ST.
ADELAIDE ST.
WINDER ST.
FISHER FWY. (UNDER CONSTRUCTION)
GRATIOT AVE.
Cass Park
LEDYARD ST.
HENRY ST.
MONTCALM ST.
COLUMBIA ST.
ELIZABETH ST.
ADAMS AVE.
Fox Theatre
Detroit Athletic Club
Police headquarters
CHRYSLER DR.
RIVARD ST.
GRAND RIVER AVE.
CASS AVE.
CLIFFORD ST.
Grand Circus Park
MADISON
BROADWAY
JOHN C. LODGE FWY.
2ND AVE.
3RD AVE.
4TH AVE
BAGLEY
1ST ST.
WASHINGTON BLVD.
WOODWARD AVE.
RANDOLPH ST.
CLINTON AVE.
MONROE ST.
LAFAYETTE ST.
FORT ST.
375
JEFFERSON AVE.
Sheraton (Book) Cadillac Hotel
MICHIGAN AVE.
Penobscot Building
CONGRESS ST.
City County Building
ABBOTT ST.
HOWARD ST.
Detroit Free Press
SHELBY ST.
LARNED ST.
Spirit of Detroit Statue
BROOKLYN ST.
8TH AVE
TRUMBULL ST.
6TH AVE
WASHINGTON BLVD.
Buhl Building
Detroit News
Cobo Arena
LAFAYETTE ST.
FORT ST.
JEFFERSON ST.
DETROIT-WINDSOR TUNNEL
MICHIGAN (U.S.)
ONTARIO (CANADA)
Detroit River
JOHN C. LODGE FWY.
SOUTHFIELD FWY.
Detroit
94
Detail
EDSEL FORD EXPWY.
Lake St. Clair
94
Detroit River
Windsor
0 8
MILES
DETROIT INDUSTRIAL FWY.
MICHIGAN (U.S.)
ONTARIO (CANADA)
WINDSOR
0 1/4 1/2
MILES
N
W
E
S
Map by Gene Thorp

The politics of the family folded neatly into that elite milieu. The patriarch, B. E. Hutchinson, had been an influential rightist who helped finance William F. Buckley's *National Review* when it was energizing and redefining the American conservative movement in the midfifties. Bill Laurie too befriended Buckley, hosting him on occasion in Grosse Pointe, sailing with him at the family's summer estate in Jamestown, Rhode Island, an island community off Newport, and keeping prized autographed copies of *God and Man at Yale* and other early Buckley books in prominent positions on the coffee tables at home. Thayer Laurie was her father's daughter, more conservative and political than her husband, and by 1963 was actively supporting Barry Goldwater for the Republican presidential nomination. Neither of them liked George Romney. Romney rose from the same Detroit auto culture, and he was now the most prominent Republican in Michigan, but he was decidedly not part of the club. The Lauries were Episcopalian, prominent members of Christ Church in Grosse Pointe, and Romney was a Mormon. More than that, his politics were too moderate for their tastes.

Laurie's house at 121 Merriweather Road showed other aspects of the man of many parts. The modernist design, so distinct from the traditional houses of Grosse Pointe Farms, was conceived by Alexander Girard, known as Sandro, a world-class architect, interior designer, and art collector who had become such a close family friend that he was David's godfather. The glistening, airy rooms were filled with an eclectic array of modern art, old American folk art, and exquisite modern furniture, much of it accumulated in trips with Sandro and his wife, Susan, or with another couple with whom the Lauries were close, Charles Eames and his wife, Ray, noted designers who had met at the Cranbrook Academy of Art in Bloomfield Hills.

There were books everywhere in the Laurie house and a built-in stereo system playing Bill's favorite music, especially the jazz compositions of Duke Ellington and a recording of Kurt Weill's *Threepenny Opera*. At the back of the house was a hexagon-shaped room—the Hex, they called it—with burlap walls and toys Thayer collected during outings with Sandro. In the dining room was a duck press with the 21 Club logo on it, a cherished gift Laurie received decades earlier from his boss at Maxon after a night at the Manhattan restaurant celebrating an advertising deal. Laurie had no idea how to press a duck but occasionally tried to squeeze oranges with the press, sending juice flying across the room. Directly above the living room was a hideaway designed like an old ship's cabin, with brass lanterns, more books, and built-in bunk beds, a motif inspired by Laurie's years as a naval officer during World War II aboard merchant marine vessels carrying munitions across the Atlantic and Arctic Oceans to Soviet allies on what was known as the Murmansk run.

Laurie was able to escape the confinements of the auto culture, but he was also tightly connected to it. He and Thayer hosted parties at the Merriweather Road house to entertain friends and clients, who often merged. Lee Iacocca was a frequent guest, among other top Ford executives. Other visitors included Tennessee Ernie Ford, the conveniently named southern singer whose Ford-sponsored television show ran on Thursday nights on NBC from 1955 to 1961 ("Bless your pea-pickin' hearts," Tennessee Ernie would drawl in closing), and Charles Schultz, who first deployed his *Peanuts* comic strip characters in ads selling the new Ford Falcon in 1959. Henry Ford II lived nearby, and Laurie was at a level professionally and socially where he could associate comfortably with the Ford boss, though he found the Deuce's carryings-on unrefined. Every fall, when the new line of Ford cars came out, two of the latest models would arrive at the Laurie house. It was always a yellow Ford station wagon for Thayer and a dark green Thunderbird convertible tricked out with leather seats for Bill. The man next door was Laurie's nemesis, a Chrysler executive, generating yearly competition about who had what in the driveway.

From his office high atop the Buhl Building, Bill Laurie could see across to Windsor, Ontario, and at closer distance the steady passage of barges and ships plying the Detroit River, one of the busiest inland waterways in America, most of the cargo related to the auto industry. Many years on the Fourth of July, after dinner at the London Chop House, he would take the family up to his office aerie to watch fireworks explode in the night sky over the water. Across from his massive desk and walls lined with naval awards, he kept a seventeenth-century antique telescope by the window for daily viewing of river activities.

Laurie knew what was going on, outside and in. Elsewhere in the Buhl Building, at a location known only to him and two men who worked in Forward Planning, was an office they called the Tomb. The room was isolated, locked off, on a different floor from the rest of the JWT operation. Only Laurie and the two forward planners had keys. Cleaning women were not allowed in. The Tomb was cleaned by building guards, but only when the forward planners were around to watch. All wastepaper was burned. It was there that J. Walter Thompson's advance team worked on the T-5, the Ford project that Iacocca had revealed to Laurie and Strouse and their second-in-command that afternoon deep in the heavily secured interior of Ford's Design Center.

The forward planners had set up shop in the Tomb months earlier, in November 1962, about one year after Iacocca and his Ford team had first begun thinking about this new car. The long process began during the early months of JFK's New Frontier in 1961, when the world was changing, the demographics of America were changing, and market researchers at Ford and J. Walter Thompson were taking notice, with Iacocca in the lead. Three trends were converging. The first was an increase in the number of young people. As a JWT memo noted, the era of World War II was long distant not only emotionally but statistically—nearly 50 percent of Americans "were not born when Hitler invaded Poland [in 1939]" and "thirty percent were not here when the Korean War started in 1950." Combined, these were the children of the postwar baby boom, the largest rising generation in American history. Second, the population was becoming more educated, with a direct correlation to car buying. Industry research showed that 46 percent of all cars were being sold to the 20 percent of the populace with some college education. A third factor was the sharp rise in two-car families. In studying these trends, Ford concluded that "there appeared no car on the market that met the spirit, the major desires of this more sophisticated, more youthful, better educated population trending toward multiple car ownership." Don Frey, Iacocca's top product planning manager, described this situation as "a market looking for a product." Laurie and Franklyn Thomas over at JWT used another description; they said it was "reminiscent of a Pirandello play called *Six Characters in Search of an Author.*"

After a few false starts with cars and mockups that were too small or sporty or narrow in their potential appeal, Iacocca passed down a mission statement along the chain of command through Frey and Eugene Bordinat, the design vice president, to stylists Joe Oros and Dave Ash and others: Come up with a car that can trump the Chevrolet Corvair Monza. The Ford Falcon was practical and a decent seller, but not sexy enough. Design a car that will appeal to the coming-of-age postwar baby boomers and men and women of all ages who want to feel young and free. Make a car that is sporty and stylish, that weighs about 2,500 pounds, costs about $2,500, seats four comfortably, uses a standard floor shift, with plenty of options.

Fear and excitement, in equal parts, fueled the drive to produce this new car. The fear was always there, what executives called "the terror of error," but it was compounded in this case because the previous creative burst from Ford was one of the defining busts in automaker history, the Edsel, which had been introduced with great expectations in September 1957 and had collapsed into history's dustbin by 1960, losing Ford scores of millions of dollars and forever turning the name of Henry Ford II's father into a symbol of failure. To get Ford to buy in again on another new car would take some doing, but Lido Anthony Iacocca was confident he could do it. Since those early days in 1961, he had been holding twice-monthly dinner meetings with his project crew, including the forward planners and a writer from JWT, at the nearby Fairlane Room, meticulously planning the concept of a car he was certain would do what the Edsel could not: hit the sweet spot of American yearning. They called Iacocca a car guy, and he held an engineering degree from Lehigh University, but mostly he was a salesman, and at age thirty-eight this would be the biggest sales job of his life.

What would this car look like? The basic answer came on August 16, 1962, when Iacocca, HF2, and other top Ford executives gathered in the secure Ford Design Center. There stood seven mockups of cars covered in canvas, rough drafts made of clay and aluminum foil, many of them finished only on one side. Only one of the seven was designed directly by Iacocca's stylists, the others done by Lincoln-Mercury or corporate's Advance Design team. The lone Ford Division mockup was put together hastily, a last-minute entry done in three days. It was the one that wowed everyone. The white model with the long hood and short deck. Somehow it transcended its inert condition. Iacocca said later that even in clay and without a motor it seemed to be rushing ahead, beauty and daring in motion. Here was the choice: Project T-5.

J. Walter Thompson's forward planning men would soon set up the Tomb, and then Laurie and Strouse would get ushered into the styling room for their first glimpse. By midspring 1963 Laurie had established a "hot project" staff at the Buhl Building in Detroit and at 420 Lex in New York, larger than the original two-man effort but still select and sworn to secrecy. The car was taking shape, but what would they call it? Cougar? Thunderbolt? TBird II? Monte Carlo? Ford K-2? Mustang? Falcon Special? Thunderstar? XTC? Colt? Panther? Allegro? Torino?

## Chapter 8

# THE PITCH OF HIS HUM

**THE CARAVAN OF** three hundred cars unwound languidly from the church parking lot at 9:30 on the morning of March 17, snaking north up 12th Street a block, then west across Euclid a half mile and right at Linwood before easing to a stop near the corner with Philadelphia. Another five hundred people waited as a greeting party outside the remodeled Oriole Theater. The slow-motion procession on this sun-dappled Sunday looked like a funeral cortege but felt like something more joyous. For the flock of New Bethel Baptist, this was the last migration in an urban rite of passage, more beginning than ending. The Oriole was their new house of worship, a gathering place that seemed entirely appropriate for a congregation led by Detroit's most theatrical preacher, the Reverend Clarence La Vaughn Franklin.

In the old days, before urban renewal, New Bethel Baptist rocked on Hastings Street in the raucous heart of Detroit's Black Bottom neighborhood, its church a spiritual colossus of warm knotty-pine paneling. Even without summer air-conditioning the church lured thousands of hungry souls inside each Sunday night, elbow to elbow from floor to balcony, with hundreds more on occasion lining the street outside and listening to the broadcast via loudspeakers. Then Hastings and its life force vanished in 1961, replaced by the concrete of the Chrysler Freeway, and New Bethel, after depositing a $200,000-plus eminent domain check from the city, moved across town to transitional quarters on 12th Street. Now the church had used part of that payoff and a loan from the National Bank of Detroit to transform the old theater on Linwood into a magisterial religious sanctuary, a remodeling that, with Franklin in the pulpit, seemed much like a distinction without a difference.

"This is a day of victory, triumph and achievement, and we are happy," the reverend exclaimed to the multitudes in his church-christening sermon. "Nothing can be achieved without conflict and trial. That is the main reason we here at New Bethel are able to say there is power in faith." Faith rewarded, a church blessed, a pastor and his people awash in good wishes, including telegrams from Martin Luther King Jr., Adam Clayton Powell Jr., and President Kennedy. With that the organist, Harold Smith, began to strike the reverberant keys, and soon the New Bethel choir was singing "The Battle Hymn of the Republic" and "Lord Will Make a Way" and "How Great Thou Art."

C. L. Franklin, who had just turned forty-eight, was at the pinnacle of his career but in the midst of personal change as the world was changing around him. He had spent much of the past decade on the road as a celebrity preacher, the marquee performer in a traveling show of sermon and song that at various times included his daughters Aretha, Erma, and Carolyn, along with Little Sammie Bryant, a three-foot-small performing dynamo, and before that the Ward sisters, led by Clara Ward, a noted gospel artist who had been the reverend's off-and-on lover. Franklin was the leading circuit flyer in black America, the modern variation of the old-fashioned circuit-riding preacher, using a plane rather than a horse and filling large auditoriums rather than one-room churches. But now Aretha was about to turn twenty-one and gone from Detroit, bursting into soul-singing stardom in New York, and Erma had left Clark College in Atlanta after her sophomore year to record on the Epic label. For their flamboyant widower father, the grind of so much travel, combined with the great expectations people had for his every appearance, as he later explained, "kind of broke me down," leaving him exhausted and susceptible to ill health. Beyond that, in the seven years since his longtime friend and colleague in the Baptist ministry, Martin Luther King Jr., intensified the civil rights movement with the Montgomery bus boycott, Franklin had been devoting more time each year to the rhetoric of equality and a bit less to the spectacle of evangelistic entertainment. The goings-on in his native South in the first months of 1963 had prompted him to seek a more activist role, at once deepening his commitment and exposing him to factional discord within the church community and the civil rights movement.

Although the story of his rise to prominence had familiar elements, Franklin stood apart from his Baptist brethren, larger than life, a splashy exaggeration of common traits. He emerged from the poor black terrain of the Mississippi Delta, in Sunflower County, and started preaching when he was sixteen, finding his way to churches in Memphis and Buffalo before reaching Detroit in 1946. New Bethel was already there, its roots stretching back to a Depression-era prayer-and-song society formed by a group of Detroit women, but under Franklin's leadership it grew into what later might be called a megachurch, with nearly ten thousand members. From its location at Hastings and Willis, amid the hubbub of Hastings, New Bethel developed a reputation as the people's palace, embracing rich and poor, upright and derelict, matron and streetwalker, foundry worker and mortician. The church was there for daily survival as well as spiritual salvation. Erma Franklin recalled how newcomers would arrive in Detroit from Mississippi or Alabama or Tennessee and ask, "Can you tell me where C. L. Franklin lives?" "They would show up sometimes twelve thirty, one o'clock in the morning, and they would say, well, you know, 'I got here, I don't have any money, I don't have a job, can you help me?' And he would take money out of his pocket and find them a place to stay."

In the early fifties, after he started his flying-circuit road show, Franklin became a man of wealth as the Detroit church grew and his national reputation spread. He looked the part of an ecclesiastical grandee, with his silk suits of cream and white, alligator shoes, diamond jewelry, and big Cadillac. The Flame Show Bar, the 20 Grand, the Ebony Room at the Gotham Hotel, the nightlife and good life—it was all as much a part of him as the sanctity of his pulpit. Smokey Robinson, a childhood friend of Cecil Franklin, recounted the time when they first met and were playing in a vacant field in the neighborhood and Cecil asked, "Wanna see my new house?" Cecil pointed to a mansion nearby. "I approach the house hesitantly," Robinson later wrote. "Once inside, I'm awestruck—oil paintings, velvet tapestries, silk curtains, mahogany cabinets filled with ornate objects of silver and gold. Man, I've never seen anything like this before." Franklin was raising five children in that elegant home; four of them—the three girls and Cecil—were his children with his second wife, Barbara Vernice Siggers, who years earlier had left him to return to Buffalo before dying at only thirty-four. There was also in his brood an adopted son, Vaughn, and, apart from the family, a daughter he had fathered with a girl barely in her teens during his Memphis years.

The Man with the Million Dollar Voice, they called C.L. And the Rabbi. And the Learned one. And the High Priest of Soul Preaching. And Black Beauty. His sermons were so well known that when he was on the road the audience would demand to hear one of his greatest hits, most often "The Eagle Stirreth Her Nest" or "Dry Bones in the Valley" or "Give Me This Mountain." People knew his sermons not only from previous performances but from radio broadcasts and the record player. His sermons had been recorded and sold as albums first on the JVB label and then by Chess Records in Chicago, with royalties to him of thirty to thirty-five cents a record. On the road, Franklin recalled during an oral interview, "I would preach whatever the [local] deejay had been playing and what was indicated to the deejay that the people liked most. At first I resented those requests. I had the attitude that I would have at the church—that people should be ready to listen to whatever I chose to preach on, but people are not like that. They want to hear what they have been hearing. . . . They usually responded strongly. Some people shouted and some people hollered at me, waved their hands, stand up and point at you. It gave me a thrill to see people react that way, because I felt that in some way it was helpful to them, if nothing more than to raise their spirits."

The interplay of story and storyteller created the Franklin magic. He was a master at building a homily with tension and expectation and using his voice as instrumental accompaniment. Rev. Nicholas Hood, his contemporary in Detroit, pastor at the more sedate Plymouth Congregational Church, would sometimes slip over to New Bethel Baptist on Sunday nights just to marvel at the theatrics, taking note of what he called "the pickup" in the sermon—"Mmmmhmmm, uuhuuuh"—that he later heard echoes of in Aretha's gospel-soul style. Franklin's momentum carried him from speech to hum to song, a style captured evocatively in a theology thesis by John R. Bryant: "The singing usually comes during the conclusion, but before he gets to that point he does what is referred to as 'tuning up.' Franklin does this by humming after every phrase. When he finds a comfortable pitch, he begins preaching at the pitch of his hum. At this time he is preaching a set rhythm and his organist will join in with chords of accompaniment. At this time one experiences what might be called black opera. It is without a doubt a spiritual art."

The pitch of his hum, in a metaphorical sense, was a bit much for many of the other black ministers in Detroit. They admired C.L.'s preaching but were jealous of his immense following and questioned his personal behavior and financial reliability. Even some members of his own parish questioned whether he had misused the urban renewal funds, but when they disclosed their findings and called for a vote of confidence, many hundreds sided with the preacher and only seven against him. Rev. Hood, who came out of New England but had led a church in New Orleans before arriving in Detroit, said his southern experience helped him understand Franklin, and he exempted himself from judging the showy reverend too harshly, even while saying, "Morally he was not up to par; he was very, very loose." Hood said he felt no direct competition with New Bethel because his own Plymouth Congregational was affiliated more closely with Detroit's black establishment, stocked with doctors and lawyers and other professionals trained at historically black colleges founded by Congregational missionaries, including Howard University in Washington, Fisk in Nashville, and Dillard in New Orleans. But as Franklin turned toward civil rights activism in the first months of 1963, Hood's attitude seemed to be an exception. To take a leadership role in the Detroit movement, Franklin would have to overcome doubters and detractors in his own community.

---

The cause of civil rights, that mighty stream of righteousness, had many currents in the Detroit of 1963. There was the local chapter of the National Association for the Advancement of Colored People, the largest affiliate in the nation, with its focus on education and the formal processes of working through the system. There was the United Auto Workers, which, under Walter Reuther and his brothers, Roy and Victor, had made an unequivocal moral and financial commitment to civil rights action and legislation. There was the Trade Union Leadership Council, an African American offshoot of the UAW chartered in 1956 and led by Horace Sheffield and Buddy Battle, with a more concentrated focus on black advancement and leadership in the Detroit labor force. There was a potent group of activist black lawyers, led by George Crockett, Damon Keith, and John Conyers Jr., who were working through the legal system with vigor and fluidity for both moderate and left-leaning civil rights institutions. There was the *Michigan Chronicle*, with its columnists and editorialists advancing the cause. There was an incipient black nationalist faction led by the Reverend Albert Cleage (rhymes with "vague," which he most decidedly was not), the outspoken pastor of Central Congregational Church, who also had a family publishing arm with the pamphlet *Illustrated News*. There was the Baptist Ministerial Alliance, an influential and mostly cautious organization of local black pastors. And there was the city leadership of Mayor Cavanagh and Police Commissioner Edwards, who had taken office committed to improving Detroit's civil rights record. All of these currents were flowing in the same general direction, but not always smoothly, when Franklin, responding to a plea over the telephone from Mahalia Jackson, decided he should lead a grand action that might bring the passion of the southern civil rights movement to the northern city. Franklin and the famous gospel singer were "like brother and sister," his daughter Erma later recalled, and when Mahalia urged C.L. to sponsor a fundraising event for the cause, he readily agreed without considering the difficulties that might entail.

The makings of a united front appeared possible at first, when Franklin, at a meeting held in the offices of the Detroit Urban League, was elected general chairman of an as-yet-unnamed local civil rights coalition. The expressed mission of this umbrella group was to sponsor an event in Detroit supporting the most recent civil rights protests in Birmingham led by King and the Southern Christian Leadership Conference, while at the same time calling attention to unmet needs of blacks in Detroit. Only a month earlier, on April 12, King had been arrested in Alabama's largest city, and while still behind bars four days later, he had written—in the margins of a newspaper and on other scraps of paper—a pivotal statement of purpose, the "Letter from Birmingham Jail," in response to seven white clergymen who had called his protest activities unwise and untimely. "We know through painful experience that freedom is never voluntarily given by the oppressor, it must be demanded by the oppressed," King wrote. "Frankly, I have yet to engage in a direct-action campaign that was 'well-timed' in view of those who have not suffered unduly from the disease of segregation." Franklin's plan was to invite King to Detroit to participate in a march and rally with the intention of raising not only consciousness but as much as $100,000 for the cause, most of it to go to the SCLC and its direct-action campaign. The leadership of Franklin's new group, while ostensibly representing a coalition, was dominated by close associates, including James Del Rio, his lawyer; Benjamin McFall, a wealthy funeral home director who was a trustee at New Bethel Baptist; and Thomas H. Shelby Jr., the minister of music at New Bethel, who was asked to assemble an all-city gospel choir for the next mass meeting, which was to be held at the new New Bethel Baptist in the refurbished Oriole Theater on May 17.

The first note of concern came two days before that second meeting, when the activist lawyers Conyers, Keith, and Crockett met at the Lucy Thurman Branch of the YWCA with a different set of pastors, including the two Congregational ministers, the mainstream Hood and more radical Cleage, along with Sheffield and Battle from the black labor group and a few white representatives of the autoworkers union. They too wanted to raise funds for King and the SCLC. Should they align with Franklin? Was he capable of running such a vital political enterprise? Would they be co-opted by him, or should they try to co-opt him? According to a memo written by Joseph E. Coles, who reported to the city's commission on community relations and was in attendance, they decided to delay answering those questions until after the mass meeting at Franklin's church. "It was thought if unity could be established by the two groups any drive would be more effective," Coles wrote.

If defined by numbers and passionate rhetoric, the May 17 meeting seemed to be a rollicking success. On a rainy Friday night, some eight hundred people filed into New Bethel for a long night of speeches, declarations, and organizational decisions. With Franklin presiding from the pulpit, it was decided to name the group the Detroit Council for Human Rights (DCHR), and an early June date was set for a Walk to Freedom down Woodward Avenue, followed by a rally at Cobo Hall, both starring King. The church collection baskets brought in five hundred dollars on the spot, with pledges for thousands more. At the end, the council issued a Declaration of Detroit that echoed King's Birmingham letter in its sense of urgency and employed some of the formal phraseology of the Great Emancipator, Abraham Lincoln, from a hundred years earlier: "Comprising nearly 30 percent of the population of this city and 70 percent of us existing in substandard housing; denied after 100 years of Constitutional freedom the full measure of the social contract, we do hereby declare before God and all men this 17th day of May in the Year of our Lord 1963, that we will no longer abide, tolerate or countenance this manifest injustice. . . . Be it also known that where in the past we have been deluded by promises, and made comfortable by small steps of progress, we shall not rest now until our lot is equal to the promises of the Constitution, not only of the United States, but of the State of Michigan, nor shall we slacken our pace while others of our color and kind, wherever they may abide, are denied the full measure of freedom."

Serious divisions became apparent soon after that meeting, from both ends of the civil rights spectrum. One problem involved the NAACP, which, though split internally, declined to endorse the march formally or join the DCHR, keeping some distance from both Rev. Franklin and

Dr. King for different reasons. Another involved Rev. Cleage, who in his speeches and pamphleteering started denouncing all elements of what he considered the complacent old-school leadership, from the NAACP to the Baptist Ministerial Alliance to elements of the labor movement, and at the same time declared that the march and rally should be a decidedly black event, with no leadership role for Walter Reuther or white city officials. Cleage, whose church was in Franklin's neighborhood, eight blocks up Linwood from New Bethel, did not see Franklin as part of that outdated set but as a populist outsider with whom he could align, at least temporarily, to push a more revolutionary agenda. Although not as outspoken as Cleage, Franklin had expressed his own critique of the black establishment as early as 1956, when he wrote a two-page letter to the *Michigan Chronicle* saying that when he got his hair cut at the barbershop he could not find anyone who knew what the NAACP was doing.

Franklin's preemptive bid to seize local leadership revealed, among other things, the vulnerability of the NAACP to a changing mood within the larger struggle. The chapter represented by far the largest and most diverse membership of any civil rights institution, with twenty-nine thousand dues-paying Detroiters. Even Cleage was on the board of directors, and the membership rolls included almost all of the city's black ministers, doctors, lawyers, and businessmen, ranging from A. A. Banks at Second Baptist to Berry Gordy Jr. at Motown. When the NAACP staged a major affair, anyone in town who supported the larger cause was expected to be there, the tickets as coveted as those to the annual black-tie Cotillion Ball. In April alone, two NAACP events had been held in the largest ballroom at Cobo Hall, each attracting crowds of more than 1,200 Detroiters, first a hundred-year celebration of the Emancipation Proclamation, with entertainment provided by Ziggy Johnson, the emcee at the 20 Grand, and Motown's Stevie Wonder, and two weeks later an annual "Fight for Freedom" dinner that brought in Dick Gregory, the activist comedian. But going to banquets was one thing, agreeing on politics and methods was quite another, and different factions within the NAACP were angling for control. In the final days of 1962, there had been an intense power struggle over the local presidency that was still reverberating months later. Edward Turner, the incumbent, had been challenged by his chapter's own nominating committee, which sought to replace him with Ernest Shell, a younger and more activist insurance executive. Turner, while keeping secret the fact that he was suffering from a fatal cancer and would be dead within a half year, was able to hold his position with the support of more conservative black ministers, who on election day turned out busloads of elderly churchgoers to vote for him.

The Detroit chapter's daily affairs were run by its executive secretary, Arthur L. Johnson, who was more aggressive than Turner but had his own conflicting impulses. Johnson had been friends with King since 1944, when they were in the same freshman class at Morehouse College in Atlanta, King as a mere fifteen-year-old who had gained early admission. They were both sociology majors, in many of the same classes, and were members of the Morehouse chapter of the NAACP. Johnson thought of young King as a quiet fellow, not a leader. He could not see then, he later noted, that "he was marked for greatness." And now, two decades later, as much as Johnson had come to admire King's bold actions and soaring rhetoric, he found himself defending the NAACP's interests against the rising power of King's SCLC. The two groups were competing not only for prestige but also for money. Franklin's idea of using the Detroit march and rally exclusively as a fundraiser for King and the SCLC bothered Johnson and others in the NAACP chapter, who were always scraping for funds. After discussing the problem at several internal meetings, they decided to dispatch a delegation led by Rev. Banks to meet with Franklin and his lawyer, James Del Rio, to see if a compromise could be reached that might also allow the NAACP to benefit from the Detroit event and at the same time tamp down criticism from Cleage, Franklin's newfound firebrand ally.

None of that worked. Franklin insisted that any money collected during the Walk to Freedom not going to the SCLC be kept for the development of the Detroit Council for Human Rights. And once Cleage heard about attempts to constrain him, he grew only more vocal. In public comments, he ridiculed Banks and the Baptist Ministerial Alliance. In the *Illustrated News*, he attacked the NAACP and "Old Guard Negro Leaders" for conducting "a continuing campaign of harassment" against the Freedom March merely because the money was going to King and the SCLC. But the event was gaining momentum anyway, Cleage wrote, and the old guard was "being left on the side of the road" and "no longer leading the freedom struggle." At a banquet in his honor at Cobo Hall (tribute banquets seemed to be biweekly rituals in black Detroit then), Cleage was joined on the podium and praised by Paul Zuber, a black attorney from Harlem. Zuber, a registered Republican who was becoming increasingly radicalized like Cleage, had led school desegregation efforts in New Rochelle, New York; Englewood, New Jersey; Chicago; and other northern outposts, constantly challenging the methodical approach of the NAACP, whose leaders considered him a smooth-talking demagogue. "The Negro revolt is on," Zuber declared at the Cleage banquet, echoing the words of the honoree. "We must tell our leaders, if you don't want to do it, get out of the way."

The combination of Cleage's assertiveness and Franklin's relative lack of experience and colorful reputation inspired several attempts in late May and early June to either dethrone Franklin or surround him with steadier hands. As the contretemps continued, there was some talk of trying to cancel the event altogether, but instead the date was pushed back two weeks to June 23, a day with haunting resonance in Detroit: it was a date close to the twentieth anniversary of the violent 1943 race riots. At one point there was an attempt to have Franklin step down from the chairmanship in favor of two men of vastly different backgrounds: John Conyers Jr., who served as counsel for the Trade Union Leadership Council and came from a family background in the UAW, where his father had been a shop steward and organizer; and Dr. Dewitt T. Burton, one of Detroit's leading black physicians, a pillar of the old-line elite whose debutante daughter's coming-out party at a lavish Pink Ball at the Sheraton Cadillac's Crystal Ballroom was covered in *Jet* magazine. But Franklin was a mountain not easily moved, and Conyers and Burton relented. In his Franklin biography, *Singing in a*

*Strange Land,* Nick Salvatore recounted an encounter Franklin had at a session of the Baptist Ministerial Alliance where he was denied speaking privileges to make his case because it was said he had not paid his dues. When the BMA president, Rev. A. L. Merritt, refused to let Franklin have the floor, Salvatore wrote, "Franklin went after him angrily and was restrained."

Franklin soon apologized, saying his temper got the best of him, and then defended himself on his Sunday night radio broadcast from New Bethel and in a letter hand-delivered to the *Michigan Chronicle* that began, "Regardless of reports, I, as the elected leader of the human rights movement, have not now, have not in the past, nor in the future plan to blast anybody of whatever stripe in the leadership trust of the Negro community." The issues were bigger than a power struggle, he said, and the times called for unity. Drawing on his southern connections, he produced a telegram from King's wife, Coretta Scott King, praising him for his work helping her husband's efforts. King's aides at SCLC headquarters in Atlanta, on the receiving end of a constant barrage of anxious calls from all sides, moved to ease the situation, in appearance if not in reality. They appointed another minister, Charles W. Butler of New Calvary Baptist, to serve as their Detroit regional director and liaison for the event, placing a buffer between Franklin and his doubters, and told Franklin that if indeed he wanted King to appear he had to demonstrate a show of confidence by having other ministers send telegrams declaring their support. Franklin accumulated endorsements from thirty Baptist ministers, ranging from Rev. Judge Lee Pastor at Abraham Missionary Baptist to Rev. D. D. Williams at Wolverine Missionary Baptist. He also included a message from Thermon Bradfield, a member of New Bethel, who wrote to King, "We believe if God ever anointed any man he anointed Rv. Franklin. We know he has done some great jobs for God we further believe this is the greatest job he has ever undertaken to do this I mean lead us out of the wilderness."

Obstacles to Franklin's leadership started to fall away one by one. Charles Diggs, the city's powerful black congressman, came out in support of the reverend and the march, saying he failed "to see a justification for the attitude taken by these Negro 'neutrals' who have not supported the movement." It was an endorsement of critical importance that brought other Detroit leaders on board and reassured King. Diggs and King had developed a strong bond since the days of the Montgomery bus boycott, when Diggs, in his Sunday night radio broadcasts from his House of Diggs funeral home, solicited funds to assist the boycott and ended up presenting King with $10,000 raised in Detroit. At about the same time as the Diggs endorsement, Horace Sheffield, Buddy Battle, and other black labor activists in the Trade Union Leadership Council switched from caution to unequivocal support of the rally. Police Commissioner Edwards issued a permit for the parade, saying there would not be a police problem and that King would be welcomed as a distinguished visitor.

Then there was the sensitive matter of Walter Reuther, the UAW president, and what role he would play. Reuther was a twelve-cylinder political engine with enormous horsepower, fully committed to the cause, and one of King's essential white allies in the civil rights movement. He could not be ignored or shunted aside. But Rev. Cleage kept insisting that it remain a black event, and there was an undercurrent of concern among other black leaders, even as they appreciated Reuther's support and worried about Cleage's stridency, that white liberals would end up dictating decisions. How could this be finessed? The task was assigned to Horace Sheffield and Buddy Battle, both of whom had come out of Ford's Rouge plant—Battle as a truck loader, Sheffield in the salvage department—to take leadership roles under Reuther in the UAW. Devising a plan that drew on one of Franklin's vulnerabilities, they invited the reverend and his lawyer, Del Rio, to meet them at TULC headquarters on Grand River. Marc Stepp, another union official, was there, and in an oral history later recounted the liquid seduction that brought Franklin around: "So the alcohol closet was right behind Buddy Battle's desk. Open the door and there's all the whiskey and whatnot. So you know, there was plenty of that there. And . . . it was hot as hell. [Franklin] was perspiring and drinking like hell and Sheffield, you know, kept playing the role of the great host, make damn sure he drank what he wanted, you know. And Del Rio was there cursing, you know Del Rio, raising hell. But anyway, we got a decent role for Walter Reuther."

The High Priest of Soul Preaching had his sermon set at the pitch of his hum. The Walk to Freedom was coming. The eagle stirreth her nest: *Oh a few more days. Oh a few more days. A few more days. Oh, Lord.*

Chapter 9

# AN IMPORTANT MAN

Certainly one of the most fertile brains in the United States of America, certainly one of the organizational geniuses of our day and time, and one of the most important men in the world, I give you Mr. Walter Reuther.

*—Police Commissioner George Edwards introducing Reuther at the Detroit Economic Club in 1963*

**WALTER REUTHER SPENT MUCH OF HIS TIME** contemplating the plight of man in the modern world, and when he thought, he wrote. Not books or many articles, but countless notes, memos, letters, telegrams, speeches, night wires; his words were dispatched in all directions at any hour. By 1963 he had worked in the public realm for more than half of his fifty-five years. He was known in world capitals from Tokyo to London to Buenos Aires, and his influence as an intellectual leader of the international trade union movement in many but not all ways surpassed the status of George Meany, his labor colleague and bitter rival. While Meany, president of the AFL-CIO, operated as a power broker out of headquarters in Washington, blocks from the White House, and loved to hang out with cronies in Miami Beach, Reuther, who served simultaneously as UAW president and AFL-CIO vice president, maintained his base with his autoworkers at Solidarity House on

East Jefferson Avenue in Detroit. That is not to say that he was a political outsider; he worked the inside game but from the liberating middle distance of the Midwest. Detroit had been his home since he arrived in the Motor City from Wheeling, West Virginia, as a teenager and began a rise through the heart of the twentieth century that took him from the tool-and-die division at Ford's Rouge plant to the top job at the United Auto Workers union.

With his red hair and boyish mug, Reuther was a confident, straight-ahead personality with a philosophical bent and a complicated take on the political swirl around him. In the smoky and alcohol-infused atmosphere of labor halls, he neither smoked nor drank. From his earliest years, his German immigrant parents, Valentine and Anna, veterans of West Virginia's coal wars, bathed Walter and his siblings in the idealistic waters of socialism. As a close friend once noted, Walter was inculcated in the belief "that working people have a right to more of the good things in life—security, dignity, standard of living, education, and that all human beings of whatever race, creed and color were equal before God and before their fellow men." His idealism came naturally, yet he prided himself on pragmatic progressivism over purity, getting things done over making noise, and during the tumultuous ideological struggles within labor in the decades bracketing World War II he staked a middle ground between communist organizers and capitalist owners. By the early sixties he could be attacked simultaneously by Goldwater conservatives in America as a "red menace" and leftist protesters in Kyoto as an "agent of American imperialism."

When Reuther was on his way to being elected president of the UAW in 1946, George Romney labeled him "the most dangerous man in Detroit" because of his ability to bring about "the revolution without seeming to disturb the existing norms of society." It was an odd declaration, as much grudging praise as damning criticism, and later Romney and Reuther found themselves at times working in concert, agreeing to the industry's first profit-sharing plan for workers. Reuther by then was not Marxist but Rooseveltian—in his case meaning as much Eleanor as Franklin. Reuther shared Eleanor Roosevelt's humanist worldview and moral righteousness, and over the years since FDR's death had also become personally close to the former first lady. Every summer or fall since the war, he and his wife, May, had made time in their crowded schedules to stay with her at Hyde Park for a week; their last visit, in November 1962, came during the final days before her death.

His connections to the Democrats now in the White House were also of long standing. Reuther had known Lyndon Johnson since the forties, when he occasionally slept on the Texas congressman's couch if no hotel rooms were available in the wartime capital. Their relationship had swung up and down and up again over the years, first bound by a common passion for New Deal politics, then strained by Reuther's wariness of the southerner on civil rights issues and preference for Hubert Humphrey of Minnesota as JFK's running mate, and finally strengthened again with Vice President Johnson's emergence as a strong voice on racial equality and economic opportunity. LBJ in most instances was a dominating personality, but according to Irving Bluestone, one of Reuther's top aides, Johnson treated Reuther as an equal, respecting his power and independence enough that "they could have a two-way conversation."

Reuther's relationship with JFK did not stretch back as far but was strong enough that in 1954, when he sent a telegram to the New York Hospital for Special Surgery, where Kennedy was undergoing back surgery, he received a two-page handwritten note from Jacqueline saying he "would never know" how much the message lifted Jack's spirits. Reuther was as habitual about flattery as he was about moralizing, but Kennedy fully understood how essential the labor leader and the UAW were to his rise and seemed to enjoy Reuther's company. "Walter and Jack Kennedy were very close," Jack Conway, a Detroiter who came out of Reuther's UAW to serve as a housing official in the Kennedy administration, recalled later. "They used to sit—sometimes two and three hours at a time—and philosophize. The thing that Jack Kennedy found in Walter Reuther was an intellectually stimulating person that he could bounce ideas off. And he felt a deep personal obligation to Walter because he and the UAW were probably the strongest supporters he had. He came to the UAW convention and said in effect if it hadn't been for that organization he would not be president." The convention was in Atlantic City, and when JFK spoke there on May 8, 1962, he did say as much, though in his own witty fashion. "President Reuther," Kennedy began, looking out at the multitude of labor comrades. "Last week, after speaking to the Chamber of Commerce and the presidents of the American Medical Association, I began to wonder how I got elected. [pause] And now I remember."

Since taking office, Kennedy had tapped the UAW leader for advice and assistance on many issues beyond the economics and politics of labor disputes. Reuther had provided a critical endorsement of JFK's push for across-the-board tax cuts for individuals and corporations, saying it would give the economy an injection of "high velocity purchasing power." On the world stage, he and his union played an important supporting role in the cold war effort by steering international trade unionists away from communism. During the Berlin crisis, the union flew one hundred of its local presidents directly to Berlin "as a demonstration of our solidarity with the people of that beleaguered city." Reuther also took a prominent role in an effort to free prisoners in Castro's Cuba after the disastrous Bay of Pigs invasion. Through a government-inspired private enterprise known as the Tractors for Freedom Committee led by Reuther, Eleanor Roosevelt, and Milton Eisenhower, the goal was to raise enough funds to buy tractors and medical supplies and send them to Cuba in exchange for 1,200 prisoners. The plan failed, but Kennedy commended Reuther's effort in a 1961 letter, saying he "successfully exposed the cynical and brutal nature of the Cuban regime. In so doing the U.S. won a major propaganda victory and advanced closer to the day when the Cuban people will once again be free."

From then on, Reuther's most pressing communications with Kennedy increasingly concerned not foreign policy but civil rights. He was constantly pressing the administration to move forcefully and quickly, receiving memos back from JFK aides explaining their goals and practical considerations, and being relied on by the White House—along with a select few other white activists such as Joseph Rauh of Americans for Democratic Action—to serve as an establishment liaison to black civil rights leaders, especially King and his southern desegregation campaigns. Reuther thought so highly of King that he brought him to Detroit in 1961 to be the main speaker at the UAW's twenty-fifth-anniversary dinner and afterward distributed pamphlet copies of King's speech to his rank and file and pressed a 33 1/3 long-playing record of it with proceeds going to the SCLC. "Please note that you have my continued support in the great work you are doing for the working man, and indeed for all of humanity," King wrote in a letter of gratitude.

The two had remained in frequent contact as civil rights momentum built month by month over the next two years, forcing Washington and the nation to deal with the issue in ways they never had before. King's Birmingham campaign of civil disobedience in April 1963 led not only to his defining letter from jail but to haunting images of brutality—peaceful protesters being knocked down by fire hoses and attacked by police dogs and club-wielding cops—that galvanized public attention. After the goals of the campaign were largely met and the rudiments of a breakthrough agreement with local leaders had been reached, hundreds of protesters still remained locked behind bars in the jails run by the city's stridently racist police chief, Eugene (Bull) Connor. The White House, needing help to resolve the Birmingham end game, turned to Reuther. Attorney General Robert Kennedy called Reuther and Rauh and asked them to provide cold cash to bail the demonstrators out of jail. Acting swiftly, the two allies rounded up $160,000, and in the evocative phrase of Nelson Lichtenstein, Reuther's most insightful biographer, "within hours the UAW staffers Irving Bluestone and William Oliver were on their way south, the cash stashed in bulging money belts around their midsections."

Of the various ways that Reuther and his union aided the civil rights effort, here was the most fundamental. Detroit and its people made many sacrifices to advance the cause of racial equality over the years, sending pastors and lawyers and lay activists to the most treacherous reaches of the Deep South. Detroiters, black and white, rode in the freedom rides, and walked in the marches and sat in the sit-ins. Rosa Parks, the steel-willed seamstress and heroine of the Montgomery bus boycott, was now a Detroiter, moving up to the Motor City to join her brother and sister-in law, Sylvester and Daisy McCauley, after failing to find work in the South. The activist lawyers Conyers, Keith, and Crockett made several trips to rural counties in Mississippi and Alabama to represent black citizens dealing with the inequalities of Jim Crow justice. On the same day that King was arrested in Birmingham, Charles Diggs was in Clarksdale, Mississippi, staying at the home of Dr. Aaron Henry, president of the state NAACP. The Detroit congressman and his host were roused from bed in the middle of the night by the explosion of a local version of a Molotov cocktail, made from cheap gasoline and a soda bottle, that had been thrown through Henry's living-room window. Two years after Birmingham, another Detroiter, Viola Liuzzo, a white mother of three, would be killed by Klansmen, shot twice in the head while driving through Alabama after coming south to help in response to the horror of Bloody Sunday, when peaceful marchers were beaten by police as they tried to cross the Edmund Pettus Bridge in Selma on the way to Montgomery.

This force of individual and collective action was crucial, the motivation powerful and often brave. Yet there was also the practical matter of money, and in that realm Detroit's contribution—mainly the work of the UAW and primarily a result of the commitment of Walter Reuther—was vital. It could be said that to a significant degree Detroit and its autoworkers were the movement's bank. Months after Birmingham, Reuther asked for and received an informal accounting of UAW funds used in the civil rights cause. The resulting document showed that the contributions had increased exponentially, multiplying fourfold year by year, from $2,925 in 1959 to more than $114,000 by the fall 1963, the money going to scholarship funds, civil rights organizations, testimonial dinners, and legal actions (including the bail money), and to cover the organizational costs of marches and protests. The amount at least trebled when in-kind contributions of manpower and publicity were included.

Money was also an important aspect of C. L. Franklin's grand notion of a Walk to Freedom. The goal of raising tens of thousands of dollars for the SCLC's southern campaign prompted Coretta Scott King to write Franklin a telegram: "It is wonderful to know that the people of Detroit will be sharing, even at a distance, the Birmingham experience."

In the days of June leading up to the Detroit rally, pivotal events were happening one after another, imbuing Franklin's idea with increasing resonance. On June 1 in Jackson, Mississippi, NAACP president Roy Wilkins and Medgar Evers, the organization's field secretary for that state, were arrested while leading a picket line outside downtown stores. On June 5 student protesters in Danville, Virginia, staged a sit-down act of civil disobedience in the mayor's office and were arrested for "inciting to riot." On June 9 activist Fannie Lou Hamer was arrested at the Columbus, Mississippi, bus station on charges of attempting to eat at a whites-only counter and was badly beaten that night in jail.

That same day, thousands of miles away, Detroit's Mayor Cavanagh was at the Hawaiian Village Hotel in Honolulu for the annual meeting of the U.S. Conference of Mayors, a group in which he was a rising star and future chairman. The main speaker was President Kennedy, and the subject that JFK had traveled "a good many thousands of miles" to discuss was race. The issue, he said, "was not northern or southern or eastern or western, but a national problem, a national challenge." The cause of equality was just, and the mayors should "be alert, not alarmed" by the civil rights protests then sweeping the nation, with more to come that summer. "The events in Birmingham have stepped up the tempo of the nationwide drive for full equality and rising summer temperatures are often accompanied by rising human emotions. The federal government does not control these demonstrations. It neither starts them, nor stops them. What we can do is seek through legislation and executive action to provide peaceful remedies for the grievances which set them off, to give all Americans . . . a fair chance for an equal life."

Two days later, on June 11, the Kennedy administration dispatched Deputy Attorney General Nicholas Katzenbach to Tuscaloosa to ensure that a few black students could register for summer session at the University of Alabama, where George Wallace, the segregationist governor, had vowed to stand in the schoolhouse door if necessary to prevent their enrollment as the state school's first black students. Katzenbach sternly and stoically endured Wallace's show of theatrics outside Foster Auditorium, saying he was there to enforce the law, and the administration deputized the Alabama National Guard to ensure the students could exercise their legal rights without state interference. At eight that night back in Washington, Kennedy went on national television from the Oval Office to explain what had happened in Alabama and to place that event in the context of the larger struggle for equality. "We are confronted primarily with a moral issue. It is as old as the scriptures and is as clear as the American Constitution," Kennedy told the nation. "The heart of the question is whether all Americans are to be afforded equal rights and equal opportunities, whether we are going to treat our fellow Americans as we want to be treated." The speech offered more than words; Kennedy announced that the following week he would send a sweeping civil rights bill to Congress that would ban discrimination in public accommodations ranging from restaurants to hotels and stores.

Hours later, returning home after a late meeting at which he watched Kennedy's speech, Medgar Evers was assassinated, shot in the back in the driveway of his home by Byron De La Beckwith, a Mississippi Klansman who had been hiding in the bushes with a high-powered Enfield rifle. It would take another thirty years for De La Beckwith to be brought to justice. Evers, who had visited Detroit several times and been interviewed frequently for stories in the *Michigan Chronicle* going back to the days of the Emmett Till lynching in 1955, became a martyr to the cause, and both Reuther and C. L. Franklin pledged donations to a scholarship fund established in his honor.

For Reuther, the Evers assassination had a chilling resonance. Fifteen years earlier, on April 20, 1948, he had survived a similar attack when a politically motivated gunman hiding outside his house on the northwest rim of Detroit shot him after he returned from work. The likely reason Reuther was not killed was that he had changed his routine and parked his Chevy on Appoline Street, entering the family's brick bungalow through the front door rather than parking on a side street and entering through the backyard, where the would-be assassin had been lying in wait for hours. Reuther was late getting home that night after spending much of the day at a UAW executive board meeting at the Book Cadillac and then stopping at Solidarity House. He had called and asked May to have a meal ready for him. She prepared leftover stew that he ate in the breakfast nook. After finishing the stew, he walked toward the refrigerator to find a bowl of peach preserves. When he turned to look at his wife, who was talking to him about one of their daughters, a bomb-like blast reverberated in the late-night softness as double-ought buckshot from a 12-gauge shotgun broke through the kitchen window, hitting Reuther in the back and right arm, shattering the arm to pieces and throwing him to the kitchen floor in a pool of blood.

Neighbors saw a man run from Reuther's backyard toward the side street, where a getaway driver was waiting in a red Ford sedan. In the violent world of Detroit labor, the suspects were many and varied. Some thought the attackers came from the left, motivated by Reuther's efforts to purge communists from UAW leadership. Others suspected racists from the right who disliked his support of racial integration in union activities, including the bowling league. Reuther had received unsigned hate letters from both groups before the assassination attempt. The crime was never solved. "Those bastards shot me in the back," he told his brothers from his bed at New Grace Hospital. Another aide, Ken Bannon, director of the UAW's Ford office, recalled dashing out to New Grace the day his boss was shot. "He's lying there, before the doctor came from Ann Arbor, he lay there and he said, 'Ken, they'll never destroy our beliefs this way. No matter how they go about it we will live on . . . and we'll make progress for people. Guns won't stop us.' The guy is just so goddamned real it's hard to believe."

The threat of violence always hovered over Reuther's Detroit. The beating he had suffered at the hands of two hired thugs who bulled their way into his apartment in 1938 when he and his guests were expecting a delivery of chop suey had been precipitated by the more infamous attack on him a year earlier by Ford security toughs outside Gate 4 of the Rouge plant. That day Reuther had stationed himself on the overpass to prepare for the arrival of a platoon of women who were soon to arrive by streetcar to hand out leaflets demanding a decent wage. They had obtained a permit from the Dearborn city clerk. Reuther described what happened next in testimony before John T. Lindsay, a National Labor Relations Board trial examiner: "A group of men approached us. They approached in a very aggressive manner. One of them, in a very aggressive voice, said, 'This is private property and get the hell off of here.' Men were coming toward us from the south part of the superstructure and we instinctively turned toward the north stairway to obey the command to get off. We didn't want violence."

He had taken three steps, Reuther testified, when he was slugged in the back of the head. "I was pounced on by ten or twelve men. I crossed my arms and tried to protect my face. I was being pounded on all parts of my head and upper body. All around me there was scuffling but I couldn't see what was happening to the others." After beating Reuther, the Ford men carried him by his hands and legs to the overpass stairway and pushed him down the stairs, then chased him through the parking lot just as the women with the handbills were walking up from the streetcar stop.

Eleven years later, after Reuther survived the assassination attempt, the union created the equivalent of a secret service unit to protect the family. They moved to a house in Detroit's suburbs that provided better protection. The security detail conducted hourly checks of the grounds outside the house. Packages "from Hudson's or some other store" would be accepted only if delivered by someone the UAW knew. All other packages were to be opened in the garage. The two daughters, Linda and Lisa, were escorted to and from school as if they were children of the president, and when they played in the front yard, a security man had to be there to watch them. At dusk the first-floor drapes were drawn and lights were turned on in the backyard. Reuther never drove again; he rode in the backseat of an armored Packard sedan, then in a midnight-blue Oldsmobile driven by Edward Torlone of the UAW's security detail, who was licensed to carry a concealed weapon. The Olds was outfitted to Reuther's specifications: mobile car phone, seat belts, tinted glass, front and rear radio speakers, padded dash, white sidewalls. But the shooting did nothing to slow Reuther's vigorous life. With the labor movement strong and growing, his most productive years were still ahead, traveling, writing, speaking, organizing, moralizing, pushing. And he was able to keep doing other things he loved; he still packed a collapsible fishing rod with his travel gear and played tennis regularly, though his grip was weakened by the buckshot wounds and friendly opponents knew to volley to his forehand.

By 1963 bigness in the modern world had become one of Reuther's central themes: big business, big labor, big cities, big government, big life in every respect. How to accommodate that bigness and make it liberating instead of oppressive was his obsession. He believed that the concentration of power, if used foolishly, could do grave harm, but if used wisely could be a force for good. The question was not power itself, but how it was harnessed. He compared power concentrations to "the genie in the lamp." It could be used for the better if humans handled it adeptly. "Contemporary men and societies must learn to live with bigness," he said in a speech that year at the Center for the Study of Democratic Institutions in New York. "Nostalgia for an earlier time of agrarian simplicity is understandable, but no substitute for ideas, policies, and programs for coping with the new technological, economic, and political revolutions transforming our lives. We have no practical option of stopping these movements, assuming it would be desirable to do so. Our great task is to attempt to guide and shape them in the interests of freedom and justice; to see to it that they enhance rather than diminish human dignity, security and liberty; to prevent them from creating new tyrannies over the minds and bodies of men."

Racial inequality was an old tyranny, with its roots in slavery and the agrarian way, and Reuther, taking the positive view of bigness, saw the big institutions of sixties America as important tools in overcoming it. Much like President Kennedy, he viewed Jim Crow segregation as a hypocritical detriment to the United States in its cold war struggle against the Soviet Union and a parallel threat to the growth of progressive labor on an international scale. While the president expressed concern that large demonstrations and marches might backfire and hinder the cause of legislative change, Reuther saw it as his role to be the insider on the outside, pushing the legislative route while participating in and helping to fund the protests, accentuating the racial diversity of the movement while attempting to temper the most radical voices that might alienate erstwhile sympathizers. In an acute observation on Reuther's alignment, his biographer Lichtenstein saw that while King "guarded his freedom and the autonomy of the movement for which he spoke," Reuther "stepped over the line" and "throughout these crucial months of 1963 . . . used his influence to serve that of the president within these councils." To some degree this showed Reuther's hunger for affirmation from the top, but from his perspective he was using the power of bigness to his and the cause's advantage.

Civil rights was not a new issue for Reuther. He had been active in the movement for two decades, going back to the racial tensions in Detroit during World War II. On April 11, 1943, two months before the city exploded in a race riot, Reuther took the stage at a rally in Cadillac Square, joining the NAACP in calling for the hiring of more blacks in the war plants. He said that industrialists were hiring white southerners who were newcomers to the city for jobs that could have gone to long-standing black residents. "No thinking American would discriminate against other Americans," he said at that rally. "It is against the Constitution of the United States, against the constitution of the UAW, and it is against the best interests of the country in winning the war. There is no manpower shortage in Detroit. All industry needs to do is to use the men and women who are already here. A great many Negro women are ready and anxious to obtain factory work."

Twenty years later, as the Walk to Freedom approached, Reuther became increasingly interested in his union's role. On June 14, the day after leading a labor delegation to the White House, where he lobbied for strong equal employment wording in the new civil rights bill, he had a letter distributed to all UAW officials in the twenty-nine locals of Region 1 and Region 1A, covering southeastern Michigan and parts of Canada, urging them to produce "large representation" at the Detroit march. "The cry for freedom in Birmingham and Jackson has excited the nation to the need for unparalleled and long-overdue action on the civil rights front," Reuther wrote. "We will personally participate in this demonstration along with Dr. Martin Luther King, leader of the SCLC." The letter also pointed out that King and Reuther would both address the rally at Cobo Hall following the march down Woodward Avenue. "This is a matter requiring special effort," he told his top lieutenants in a cover letter. (Wittingly or not, that last comment accurately reflected not only Reuther's convictions but also the gap between his commitment and that of much of the rank and file. For every action there is a reaction. On Reuther's home turf, that reaction eventually would involve autoworkers bailing out of the city for the suburbs and rejecting their leader's liberal philosophy, many of them later voting for George Wallace and then Ronald Reagan. More immediately and narrowly, Reuther's actions made it easier for manufacturers in the South to campaign against organizing. As his brother Victor later recounted, "Employers in the South printed [a] leaflet saying don't vote for these nigger lovers who gave $160,000—to help . . . Martin Luther King. In the middle of an election, they would print those leaflets. Well, we'd lose some southern elections over that issue—but it never changed Walter's thinking about it.")

If the liquored discussion at Buddy Battle's office bar involving C. L. Franklin and the UAW officials pried open the door for Reuther's involvement in the march, he was now fully inside and trying to bring others with him. Beyond that, he was furtively trying to set up a longer-term alternative to the Detroit Council for Human Rights, which he and others feared would be sidetracked by Franklin's inexperience and Cleage's militancy. On the Thursday evening of June 20, three days before the Walk to Freedom, he convened a meeting of what might be called Detroit's liberal establishment in the English Room at the Detroit Statler Hotel downtown "for the purpose of discussing and comparing notes on what we might do as citizens to be helpful and constructive in assuring meaningful progress in our community on this great moral issue." He wanted the meeting to be "informal and unpublicized" and did not tell Franklin or Cleage about it, but did invite Ed Turner and Arthur Johnson and other representatives of the NAACP, along with various black and white doctors, judges, lawyers, clergy, labor leaders, and representatives of the auto companies, utilities, Hudson's department store, the newspapers, and the League of Women Voters. According to notes of the meeting archived at the Walter P. Reuther Library at Wayne State, Reuther recommended forming a "small ad hoc" committee that could "provide info re total activities," facilitate existing programs, and "eliminate potential explosive situations." The general sense among those Reuther brought together was that expectations were heightening and it was time to get things done.

That Saturday, June 22, Reuther was back in Washington for another meeting with President Kennedy. He was accompanied by his brother Roy and William Oliver, one of the two UAW officials who had carried the cash south two months earlier to bail the Birmingham demonstrators out of jail. At the White House, they joined a diverse group of civil rights leaders that included King, Roy Wilkins of the NAACP, John Lewis, the young chairman of the Student Nonviolent Coordinating Committee, and A. Philip Randolph, head of the Brotherhood of Sleeping Car Porters and chief organizer of a March on Washington planned for late August. A huge civil rights demonstration in the nation's capital was something that Randolph, now seventy-four, had been thinking about for more than two decades, going back to 1942, when a march he had been organizing was canceled at the last minute after President Roosevelt defused the protest by issuing Executive Order 8802, calling for fair employment in the defense industry. History was repeating itself in terms of presidential caution. Kennedy, like Roosevelt, feared that a rally of predominantly black demonstrators in Washington could backfire. In point 5a of a memo preparing JFK for the meeting, Lee C. White, the chief White House aide on civil rights, wrote, "Consider negative impact of march on Congress."

White House minutes show that Kennedy arrived in the Oval Office at 9:07 that morning, accompanied by his brother, the attorney general, whose Justice Department was in the middle of the civil rights action. Much of the first hour and a half was spent in private huddles before the larger meeting, including one with Reuther, but the Kennedy brothers spent most of that time with King. There were two problems they feared might hinder their cause and weaken them politically at the same time, and King was at the center of both. The first was a deeply private matter that Robert Kennedy broached first, and when that had little effect the president took King for a walk alone in the Rose Garden. The White House believed, based on information provided by FBI director J. Edgar Hoover, that two men in King's inner circle, including his New York lawyer, Stanley David Levison, were communists. "I presume you know you're under very close surveillance," the president told King. The FBI, with Bobby Kennedy's approval, had been tapping Levison's phones and bugging his office for fourteen months. Mentioning the two King associates by name, Kennedy said, "They're communists, you've got to get rid of them." King received the news without betraying emotion, questioned the accuracy of the report, and gave no indication of what he might do in response to the president's demand. The second concern for the Kennedys took up much of the time at the larger meeting and went back to point 5a in Lee White's memo: fears that the August demonstration would hurt rather than help the legislative effort. "We want success in Congress, not just a big show at the Capitol," JFK said. The wrong demonstration at the wrong time might turn off some otherwise potentially sympathetic congressmen.

Wilkins shared that concern, but for most of the other civil rights leaders this was old and hollow advice they had had to deal with month after month, year after year, a variation of the expressed fears of white clergy that compelled King to write his "Letter from Birmingham Jail." Randolph told the president that "the Negroes were already in the street," and it was better that they be led by serious, nonviolent veterans of the movement than by rabble-rousers "who care nothing about civil rights nor about nonviolence." King expressed exasperation at being told again and again the time was wrong. That might be so, he said, "but frankly, I have never engaged in any direct action movement which did not seem ill-timed. Some people thought Birmingham was ill-timed." Reuther said that local demonstrations, such as the Walk to Freedom planned for Detroit the next day, were needed to build support for legislation, but he stressed that the Washington demonstration had to be inclusive and free from infighting. Momentum was building along with expectations, and it was apparent that nothing the White House said would stop the march. They were all putting "a lot on the line," Kennedy said, and they had to make sure that they preserved good faith in each other. "I have problems with Congress, you have yours with your groups."

When it was over and his guests had left, Kennedy stepped out the back door of the Oval Office. He was leaving for a trip to Europe, starting in Germany (where he would give his *"Ich bin ein Berliner"* speech). Reuther and King and several others gathered for lunch at Reuther's Washington hotel suite to rehash the discussion and solidify plans. Traveling separately, Reuther and King had the same event and destination listed next on their itineraries: the Walk to Freedom in Detroit. Reuther left that night at six, home in time to read the *Free Press* editorial supporting the march, saying that Detroit, "a great American industrial city," could stir the nation by its actions. "Elsewhere—in Birmingham, Jackson, Savannah, Cumberland—the mass marches of citizens have uniformly been protests. Negroes have sought this way to demonstrate their desire to be treated as citizens. Detroit is different. This is not a march of one race against another, but a march of people of good will of all races, protesting injustice against their fellow men. . . . Though we do not believe that a march is the best way of achieving these rights, it is one way. It is a way which has proved effective under the leadership of Dr. Martin Luther King and his policy of discipline and non-violence."

King was on his way. He was to arrive on a Northwest flight early Sunday afternoon.

Mayor Cavanagh had returned from Hawaii by then. He and his wife, Mary Helen, had stayed an extra twelve days after Kennedy's speech to the U.S. Conference of Mayors but made sure to get home in time for the big march. They usually traveled on separate planes, as a family precaution, but made an exception this time. At the airport they were loaded down with souvenirs for all seven kids, including the youngest, Jerome, who was only two months old. His middle name, as it turned out, was Celestin, not Olympic. Since the mayor's hospitalization in January, Mary Helen had been pushing him to slow down, and the extra days on Oahu served that purpose. Now he was eager to get to work and excited about the Sunday event. He noted that in Honolulu, with its diverse population, he saw "many examples of racial harmony" that could serve as a model for the nation. He held the same expectations for the Walk to Freedom and urged "the total participation of all citizens in Detroit." The drive for racial equity was the force that had propelled Cavanagh into the mayor's office, and once there he had established his priorities with his first two appointments, Edwards to head the police department and Alfred M. Pelham as city controller, the first African American to hold that position. For Cavanagh, who had higher aspirations, the issue of race served as a potent convergence of ambition and idealism.

At the airport Jim Trainor, the press secretary, was there to greet the mayor and his delegation, which included Ray Girardin, the mayor's executive secretary, another former Detroit newspaperman, who had expressed interest in the police commissioner job if and when Edwards left for a federal judgeship. Trainor had been the acting mayor while they were away, and aside from the various city actions preparing for the march and rally on Sunday, there had been another big story in the city. It was the banner headline in the *Free Press* that very day: "Gambling Czar Charged with Bribes: Police Spy Used to Crack Case."

As soon as they saw Trainor at the airport, Cavanagh and Girardin pumped him for everything he knew about the arrest of the Party Bus mobster Tony Giacalone.

Chapter 10

# HOME JUICE

**ALONG WITH MARKING** the demise of a legendary black establishment, the gambling raid at the Gotham Hotel produced one unexpected and fruitful piece of information. In the bounty of confiscated betting slips, felt counting tables, adding machines, and tens of thousands of dollars in cash, the cops found a black book with an unlisted telephone number in it. The number belonged to Tony Giacalone. Here was a vital connection for Police Commissioner Edwards and his criminal investigators at 1300 Beaubien. It proved what they had believed before the November raid, that Tony Jack, as a capo in the Detroit partnership, controlled the numbers racket in Detroit, all of it, black and white. And it provided them with the means to set the trap to prove it.

Going back to the bootlegging of the Prohibition era, the Detroit mob had tried to stay one step ahead of the law by paying off dirty cops. Giacalone, who grew up on Detroit's east side, the son of a vegetable seller, and rose through the underworld ranks as bartender, bodyguard, chauffeur, bookie errand runner, and street boss, was known to be paying off policemen since at least 1954, when he was arrested for bribery and served eight months behind bars. Before that he had always beaten the rap, fourteen arrests going back to a car theft in 1937 and no convictions. Edwards and his aides were determined to get him locked up again and out of Detroit for a longer stretch. Certain that the bribe-to-survive policy was still in use, they recruited a sergeant working vice at the McGraw Station, known as the cleanup squad, for the dangerous assignment of ingratiating himself with Giacalone and his men by posing as an officer on the take.

That role was given to James W. Thomas, who at age thirty-eight had already been on the force for sixteen years and seemed perfectly average in every respect: average height, average weight, dark hair, unprepossessing demeanor. Average in every respect except one. He was a former marine who fought at Iwo Jima and was known on the Detroit force as someone who would not flinch in a pinch. His task was made easier by the fact that even before Edwards gave him the assignment he had been approached by Giacalone underlings to see if he could be bribed.

Sergeant Thomas did not act alone. He was supported by members of the Criminal Investigations Bureau who worked in shifts monitoring Giacalone's movements with electronic surveillance. The first contact Thomas made, on February 28, was with Claude Williams, one of Tony Jack's top numbers runners. Thomas set a price for his protection at fifty bucks a month, and for reassurance asked to talk to Williams's boss. Soon thereafter he had a classic underworld conversation that went like this:

T: Wait, now, who am I talking to? So I know.

G: Tony.

T: Just Tony, huh.

G: You heard of me?

T: Yeah. I don't know if I heard of you or not.

G: Yeah. You've heard of me.

T: If you said I did, I guess I did.

G: Yes, you have heard of me. What's your first name?

T: Jim.

G: Jim. All right. Listen, Jim. You've heard of me. You've heard of Tony Giacalone.

T: Tony Giacalone?

G: That's me.

During March and April, Thomas worked his regular shift with the cleanup squad while also playing his role as the dirty cop. He got his first fifty-dollar payment on time, but before the second payment arrived, the police arrested Williams and charged him with possessing numbers tickets. Thomas was not sure if the arrest was part of the sting or incidental to it, but he played it to his advantage, explaining to Williams that the cops would lay off if he got paid on time. Soon came another call from the boss, who by now was calling Thomas "buddy." Thomas took the call at a telephone booth at the corner of Schoolcraft and Chatham.

G: How are you, buddy?

T: This Giacalone?

G: Yeah. How you feel?

T: Yeah. I wonder what's going on.

G: Well, it's just what I told you. I'd call you around this time. Where you at? In an outside station?

T: Yeah. I'm in a pay station.

G: How you?

T: Okay.

G: Listen. Have you got an address where I can send that to you?

T: Oh.

G: I got to send you $150.

The investigators now had clear identification of Giacalone and proof of a bribe. In a meeting with Williams, recorded by the police, Thomas showed the numbers runner a photograph of Giacalone, and Williams confirmed that was his boss. But Edwards needed an airtight case to get a Giacalone conviction. No more beating the rap. Through this investigation and the loosely connected probe of the Giacalone brothers and the Party Bus and the Lions, the police commissioner had come to despise the mobsters and the sinister effects of their criminal enterprise. During the Party Bus investigation, Edwards had already taken the precaution of writing letters for the publisher of the *Detroit News* and Robert Kennedy to open in case of his untimely death. Now the surveillance showed there might be reason for concern. On one recording, Tony Jack could be heard telling an associate that he was in favor of killing policemen.

Giacalone lived in a redbrick palace on Balfour Street in Grosse Pointe Park between East Jefferson and the Detroit River. Only the highest-ranking mobsters, of whom he was one, had homes there. The Zerillis and Corrados had moved into the neighborhood before him, all following the same path from petty street crime to the top of the heap, from impoverished Sicily to promising America, from Terrasini Favarotta to booming Detroit. *Favarottado,* they were called. Within the Detroit branch of the Mafiosi, it helped to be a *Favarottado* like Tony Jack and Billy Jack, whose parents immigrated from the small village near Palermo. In Grosse Pointe Park, Tony Giacalone was respected as a family man. A local judge once gave him a reprieve using those very words. Fanny Fierimonte, the wife of a Detroit cop, grew up near the Giacalone kids and attended Catholic elementary schools with them: "We were all just one big happy family, even though my mother would say, 'Are you running with the Dagos again?' She knew the kinds of troubles the fathers had. They [the children of the Giacalone clan] always said, 'Dad's at a meeting.' The Giacalones were very private people. They really stuck with the Italians. They didn't move out of their circle much at all. And the other Italians orbited around them. They were the sun and the others were all the planets." In that environment, as the Italian family man, Tony Giacalone would not be seen with the tools of the enforcement trade that he was said to have available in his trunk: the blackjack, brass knuckles, or rock-hard slab of deer leg.

He was a busy man with several offices. His main office was in Greektown, at 1013 St. Antoine, with paneled walls and carpeted floors. There he watched over his interests in what were considered legitimate enterprises, including Detroit Stevedoring and Lightering on East Jefferson, Snow Pest Control on Livernois, and Home Juice Company on East Palmer. Until the cops shut it down, his gambling hangout was the Lesod Club on West Columbia, where the specialty of the house was a dice game called barbut. Edwards became obsessed with the brazenness of the Lesod and made it his mission to close it. Earlier that year, when William O. Douglas, the Supreme Court justice, was in Detroit to deliver a speech, he asked Edwards to show him the police department in action. "How about we go out with the late shift and stake out a gambling parlor?" Edwards asked. Douglas was game. In a speech he delivered to the Advisory Council of Judges in New York in May 1963, Edwards picked up the story from there: "At one a.m. on the night in question, we showed him the security arrangements at the Lesod Club, one of the most aggravating and persistent operations of organized crime with which we had to deal in Detroit. The club possessed a state charter as a social club but was actually the medium through which the two top gambling bosses in our area—the Giacalone brothers—ran a barbut game. At one a.m. the scout car we were in pulled up near 106 W. Columbia in downtown Detroit. Two-story building in a business block. Lights shone through drawn shades on the second floor. In front of the door was an auto with [a] driver at the wheel and directly behind was another—our unmarked vice squad car. The officer wandered over and I introduced him to the gray-haired man with weatherworn face who was my companion. Vice then showed and explained some of the defense mechanisms of modern organized crime to Justice Douglas. He identified by name the lookout at the wheel and gave the record for gambling convictions. All customers have to check in first with the lookout posted at the door. If properly identified the lookout rang a bell on the downstairs door, gave [the] proper signal with eye-to-eye contact with the doorman looking out the door at the head of the stairs, who pressed a buzzer to open the downstairs door. Then another lookout followed the same procedure on the second floor." Not long after that unlikely scene, Edwards and his men cracked the fortress and busted the Lesod, though Tony Giacalone was not there that night.

Giacalone's unofficial office was the back room of Grecian Gardens, at the table where the Detroit cops happened to see him sitting with Lions linebacker Wayne Walker and Lindell Cocktail Bar owner Jimmy Butsicaris the previous August. The Gardens is where Tony Jack held court, made deals, collected debts, and when the mood struck slipped out onto his Party Bus. At whatever office, Giacalone carried himself with the same self-assurance, dapper and cold and intimidating at six feet and two hundred pounds. The piercing look in his brown eyes could chill a man. His suits came from the same haberdashery that Mayor Cavanagh used. He always had a fresh silk handkerchief in his breast pocket. He had his hair cut twice a week at Jimmy the Barber's place in the Seville Hotel, where the shoeshine man knew to shine the soles of his shoes.

After several dealings with Giacalone, Sergeant Thomas became anxious. In one telephone conversation, they both talked about how they were starting to feel exposed. Edwards and his men decided it was time to move in. On the Thursday afternoon of June 20, Tony Jack was hanging out at the Home Juice Company, which, according to word on the street, his brother Vito had won in a dice game. The brothers served as vice presidents. Home Juice was based in Chicago and clean of mob ties there, but the Detroit franchise, with the Giacalone brothers involved, was their most profitable branch. It was there that the Detroit police found Tony Giacalone that afternoon, wearing a flashy blue suit and freshly shined shoes. They placed him under arrest on charges of bribing a police officer and took him downtown for arraignment at Recorder's Court, where Judge Paul E. Krause set bond at $5,000. When Giacalone's lawyer protested that the bond was excessive, the judge held out a sheaf of papers documenting his previous bribery conviction and fourteen other arrests. "He has this," the judge said.

Giacalone showed nothing.

Sergeant Thomas was not at the scene, but his actions had made it possible, and Edwards, in keeping with his theory that publicity was his best weapon, offensive or defensive, immediately gave him a battlefield promotion to lieutenant and announced it to the press. Giacalone made bail and went back to Grosse Pointe Park. There was no love lost between the commissioner and the capo. Edwards had listened to the tapes, and one had a special resonance. It was when Giacalone brought up Edwards in the context of his attempts to ease racial tensions in the city and his outspoken support of Martin Luther King and the upcoming Walk to Freedom. "Well, you know what I mean. He's for the niggers," Giacalone said to Sergeant Thomas. "You're not for the niggers, are you?"

George Edwards was for a lot of things, but none more than the cause of racial justice. To that extent, if one can move past the racial slur, Tony Jack knew his nemesis. The lessons of race in America were seared into Edwards's consciousness from birth. He grew up listening to his father, a lawyer in Dallas, tell the story of his first criminal case in 1910, when he was defending an elderly black man who had been accused of assaulting a child. "Before he had reached the room to which he was going in order to interview the client, whose life he was required to defend, a mob broke into the court house, into the courtroom, into the jury room, and seized the man, tied a rope around his neck, threw him out a third story window, dragged him up the main street of Dallas, and hanged him from an arch built for the Elk's Temple national convention." Edwards recounted that story in a speech he delivered to a conference on police-community relations at Michigan State University in late May 1963, around the time of Giacalone's comment and one month before the Walk to Freedom.

In that speech Edwards also recalled how his father's last case, in 1959, when he was seventy-nine years old, was in defense of the rights of the NAACP in Texas "to continue to exist and function there against a petition and injunction filed by the attorney general in Texas." And he recounted how he himself was on the Detroit City Council in 1943 when "unreasoning animosities and hatreds" led to the race riot. "Think about what we are doing in this America of ours," Edwards concluded. "Think real hard about what we're talking about today. Because I say to you in as earnest terms as I can say it, there is no other road for these United States of America than to make good its promises of equality and freedom to all of its people, and to make good its promise of order to all of its people. Now, if you say that's tough, I couldn't agree with you more. But I also say to you it's possible and it's necessary and that's the job we all have ahead of us."

Equality and order. Like his friend and mentor Walter Reuther, George Edwards tried to walk a straight line between the two, but there was always some human imperfection in the way.

## Chapter 11

# EIGHT LANES DOWN WOODWARD

**SINCE THE PLANE** from Washington, due at one-thirty, was running late, Police Commissioner Edwards went to the airport with a phalanx of motorcycle cops to retrieve Martin Luther King instead of meeting him as planned at a downtown hotel before the march. Lt. George Harge came along, his presence signaling that Detroit would be a safe haven for the civil rights leader. Harge had been promoted months earlier as the highest-ranking black officer in the Detroit Police Department, and his assignment now was to serve as King's bodyguard throughout the day. Edwards led the small greeting party on the tarmac, with Harge at his side, when King deplaned with his traveling aide, Walter Fauntroy, an SCLC regional director and pastor of the Washington version of New Bethel Baptist. Michigan's political leadership wanted to make it clear that this was not the South. Governor Romney had issued a proclamation declaring Sunday, June 23, 1963, "Freedom March Day." Mayor Cavanagh had offered King the use of his limousine. And Edwards extended a greeting that sharply differentiated his force from the ugliness King had endured in Birmingham. "You'll see no dogs and fire hoses here," he said.

With a police escort clearing the way, the official party moved swiftly into the city and down to the Sheraton Cadillac at the corner of Michigan and Washington, skirting crowds already massing along Woodward. King washed up, changed clothes, and relaxed in his suite while granting a brief interview to a reporter from the *Free Press.* Dressed "somberly in black," he talked about his Oval Office meeting with President Kennedy the previous day at which they discussed the administration's civil rights bill. Alluding to the Walk to Freedom that was about to take place on the streets of Detroit, King also stressed how vital mass protests were in pushing the cause, an idea not exactly endorsed by JFK. "The president solicited our support of his legislation. He wants Negroes to mobilize to help pass the bill," King said. "The president told me some congressmen feel this would be more harmful than helpful. I insisted it would not be harmful. He expressed concern over the fact that some demonstrations have led to violence. I told him the demonstrations have been amazingly nonviolent and it was spectators and others who were violent."

By "others" King was referencing Bull Connor and other southern officers of the law who had been upholding Jim Crow segregation through violent means. Proof that Detroit would be different went deeper than the protective assignment of Lieutenant Harge. Edwards had devoted significant time and attention to how his department would handle the march. By haunting coincidence, this very week marked the twentieth anniversary of the violent race riot that wounded Detroit in 1943, when Edwards was on the city council, a progressive shaken to his core by that deadly reminder of man's inhumanity to man. Two decades later, he wanted to minimize the possibility that his officers would provide a spark. "I want this event to be peaceful and happy," he told Paul Sheridan, the Central Station inspector placed in charge of the parade detail. "I want you to talk to every one of your details personally. Tell them we expect no trouble. Tell them to leave their clubs in the station house, and Paul, tell them all the time they are on Woodward Avenue to smile." At roll call that day, Sheridan dutifully passed along the sentiments of his boss, along with this written reminder: "It is no secret that we can never retract a spoken word, so you are hereby instructed at this time to be absolutely certain that any conversation had by you at any time you are on this detail shall be strictly in the best police manner possible."

With the marchers expected to be predominantly African American, all available black officers were assigned to the event, but that still amounted to only twenty, a minuscule percentage of the five hundred–plus detail that included two deputy inspectors, eight lieutenants, twenty-eight sergeants, twenty-three detectives, and 452 patrolmen. Edwards wanted no trouble, but he also wanted the means to respond if trouble arose. His biggest fear was not that his force would misbehave but that antimarch hecklers might appear along the route. Hate mail was already starting to pile up in his office. Just in case, he had one hundred commandos stationed in the garage at 1300 Beaubien, out of sight but connected by open line to Cobo Arena, where the rally was to end.

An event that six weeks earlier was no more than C. L. Franklin's hazy idea and had been on the verge of collapse many times during the contentious planning stages, was now becoming a reality beyond even the extravagant reverend's imagining. It seemed that everybody and everything were cooperating, even the weather. The early summer sun radiated in a high blue sky. Franklin's Detroit Council for Human Rights had evolved into a vibrant coalition joining forces for this day, from the Jewish Community Council to the Roman Catholic archdiocese, from the United Auto Workers to a group of local Teamsters, from the Urban League to—reluctantly, but in the end demonstrably—the NAACP, from New Bethel Baptist to Plymouth Congregational, from the Booker T. Washington Business Association to the Wolverine Bar Association, from the Conant Gardens Property Owners Association to the Cortland Block Club, from the Detroit Police Department Band to the Cass Tech Marching Band.

Churches, schools, social clubs, civic groups, small businesses, labor unions—all had their own marshals and armbands and signs and staging areas in a twenty-one-block area off Woodward that stretched north along the avenue from Adelaide to the intersection with Warren several blocks below Wayne State and the Detroit Institute of Arts, about three miles away from the final destination at the riverside arena. At first the march had been scheduled to start at four, then it was moved up to three, but by as early as noon the staging areas were throbbing with energized masses eager to pick up their feet. Early crowds became so thick around Hudson's in the Woodward shopping district that horses from the Police Mounted Bureau were diverted from their original mission there and clip-clopped down to the more spacious areas near Cobo to pull traffic duty. The optimistic talk beforehand was of bringing out 100,000 people; now it would be that and more, from a quarter again more to twice that many, depending on who did the counting.

The march had begun prematurely by the time King and his entourage left the hotel. An early platoon had already reached the corner of Woodward and Michigan at Campus Martius when the limo carrying King and Edwards approached. As the two men emerged from the backseat, thinking they had missed half the procession and should get to the front, a raucous shout—"There he is!"—sent a swarm toward King with the exuberance that would overwhelm him the rest of the day.

Some people started singing "God Bless America" as he took to the street. But just then Edwards heard on his radio that the other leaders of the march were waiting for them back at the Adelaide starting point. He motioned to King, who swiftly retreated with him into the limo, their faces shrouded by tinted windows as the vehicle maneuvered the back streets to get to where they were supposed to be. Fifteen minutes later, King and Edwards took their places in the front line, locking arms with C. L. Franklin, Charles Diggs, Benjamin McFall, Albert Cleage, James Del Rio, James Swainson, and Walter Reuther and taking the first steps forward, a mass of humanity behind them, eight lanes wide, nearly a mile deep, as they moved down Woodward Avenue on the Walk to Freedom. Mayor Cavanagh marched with other dignitaries in the second row, directly behind King. Del Rio, who was in charge of arrangements, later claimed that he had assigned Cavanagh to the tenth row but the ambitious mayor had elbowed his way up. Possible but unlikely. Del Rio proved to be an unreliable narrator, also later asserting that the march was more than twice as large as the most generous estimates. What his claim about Cavanagh revealed, if nothing else, was the sentiment he shared with Reverend Cleage: this was to be a black-oriented event not overshadowed by white leaders. The enormity of the march made that concern seem inconsequential, just as it overwhelmed all of the infighting leading up to that moment.

The surge behind Reuther and Franklin and King was so great that they all described being lifted off their feet and carried forward as if pushed by a great torrent. Erma Franklin recalled, "There were so many people it was almost like you were kind of scared to get in there, or you got there and there were that many people and then say ten minutes later you look behind you and you couldn't see the end of the line!" The size and velocity of the crowd made it seem "as if a huge dam had burst," reported the *Detroit News*. At some point the mayor's wristwatch fell off and was trampled by the advancing army. There was so much noise and commotion around the leaders that talking was futile. Shouts of "Hang on! Hang on!" reverberated down the line. Del Rio held up a bullhorn and shouted "Back off! Back off!" to no avail. Lieutenant Harge and another policeman, Sergeant Tetrault, tried to protect King and his cohort, walking directly behind them, but were pushed around with everyone else. Harge became winded. From no ill intent, just the force of the moment, Tetrault was knocked to the ground, scraping his hands and knees. If you got pushed out of line, the best way to get back in place was to race through a relatively empty alley paralleling Woodward and try to meet the wave again as it rolled down the avenue. People were singing all along the route, alternately somber and joyous as they went through the verses of "We Shall Overcome" and "The Battle Hymn of the Republic." There were signs everywhere: *Time is Running Out; Let's Move to Grosse Pointe; I'm Ashamed I Live in Dearborn; Don't Tread on Me, White Man; Detroit Needs Strong Housing Laws; UAW Supports Pres. Kennedy's Civil Rights Program; Evers Died for You; Stop Jim Crow; Fight for Freedom; Down with Segregation.*

Some of those signs, quite noticeably, displayed five letters at the top: NAACP. This was the Machiavellian work of Arthur Johnson, executive director of the Detroit chapter, a group that had no role in planning the march and spent considerable time beforehand diminishing its importance, with some of its members forcefully trying to scuttle it and feuding with Reverend Franklin. "As the excitement about the march grew in the community, we understood that it was bound to be a milestone for the city and the nation," Johnson explained later. "We supported the march but had to recognize that we did not have leadership participation in it. Because the branch was at the forefront of all the issues of segregation, discrimination, and police brutality, not being a part of this landmark civil rights event particularly concerned me, and I knew that I had to do something to advance the NAACP's interest." That something, Johnson decided, would be thousands of placards with "NAACP" printed on them for people to carry on the march. He found a silkscreen company that could handle the order for $750 and called a closed-door meeting of his executive committee, which endorsed his plan and agreed to keep it secret. Early on the morning of the march he and an aide brought the placards to the staging areas and spread the word that anyone could carry them. "Within minutes," Johnson noted, "all one thousand signs were gone." If Franklin was upset by the maneuver, he never mentioned it; there was too much going his way at the moment for him to bother with the unbrotherly cageyness. Even the outspoken Cleage let it go, for once.

What does a march signify in the larger scheme of things? It does not do the work of legislation, changing the laws and norms of society. It does not promise a transformative effect on an individual life, nor a lasting impact on a city, the way that education can, or money, smart leadership, community responsibility, or an effective social program. A march is ephemeral and symbolic. When stripped bare, it is nothing more than a parade of people. But that does not render it meaningless. In retrospect, the Walk to Freedom on that fine June day can seem hollow, considering all that was to happen in and to Detroit in the following years, from the 1967 riot to the decline and fall toward bankruptcy a half century later. But a moment like that collapses time and represents its own reality, apart from the day to day, transcending the harsh judgment of literal and practical perspectives. No one who participated in the march forgot it, and as they moved eight lanes down Woodward toward Cobo they carried with them stories that were defined and deepened by the events of that day—and that its aftermath could not diminish.

Rev. Nicholas Hood of Plymouth Congregational, an establishment institution not inclined toward political demonstrations, found himself leading nearly a hundred members of his church who had surprised him by turning out for the march. Plymouth was just then emerging from a difficult eight-year stretch of dislocation and disillusionment precipitated in part by the mayoral administrations of Jerome Cavanagh's predecessors, Republicans Albert Cobo and Louis Miriani. The congregation's old church, a former synagogue, had been demolished as part of the urban renewal that leveled wide swaths of Black Bottom and Paradise Valley to make way for hospitals, parking lots, and the Chrysler Freeway. Hood always tried to look on the positive side—he called himself "a bridge builder, not a bridge burner"—but he considered urban renewal, or "Negro removal," the most overt indication that "there was a total disregard for anything black in this community." Before the bulldozers came, he was shown a detailed planning map of a three-hundred-acre area that identified properties block by block yet failed to indicate the presence of black churches, of which there were more than a dozen.

One way his church reacted was by saying, as he put it, "Yes, urban renewal is Negro removal, but we're going to make it work for us." He fought for the right to rebuild in the same area and to surround his new church with affordable housing, a rarity in the renewal zones. The other way he reacted was by getting more political. The wave that brought Cavanagh into office in 1961, defeating Miriani in an upset, was largely powered by black voters. Hood now contemplated a role in city politics himself, a possibility that he said came in part because of King and the civil rights movement rolling across the South. The movement, Hood said later, not only challenged Jim Crow segregation; it also awakened and emboldened northern blacks to action on their home turf.

As he took his place in a staging area several blocks behind King and the leadership row, his two young sons tagging along, Hood looked out in wonder, thinking to himself, *Where did all these people come from?* Establishment black churches like his had not organized the march. The NAACP was not behind it. But the black citizens of Detroit had clearly rallied, whatever their affiliation. "They had been pent-up for so long," Hood recalled. "And when King asked them to do something, they were happy to get out on the street. They could sing and dance. I led my church out there, singing to the top of our voices. It was a joyous experience. We sang all the way. It was bigger than the Thanksgiving Day parade. I had never seen anything like it, just unbelievable. But I think part of it was the pent-up emotion. These were peace-loving people. These were not people throwing Molotov cocktails and that kind of foolishness. People who just wanted an opportunity to express themselves. Where are they coming from? Where are they coming from? Everywhere."

A block or so in front of Hood and his contingent were Booker Moten and his Kappa Alpha Psi fraternity pledgemates. Moten was eighteen, a freshman at Wayne State, and an amateur photographer who wanted to capture the day on film as part of his portfolio of his hometown. He had grown up near Outer Drive in the southernmost point of Detroit's west side but was smart enough to get accepted at Cass Tech near downtown, where one of his classmates was Diane Ross (before she became Diana), who lived in the Brewster projects. Race was a constant topic of conversation at church and at the dinner table, led by his father, Pops Booker, who had arrived in Detroit with a master's degree in mathematics but had to take a job as a busboy at the YMCA. At the center of the discussion was housing and the demographics of the city. "In the black community housing segregation was so distinct that we knew block by block when a black family moved into a new neighborhood," Moten recalled. "That was always news in black society." Jobs and housing had been the fundamental problems, along with difficult relations with police, but by the time Moten reached college he was looking at how racial issues played out beyond his own experience. At the time of the march, he and his friends were talking about boycotting the local Kresge's in sympathy with lunch-counter protests in the Jim Crow South. Like Reverend Hood, he felt that King and the southern movement empowered his northern cohort as well. They talked that month about picketing theaters showing *Cleopatra*, a movie just being released with Elizabeth Taylor in the lead role. "We were developing a

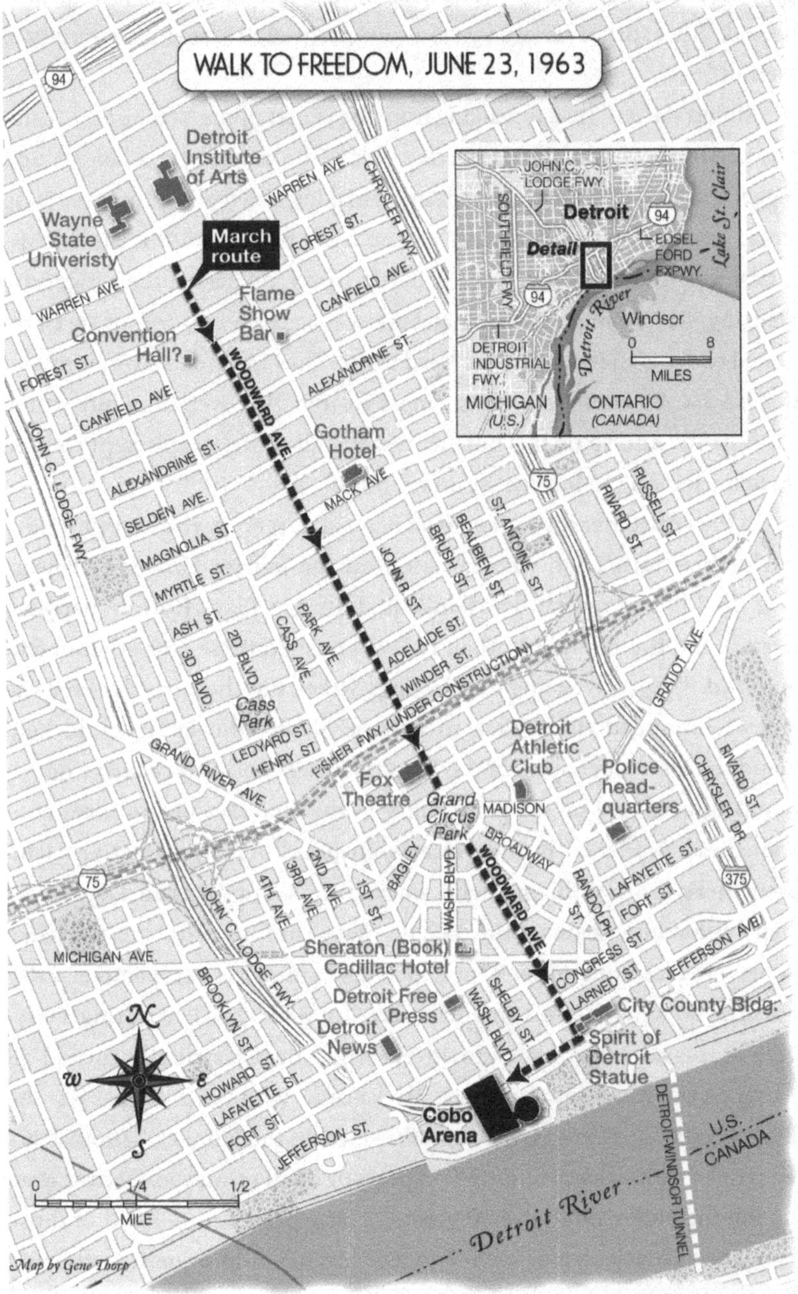
WALK TO FREEDOM, JUNE 23, 1963
Detroit Institute of Arts
Wayne State Univeristy
March route
Flame Show Bar
Convention Hall?
Gotham Hotel
Cass Park
Fox Theatre
Grand Circus Park
Detroit Athletic Club
Police head-quarters
Sheraton (Book) Cadillac Hotel
Detroit Free Press
Detroit News
City County Bldg.
Spirit of Detroit Statue
Cobo Arena
WOODWARD AVE.
WARREN AVE.
FOREST ST.
CANFIELD AVE.
ALEXANDRINE ST.
CHRYSLER FWY.
MACK AVE.
SELDEN AVE.
MAGNOLIA ST.
MYRTLE ST.
ASH ST.
3D BLVD.
2D BLVD.
CASS AVE.
PARK AVE.
JOHN R ST.
BRUSH ST.
BEAUBIEN ST.
ST. ANTOINE ST.
RIVARD ST.
RUSSELL ST.
ADELAIDE ST.
WINDER ST.
FISHER FWY. (UNDER CONSTRUCTION)
LEDYARD ST.
HENRY ST.
GRAND RIVER AVE.
GRATIOT AVE.
CHRYSLER DR.
MADISON
BROADWAY
RANDOLPH ST.
LAFAYETTE ST.
FORT ST.
CONGRESS ST.
LARNED ST.
JEFFERSON AVE.
JOHN C. LODGE FWY.
4TH AVE.
3RD AVE.
2ND AVE.
1ST ST.
BAGLEY
WASH. BLVD.
SHELBY ST.
MICHIGAN AVE.
BROOKLYN ST.
HOWARD ST.
JEFFERSON ST.
DETROIT-WINDSOR TUNNEL
U.S.
CANADA
Detroit River
94
75
375
N
E
S
W
0
1/4
1/2
MILE
JOHN C. LODGE FWY.
SOUTHFIELD FWY.
Detroit
Detail
EDSEL FORD EXPWY.
Lake St. Clair
Windsor
DETROIT INDUSTRIAL FWY.
MICHIGAN (U.S.)
ONTARIO (CANADA)
8
MILES
Map by Gene Thorp

growing black sensibility about a white woman playing an African queen," he said. "That sort of racial consciousness permeated students in the city of Detroit."

Moten started the day walking from the center of the Wayne State campus a mile above the official starting point. The crowds grew "bigger and bigger and bigger" as they moved south, making him feel part of something larger, a massive flow of energy that could not be denied. But the full historical weight came to him mostly in retrospect. As part of their fraternity pledging, Moten and his classmates were assigned a uniform of sorts, required to dress all in white from head to toe. They looked like vendors, and this is what he would remember most clearly: "We were in white shirts, white pants. And so on this hot day, wearing all white, people kept coming up to me looking to buy ice cream or sodas."

In the crowd nearby walked Ron Scott, a sixteen-year-old sophomore at Northwestern High who came out of the Jeffries Housing Projects near the Lodge Freeway. His family first lived in Black Bottom between Gratiot and the river, but urban renewal pushed them from that neighborhood. They moved up near Hastings Street, but the Chrysler Freeway renewal bounced them back to Jeffries. Scott, who later would help found the Detroit chapter of the Black Panthers and evolve into a television producer and media personality in the city, had his political consciousness awakened in the projects, inspired first by an activist who lived there, Lois Williams, who worked for Congressman Diggs, and then by hanging around the Wayne State campus with his pal Mike Evans. He cited one other experience in shaping his perspective: a day late in 1960 when he and an uncle were stopped by police during a city-wide stop-and-search crackdown on crime that essentially turned all blacks on the street into suspects. Black crime, white cops—that was the difficult mix. The *Detroit News* and *Free Press* in the winter of 1960–1961 reported that blacks committed 65 percent of all crimes in Detroit even though they were not quite 30 percent of the population. Most of those crimes were black on black, but two murders of white women dominated the coverage and ignited the police action. As Scott recounted it, a cop put a shotgun to his face and said, "Nigger, if you move I'll blow your head off."

That was in the era before Commissioner Edwards, and the frequency of similar encounters helped fuel the electoral uprising that sent Cavanagh into the mayor's office and Edwards into the top job at 1300 Beaubien—while, at the same time, a contagion of fear generated by that earlier crime wave had helped propel a countermovement of whites to the Detroit suburbs.

The first thing young Scott heard about the march was that many ministers were not supporting it. The fact that C. L. Franklin had organized it was enough for him. He identified with the High Priest of Soul Preaching from his days on Hastings Street. "We knew people who went to his church, and we knew Aretha, and it seemed very significant that he was involved," Scott recalled. "I was highly motivated on that walk." As he hiked down Woodward, he was thinking about those parts of his own experience—urban renewal, police attitudes, and the racial segregation of his northern city—that took him to that moment, but the presence of so many others with him on the street brought elation along with anger. The feeling, he said, "was a combination between a vision and a festive atmosphere . . . a solemnity, but really it was kind of exciting. There were a number of people in our age group marching. We were just part of the mass. I was already simmering by the time of the march. It just enhanced the spark."

Covering the march for the *Michigan Chronicle* was Ofield Dukes, their ace reporter and editorial writer on civil rights, who would go on to a White House job in Washington and a long career in public relations and civic engagement, including a key role decades later in establishing King's birthday as a national holiday. His Rolodex in 1963 had the telephone numbers of many key figures in the movement, from the late Medgar Evers and Aaron Henry and James Meredith in Mississippi to Martin Luther King, Ralph Abernathy, and Andrew Young in Georgia. He covered the national scene but was intimately familiar with the Detroit players and wrote several stories about Reverend Franklin and his skeptics in the city's black Baptist hierarchy. Even as he reported that day, Dukes walked with his own race story. He was born in Alabama and came up to Detroit's Black Bottom neighborhood during World War II with his mother and three siblings to join their father, who had taken a job at the Ford plant. At Miller High, then the city's only all-black high school, he was vice president of the senior class and manager of the championship basketball team. After graduating he tried to get into Wayne State but failed the entrance exam and ended up with the army in Korea, where, he later recalled in an oral interview, he spent most of a year reading books on philosophy—his favorite was William James on pragmatism—while stationed "on a lonely hill overlooking the Chowan Valley about five miles from the front." After his service, he took the college tests again, got accepted at Wayne State, and graduated four years later with a B average and a degree in journalism. There were nine journalism grads, he said, and the eight white students found jobs on the *News, Free Press,* and *Times*. None would hire Dukes, so he joined the *Chronicle*. "You always have two strikes against you," a mentor told him. "It's just a question of what you do with that third strike." At Detroit's leading black newspaper, he used that third strike to full advantage. "Nothing happened in this city, politically, without people coming by the *Michigan Chronicle*," he said, and no one knew black Detroit more intimately than Dukes. Now, as he surveyed the marchers moving down Woodward, he concluded that this "was a C. L. Franklin crowd." He saw blacks "of all classes—street walkers, doctors, school children, senior citizens, drunks, clergymen and their congregations [who] came from near and far to walk for freedom."

For Russ Cowan, another veteran *Chronicle* reporter, the march satisfied two yearnings at once: the huge crowd buoyed his hope for the cause, and the physical act itself pleased him for a wholly personal reason. "For a long number of years, I had cherished the desire to march down Woodward to the stirring tunes of a band," Cowan revealed. He went to the march with his son and along the route joined forces with Dave Clark, a former welterweight who had trained at the Brewster Recreation Center with Joe Louis, learning the left jab–right cross–left hook technique that became known as the Detroit style, and Clarence Gatliff, an accomplished swimmer who ran the Brewster rec program and had worked to integrate Detroit's pools and recreation facilities. Gatliff and Clark carried a banner that read "Brewster Old Timers." Nearby was another old-timer, Myrtle Gaskill, society editor of the *Chronicle*, who called her participation in the march "absolutely an ablution for my shame in my generation which had no spirit to generate such magnificent solidarity of purpose." It had never occurred to her, she wrote, "to be proud of what should be obvious, but I WAS proud of this tangible evidence that my race is in accord with what we should have initiated decades ago." Walking down Woodward, she said, made her feel that she belonged.

June Brown, who worked in classified ads, had a different reaction as she marched down Woodward. Like Reverend Hood, her first question was "Where did all these people come from? If there is strength in numbers, then we are very strong." The next thing she thought was "Wouldn't it be great if all of us turned out like this every Election Day?" And her third thought subsumed any sense of satisfaction she experienced along the way: "What do we do now?" Ray McCann, a general assignment reporter for the *Chronicle*, was less concerned with that question. He found the march impressive for a number of reasons: "First, it demonstrated that if properly notified, Negroes will support civil rights groups. Second, it demonstrated the ability of Negroes to organize properly and manipulate a crowd in excess of 100,000 people. And finally the participation by so many whites of all ages points out that many Americans realize that the problem of civil rights is a problem for this whole country to settle." There in fact were many whites in the crowd, at least several thousand, including Protestant ministers, Jewish rabbis, and Catholic priests, along with clusters of their followers. Peg Edwards, the wife of the police commissioner, marched with an integrated but largely white group from the Michigan chapter of the Episcopal Society for Cultural and Racial Unity. In such a massive crowd, the white participants appeared slightly more in percentage than black members of the police force, and as many whites might have been observing the march from the downtown sidewalks as taking part in it.

There was remarkably little heckling and no violence whatsoever. No need to summon the hundred-man commando team from the 1300 Beaubien garage. Some bystanders brought stools, coolers, and radios, as though this were a holiday parade, and had their radios tuned to the warmly crackling voice of Ernie Harwell calling that afternoon's Tigers game against Kansas City (Detroit won 11–2; Mickey Lolich went the distance; Rocky Colavito smacked a homer; some scrub named Tony LaRussa pinch-ran for the Athletics). Along the route, three observers were injured in falls, seven marchers fainted from heat and exhaustion, twenty-six children were separated from their parents, and four people were arrested, including two drunks and a pickpocket. The fourth arrest involved a man who stepped from the sidewalk at Woodward and Grand River, saying he had a message for King, and started scuffling with officers when they sought to get him away from the curb. The message that Joseph Lalibert, a house painter, said he had for King was to go slow pushing for integration in suburbs like his neighborhood in Berkley out near Royal Oak. Lalibert never got close to King, but many other people did, without serious incident. "Everywhere he went, people shouted, pressed in to touch him, shake his hand, stand close to him, or just look in his face," the *Detroit News* reported. At one point he was overheard saying, as a bookend to Commissioner Edwards's greeting at the airport, "I've faced so many mobs of hate in the South, this was kind of a relief."

It took an hour and forty-five minutes for all of the marchers to reach their destination. By then Arthur Johnson, the NAACP official, was watching from the roof of Cobo Hall. "It was a breathtaking experience and tears of joy welled in my eyes." He also felt "a deep irony at work" as he watched the marchers file into Cobo. "This venue, named after a racist mayor [many Detroit blacks shared that opinion of Albert Cobo], was transformed by a man who would become the iconic voice for racial justice. Twenty years ago on this same day, the worst race riot in U.S. history happened in Detroit. The Walk to Freedom was a model of peaceful protest and racial cooperation." Another irony, of course, involved his own organization: the largest civil rights rally to that point in U.S. history was staged without the full support of the NAACP.

By the time the marchers finished, there was no room inside for them. The arena was jammed to the capacity fire officials would allow, every one of the sixteen thousand seats filled, with another ten thousand finding seats in the adjacent hall. May Reuther, the labor leader's wife, was in the arena's front row with her daughters, Linda and Lisa. Commissioner Edwards found a place to stand. Erma Franklin, the second most famous singing daughter of the preacher, was backstage with a sterling cast of performers, but her sister Aretha, who had returned home from New York a month earlier to perform for a week at the Flame Show Bar, could not make it back again. Official programs were handed out with special acknowledgments to the United Auto Workers, the Detroit Federation of Musicians, Cleage Printing Company, and Gordy Printing Company. Many marchers who could not get inside straggled toward home, thirsty and exhausted, but at least ten thousand more remained, spreading out in a vast semicircle around the building. Booker Moten and Reverend Hood were among those who stayed to listen to the rally as it was broadcast on loudspeakers outside. One could hear the proceedings, the other could not because of the hubbub around him, but both would be able to say they were there when Martin Luther King rehearsed the most famous refrain of his life.

Chapter 12

# DETROIT DREAMED FIRST

**WITH EVERY SEAT OCCUPIED** and people standing in back and pressed against the sidewalls, Cobo Arena was uncomfortably dense yet improbably calm. The mood was softened by a communal sense of accomplishment after that long walk down Woodward and by anticipation of what was to come, a program of songs and speeches culminating with an oration by Martin Luther King. Women fanning themselves, babies crying, well-dressed men holding canisters to collect the day's offering—it felt like a Sunday morning at New Bethel Baptist. A ring of policemen stood sentinel outside to keep back the throngs, but there was no pushing and shoving beyond the unavoidable nervous jostling of an overflow crowd.

The speechifying part of the program started an hour later than scheduled, but the prelude was filled with music that provided reason enough to be there. The lineup included the Ramsey Lewis Trio, in town from Chicago to perform at the Grand Show Bar, a new jazz club out on Joy Road. Lewis, a pianist, and his partners, drummer Redd Holt and bassist Eldee Young, were moved by what they had experienced that day in Detroit. Young felt the march had "a tremendous emotional impact" on him. Holt called it "a great stride toward equality." And Lewis stressed the importance of entertainers showing their commitment by refusing to play at segregated nightclubs or "to accept privileges not afforded other Negroes." The jazz trio entertained the crowd with songs from their latest album, *Pot Luck.*

Then there was Dinah Washington, who had moved from Chicago to Detroit to live with her soon-to-be seventh husband, Dick (Night Train) Lane, the star defensive back for the Detroit Lions, who was in the Cobo audience. The exotic queen of the blues and the hard-tackling Night Train were to get married ten days later in Las Vegas. Washington, who was performing that week at the 20 Grand, was drawn to the rally mostly because of her close friendship with Reverend Franklin and his daughter Aretha. She was also a favorite of Berry Gordy, who before his Motown days had been a doting fan of her performances at the Flame Show Bar, entranced by how "she actually would shake her booty onstage and move from place to place and talk about men." Also on the bill were the Four Tops, a popular local quartet about to join Gordy's Motown assemblage, and Liz Lands, a soul singer from New York with a stunning five-octave range, also soon to fall into the Motown orbit. Chairman Gordy himself made arrangements to record the program, not for the music so much as for the words of Dr. King.

It would take some time to get to King. Reverend Franklin, who already had occasioned a miracle of sorts with the successful and peaceful march, accomplished something equally extraordinary now, sublimating his ego by serving as emcee rather than main attraction. There were those who had heard both who thought Franklin could outperform King onstage or at the pulpit, but the pitch of his hum now was limited to brief remarks interspersed among more than twenty speakers, a too-long list that was an unavoidable result of his desire to keep his coalition together in the fractious days before the event. After introductions, a prayer, a spiritual reading, and a resounding rendition of "Lift Every Voice and Sing," the black national anthem, from the Rock of Ages Gospel Choir, Mayor Cavanagh stepped to the podium to issue the city's formal welcome.

This had been a long Sunday for the mayor. Before securing his place in the second row of marchers, three feet directly behind King, he had spent the morning dedicating a new wing of the Detroit Public Library, where he honored "the enduring nature of knowledge and wisdom" in an age of skepticism. Now, at Cobo, he spoke of the struggle between enlightenment and ignorance and the power of nonviolence and legislative action: "This gathering is a tribute to Dr. Martin Luther King and to those men of goodwill who march for freedom and justice throughout this nation. If a symbol were needed of intelligent, enlightened leadership, Dr. King has dramatically filled that need. The hunger for equality, the thirst for justice, the struggle for the right to sit at a lunch counter and the yearning for educational and job opportunities has generated tremendous antagonisms. But the reaction to brutal treatment, to mass arrests of peaceful marchers, to the denial of fundamental human rights as citizens, has been swift and decisive. No longer can the courts alone carry the brunt of the burden. No longer can this nation tolerate legislative indifference to blatant constitutional violations. President Kennedy has challenged the Congress to enact the laws needed to help achieve equality. I believe a national consensus supports these proposals."

The various speakers and agendas that followed over the next ninety minutes reflected the complicated racial realities of that momentous summer and the frailties of a broad coalition. Radicals interspersed with moderates, politicians mixed with street rhetoricians, those who believed in the system and the legislative process and those who thought salvation came only from a rising of the people. On one end was Reverend Cleage, who had tried and failed to make this a blacks-only event and now said that he and his people were readying themselves for the liberation struggle. On the other end were two Republicans representing George Romney, the Mormon governor who was absent because this was a Sunday, the one day he did not make public appearances. When Franklin, as emcee, first mentioned Romney while introducing Leo Greene, one of his aides who had come down from Lansing, there were scattered boos and catcalls from the audience. "Be kind now," Franklin said. "Be sweet." The booing recurred each time Greene mentioned Romney. There was a warmer response when Stanley G. Thayer, the Republican state senator from Ann Arbor, a moderate and strong supporter of civil rights, as was Romney, presented King with a proclamation welcoming him to the state. And even more to the crowd's liking was John B. Swainson, the former governor who had lost both legs as a young soldier in World War II and walked down Woodward on his prosthetic limbs. "If Americans can fight and die together, they can live and work together," Swainson told the receptive Cobo audience.

Soon came Reuther, who as the summer began was allowing as little room as possible between himself and Dr. King. The day before, at the White House, he had supported King's defense of large-scale demonstrations in the face of President Kennedy's wariness on the subject, and he reiterated that position now, while broadening the civil rights cause to all races and regions. This was "a fight for every American," he said. "Let's keep the freedom marches rolling all over America. We shall not rest until we have full freedom for every American."

The assembled choirs sang Rossini's "Inflammatus" during a break for passing the offering buckets, and then Congressman Diggs introduced the main speaker. The arena roared with shouts and applause. King, at five-seven, stepped up on a small box to reach the bank of microphones placed before him on the podium. "God didn't make me tall enough," he said. The large room grew close, bathed in shadows and light. "My good friend, the Reverend C. L. Franklin," he began, "I cannot begin to say to you this afternoon how thrilled I am, and I cannot begin to tell you the deep joy that comes to my heart as I participate with you in what I consider to be the largest and greatest demonstration for freedom ever held in the United States. And I can assure you that what has been done here today will serve as a source of inspiration for all of the freedom-loving people of this nation."

The call-and-response had begun, with shouts of "All right!" and "Amen."

King was still in the moment, struck by what he had seen and heard that day: the greeting Police Commissioner Edwards gave him at the airport, promising there would be no dogs and hoses; the city's protective embrace symbolized by his assigned bodyguard, the black lieutenant, George Harge; the buoyant throngs lifting him up as he walked down Woodward. "I think there is something else that must be said because it is a magnificent demonstration of discipline. With all of the thousands and hundreds of thousands of people engaged in this demonstration today, there has not been one reported incident of violence." More applause and approving shouts. "I think this is a magnificent demonstration of our commitment to nonviolence in this struggle for freedom all over the United States, and I want to commend the leadership of this community for making this great event possible and making such a great event possible through such disciplined channels."

The internecine squabbles, the discussions and telegrams between Detroit and SCLC headquarters in Atlanta, the doubters who thought the occasion was too important for C. L. Franklin to handle, the fears that something unfortunate would occur along the route—all that was gone now, transformed by King into a redemption story as he stood on his box and spoke of hope and struggle and a dream.

King wended his way to that dream, moving slowly and steadily toward it. He talked about the protests in Birmingham, the cancer of racial segregation, and the rising sense of dignity among black citizens, who had come to realize that "every man from a bass-black to a treble-white is significant on God's keyboard." He employed a Motor City metaphor to describe his response to those who say *Cool off; Put on the brakes; You're moving too fast.* "The only answer we can give to that is that the motor's now cranked up and we're moving up the highway of freedom toward the city of equality." He expounded on the power of nonviolence as a means of disarming the opponent. "If he doesn't put you in jail, wonderful. Nobody with any sense likes to go to jail. But if he puts you in jail, you go in that jail and transform it from a dungeon of shame to a haven of freedom and human dignity." He evoked the martyrdom of the recently slain Medgar Evers and said, "If a man has not discovered something that he will die for, he isn't fit to live."

He extolled the new militancy in the black community but cautioned that it "must not lead us to the position of distrusting every white person who lives in these United States. There are some white people in this country who are as determined to see the Negro free as we are to be free." While acknowledging that he understood the motivations of the Nation of Islam, which was founded in Detroit, he urged his audience to reject racial separation, whatever the cause. "Black supremacy," he said, "is as dangerous as white supremacy" and would not help transform "this jangling discord of a nation into a beautiful symphony of brotherhood." Working to end discrimination in Detroit was as important as his work in the South. "Now in the North it's different in that it doesn't have the legal sanction that it has in the South. But it has its subtle and hidden forms and it exists in three areas: in the area of employment discrimination, in the area of housing discrimination, and in the area of de facto segregation in the public schools." Detroit could also help the cause by supporting the civil rights bill that Kennedy had proposed and by putting pressure on Congress to pass it. That pressure, he said, included coming to another march, this one to the Lincoln Memorial in the nation's capital. (Inserted into the official programs for the Walk to Freedom were brochures outlining travel arrangements for Detroiters to attend the March on Washington, leaving by train at seven on the night of August 27 and arriving at Union Station at ten on the morning of the event, at a cost of $28.25 per person.)

All this led to his final prose poem of a dream: "And so I go back to the South not with a feeling that we are caught in a dark dungeon that will never lead to a way out. I go back believing that the new day is coming. And so this afternoon, I have a dream."

"Go ahead," someone shouted.

"I have a dream deeply rooted in the American dream."

This was nine weeks before the March on Washington, when King would deliver another version of the same refrain that would become etched in history, eventually considered the most famous American speech of the twentieth century. What he said at Cobo on that Sunday in June was virtually lost to history, overwhelmed by what was to come, but the first time King dreamed his dream at a large public gathering, he dreamed it in Detroit. His riff at the Walk to Freedom was a planned part of the speech. In Washington, where it earned its fame, it was not even in the official text. The refrain would draw divergent reactions from his inner circle. Mahalia Jackson, his favorite spiritual singer and a confidante, loved its majesty and inspired King to use it in Washington, by some accounts urging him on from her perch behind him at the Lincoln Memorial. Wyatt Tee Walker, executive director of the SCLC, thought it was cliché-ridden and tried to discourage him from falling back on it. When King soared into his dream sequence he was preaching, not lecturing, drawing on rhythms and images more than thoughts and arguments. The people in Detroit took to it heartily. They were hearing it for the first time, but many of them were also hearing familiar rhythms, reminiscent of the pulpit oratory of Reverend Franklin.

*I have a dream that one day, right down in Georgia and Mississippi and Alabama, the sons of former slaves and the sons of former slave owners will be able to live together as brothers.*

King would enrich this image in Washington nine weeks later, changing it to "that one day on the red hills of Georgia sons of former slaves and the sons of former slave owners will be able to sit down together at the table as brothers."

*I have a dream this afternoon, I have a dream that one day . . .*

The Detroit crowd was at church now, applauding, anticipating.

*. . . one day little white children and little Negro children will be able to join hands as brothers and sisters.*

The Washington version would have a more evocative rendering of what needed to be overcome, extending the dream phrase to say "that one day in Alabama, with its vicious racists, with its governor having his lips dripping with the words of interposition and nullification, one day right there in Alabama little black boys and black girls will be able to join hands with little white boys and white girls as brothers and sisters."

*I have a dream this afternoon that one day . . .*

More applause.

*. . . that one day men will no longer burn down houses and the church of God simply because people want to be free.*

In his ad-libbed version in Washington, King deleted that line.

*I have a dream this afternoon, I have a dream that there will be a day that we will no longer face the atrocities that Emmett Till had to face or Medgar Evers had to face, that all men can live with dignity.*

The Evers assassination eleven days earlier was fresh in the minds of the Detroit marchers, many of whom carried signs in his honor. That line was also missing when King spoke in Washington.

*I have a dream this afternoon that my four little children, that my four little children will not come up in the same young days that I came up within, but they will be judged on the basis of the content of their character, not the color of their skin.*

Here was the most famous phrase in the speech, though its order was flipped for posterity in the Lincoln Memorial version. Just as JFK had delivered a variation of his famous "Ask not" line first in Detroit, but then inverted the words to lend it more rhythmic power in his inaugural address, King enhanced his immortal line between Detroit and Washington, turning it into "they will not be judged by the color of their skin but by the content of their character."

*I have a dream this afternoon that one day right here in Detroit, Negroes will be able to buy a house or rent a house anywhere that their money will carry them and they will be able to get a job.*

Wild applause and shouts of "That's right!"

The housing issue was about to dominate Detroit city politics that summer. Two members of the Common Council had drawn up open-occupancy legislation prohibiting landlords or house sellers from discriminating on the basis of race.

*Yes, I have a dream this afternoon that one day in this land the words of Amos will become real and "justice will roll down like waters, and righteousness like a mighty stream."*

This verse from Amos 5:24 appeared again in the Washington speech, but in the main text well before the dream sequence. The refrain introducing it began, "No, no, we are not satisfied, and we cannot be satisfied until . . ." The verse was a staple in King's greatest speeches. He used it to close his antiwar address, "Beyond Vietnam," delivered at Riverside Church in New York on April 4, 1967, and returned to it in "I've Been to the Mountaintop," the emotional speech delivered in Memphis on April 3, 1968, in which he seemed to foretell his own death. He was assassinated the next day.

*I have a dream this evening that one day we will recognize the words of Jefferson that "all men are created equal, that they are endowed by their creator with certain inalienable rights, that among them are life, liberty, and the pursuit of happiness." I have a dream this afternoon.*

In Washington, King opened his dream sequence with a shorter version of that thought, building off the introductory phrase that his dream was deeply rooted in the American dream: "I have a dream that one day this nation will rise up, live out the true meaning of its creed: 'We hold these truths to be self-evident, that all men are created equal.'" Much earlier in the Washington speech, he had already used the "life, liberty, and pursuit of happiness" line from the Declaration of Independence, saying it was a promissory note from the nation's founders that turned into a bad check for blacks that came back marked "insufficient funds."

*I have a dream that one day every valley shall be exalted, and every hill shall be made low; the crooked places shall be made straight, and the rough places plain; and the glory of the Lord shall be revealed, and all flesh shall see it together.*

In Washington, King ended his dream sequence with that line. In Detroit, he found one final dream:

*I have a dream that the brotherhood of man will become a reality in this day.*

In Detroit there was only one more paragraph carrying King to the end. In Washington he drew out the climax with a "Let freedom ring!" refrain taking him on a geographic tour of America the beautiful. Both speeches closed the same way, with his call of the spiritual, "Free at last! Free at last! Thank God almighty, we are free at last!"

What do reporters look for in a speech as they write a first draft of history? The *Washington Post* coverage of the March on Washington failed to take note of "I Have a Dream." King's speech warranted only fleeting mention in the fifth paragraph of a story on the day's rhetoric on page A15, and even there the dream sequence was not quoted. Nine weeks earlier, the *Detroit News* fared slightly better covering the Walk to Freedom, noting that King "ended his 48-minute talk repeating 'dreams' of a better world united in brotherhood." The final refrains, the *News* added, "brought a wild response from the overflow crowd and Dr. King was quickly whisked out of the auditorium and to his hotel for a shower and change of shirt."

Reverend Hood, who never made it inside the arena but huddled with his Congregationalists and thousands of other marchers during the long program as it aired over outdoor loudspeakers, would be asked many times in the ensuing years what he thought of King's first dream in Detroit. Fifty years later he was asked one more time during an interview for this book. He was ninety then, and one of the sons he had taken with him on the Walk to Freedom had followed him as pastor of the same church. What did he remember about the dream? "In all honesty, I couldn't even hear it," he acknowledged. "But I certainly enjoyed the fellowship, the joy, the feeling of freedom. Oh, yeah." Booker Moten, in his white-on-white fraternity outfit, was closer to a loudspeaker and was able to hear King's words. He remembered a political type standing near him who, during the middle of the dream riff, blurted out, "God, I wish I could give a speech like that just once in my lifetime!"

Arthur Johnson of the Detroit NAACP, who had watched the march unfold from the Cobo roof, ventured down into the arena to hear King's speech and came away realizing that his old college classmate had risen to a new level. "Martin's voice this day in Detroit was never better," Johnson noted later. "He had worked out the structure, rhythm, and climactic parts of the speech so that it moved like a great piece of music. We were all utterly spellbound." Johnson encountered King later that evening and congratulated him on the speech. The complications of the civil rights movement, the jealousies between Johnson's NAACP and King's SCLC inevitably placed a strain on their relationship, but Johnson realized that he had seen and heard greatness. "We spoke as old friends, and as usual, I addressed him as M.L.," Johnson recalled. "He wanted my advice on an important matter, but time and his pressing commitments did not permit that conversation then. . . . My former and young classmate at Morehouse College was now, without a doubt, the indisputable leader of the civil rights movement."

Four days after the Walk to Freedom, Mayor Cavanagh was at the Sheraton Cadillac, speaking at a noon luncheon of the National Newspaper Publishers Association, which was holding its convention in Detroit. "I know it must have been decided some time ago to conduct this particular meeting in Detroit, but your foresight has brought you here at a high point in Detroit's history," Cavanagh said. "Just last Sunday, as you are no doubt aware, Detroit showed the nation and the world that men of goodwill—no matter what their color—can band together peacefully to protest the stifling evil of prejudice." Cavanagh described the march down Woodward Avenue with Martin Luther King, and how there were white marchers along with blacks, and how the march commemorated a new spirit of fairness and fellowship in the city.

"We Detroiters know that in many ways we are ahead of the nation in respecting the rights of man," he added. "But we are not so presumptuous that we are satisfied. We know there is much to be done." The large numbers who attended the march offered reason for hope and optimism. "But consider too another aspect of the march that is perhaps even more significant.... This huge crowd of dedicated people, people with fervor, marched through our city without one incident taking place that is worthy of mentioning. Not one. Think of that. Could that happen in a city where there is deep-seated racial distrust, where men fear their fellows of another color?"

Hate letters were arriving by the bundle at Cavanagh's office as he spoke those words. One out of the many was this:

*Mayor Cavanagh,*

*Never thought I'd live to see the day that a white, Catholic mayor would discriminate as you are doing against the white people. I am ashamed for you—to lead a horrible parade as you did Sunday. Behind that hypocrite—Luther King—at least he does it for money. But you, you are doing it for the Negro vote. Well be careful that by doing so you are not losing the white vote. You are doing nothing but cheapen Detroit, by your actions. I've paid taxes in*

*Detroit for 46 years, but at the rate you are allowing the nigger to take over Detroit I want no part of Detroit any longer.*

*Estelle Thomas, 8903 Birwood, Detroit, Michigan*

Ray Girardin, the mayor's executive assistant, wrote the response:

*Dear Mrs. Thomas,*

*I notice the five cent postage stamp on your letter to Mayor Cavanagh bore the slogan of "Food for Peace" and "Food for Hunger." Perhaps you didn't read these when you affixed the stamp. But isn't that just about what the Negroes were marching for in our city? I am at a loss to explain how you can possibly call a peaceful march in protest against brutalities and inhumanities a "horrible" parade. I trust, Mrs. Thomas, that you will somehow find a way to rid your heart of its bitterness towards other human beings.*

The hot summer had begun.

Chapter 13

# HEAT WAVE

**MOTOWN WAS ROLLING** in the summer of 1963. Berry Gordy Jr. was not just paying his bills, he was turning a profit and expanding his empire, and one indication that he had made it came that June when he bought a five-story neo-Gothic building that occupied most of a city block. The gray terra-cotta structure at the corner of Woodward and Canfield had deteriorated over the past decade, and its glory years seemed long gone, but its ballroom was familiar to all Detroiters and recognized throughout the music world for its rich history.

G
R
A
Y
S
T
O
N
E

That was the vertical sign out front on Woodward. Some at Motown thought the Graystone Ballroom and Gardens had outlived its purpose and needed not just a renovation but a new name. But Graystone meant something special to Gordy. He could be a skinflint businessman, but he was also a softhearted sentimentalist, and the ballroom touched his romantic side even as it reminded him of Detroit's segregated past. For more than three decades, from its opening in 1922 until the mid-1950s, the Graystone was the largest and most popular dance hall in the city, its cavernous ballroom hopping and swirling with as many as three thousand dancers at a time. All the big bands played there, from Jean Goldkette to Count Basie, from Glen Miller to Duke Ellington. But off the bandstand, the races did not mix at the Graystone, reflecting the de facto segregation in northern cities that was often as prevalent as Jim Crow laws in the South. The ballroom was for white dancers only on all nights but Monday, which was reserved for blacks.

"It was the most beautiful ballroom," Gordy recalled in an interview for this book. "The bigger bands went to the Graystone. That was classy. It was just bigger than life. And the people were dressed to kill. It was the place to go Monday nights. Save up and go. And I would just see the most beautiful people and the most beautiful girls. And that's where I would try to dance with girls. I would go out on the dance floor and see a girl who had just finished dancing and was walking in the other direction and I would walk up to them and say, 'Can I have the next dance?' They would always say, 'No, I'm through dancing for the night. I'm not dancing.' My best friend, Billy Davis, I would go with. He could dance. And I was square. He was an east side kid, so cool. And they would say to me, 'No, I'm not dancing anymore.' And I would walk back with all the people with me laughing at me. And then I came up with the *Two out of Ten* rule. I said to myself, 'Look, that's okay. If I ask ten girls to dance, two will dance. I'm not going to stop.' "

Cause and effect is never so simple, but there seems to have been more than a suggestion of the *Citizen Kane* "rosebud" in that recollection, a clue to the motivation for all that was to follow in Berry Gordy's life. As a teenager he was short and unprepossessing and could not dance. But he was persistent, developed a plan, and now here he was, chairman of a music empire, author of a song that mocked his adolescent failings, the Contours's rollicking "Do You Love Me (Now That I Can Dance)?," and owner of the very ballroom of his humiliation, set to transform it into Motown's grand rehearsal hall and hometown stage. Do you love me? *Now I am back to let you know, I can really shake it down!*

Gordy set up the Rayber Corporation to handle the Graystone and installed his big sister, Esther Edwards, as the treasurer, and her husband to help handle the books and ticket sales. Then he started planning events for his artists, friendly battle-of-the-bands competitions along the lines of the boxing matches he was involved in as a young man. He knew he had more than enough high-caliber Motown talent to put up on the Graystone stage. The breakthroughs had begun in the three previous years, but the second half of 1963 brought Motown its brightest glow, corresponding with the resurgence in the automobile industry. Ten Motown singles rose into *Billboard*'s Top 10 that year, and eight more into the Top 20. The boom was led by Gordy's unusual live recording of his twelve-year-old phenom, Little Stevie Wonder, whose "Fingertips (Part 2)" was rocketing up the charts and before the summer was out would reach No. 1.

The wonder of this record began with its conflicting origin stories. There is no doubt that "Fingertips (Part 2)" was recorded during a Motown show at the Regal Theater at 47th and South Parkway in Chicago, but music experts differ on when, citing two Motown shows there nine months apart. Some say the performance was in mid-June 1962 during a preview trip months before the first *Motortown Revue*. Others say it was "probably" recorded during another Motown show at the Regal on March 10, 1963. In either case, the rest of the story is equally unusual, although Little Stevie's behavior was rambunctiously predictable. Ever since Gordy signed the talented Wonder, Motown had been trying with little success to get him a hit. Concluding that there was an electricity to his live performances that for various reasons was not duplicated in the studio, Gordy scavenged through his box of tapes searching for something from Wonder that captured his magic and settled on the Regal version of "Fingertips," a song whose studio version had attracted little notice on Wonder's previous album.

The band that day at the Regal was conducted by Clarence Paul, who escorted Little Stevie onto the Regal stage with his bongos and harmonica.

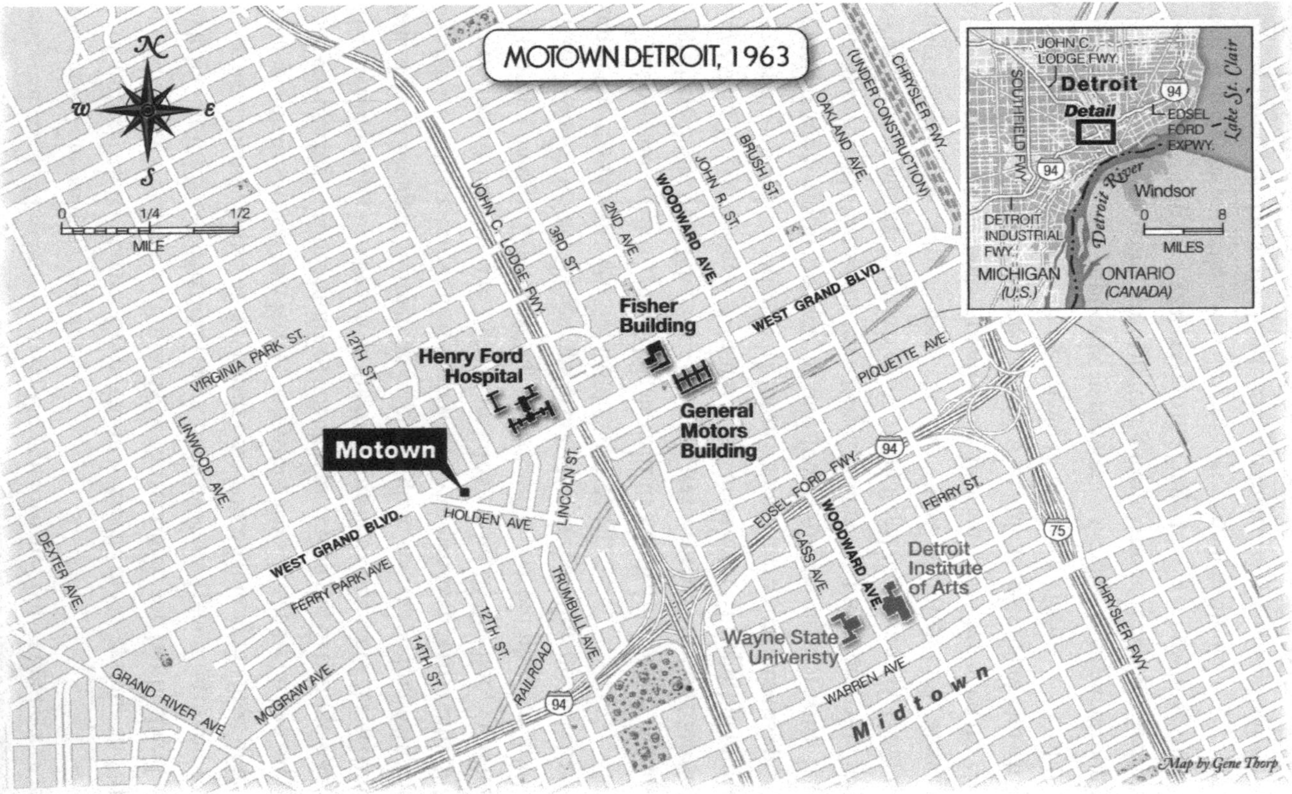

MOTOWN DETROIT, 1963
N
W
E
S
0
1/4
1/2
MILE
JOHN C. LODGE FWY.
3RD ST.
2ND AVE.
WOODWARD AVE.
JOHN R. ST.
BRUSH ST.
OAKLAND AVE.
(UNDER CONSTRUCTION)
CHRYSLER FWY.
VIRGINIA PARK ST.
12TH ST.
Henry Ford Hospital
Fisher Building
WEST GRAND BLVD.
PIQUETTE AVE.
General Motors Building
LINWOOD AVE.
Motown
HOLDEN AVE.
LINCOLN ST.
EDSEL FORD FWY.
94
FERRY ST.
75
DEXTER AVE.
WEST GRAND BLVD.
FERRY PARK AVE.
CASS AVE.
WOODWARD AVE.
Detroit Institute of Arts
12TH ST.
TRUMBULL AVE.
14TH ST.
RAILROAD
Wayne State University
CHRYSLER FWY.
GRAND RIVER AVE.
MCGRAW AVE.
94
WARREN AVE.
Midtown
Map by Gene Thorp
JOHN C. LODGE FWY.
Detroit
Detail
SOUTHFIELD FWY.
94
EDSEL FORD EXPWY.
Lake St. Clair
Detroit River
Windsor
DETROIT INDUSTRIAL FWY.
0
8
MILES
MICHIGAN (U.S.)
ONTARIO (CANADA)

Comedian Bill Murry, who had accompanied the Motown troop on its first *Motortown Revue,* was also the emcee at this performance and introduced the young genius, who in his infectious high voice said, "Yeah, yeah. . . . A song from my album, *The Jazz Soul of Little Stevie.* The name of the song is called, uh, 'Fingertips.' I want you to clap your hands. Come on, yeah! Stomp your feet, jump up and down. Do anything you wanna do!" And with that he and the band were off on their wild, contagious ride. It is hard to say that "Fingertips" is a song so much as a feeling. There is no story to tell, no poetic lyrics, no memorable melody, just a jumping, joyous, musical jaunt, with Little Stevie starting on his bongos, horns soon firing behind him, then sliding into harmonica riffs. (Gordy's strongest first impression of Stevland Morris was of his unique talent on the harmonica: "I didn't even like his singing, but I loved his harmonica.") When the audience was up and dancing and with him all the way, he started playing with them in a church-style call-and-response with his urging "Everybody say yeah." Parts of it were clearly orchestrated, parts improvised. At one soft interlude Wonder threw in the first lines of "Mary Had a Little Lamb"—wittingly or not, a nod to where it all began, back to the Lincoln-Mercury assembly line where Gordy had used the simple notations of that nursery song as he composed the first pop tunes in his head.

The climax came soon, or was supposed to, with Murry shouting, "How about it! Let's hear it for him, Little Stevie Wonder! Take a bow, Stevie." Wonder already had a reputation for hogging the stage, upsetting the acts that were to follow. It became part of the routine for Clarence Paul to grab the kid's elbow and escort him off, not unlike a principal strong-arming a recalcitrant student into his office. But this time Little Stevie wiggled free and began honking back into "Fingertips" with his harmonica. What followed, as music writer Mark Ribowsky so aptly put it, were "a few confusing seconds—and music history bliss." Wonder's band members had put down their instruments and were clearing the stage for the musicians who would accompany the next act. Ribowsky said that was Mary Wells. The liner notes for *The Complete Motown Singles,* Volume 3, say it was the Marvelettes. In either case, the confusion was recorded as Little Stevie kept going and the musicians scrambled to get back into the groove, with Joe Swift, a bass player, heard shouting, "What key? What key?" And off it all went again, pushing the eight-minute mark when Murry was sent out to sign off again, and Paul walked over again to lead Wonder out, this time for good.

When Gordy months later pulled the tape out of oblivion and turned it into a single, he broke the eight minutes into two sides. What was intended to be the B side began with "Mary Had a Little Lamb" and went through the confusion and the shouting and on from there. But disc jockeys and listeners loved the ad hoc vibrancy of that flip side so much that Gordy rereleased the single a few weeks later with that as the feature. Little Stevie finally had his breakthrough hit, with the obstreperous "Fingertips (Part 2)" rising and on its way to the top.

Wonder's first big hit was conceived in Chicago and created in Detroit, but the seven-inch 45 rpm record itself, like many other Motown vinyls, was pressed not in the Motor City but 533 miles away in another music city, Nashville. Here was another small but noteworthy way that rock and roll and rhythm and blues cut across the racial currents of America in the sixties. Nashville, home to the Grand Ole Opry, a cultural icon of the old South, was also a seminal outpost in the civil rights movement of that era, training ground for activists and embarkation point for freedom rides deeper into the Jim Crow states of the former Confederacy. As in Memphis, its Tennessee neighbor to the west, though to a lesser degree, Nashville's recording scene could be more progressive than the society surrounding it. A prime example was Southern Plastics and its industrial plant on Chestnut Street that was busily stamping out Motown records along with country and rock and even the earliest Beatles records distributed in the United States.

The impulse was business, not politics, but nonetheless Southern Plastics and its white owners—John Dunn, Joe Talbot, and Ozell Simpkins—went well beyond the impersonal transaction of turning analog tapes into vinyl records in their dealings with Motown. On the second floor—above the steam boilers and lathes and lacquers and resin and metal disks and stampers of the recordmaking trade—was a set of rooms that came to be known after the fact as the Motown Suite. Two single beds, bathroom, pine paneling in living room/kitchen with Formica table and black-and-white television. Hotels in Nashville were segregated, and there were no public accommodations downtown for Motown's black executives, including at times Gordy and Smokey Robinson (nor for the rhythm and blues operators of Vee-Jay records in the Chicago area), so during visits to Nashville to check on production and distribution, and occasionally even for release parties held at the factory, they would spend a night or two in that second-floor suite.

To borrow a phrase from Vince Lombardi, the football coach who had been assembling a powerhouse football team up in Green Bay during that same period, Gordy was developing a system at Motown in 1963 that nurtured freedom through discipline. His musical assembly line operated on a routine. Everything was framed by a structure devised by Gordy and his influential sisters, but within that structure lay a sense of creativity and possibility, just as there was a surprising amount of freedom within Lombardi's disciplined playbook. The parallel goes one step farther. The Packer athletes were an eclectic bunch of roustabouts, playboys, cutups, and straight arrows, and so too were Motown's artists, but Lombardi and Gordy both knew how to get the best out of all of them and keep them going in the same direction, at least for a time. Eventually success would become an addiction for the leaders, some of the athletes and artists would yearn to bust free of the structure, and issues of control and money and self-expression would complicate matters, but not yet.

The structure of activities on West Grand Boulevard followed a weekly pattern. On Tuesdays, Esther Edwards led a meeting of the management department, known as ITMI (International Talent Management Inc.), at which she and her team went over touring schedules and publicity appearances, trying to match those with the career needs of the artists. On Thursdays, members of the publicity and marketing departments gathered to talk about what they could do with deejays, radio spots, and print and radio advertisements to push records then hitting the stores. And on Fridays, at precisely nine in the morning, Gordy assembled his product evaluation committee to listen to demo records and vote on whether they should be released. He even had his own version of what in Green Bay was known as "Lombardi time." If you arrived at a Packer meeting on time, you were ten minutes late and subjected to a fine. At Motown, if you arrived at the product evaluation committee meeting five minutes late, you were locked out, no excuses. There was always a tension in the room between ambition and objectivity. Gordy wanted it to be like quality control on an assembly line. He wanted to rid the room of jealousy and reprisal: "No lobbying and no holds barred. If you voted against me, it didn't matter. The best record wins. No egos or politics involved. I was frantic about that." But of course these were human beings, not automobiles, and jealousy and elbowing unavoidably were part of the scene. Gordy himself would carry little grudges for decades against his own sisters, who frequently voted against him, especially Esther, who, whenever there was a choice between a record Smokey Robinson had written or produced and one that her brother had written or produced, seemed always to vote for Smokey.

The Motown team was never more talented than that summer. Earl Van Dyke had joined the house band, the Funk Brothers, providing leadership and virtuoso keyboard to a boisterous group that included Benny Benjamin and Pistol Allen on drums, James Jamerson on bass, Mike Terry on saxophone, Jack Ashford on vibes, Patrick Lanier and Paul Riser, still a teenager out of Cass Tech, on trombone, Marcus Belgrave and Russell Conway on trumpet, and guitarists Robert White, Joe Messina, and Eddie Willis. The Four Tops were signing up with their soulful four-part harmony and pulsating lead singing from Levi Stubbs. The Temptations and Supremes were about to come into their own; the always underrated Velvelettes, a five-girl group with a velvety sound that came to Motown via Western Michigan University in Kalamazoo, were getting regional play for "There He Goes"; Little Stevie (he would drop the diminutive the following year) was fingertipping to the top; Smokey and his Miracles had another hit with a show-closing dance number called "Mickey's Monkey"; Mary Wells was still on the rhythm and blues charts with "Your Old

Standby," as usual a song Smokey wrote for her; Marvin Gaye was in the studio recording "Can I Get a Witness," with the Supremes singing backup. (The Rolling Stones would soon appropriate the song for their first album, part of a trend of popular British rock groups consistently endorsing and covering songs from Motown and other black American artists.) And Martha and the Vandellas were emerging from the West Grand studio with Holland-Dozier-Holland's "Heat Wave."

If "Come and Get These Memories" established the quintessential Motown sound, "Heat Wave," with its irrepressibly joyous momentum, did something more important for Martha Reeves, Rosalind Ashford, and Annette Beard. It propelled Martha and the Vandellas toward stardom. "Marvin, Smokey, Mary Wells, my pal Little Stevie Wonder—they were all hot, and finally so were we," Reeves noted later. Rock critic Dave Marsh, who was born in Detroit and grew up with Motown, later worked a writing riff of praise off "Heat Wave's" most buoyant stanza—"has high blood pressure got a hold on me, or is this the way love's supposed to be?"—by confessing, "Personally, I'd be willing to endure hospitalization for a few weeks just to feel the way [Mike Terry's] baritone sax sounds." "Heat Wave" was released just as a true heat wave roasted Southern California, prompting L.A. weathermen to use it as background music for their nightly reports, boosting its popularity. In Detroit there was another heat wave of a more troubling kind.

Anyone familiar with the late-night street life on John R knew Cynthia Scott—all the pimps and johns and cops. She was a singularly imposing prostitute, standing over six feet without heels, and weighing nearly two hundred pounds. At three on the morning of July 5, two young patrolmen in the First District, Ted Spicher and Bob Marshall, arrived at the corner of John R and Edmond in what was officially called a disorderly persons car. The cops called it a whore car. Their job was to clear out and, if the opportunity arose, arrest the passel of prostitutes who walked John R from Edmond to Brush until dawn soliciting johns, mostly white and mostly from the suburbs, including regulars on their way to or from the Fisher Body plant. They operated in an underworld of nicknames. One pimp went by Black Diamond, another by Big Tiny Little. One of the prostitutes, who also doubled as an informant for the cops, was called the First Lady. And Cynthia Scott was known as St. Cynthia. Her sainthood included seven arrests for prostitution and one for destruction of property when she obliterated everything in her path during a drunken rage in a bar.

Scott was with a john when patrolmen Spicher and Marshall spotted her in the early morning darkness on John R. She seemed to be hugging the man with one arm while holding a wad of bills in her other hand. Was she robbing him? They approached and attempted to escort her to the whore car. She resisted—and ended up dead, shot by Spicher. The official report went like this: Scott pulled a knife on the officers as they tried to get her into the car, sliced a gash in Spicher's hand, and started to run away. Both patrolmen chased after her and ordered her to stop. Scott flashed the knife again, lunged at Spicher, and as she turned to flee across the street, Spicher shot her. She was walking, not running, when the bullet entered her back and pierced her heart.

At the time of the shooting, Police Commissioner Edwards was with his wife, Peg, far from Detroit, on an ocean liner making its way across the Atlantic. Their plan was to spend a month in Europe, starting with a judicial conference in London. Edwards had been Detroit's top cop for eighteen months by then and left for the working vacation confident that he had made significant progress easing racial tensions between the police force and the city's black citizens. That cause had been his obsession, the main reason he had heeded Mayor Cavanagh's request and resigned from the Michigan Supreme Court to take the police job in the first place. He was still aboard ship when he received a situation report from back home, including word of the shooting. Everything was under control, he was told. The policeman acted appropriately, no reason for concern.

Wishful thinking, or narrow thinking, or no thinking. The shooting of Cynthia Scott was not so easily dismissed, not with the long and difficult history involving Detroit cops and the black community. St. Cynthia quickly became a martyr, a victim of police brutality. Her funeral service on July 13 drew hundreds to St. John's African Methodist Episcopal Church on Woodward, and an even larger throng gathered outside 1300 Beaubien that day to picket police headquarters, where the leader of Detroit's Nation of Islam temple, Wilfred X, brother of Malcolm X, spoke to the angry crowd. The *Michigan Chronicle* ran front-page stories and editorials. Scott, the newspaper argued, "was not a felon but a known prostitute." Spicher suffered no more than a finger cut. "The situation did not warrant extreme measures." Letters and telegrams of protest flooded police headquarters and the mayor's office. Congressman Diggs said the city had to take action "to prevent citizens from taking the law into their own hands against trigger-happy cops." The Wayne County district attorney and the Michigan attorney general's office both looked at the case and declined to take action against Spicher. And soon enough Edwards got an urgent call from an old labor friend saying that things were falling apart, no matter what his police aides told him, and that he had to cut short his European sojourn and return to Detroit.

The situation was so dire by the time Edwards got home on July 28 that reporters met him at the airport gate with questions about the Scott case. "We want no reckless or wanton use of deadly weapons by anyone, least of all by police officers," Edwards said. "But we have also assured our police officers that when they follow the police manual they are protected by the law." He spent the next week investigating the case himself, interviewing the cops and other witnesses and examining the county and state decisions not to prosecute. In the end, he reached the same conclusion they had: Spicher feared for his life when he fired at Scott, who had already assaulted him. His decision to shoot was regrettable and unwise, Edwards said, but by the standards of the law it was justified.

The Nation of Islam and another group loosely affiliated with Reverend Cleage called for the commissioner's resignation, but Edwards had built up enough goodwill in the black community that most key institutions, including the *Chronicle*, the Baptist Ministers Alliance, and various black business associations, supported him, even as they disagreed with his conclusions about the case. But there was something deeper that now haunted Edwards. He regretted that he had been out of town when the shooting happened, calling it "one of the worst mistakes of my life." He wondered whether he could have somehow prevented it, or at least have stepped in immediately to ease the tension. Now it was too late, and everything that he had worked so hard to achieve seemed in jeopardy. The distrust was there again, and might deepen with every new confrontation or controversy. He and Mayor Cavanagh began with good intentions, but here was a reminder of how vulnerable their intentions were to the vagaries of daily life.

With the ramifications of the Scott incident, Edwards was feeling squeezed from all sides. He ended up supporting his officers, but by that time his liberal attitudes and determined effort to rid the department of its old guard had caused morale problems with the rank and file and diminished his support in the high command. Earlier that year he had tried to foreclose resistance from the old guard by transferring its two lead actors, the Berg brothers, Louis and James, who had served in the number two and three positions, superintendent and deputy superintendent, to the Traffic Bureau, demotions that forced their resignations. But the sensibility of the Berg brothers, who had resisted all of Edwards's efforts to improve the department's reputation in the black community, ran deeply through the department. The cops on the street, several levels below the commissioner, believed that nobody who was not in their position, and certainly not Edwards, who had come out of the judiciary, could understand the pressures and strains of their assignment.

"What needed to be recognized is that the police were on the front line and trying to hold it together, but they could sense things falling apart," John Tsampikou, who joined the force a year before the Scott shooting, recalled more than a half century later. "Things were changing then, and the police department was a lot of old school guys. Not idiots, not by a long shot . . . but predominantly conservative people who were self-disciplined, all with military training and work ethic. When I hit the streets, the rookies, we tended to be more compassionate until we got the message, 'If you feel that way keep your mouth shut.' You could sense things changing on the street. The civil rights movement. The increase in crime. To the average cop, this was all part of the same thing. We didn't know how to separate it. Then the Cynthia Scott thing came along. I knew Ted Spicher after the fact, the kid who did the shooting. He climbed into the bottle. Whether he was a drinker before I don't know. I think it had a direct impact on his life forever. Shooting at a fleeing suspect was the law. I am not saying Spicher was right or wrong, but the administration in those days supported the troops very well. You never heard of a policeman being charged criminally."

Another young Detroit cop then was Anthony Fierimonte, whose girlfriend was the daughter of the First District inspector. "I was over at her house one day," Fierimonte recalled, "and the inspector called home and said, 'Well, I'm not going to make it home, we're involved in this big mess, rioting going on. Somebody shot the whore over here and now everyone's going crazy that she was a good young girl and should not have been shot. On the news broadcasts it was totally liberal: 'Oh, this poor black woman got shot, and no sense to the shooting.' We were looking at each other and saying 'She was a streetwalker and got in trouble.' They just didn't know what was really happening."

David Wright was a rookie cop in the adjacent 13th Precinct near Wayne State. "I worked a whore car for a while. There were three thousand [prostitutes] by fingerprint just at John R. And then white whores on Cass and Third Avenue." The cops called the hookers "nooners," Wright said. They would arrest them, take them down to the station, test them for venereal disease, and then release them at noon the next day. "If you went by the courthouse at noon, there'd be like a hundred that came out." Most prostitutes accepted the routine and did not fight back. Cynthia Scott was different, according to Wright. She was big and a fighter, and she ran. "Most whores never fought. You'd say, 'Come on, let's go.' The big sin was running from the police. What it was was, and people still don't get this today—the fact that you shoot somebody in the back doesn't mean shit. You are moving, they are moving. It's an all-out panic situation."

If the cops considered it a battle out there on the streets of Detroit, it was an uneven fight. They had the far superior firepower, led by what was called "the Big 4"—unmarked police sedans, Chryslers or Buicks, carrying four officers, one in uniform, three in plainclothes, fortified with a store of weapons including ax handles, baseball bats, shotguns, and a Thompson submachine gun. Big 4s roamed the streets day and night in six of the city's high-crime districts, which were predominantly black but also included an area populated by white immigrants from Appalachia. David Wright, who joined the department in 1961, worked on a Big 4 crew with a partner nicknamed Rotation Slim and another cop who liked to quote Shakespeare. "When police needed help, they called in the Big 4," Wright recalled. "It was nice if you were walking the beat and there was a crowd forming. 'Get inside or I'm gonna call in the Big 4.' The Big 4 didn't do public relations, they just started kicking ass."

In the weeks after the Cynthia Scott shooting, just before roll call in the First District, an officer would get out his guitar and sing a little ditty that began:

*Run, Cynthia, run*
*Spicher gone to get his gun.*

George Edwards had taken the job at 1300 Beaubien with the zeal of a missionary and from the beginning understood that his reform administration could be effective for only so long. Two years maximum as police commissioner, he thought, and then time to move on. But his great ambition, as he said during that speech at Michigan State a few months earlier, was to create an atmosphere in Detroit that honored both full equality and law and order. He had left for Europe on a high, boosted by the success of the Walk to Freedom and a glowing note he had received from Martin Luther King. "As one who bears both the physical and psychological effects of brutal and inhuman police forces in the South, I was both uplifted and consoled to be with a police force that proved to be a genuine protector and a friend indeed," King wrote. "I am sure that a great deal of the success of the march can be attributed to you and the significant leadership that you have given the police department of Detroit. You have proved to the Negro citizenry of your community that you are a friend rather than an enemy." Now that praise seemed hollow, as Edwards faced the depressing realization that his hopes for equality and order might never be achieved, undone by the shooting of St. Cynthia less than a month after the great demonstration of interracial respect.

"Heat Wave." Not from love, but from fear and misunderstanding, it seemed once again that high blood pressure got a hold on the city of Detroit.

## Chapter 14

# THE VAST MAGNITUDE

**WORK STARTED EARLY** for most of the men at the top of Ford. By seven each weekday, a stream of black limousines began flowing from Bloomfield Hills down to the Glass House, the company headquarters in Dearborn. Much like their GM and Chrysler counterparts, these were job-driven car guys who rarely drove; instead they were chauffeured from their suburban estates to the office and on toward downtown for their ritual appointments at the Detroit Athletic Club, nerve center of the business elite, a fleet of sedans double-parked outside while executives lunched or played their clubhouse games as members of the Three Bs: Beavers (swimmers), Blackballers (handball and racquetball), and Bowlers. For those who accepted the order of things, all still seemed golden in the summer of 1963, their work and play sealed off and protected. To them urban renewal meant a faster ride into the city and back.

Holmes Brown, then a Ford public relations man, later called the company subculture of that era "the most isolated and insulated community I ever saw. It was, they thought, the 'Big Operation.' . . . Everybody was insulated within the company. . . . My wife fought it and hated it. She fought it all the time. She hated Detroit and Grosse Pointe, and the private schools where all the Ford kids would go, the wives saw only the wives and there was a pecking order, level by level, and there were meetings with [car] dealers, which were monstrous. Everyone wore the same coat among the wives.

It was like a uniform. Not only did the men have a uniform with their suits but the women had the same.... It was something that no one ever told you to do. It was something you knew. You had to play golf or bridge if your boss did."

At the very top, the big boss might have been sympathetic to Mrs. Brown. Henry Ford II, in his own way, was rebelling against the regimented mores of his time and place. Typically he was still asleep at seven when his Ford men went off to work. He rarely woke before seven-thirty and did not leave his lonely mansion at Grosse Pointe Farms for another hour. The company defined his life, but the social expectations of Detroit's auto society bored him. He was spending more time overseas, especially in Italy, home of his mistress, Maria Cristina Vettore Austin. Behind a crusty vocabulary that could sound jingoistic—"I don't like frog tires," he once snapped at an underling who put Michelins on a Ford—was a man of the world who spoke fluent French and was learning some Italian, had bought a $700,000 yacht, and was living out of a suitcase more and more. He and his wife, Anne, were separating that summer, and he was searching for new and sexier things, even toying with the idea of acquiring an Italian car company. "He was tired of being a suburban husband in a suburban city," said his daughter, Charlotte, who lived in New York. "He envied café society, [envied] the owner of Fiat, who was having a good life, a boat everywhere—I think it was very hard on him. He was another suburban businessman in Detroit and he was bored with it and you could almost see it happening. At the end it was real hatred in the marriage between him and Anne because he started to see Cristina. Cristina was the reflection of the desperate desire to get out of Detroit, and she was the perfect person at the perfect time."

The perfect time for Henry Ford II came during a period of automobile world bounty. Car sales were booming, the future seemed to promise only more of everything—more cars, more roads, more people, more drivers—and a series of anniversaries coincided as reminders of Ford's consequential history.

On the second to last day of July, the Deuce's Lincoln limousine followed its regular route to the Glass House, traversing the Edsel Ford Expressway for part of the trip, a road named for his father, an unavoidable reminder of how city and family were inextricably linked. His grandfather, the original Henry Ford, was born during the middle of the Civil War, less than a month after Gettysburg, and this July 30 marked the centennial of his birth. It was also the sixtieth anniversary of the founding of Ford Motor Company and the fiftieth anniversary of Ford's world-changing mass assembly line. Threes all in a row: 1863, 1903, and 1913. And there was another three in the mix: 1943. It had been twenty years since Edsel Ford, then president of the company and an underrated force in the building of the Arsenal of Democracy, died of stomach cancer at the too young age of forty-nine and young Henry was called back from navy training to join Ford's management team. All of this, especially the centennial, could not go unnoticed in the Motor City Ford helped make famous. Mayor Cavanagh proclaimed July 28 to August 3 Henry Ford Centennial Week, a plaza to the west of downtown's Ford Auditorium was renamed Henry Ford Plaza, local museums staged exhibits related to his work and hobbies and homes, the newspapers ran special sections recounting his biography and the creation of the automobile industry, and the political and business elite were now gathering with the namesake grandson to celebrate the founder's memory at a hundredth-birthday anniversary luncheon at Lovett Hall in Greenfield Village.

To one side of the Deuce at the speakers' table sat Lenore Romney, Michigan's first lady. To the other side was Cavanagh. As the audience spooned desserts of lime ice and crème de menthe, Detroit's mayor described how his life, like so many thousands of others, had been shaped by Henry Ford. "It was fortunate for us in Dearborn and the Detroit area that Mr. Ford was born here one hundred years ago," Cavanagh said. "There is no question that southeastern Michigan would be a different place today if Henry Ford had not been a native son. In so many ways Henry Ford has touched our lives. In my case, for example, my father was an employee of the Ford Motor Company for forty-two years. . . . I was made aware early in life of the vast magnitude of Henry Ford's company. I also have worked as a guide here at Greenfield Village. As a guide I was proud to show the hundreds of thousands of visitors who came here each year the irreplaceable examples of America's heritage which we owe to Mr. Ford and his love of his country."

"We shall have reproduced American life as lived," old man Ford once said of his museum and village, and after lunch his grandson and the mayor and the other centennial celebrants dutifully boarded buses for another tour of that vision of American life. Here was the farmhouse where Henry Ford was born, transplanted from its original location on Greenfield Road a few miles away and restored on the faux village property. There was the Connecticut house where Noah Webster completed his dictionary. The Ohio bicycle shop where Orville and Wilbur Wright tinkered with their first flying machine. The Pennsylvania birthplace of William Holmes McGuffey, author of Americana's sacred texts, the *McGuffey Readers*. The rural Illinois courthouse where Abe Lincoln practiced law. A replica of inventor Thomas Edison's laboratory in New Jersey. Life mythologized and sanitized, as insulated from the changing world of the sixties as those Ford men riding down from Bloomfield Hills in the backseats of black sedans.

Jerome Cavanagh might have felt indebted to the Ford Motor Company, but the mayor and the city he loved were excluded from the founder's American myth. This was the infected heart of the Detroit story. Henry Ford, whose cars transformed the American landscape, whose assembly line stood as a symbol of the industrial age, whose Rouge plant lured hundreds of thousands of people off the farms and out of the small towns and into the metropolis, and whose cars made it easier for millions of people to escape to the suburbs, did not value urban life. He was a leading propagator of the pastoral idyll, the notion that urban life was not the good America, not the real America. And who was accepted and who was rejected in his real America? There the myth grew more sinister. Henry Ford II realized this long before he led the festivities honoring his grandfather's hundredth anniversary. The grandson had been the beneficiary of the company's "vast magnitude" more than Mayor Cavanagh or anyone else, but also more than anyone he had had to spend his life trying to overcome if not erase the vast malignancy attached to that Ford legacy. The flip side of Henry Ford's rural sentimentality was a virulent, obsessive campaign against people he felt threatened by, especially Jews. He was the first of the automakers to hire blacks and also brought in large numbers of immigrants from Lebanon, eventually turning Dearborn into a national center of Arab America, but his attacks on Jews transcended these other characteristics of diversity. He might have offered Martin Luther King a job had King's family made the migration to Detroit, but his dreamscape could not have differed more from the one King evoked after that walk down Woodward a month before the centennial celebration.

It is difficult to overstate Ford's anti-Semitic malevolence, documented for posterity, far from the sight of Greenfield Village tourists, in old issues of the *Dearborn Independent,* a newspaper he owned and used as his primary propaganda tool during the twenties. In ninety-one consecutive issues starting in May 1920, Ford's paper ran article after article attacking Jews as "the world's problem." Using the editor, William J. Cameron, as his mouthpiece, Ford set forth a worldview that blamed Jews for everything from the despoilment of baseball to the assassination of Abraham Lincoln, from the betrayal of Christopher Columbus to the creation of the evil Jewish state of the Soviet Union, from the corruption of Anglo-Saxon culture through jazz and provocative movies to the evil of Jewish bankers who he claimed started and prolonged World War I. In the pages of the *Dearborn Independent,* anything wrong in the world traced back to a conspiracy by the Jews.

Ford found an audience for these diatribes at home and abroad. In Munich leaders of the rising Nazi Party spread the columns to followers in *The International Jew: The World's Problem,* an anthology translated into German. The *New York Times* reported that Adolf Hitler kept a well-used copy of the book in his library and hung a portrait of Henry Ford on his wall. Back in the United States, where the Ku Klux Klan contemporaneously was surging as a nativist force, the columns were distributed at rallies, and Ford was promoted as a presidential candidate. At the same time, he was developing a nationwide network for the newspaper by instructing Ford car dealers in cities and towns across America to sell subscriptions along with automobiles. At its peak the *Dearborn Independent* reached nearly 700,000 subscribers. In parallel with the propaganda effort, Ernest G. Liebold, who served as general manager of the newspaper and one of Ford's personal henchmen, set up a private squad to identify and investigate Jewish radicals, and was so connected to the Nazis that he had a box of swastikas shipped to his Dearborn office. Later, as Hitler was preparing his invasion of Europe, he honored Ford with the Grand Cross of the German Eagle, presented to the American industrialist on his seventy-fifth birthday, a quarter-century to the day before the centennial celebration at Greenfield Village. By that time Ford's virulence was outpaced by another fearmongering Detroit figure, Father Charles Edward Coughlin, a prominent fascist sympathizer who laced his nationally popular radio commentary on *The Golden Hour of the Shrine of the Little Flower* with attacks on Jews and blacks and Roosevelt's New Deal.

Although Ford had issued an apology of sorts for the screeds, relying on a claim that he did not know all that the *Dearborn Independent* had been writing in his newspaper, the apology was never fully believed or accepted by his wounded targets, and intense hostility toward Ford Motor Company was something Henry Ford II had worked to overcome from the moment he took command from his grandfather near the end of World War II. What had started as angry boycotts became a deeply embedded matter of pride and faith in the Jewish culture. You did not buy a Ford. "I started right out to change that," Henry Ford II recalled in an oral interview with company historian David Lewis, a transcript of which is archived at the Benson Ford Research Center. "I spent a lot of time on the West Coast working on the movies because of their propaganda influence. The four Warner brothers ran Warner Brothers. Harry Warner, who was a sort of chief, wouldn't allow an employee to drive a Ford product. Gary Cooper, who was a friend of mine, couldn't drive his Ford product into the Warner Brothers lot. I made a great effort to straighten out this situation. . . . It was bad. I don't know whether this is true or not, but I was told that Bernie Baruch [Bernard Baruch was a noted Jewish financier and presidential adviser who had been assailed in the *Dearborn Independent* as "the pro-consul of Judah in America"] at one time was riding in a taxicab and a guy with him said, 'This is a Ford,' and Baruch stopped the cab and got out." Old man Ford died, senile, in a Detroit hospital named for him, and it was left to the grandson to pay penance, which he did through words and deeds. He immediately fired Cameron, the *Independent* editor, then set about supporting Jewish antidefamation organizations, contributing to Yeshiva University, establishing business dealings in Israel, and courting Jewish advisers.

The reshaping of the Ford image by Henry Ford II also involved the company's approach to labor. Ford had been the last of the Big Three to have its workers unionized, and during the thirties and early forties had tried, ferociously and at times violently, to repress the efforts of the United Auto Workers. When company thugs attacked Walter Reuther at the battle of the overpass in 1937, it was not an isolated incident but part of a concerted effort by Ford to harass, intimidate, and injure union leaders. Just as Henry Ford had set up an external ring under Liebold, the Nazi sympathizer, to track radicals, he established a larger internal network of spies and goons in his Service Department, under the iron grip of Harry Bennett, to control activities within his own company. Bennett, a pug boxer picked up off the streets of New York who knew nothing about cars, proved so valuable to Henry Ford as the in-house enforcer that he rose to the top of the company and thought he would be the founder's successor. The Deuce fired him the day he took control. "I simply said to him, 'Harry, we've got to part company.' His reaction wasn't very good," Ford later recalled. More than a thousand "Bennett men" were fired along with the head thug.

In 1946, less than a year after HF2 became president of Ford, Reuther was elected president of the UAW, and Ford took a quiet but unconventional first step toward calming the company's approach to the union. "When Walter was elected president of the UAW, the first thing I did was pay a call on him at *his* office," Ford recalled in the oral interview. "Everybody [in the executive suites at Ford] thought that was heresy. But I said, 'Well, hell, aren't you guys working with him? Doesn't he run your plants for you? Might as well find out about the guy and see what kind of guy he is.'

So Walter and I had a very good relationship over many, many years. But Walter was left of center by a long ways. I didn't believe what Walter believed in. But as far as being a guy that you could work with, or sit down and talk with, Walter was as reasonable as any. And a very decent and nice guy."

The inevitably contentious push and pull of labor-management relations would persist, but in a less poisonous environment. "Labor unions are here to stay," HF2 had said in one of his early speeches as company president. Ford Motor Company was not going to try to turn back the clock or break the union, he insisted, but deal with Reuther and his UAW in the same professional negotiating manner that the company would use in any other business transaction. It was under Reuther and Henry Ford II that the UAW and Ford Motor Company reached what would become one of the defining collective bargaining agreements in American labor history, a contract in 1949 that for the first time provided full pension benefits, funded by the company, along with medical and hospital insurance and wage increases tied to the inflation index. In exchange, the union agreed to a five-year contract that would promise the automaker a period of stability and labor peace. Chrysler, after a 104-day strike, accepted the same agreement, and finally General Motors signed on for what became known as the Treaty of Detroit, establishing a set of conditions that as much as anything lifted hundreds of thousands of working people into the middle class and made it possible for millions of workers across the nation to share that dream. When considering all that Detroit has meant to America, along with cars and music and civil rights, it can be said in a profound sense that Detroit gave blue-collar workers a way into the middle class, and that Henry Ford II and Walter Reuther, two giants of the mid-twentieth century, were essential to that result.

Ford and Reuther. It was not a coincidence that Reuther's first appearance at the Detroit Auto Show banquet in October 1962 came when HF2 was president of the Automobile Manufacturers Association. They were far from social friends, coming from wholly different backgrounds and perspectives, but they remained in frequent contact over the years through notes and letters and occasional visits. After a trip to London in 1961,

Reuther sent Ford a copy of the "Proposed British Charter of Industrial Relations," a gift that Ford received with thanks and at face value. A year later Ford sent Reuther copies of photographs he had taken in London during a visit with Sir William Carron, president of the Amalgamated Engineering Union, whose trade unionism was so moderate that he was knighted in 1963, appointed to the Bank of England, and disparaged by British socialists as a capitalist tool. Although Reuther was more militant than Carron, his comfort with the American establishment also drew criticism from his left flank.

One day in mid-July 1963, eighteen years after his first visit, HF2 again met Reuther on his union turf. This was two weeks before the Henry Ford centennial anniversary celebration at Greenfield Village. When Ford first visited Reuther back when they were both new to their jobs, UAW headquarters was on Milwaukee Street in the shadows of the General Motors offices, one block west of Woodward and south of West Grand. Now Solidarity House was located at 8000 East Jefferson on property that was hauntingly familiar. Edsel and Eleanor Ford once had owned a riverfront mansion on that very site. The family moved there when Henry II, the oldest of four children, was four, and left when he was nine, moving on up to a new mansion in Grosse Pointe Shores designed by Albert Kahn. The old place on East Jefferson was gone now, but the original boathouse still stood in back of an undistinguished building that looked more like a cut-rate motel than UAW headquarters, a center of the labor movement.

Reuther, who had just returned from Washington, where he had testified before Congress on behalf of JFK's civil rights bill, showed Ford around the building and grounds for more than an hour before they sat down to talk. Rumors spread afterward that they had broached the subject of Ford-UAW contract negotiations, which would come around again in 1964, but both men denied it and said they discussed political issues, including civil rights, and the national scope of matters they dealt with as colleagues on Kennedy's Advisory Committee on Labor-Management Policy. The intent of that committee, the brainchild of Arthur Goldberg, the secretary of labor, was to enable high-level communications between business and labor leaders on a routine basis in hopes that this might create a sense of common purpose and avert national crises similar to the prolonged 1959 strike in the steel industry. "We used to remark lightly that it's important that Henry Ford II see that Walter Reuther doesn't have fangs; and it was important for Walter Reuther to see that Henry Ford can be a reasonable man," recalled David W. Burke, who served as executive secretary for the advisory committee. "So my belief was that the main purpose of the committee was to forestall future labor disputes that had a serious economic impact upon the country."

In an oral history interview for the John F. Kennedy Library, Burke offered sharp insights into the different ways Ford and Reuther approached their committee work. Ford, he said, always came well prepared by his staff with talking points and briefing documents and was eager to contribute but was not comfortably fluent in the nuances of the discussion. "I always felt that Henry Ford came so well prepared that he knew what the bottom line was that he was supposed to maintain but not knowing entirely how he got there, he didn't know how to back off it." When the committee tried to reach a consensus, Burke noticed, "Ford was always very brittle in that situation because if you don't know how you got to your position, then you don't know how to come off it, by issue, to accommodate a resolution." Reuther, by contrast, appeared to Burke to be "terribly thoughtful, he was innovative, he was looking for new ways to do things" and was more fluid reacting to changing circumstances. But he also seemed to have a strong need to prove himself, in different ways, to the two people on the committee who were most immediately relevant in his sphere: Ford, his nominal opponent in management, and George Meany, the AFL-CIO president, his nominal ally but visceral antagonist.

The conflicts on the committee were often between Meany and Ford, not Reuther and Ford, and even more between Meany and Reuther, Burke said. "I always felt that Meany took on Ford more than Reuther to make some kind of point that I'm not willing to speculate about. It was sort of, 'I'll show you, Walter, how to deal with this fellow.' And he'd go and do that." Reuther often tried to ignore Meany and direct his thoughts toward

Ford. "He was trying to prove something to Henry Ford. . . . He didn't have to prove that he was more intelligent, but he also had to prove that he had a lot of other interests in mind other than just the union that he represented, which is a hallmark of the United Auto Workers"—a sensibility that only further irritated Meany, with his narrower us-versus-them mentality.

Reuther considered himself a visionary and focused his attention on the major issues that he thought would define labor in America and the world for the rest of the century. A stump speech that he delivered in various forms in Detroit, New York, and abroad during the spring and summer of 1963 involved automation, technology, and the meaning of work—the vast magnitude of the future. Unions, he said, were on their way to becoming less economic organizations than socioeconomic forces working to improve the quality of life. They would be functioning in a rapidly transforming society in which there would be more technological change in the next quarter century than there had been in the previous 250 years. To adapt and survive in this period of flux, Reuther thought that unions, employers, and the government had to work together to bring about four essential conditions: meaningful and creative employment, adequate educational facilities, equal rights regardless of race, and a full measure of economic security for the aging. Medicare was three years away. The civil rights bill was in committee. The rising postwar baby boom generation had flooded the school systems and created a surge in government funding and parental involvement in education. Meaningful and creative employment was another matter. From the time Ford installed the first assembly line in 1913, it had been difficult to make routinized factory work anything but tedious and soul-sapping, if not dehumanizing and dangerous. "Three young men in dirty work clothes," Philip Levine, the Detroit native who became the great poet of the autoworkers, wrote in "Salt and Oil,"

*on their way home or to a bar*
*in the late morning, this is not*
*a photograph, it is a moment*
*in the daily life of the world,*

*a moment that will pass into*
*the unwritten biography*
*of your city or my city*
*unless it is frozen in the fine print*
*of our eyes.*

They could have been leaving the Rouge plant on their way to Salamie's or Johnny's, walking past young Bob Ankony as he was going the other way, playing hooky, the image of the three men in grimy work clothes freezing in the fine print of his eyes, reminding him, despite all the talk about the dignity of work, precisely what he did not want in his own future, just as it reminded the poet. Work, yes, but not that life. Morning after morning, week after week, year after year, the unwritten biography of Detroit. There had to be a better life outside the factory, Reuther believed. The work clothes might not be as dirty in the technological future, but the jobs could be just as numbing, or more so. In 1961 he had proposed that autoworkers with seniority get a lengthy sabbatical every now and then, and he was thinking of pursuing it again in the 1964 negotiations now that the United Steelworkers of America had won something similar in a contract agreement announced that summer on the same day as Detroit's Walk to Freedom. Steelworkers with fifteen years seniority would get a thirteen-week vacation every five years. This concession came in exchange for two years of labor peace and no wage increases. The sabbatical would not only refresh workers but would expand the workforce through replacements. Fringe benefits of that sort energized Reuther in a way that fights over dollars and cents could not. The steelworkers deal was also received well by a spokesman for Ford, reflecting the interests of the industry, who said the company was "pleased, of course, that there will be no strikes in the steel industry"—strikes that had a debilitating secondary effect on the automakers. And Pierre Salinger, the White House press secretary, said that President Kennedy was "gratified" by the agreement. Perhaps it was working, that labor-management advisory committee of which Reuther and Henry Ford

II were such key members. Since 1960, according to the Department of Labor, the United States had enjoyed a sustained period of minimal strike activity unparalleled in modern peacetime.

After arriving at Ford Motor Company a decade and a half earlier out of graduate school at Princeton, Lee Iacocca had sprinted up the marketing ranks until he had real power as the Ford Division general manager. He was a star, his rise seemingly inexorable, but he was never a Ford protégé. There was something about him that irritated the Deuce despite the obvious talent. Reuther was the respected enemy, but Iacocca was something less pleasing. Some of it might have been social and cultural. Iacocca never felt fully comfortable among Ford's WASPy set, and associates of the Deuce could recall times when they heard Ford calling Iacocca "that goddamn wop." But mostly it was a conflict of ambition and style. Like many very rich people, Ford did not have to sell himself; Iacocca knew no other way. "He had a lot of ability," Ford later said of Iacocca. "Unfortunately his ability lies ninety-nine percent in sales. But it isn't only in selling cars—it's selling everything. It's selling himself, it's selling an idea, selling anything—the Brooklyn Bridge, if you will. When he started to talk he could talk interminably, selling something, and he did a good job. Now if he was really wound up I think at the end he forgot what he started with, but he was still selling something at the end. It didn't make much difference because it usually got sold."

Iacocca could talk cars nonstop, but marketing was his most comfortable domain, and the language of dealers and advertisers his native tongue. From the time he had made his name in Ford's mid-Atlantic region with a *56 in 56* marketing campaign—$56 a month for the 1956 Ford—he was considered the Ford favorite among ad men. HF2 could be crusty, wondering why he was spending so much money on marketing, questioning the value for the cost. There was a bit of us versus them, substance versus style in his outlook, but Iacocca looked at it from a more mutually dependent perspective. His philosophy was encapsulated in a speech he later delivered to the American Association of Advertising Agencies called "The Four Freedoms of Advertising." From the perspective of ad agencies, no declaration could have been more sympathetic to their cause. Iacocca's four freedoms called for total immersion and involvement of the ad men in the process from beginning to end. Freedom of access. Freedom of involvement. Freedom to experiment. Freedom to persuade. From the time he rose to power within the Ford Division, he said, "we've had a formal setup to make sure our agency people are involved in the development of our products darned near as soon as we are. Wouldn't it be ridiculous to call the agency in the sixty days before our new model introduction and tell them to come up with some fresh ideas? Advertising men are a vital link between us and the customer. They help us figure out what the customer wants.... You have to live with the car for a long time before you can decide what it really has that will make news to the customer. You have to experiment—take pictures, write copy and see whether they look good or make sense."

And so it was with J. Walter Thompson and Project T-5. Bill Laurie's team in Detroit and their creative counterparts in New York had been immersed in Iacocca's new car from the beginning, starting with the Fairlane Room dinner meetings and the secure work inside the Tomb in the Buhl Building. By midsummer 1963 the agency had assigned hundreds to the project. By then Laurie's ad men had been told that key decision makers at Ford were leaning toward naming the car Torino, after the city in Italy more commonly known in the English-speaking world as Turin. In some important ways, the name made sense. Italian fashion was considered the best in the world, Italian cars were highly regarded for their coachwork, and this Ford model evoked an imported look. Franklyn Thomas, Laurie's deputy, recalled what happened next: "To fire up the enthusiasm of our 'hot project' staff, we needed film, lots of film on the car. We asked Ford for a running prototype of the car to establish a pictorial emotion and personality platform for the product. The Ford staff agreed."

There was only one prototype model in full operation, and a quirky model at that. It was virtually handmade, away from the assembly line, at a cost of about $200,000. No shock absorbers. Bucket seats bolted into the farthest back position. Windows that did not roll down. A right door that did not open. On the Fourth of July weekend, Ford slipped the prototype into a closed transport van and hauled it to the Romeo Proving Grounds northeast of Detroit. A team of twenty-five artists, writers, and photographers from JWT were there waiting for its arrival. "For three days and part time nights, everybody sweated off pounds shooting secret film around the clock and around the car," Thomas recalled. "This frantic photo safari brought in over a thousand still shots and 5,000 feet of motion picture film, all in color. We needed this film to convey to top Ford management all the excitement we knew was in this product... to bring that product out of the garage where the client had been seeing it and put it in action in the proper environment on highway and byway."

Was this essentially a family car or a sports car or some combination of the two? Sentiments at Ford and JWT differed on that question, so it was decided to get an early read on what the public thought. Sworn to secrecy, fifty-two couples with young children were brought to Ford to look at the T-5 model. At first their consensus seemed to be heavily on the side that this was a sports car, not for families. "They loved the styling but decided it wasn't their cup of tea," according to Thomas. "Too impractical." Then they were asked to guess the price. Their estimates came in at least $700 above the planned sticker price, with most guesses more than $1,000 too high. When informed of the price, these same couples "walked back for another look and began rationalizing about how practical the car would be after all."

With Torino as the working name, and a vault of photographs and video from the test run at Romeo to work with, JWT's creative staff started concocting newspaper and magazine ads.

> BRAND NEW IMPORT... FROM DETROIT
>
> Scusi, Signori, may I introduce my Torino. Inspired by Italy's great road cars but straight from Detroit. Bucket seats of GT design. I could have floor mounted 3 speed shift. I could have...

What price is this eleganza de Italia?

Only 1,478,000 lire.

(There it was, forty-eight years before the Chrysler ad with Eminem and the Diego Rivera murals and the Joe Louis fist and the black choir at the Fox Theater, a first iteration of "Imported from Detroit.")

Another ad:

TORINO BY FORD

It looks like one of the great Italian road cars—with a price to match—but don't be misled. Torino is built in Detroit—a small luxury car that also happens to be small in price. Its style may speak with an Italian accent, but it is pure American in the way it translates economy into pleasure, savings into comfort, thrift into luxury.

All destined for the dustbin of advertising history.

In his later remembrances, Lee Iacocca might have taken a certain satisfaction in recounting how the Torino name was ditched, considering his less than bosomy relationship with HF2. As the Torino campaign was being prepared, Iacocca received a call from one of Ford's public relations men, who told him they would have to pick another name for the car because the Deuce was "in the midst of divorce and keeping company with Cristina Vettore Austin, an Italian jet-set divorcee he had met at a party in Paris. Some of his underlings felt that giving the car an Italian name would lead to bad publicity and gossip that would embarrass the boss."

At JWT, John Conley, one of the forward planners in the Tomb, was a resident expert on brand names, the ad man who had helped Ford come up with the name Falcon. Now, with Torino off the boards, he went to the Detroit Public Library and spent several hours poring through books in search of something suitable. He emerged with Bronco, Puma, Colt, Cheetah, Cougar, and Mustang. Back where they had started. A prototype sports car that Iacocca and his team had conceived two years earlier—a two-seater, but in the lineage that led to the T-5—was named Mustang 1. That earlier version was meant to evoke the warplane; now the image was of a wild horse. In making the case to Iacocca, Laurie and Conley and the J. Walter Thompson men said "Mustang" "had the excitement of wide open spaces and was American as hell."

There is a story told by Walter Murphy, the Ford Division's in-house public relations man, about how Iacocca sold the name to HF2: On the night before Iacocca was to make another key sales pitch on the new car, he met one last time with the planning group at the Fairlane Room. "What I need are some fresh grabbers for my meeting tomorrow with Henry at the Glass House," Murphy recalled Iacocca saying. Some suggested he lead off with the new name. Others suggested he should emphasize that the car would "kick GM's Monza square in the balls." At that point Iacocca closed his research binder and declared that he had figured out his pitch.

The next morning, in Murphy's account, Ford was "stretched out in his leather chair, fingers clasped upon his expanding belly." "What have you got, Lee?" he asked.

Partway through his pitch, Iacocca came to the line that had crossed his mind at the planning meeting, a line that made him close his binder and say he was ready. "Now this little pony car, the Mustang, would give an orgasm to anyone under thirty," he said.

Ford "sat upright, as if jabbed by a needle."

"What was that you said, Lee?"

Iacocca repeated the orgasm line.

"No, not that crap," Ford said. "What did you call the car?"

"It's the Mustang, Mr. Ford."

It is wise to consider the reliability of that account in the context of who was telling it: a lifelong public relations man. But it sounded like Iacocca and it sounded like Ford. So did another version told by Donald Frey, the product planning manager, who remembered Ford telling him before the meeting, "Frey, I'm tired of your fucking car. I'm going to approve it . . . and it's your ass if it doesn't sell well."

## Chapter 15

# HOUSES DIVIDED

**GEORGE ROMNEY, HAIR SLICKED BACK** from his broad forehead, his tanned mug exuding executive-class prosperity, came to Grosse Pointe ready to hit the streets as a protester. Earlier that summer at the end of the Walk to Freedom, mention of the governor's name had been greeted with a ripple of boos in Cobo Hall, even though he had issued a proclamation honoring the event and had sent a delegation to represent him. That was on a Sunday, the one day of the week he did not make public appearances, citing his religious beliefs as a Mormon. Now it was Saturday, and there was another civil rights march, this one in support of open housing, and he was there. This time the marchers were not rolling down Woodward Avenue by the tens of thousands but strolling from a shopping center through the leafy side streets of the region's most exclusive suburban enclave, home to Henry Ford II and William D. Laurie of J. Walter Thompson and other members of Detroit's ruling elite. No more than 250 marchers participated, about the size of the crowd watching from the sidewalks in a less than welcoming manner. The organizers did not even know Romney would appear. "I came because I believe any American should have equal rights with any other American," he said. "There is an excessive amount of discrimination in housing. Some practiced in this particular part of the state is particularly reprehensible."

The practice he alluded to was known as the Grosse Pointe point system, a real estate contrivance that held the dubious distinction of being the Detroit area's most egregious form of discrimination in a realm of human interaction that proved to be the most stubbornly segregated. Determined to control who was allowed to live there and to keep out "undesirables," the Grosse Pointe Brokers Association in 1945 devised a system that involved hiring a private investigator to probe the background of prospective homebuyers and then having a secret three-member panel rate them on a point scale based on occupation, country of origin, appearance (including level of "swarthiness"), education, and whether their "way of living" was sufficiently "American." WASPs were basically in free, if they had the money, while blacks, Asians, and Mexicans were not even scored; they had no chance whatsoever. The system was also rigged against Jews, who had to score more points than people of Greek and Italian descent, who had to score more than Poles and other East Europeans, though it was rare for any of them to make the cut, aside from a few wealthy mobsters like Tony Giacalone. The Grosse Pointe point system persisted for fifteen years, until it was challenged in court and by the state administration of G. Mennen Williams, a liberal Democratic governor, in 1960, but the remnants of it were still evident three years later when Romney came to join the protests.

As historian Geoffrey Kabaservice has astutely noted, Romney could be "willful, bad-tempered, blustery, moralistic, inarticulate, self-aggrandizing, and self-contradictory," but he also showed foresight, courage, and persistence in dealing with civil rights, especially considering the context of his public and private circumstances. His rise from the corporate world to Republican politics paralleled the ascent of Barry Goldwater and a conservative movement that opposed the use of laws and government regulations to ban discrimination and enforce racial equality. In his private life, Romney remained unflinchingly devoted to the teachings of the Church of Latter-Day Saints and served as president of the Church's Detroit stake, but he spoke out against the Mormon practice of denying the priesthood to blacks and worked for decades to improve the institution's civil rights image.

Since arriving in Detroit in 1939 at age thirty-two, George Wilcken

Romney, born to Mormon parents living in a church colony in Mexico, had never been your average Motor City executive, though he fit the mold in some ways, living in Bloomfield Hills and sending his sons to the exclusive Cranbrook Schools. His religion tended to separate him, but so did his decisions as a car guy and his activities in the civic sphere. His support of civil rights extended back to World War II, when he worked as chief spokesman for the Automobile Manufacturers Association and expressed his distaste for segregated public housing in Detroit's defense industry, an issue that served as the backdrop for the 1943 Detroit riot. As an executive at American Motors Corporation, where he became president in 1954 and bucked the Big Three by manufacturing smaller and more fuel-efficient cars, he also endorsed the goals of the Fair Employment Practices Act and headed up a civic committee seeking more funding for Detroit public schools. During his gubernatorial campaign in 1962, he ventured into black precincts in Detroit at the side of Rev. A. A. Banks, the prominent Republican minister of Second Avenue Baptist, and gave a strong civil rights speech at an event sponsored by the Trade Union Leadership Council, the progressive African American wing of the UAW. Some critics asserted that his stance was more political than moral, just as some believed that his push for small cars was as much a matter of pragmatic necessity as environment-conscious philosophy. Certainly there was some of both. But in the end he might have lost more votes than he gained, and he took his campaigning in the black community only so far. A memo from Charles M. Tucker, a black campaign aide, noted that he won only a "fractional rise in the Negro vote" and that "too much solicitude on the part of Mr. Romney for Negro support could have reduced the enthusiasm for him in such places as Dearborn and like areas."

After winning the election and gaining national notice as a rising Republican star, he continued his civil rights push by galvanizing support for a new Michigan constitution that created a bipartisan civil rights commission and included an equal rights clause prohibiting discrimination "because of religion, race, color, or national origin." His first public appearance as governor, on January 3, 1963, two days after his inauguration, was in

Detroit at the Metropolitan Conference on Open Housing, where he called open-housing laws crucial to the furthering of civil rights: "Housing discrimination in Michigan admittedly is a massive problem and clearly the core of the problem is discrimination based on race." The two previous Democratic governors, first Williams and then Swainson, had attempted to outlaw blatant discriminatory practices such as the Grosse Pointe point system through a state Corporation and Securities Commission regulation known as Rule 9 that prohibited "unfair dealing" by real estate brokers. When that regulation was struck down by the state supreme court in February 1963, Romney pushed the legislature to enact a version into law, and when that failed Michigan's attorney general, a Democrat, ruled that the new Civil Rights Commission would have the power to enforce civil rights in private housing.

When President Kennedy delivered his prime-time speech on June 13 outlining the administration's proposed civil rights legislation, Romney was among those Republicans who praised him and promised his support. "There is no question where the people of Michigan stand on this great moral and civic issue," the governor noted in a letter to the president that also served as a form of self-congratulation. "Through action at the polls on April 1, 1963, they have given unprecedented voice to the most comprehensive, exhaustive, and clearest expression of belief in the basic human rights of all people ever expressed by the people of any state of which I am aware."

If Romney was correct in boasting about his state's firm moral stand on civil rights, the archive holding his papers at the University of Michigan's Bentley Historical Library shows just how far from unanimous that feeling was in his state and elsewhere. Four thick folders there contain letters he received from former supporters regarding the Grosse Pointe march and other civil rights issues. The vast majority of them would be characterized as hate mail.

One of his early correspondents was E. V. Hogge, who lived on Riverdale Drive in Detroit and spiced his diatribe with a bitingly sarcastic jibe about upper-class hypocrisy: "Now that the people of Michigan have elected you and are going to supply you with a Governor's mansion, which some white people also helped pay for, then it stands as a fact that your mansion in the silk stocking unintegrated community of Bloomfield Hills will be vacant for extended periods of the year. Perhaps you will strike the first blow for integrated housing by leasing your home to needy colored for a nominal fee. Or perhaps even better, donating it as a welfare shelter for the indigent colored. With its vastness, it could accommodate very many."

A. B. Gilchrist, who provided no return address, clipped an Associated Press account of Romney's appearance at the Grosse Pointe open-housing rally and typed above the headline, "Politics!! But this won't get you the negro vote. You are a 'dead duck' for 1964." E. G. Brennan, who lived on Parkside Drive on the edge of the all-white Detroit Golf Club, called Romney "the worst version of a double crosser," and added, "I voted and worked for you and the new Constitution and regret it exceedingly. Your version of the Rule Nine and Civil Rights suits me no better than the Democratic one. The negroes' hocus-pocus will ruin this country. If you are trying to gain voters, you are self-defeating, because the whites have more votes, and we are not going to take this lying down. Walter Reuther does not speak for labor, nor will me-tooism conquer." The slap at Reuther, whose UAW leadership was far in front of its rank and file on civil rights, presaged a divide that would grow wider year by year. Brennan closed his letter with a line that underscored a companion development: the future popularity of a southern demagogue in Michigan presidential primaries. "Yours for Gov. Wallace," he signed off.

The mail on August 1, 1963, brought a letter from Don E. Bruner, a lawyer in Albany, Georgia, battleground of one of the early civil rights campaigns. Bruner was aghast at the news that Romney had spoken at a memorial service for Medgar Evers, the civil rights activist who had been murdered in Mississippi hours after JFK's prime-time civil rights speech. Bruner also happened to be a Mormon, an affiliation that permeated his comments to Brother Romney: "We southern Mormons find it difficult to believe that any Mormon Elder could ever advocate integration and subsequent amalgamation of the races. We, as southerners, viewed your rise in national politics as possible fulfillment of the prophecy made by the Prophet Joseph Smith concerning the constitution of the United States. In essence, the prophecy stated that the constitution would hang by a thread, and if it were saved, it would be by the Mormon Elders. Many of us felt that you perhaps were that Elder to fulfill the prophecy. But after Evers . . . we feel that you have deserted the teachings of your Church, of which you are a holder of the Melchizedek Priesthood, in a cheap effort to further your political career. How many Negro Priesthood bearers do you have in your Ward? All of this, Brother Romney, presents manifold the opportunity for mixed marriages and of white children who are forced to give up all their endowments in the church that their one white parent entitled them to because they have some small part of Negro blood in their veins."

Many of the letters elicited responses from the governor's staff, but that one he answered personally. "Dear Brother Bruner," Romney wrote back. "You will find that the first section of the Doctrines and Covenants makes it clear that the revelations of the gospel were for all. Furthermore, the Book of Mormon makes it clear in several places that God is no respecter of persons and that his plan of salvation is for the people of all colors, both black and white. I am fully aware of the Church doctrine, and I know nothing in our Church doctrine that denies negroes or anyone else full rights as American citizens."

Houses falling and rising. On August 2, the day after Romney's Mormon exchange, work crews were hauling debris from the final demolition of the Gotham Hotel, a Detroit institution that would never be replaced. John White, the owner, was on his way to prison on federal gambling charges, broken and sick. That same day another pile of rubble was cleared from a lot where once stood the Lansing, the first apartment building in Detroit to house black tenants back in 1930. By the time of its demise in the summer of 1963, the six-story structure had become a hangout for prostitutes and drug users. That night, on Woodward Avenue, crowds poured into Berry Gordy's new pride and joy, the restored Graystone Ballroom, to hear a big Motown dance concert featuring Smokey Robinson and the Miracles and Martha and the Vandellas. And across town at New Bethel Baptist, C. L. Franklin convened another meeting of his Detroit Council for Human Rights, the umbrella group that staged the Walk to Freedom. The police shooting of Cynthia Scott had discombobulated the dynamics of race in the city. Any communal black and white sensibility resulting from the June 23 rally had dissipated, and the prevailing feeling was again us versus them.

Now came reports that police were using a passive-aggressive tactic to respond to the black protests. "Prostitutes Run Wild on John R at Canfield," blared a headline that week in the *Michigan Chronicle*. The article began, "Is the Detroit Police Department using the Cynthia Scott protests as a pretext to permit wholesale prostitution to pollute Negro communities? This is a major question which Detroit must consider and face immediately and a consequential problem to which official attention must be paid." One night that week, a reporter stood at the corner of John R and Canfield at midnight, right outside the Flame Show Bar, and observed "a market traffic jam" as eighteen prostitutes worked their trade. "In minutes... prostitutes were picked up by motorists, all of them white, and whisked off into the night. The pickups, accompanied by loud and obscene verbal exchanges between the prostitutes and customers, disrupted traffic, flared tempers and brought chaos to the brightly lighted area." The word was that vice cops were now reluctant to arrest the prostitutes. The whore car was nowhere to be seen. If blacks did not like what happened to St. Cynthia, the police seemed to be saying, this is what they would get. Franklin and others at the Detroit Council for Human Rights meeting complained that the powers that be, from the Romney regime in Lansing to the Cavanagh administration in Detroit, were negligent, not doing enough to investigate the shooting and respond to their demands for remedial action.

The larger purpose of the meeting that drew three hundred citizens to New Bethel Baptist was to discuss the aftermath of the Walk to Freedom. Although the march exceeded expectations in terms of participation, the practical matter of raising money for King's SCLC and Franklin's local organization fell short of projections. The reverend had set a goal of raising

$100,000, but the latest financial report listed pledges of slightly above $37,000, minus expenses of $5,256, including the cost of renting Cobo Hall. About $18,000 of that amount made its way down to King's offices in Atlanta, according to the SCLC's receipt. It was better than nothing, and considering that events of that sort tended to draw more publicity than money, Franklin was not discouraged. His goal, he announced at the DCHR meeting, was to stage another big march the following June.

Houses divided. Franklin's optimism belied the chaos around him. Amid continued rifts between Detroit's civil rights factions, his grand coalition was collapsing from pressures left and right. At a national gathering of the NAACP in Chicago in mid-July, where Detroit delegates might have been expected to bask in the glow of the June rally even if their organization did not sponsor it, they instead engaged in an internecine dispute that disrupted the convention. More than one hundred delegates, including Detroit's NAACP leaders and the national president, Arthur Spingarn, walked out of a session on housing in protest of the presence on the panel of James Del Rio, Franklin's outspoken lawyer, who had further irritated the Detroit chapter by declaring that the success of the Walk to Freedom was a "direct repudiation" of the NAACP. A *Michigan Chronicle* reporter covering the convention took note of a "prevailing new mood of militance." Who knew that a walkout, a tactic usually associated with militants, would be staged by moderates? John Conyers, the activist Detroit lawyer, was quoted saying he was bothered by the walkout and felt the local dispute should not have been played out so dramatically in front of the national host.

On the *Chronicle*'s op-ed page in that edition, Dr. Broadus N. Butler dismissed Del Rio and his preacher cohorts, Franklin and Cleage, as "by-nighters" and "self-anointed opportunists." The divisions were becoming more vitriolic and apparent day by day, and not just among Detroiters. On that same page was a column by Jackie Robinson, the baseball legend, deploring the fact that Dr. King had been booed and pelted with eggs earlier that summer by a black crowd outside a church in Harlem. Robinson felt the hostile reception was inspired "in some degree" by Malcolm X, the spellbinding black Muslim leader who ridiculed the concept of black nonviolence in the face of white oppression. The timing of the egg-pelting of King reflected the swirling crosswinds of politics that summer—it came only one day after his triumphant walk down Woodward and the "dream" speech in Detroit.

By August, Franklin was uncomfortably stuck in the middle of all this and unable to find a way out. He greatly admired King and espoused nonviolence, and though he had his own problems with the NAACP his greater problem now was with his militant flank. He felt unjustly accused of being divisive and tried to tamp down criticism of the NAACP by Reverend Cleage and Del Rio. Cleage, angered by what he saw as Franklin's capitulation to power, was notably absent from the August 2 meeting. It soon came out that he had resigned from the DCHR board of directors and affiliated himself with a new black nationalist organization, the Freedom Now Party. Franklin and Cleage had been working together on the idea of hosting a Northern Negro Leadership Conference in November but sharply disagreed over what it should entail. Franklin saw it is a northern version of King's SCLC, but Cleage thought it should be more militant, less committed to nonviolence, and more closely aligned with Malcolm X. He wanted the conference to be open to all black groups who were interested.

According to a report of the dispute in *Illustrated News*, a 35,000-circulation newspaper affiliated with Cleage's family, "Franklin was afraid it might be infiltrated by 'black nationalists and other radical groups' from the East who would hold positions on which he could not agree. 'This must be prevented at all costs,' he said. Franklin wanted to keep out the Freedom Now party because as chairman he could not 'afford to be labeled as a black nationalist like Marcus Garvey.' Rev. Cleage pointed out that he belonged to the Freedom Now party and had invited national leaders to the conference with approval of the board. Franklin said he could not consider black nationalism or criticism of the theory of nonviolence. He said he was disgusted by an article in [New York–based] *Liberator* magazine criticizing King's philosophy and strategy. Cleage said the same fear of offending white people which crowded [the Walk to Freedom] platform with white liberals, labor leaders and politicians now forces it to repudiate the black revolution and its aspirations."

Here was an early formulation of a dispute that would persist throughout the decade.

Almost beyond dispute was the rising talent of Reverend Franklin's daughter Aretha. She was twenty-one now, old enough to sing in clubs, and came home from New York that August for a week-long appearance at the Club Stadium at Puritan and Wildemere, described as "northwest Detroit's newest exciting show spot." Aretha had married Ted White, a smooth-talking hustler-manager, and was a mother again (Ted Jr. was ten months old; she had had her first child as a young teenager in Detroit), and was telling everyone about how she loved to play golf with Ted and travel with him to her new favorite place, Beverly Hills, California. She was of Detroit, her music arose from the city and from her preacher father and the pitch of his hum, but she was not part of the city like her childhood friend Smokey Robinson. She recorded with Columbia, not Motown. C.L. knew the Gordy family, but he never felt that Berry Gordy Jr.'s enterprise was good enough for Aretha. Since winning *DownBeat* magazine's new star award in 1961, she had operated in a different realm from the Motown artists, not selling as many records, not yet, but developing a style that went beyond pop. At Club Stadium she was trying out a new set of blues ballads that had fans lining the sidewalk outside, waiting to get in to listen to her sing.

In the days and weeks after the Walk to Freedom, Berry Gordy had spent many hours listening to King's speech at the Motown studios on West Grand Boulevard. He knew a hit when he heard one, and he thought the "dream" might be a hit, with memorable lyrics delivered by a melodious and familiar voice. Motown technicians had recorded it live and were now producing it as an album. This was not a new idea. As early as September 1962, Esther Gordy Edwards had written to King proposing the "the possibility of recording some of your literary works, sermons, and speeches." It was left to her brother now to work out the deal with the talent, and in this case Martin Luther King and his aides proved touchier to deal with than the most assertive Motown artists. Letters, telegrams, phone conversations—the negotiations went back and forth for weeks, involving everything from the wording of the liner notes to the royalty rates. Gordy considered King a friend and had been flattered months earlier by a warm note the civil rights leader had sent him after he had won a business award. "Your contribution as a purveyor of our culture is as important to the Freedom Movement as your creation of a sound financial institution for the employment of our people," King had written. "May God continue to empower you with wisdom and energy for this service." Words to make Gordy proud, but when it came to money and authority, there was still some haggling to be done.

"I became concerned when you called on Wednesday to raise some questions about the production of the album and about the royalty rates," Gordy wrote to King's SCLC aide, Wyatt Tee Walker, during the middle of the negotiations. "I can appreciate your concern about the quality of the album and I assure you that we share this concern. We had promised Reverend King forty cents on each album sold and an advance on 1,000 albums when they are released. If you investigate I am sure you will find this is a more than equitable arrangement. We are a growing record company and in the years since our founding we have built a reputation for integrity and a high quality of products. At the present time, we have single records and albums that are among the top-selling in the country."

All to get around to the point that Gordy was not going to budge on the royalty rates. "If we expected a series of conferences on the rates, we would have started at a much lower rate and allowed room to bargain," he argued, revealing his normal negotiating practice. "We gave you a straightforward, honest deal, considering all of the cost factors involved in producing the album. The starting rate of forty cents per album is the best rate we can give you and hope to realize a profit. Although we were motivated by messianic desires to do the album, as a business option we could not become involved in manufacturing an item of quality without expecting a profit." That "messianic desire" was one of three considerations that inspired Gordy to produce the record, he acknowledged. "First, we felt that by releasing the album through our domestic and overseas distribution centers, we could make an additional contribution (we made a $500 donation at Cobo Hall) to the cause of human decency and build both Reverend King and the organization internationally; secondly, we wanted your album to be the first in a series of albums that our company will release on the freedom struggle; and finally, because we are an aggressive young company, we like to be the first with the best for commercial purposes."

The contract was finally signed on August 5, with no change in the royalty rate. A few weeks later Gordy traveled to Atlanta to present the first copy of the album to King at a benefit concert staged in support of the March on Washington. He announced there that the record would be released on August 28, the day of the march, and was to be the first in what he called a Freedom series. "Realizing that in years to come, the Negro revolt of 1963 will take its place historically with the American Revolution and the Hungarian uprising we have elected to record the statements of the movement's leaders," Gordy said. "We are delighted that Reverend King's Detroit speech is to be the first in the series." Words and music from the big event in Washington might come next.

Detroit was already deeply involved in the March on Washington, with Motown playing its supporting musical role. Gordy was not an overtly political creature. He did not march or speak or lend his reputation to the movement in the same way that Harry Belafonte, Ossie Davis and Ruby Dee, Dick Gregory, and other black entertainers did. As his letter to Wyatt Tee Walker made clear, he was not about to let anything override his business interests. Still, his contribution can be too casually dismissed. Historian Suzanne Smith makes the insightful point in *Dancing in the Street* that Gordy came closer to fulfilling the black nationalist ideal of self-sufficiency than many other blacks in the music industry who nonetheless are more often associated with movement authenticity. In his own orbit, Gordy did what he could do best: spread the word through recordings and encourage his artists to take part. Little Stevie Wonder, whose "Fingertips (Part 2)" had moved up to No. 1 on the national charts, was plucked from Gordy's stable of singers to perform at an all-star fund-raising show in New York five days before the march. On the bill with him were Paul Newman and Joanne Woodward, Billy Eckstine, Tony Bennett, Ahmad Jamal, Carmen McRae, and Quincy Jones and his orchestra. Stevie was only twelve then, but his readiness to assist the March on Washington started a bond with Martin Luther King that would culminate exactly twenty years later with his prominent role in making King's birthday a national holiday.

Proceeds from the New York event were to help transport people to Washington for the march. Detroit had its own sponsors, including the NAACP (in on this one from the beginning), the Detroit Council of Churches, the Detroit branch of the Congress on Racial Equality, the UAW, and the Trade Union Leadership Council. Reverend Hood and his Plymouth Congregational Church, who marched a hundred strong down Woodward, were assisting with the bus reservations. The UAW and TULC expected at least two thousand autoworkers to make the trip, along with another thousand or more from Detroit churches and civil rights organizations. Most would ride on a fleet of chartered buses or an overnight train that left Detroit at seven on the night of August 27 and arrived at Union Station in Washington a few hours before the event started.

Reuther and the UAW played a more central role in the March on Washington than they had in the Walk to Freedom. At the Detroit event, even though Reuther walked in the front row with King and delivered a speech at Cobo Hall, he was only tangentially involved in the organizing and was not made to feel welcome by Reverend Cleage and the black militant wing of the DCHR. Like many politicians, his status on the national stage was perhaps greater than among the locals. He and his union were also important to King's nonviolent coalition, both in bringing white support and in funneling money and resources to the cause.

In Detroit it took an after-hours drinking session at the TULC bar to persuade Franklin that Reuther deserved a place in the program, but for the Washington march he and the UAW were there from the start. His mission was much the same in both cases: to broaden the coalition and try to ensure that the march remained peaceful and did not alienate mainstream whites or members of Congress who might support the pending legislation. One key decision that Reuther influenced, working through Jack Conway, his longtime aide, was to move the rally from the Capitol to the Lincoln Memorial, a setting that at once was farther removed from the lawmakers and provided a less threatening and more inclusive historical resonance. A key factor in persuading leaders of the march to agree to the move was that Reuther (using funds from the AFL-CIO's Industrial Unions Department, which he headed) agreed to pay the nearly $19,000 it cost for a sound system that could be heard over the vast expanse of the reflecting pool below the Lincoln Memorial steps. Here was another example of how Detroit served as the movement's bank during that crucial summer.

Reuther had wanted the entire AFL-CIO to endorse the march, but George Meany opposed the idea and led a resounding vote against it at an executive council meeting held on August 12. The most Meany would do was issue a release saying the union supported civil rights legislation and that individual unions could act on their own if they wanted to participate. No love lost between Reuther and Meany, ever, and here again was cause for their rupture to go public. Meany's endorsement, Reuther said, "was so weak that they will have to give it a blood transfusion to keep it alive long enough to mimeograph it." Several large unions, including the International Ladies Garment Workers Union, did participate, but none more than the UAW, whose leadership virtually moved en masse from Solidarity House in Detroit to a honeycomb of hotel rooms in downtown Washington to work with the coalition of march organizers.

Earlier that year, in April, Reuther had sent a straight wire to President Kennedy urging him to withdraw all federal funding from Mississippi on the grounds that the "constitutional guarantees and rights of so many citizens are being openly and flagrantly violated" by the state's policies of segregation. In July, when he testified before the House Judiciary Committee on the civil rights bill, he spoke out against any form of compromise, saying, "If you compromise one principle in this bill, if you weaken it one scintilla, you will have failed a nation urgently looking to you for leadership." Those were two of several instances where Reuther went farther in his aggressiveness than the White House was willing to go. But his philosophy of social change relied on the use of government power for the public good, and he was generally careful not to stray too far from the Kennedys. In the final hours before the Washington rally, he essentially served as their agent in tamping down the rhetoric of one key speaker, John Lewis, president of the Student Nonviolent Coordinating Committee. A draft of Lewis's speech found its way to Bobby Kennedy's Justice Department and Reuther's UAW staff the night before the event and set off alarms in both places. In the draft of his speech, Lewis disparaged Washington as a place of "cheap political leaders who build their careers on immoral compromises," dismissed the civil rights legislation as too little too late, and declared, "If any radical social, political, and economic changes are to take place in our society, the people, the masses, must bring them about." To Reuther, as he explained later to his UAW leadership, it sounded as though the SNCC chairman was "calling for open revolution."

The rhetoric was unacceptable to mainstream white religious leaders who had been brought into the coalition. When Patrick Cardinal O'Boyle, the archbishop of Washington, saw a copy of Lewis's draft, he said he would not perform the invocation. Reuther forced the issue at a meeting with King and other march leaders on the morning of the march, saying, as he later recalled, "If John Lewis feels strongly that he wants to make this speech, he can go someplace else and make it, but he has no right to make it here because if he tries to make it he destroys the integrity of our coalition. . . . This is just immoral and he has no right to do it and I demand a vote right now because I have got to call the archbishop." To say that Lewis capitulated would be an overstatement. His speech remained strong and scathing of the establishment, but it was softened just enough that O'Boyle relented, and in the end the day was remembered not for any friction but for King's dream, the enriched version of what he had said in Detroit.

Reuther also spoke that afternoon, immediately following Lewis. "I am for civil rights as a matter of human decency, as a matter of common morality, but I am also for civil rights because I believe that freedom is an indivisible value, that no one can be free unto himself," he said. "And when Bull Connor, with his police dogs and fire hoses, destroys freedom in Birmingham, he destroys my freedom in Detroit. . . . Let us understand that we cannot defend freedom in Berlin as long as we deny freedom in Birmingham. This rally is not the end, it is the beginning. It is the beginning of a great moral crusade . . . to finish the unfinished work of democracy." Nelson Lichtenstein, Reuther's biographer, later described it as "a good speech" but also noted that it might have marked "the end of something." In Lichtenstein's analysis, "two decades of such talk had long since devalued Reuther's brand of social democratic rhetoric. Indeed, the summer of 1963 may well be taken as the moment when the discourse of American liberalism shifted decisively out of the New Deal–Fair Deal–laborite orbit and into a world in which the racial divide colored all politics."

At the end of a long day of festivities that began with loudspeakers on the Mall playing Little Stevie's "Fingertips (Part 2)" and ended with King's "dream" oration, dusk settled softly over hallowed ground and more than a quarter million people trudged back to buses and trains and cars that would carry them home to New York, Philadelphia, Pittsburgh, Chicago, Atlanta, and Detroit. King and Reuther and the other leaders of the march were invited to the White House to meet again with JFK. The last time they had all been there, on the day before the Walk to Freedom in Detroit, the president had expressed his concern that a demonstration in Washington might backfire and hinder civil rights legislation. Now the march had succeeded without serious incident, and King had electrified the nation with his speech, overwhelming all else that was said that day, and here in the Oval Office he not so subtly tried to redirect the spotlight by asking the president if he had heard Walter Reuther. "Oh, I've heard him plenty of times," Kennedy said.

It did not take Berry Gordy long to realize that his first recording of King had been rendered irrelevant and essentially unsellable on the first day it was to go on sale, overtaken by the speech in Washington. Who cared about a dream in Detroit that no one outside that city even knew about when there was now a stronger version becoming the talk of the nation?

Perhaps the *Washington Post* had utterly missed the moment in its main story, but King's words reverberated in a way that few had before, and within a week his speech took on a permanent title, "I Have a Dream." If the Detroit dream was suddenly obsolete, the sequel from Washington was certainly worth a recording, though this time the difficulties went beyond financial bickering over royalties. Motown and two other recording companies who pressed recordings of King's speech, 20th Century-Fox and Mister Maestro, ended up being sued by King and the United Civil Rights Leadership group that organized the march for infringement of copyright. "If these infringing records are allowed to remain on the market, they will severely damage the ability of the Council for Civil Rights Leadership to obtain funds derived from the proceeds of the marketing of recordings of the plaintiff's speech, I HAVE A DREAM," they argued in court papers.

King himself eventually provided an affidavit in the case, offering some facts that illuminated how he differentiated this speech from what he said in Detroit. His lawyers were arguing that the fact that the Detroit speech was not copyrighted did not taint his rights to the second speech, and that Gordy in hindsight was taking advantage of his immortal phrase. "On June 23, 1963, following a peaceful willing assemblage of thousands of people through the streets of downtown Detroit, Michigan, I delivered a speech in an auditorium called Cobo Hall to the participants in said peaceful walk," his affidavit said. "The speech which I gave in Detroit as hereinabove described was recorded with my consent by Berry Gordy Records, a division of Motown Record Corporation, 2648 West Grand Boulevard.... During the course of said speech as recorded by said Berry Gordy Records, I said the phrase or words 'I have a dream'.... My speech in Detroit was not entitled by me 'I Have a Dream.' The use of said words as the title for the excerpt from my Detroit speech was done by Berry Gordy Records... after said Berry Gordy Records saw the widespread public reception accorded said words when used in the text of my address to the MARCH ON WASHINGTON."

While the use of the "dream" phrase and other wording was similar in the two speeches, King argued in his affidavit, the Washington speech "in its complete text was a completely distinct and different address from my address in Cobo Hall in Detroit. . . . While many of the words and phrases in the latter part of my August 28th Washington [address] were similar to these in the latter part of my Detroit speech, there are many words in the latter part of my Washington speech which are not identical to those in my Detroit speech. My consent to the recording, distribution and the sale of any excerpt from my Detroit, Michigan, speech was and is not regarded by me as a sound recording of the text of the speech . . . delivered by me on August 28."

Gordy sent a telegram to King after the suit was filed stating that he had been operating under the impression that King's lawyer, Clarence Jones, had said they could go ahead with producing the album, but "if this is not true we will remove our album from the market immediately. The removal of this album will represent a financial loss to us but we are prepared to do this as our contribution to the cause of unity among civil rights organizations." Instead a deal was worked out and Motown was able to produce the record, with a better royalty arrangement for King than he and his organization had for the now all but forgotten Detroit recording.

Among the few thousand Detroiters who participated in the March on Washington were two members of the City Council, Mel Ravitz and William T. Patrick Jr. The two local politicians, one white, one black, stood together on the Lincoln Memorial steps after the event, hand in hand, and sang freedom songs, then returned to Detroit with an even deeper commitment to push open-housing legislation they had cosponsored that summer. Patrick was the lone black member of the council. Ravitz, with a sociology doctorate from Wayne State, had spent his academic and political careers studying the dynamics of a city and ways to improve the lives of its residents. The troubles of Detroit, past, present, and future, were his life's calling; he saw not only what was happening but what was to come. His expertise was in neighborhoods, their pathology and means of restoration. In the midfifties he had worked for Detroit's planning commission attempting to turn around an east side neighborhood along Mack Avenue.

Ravitz, known on the council as Mr. Egghead, had the look of a professor with his horn-rim glasses and pipe. He was at once passionate and clear-headed. His sympathies were with the poor and forgotten citizens of Detroit, but he saw the complexities and interconnections of problems that could not be solved with the magic wand of good intentions. He wrote a paper for the *Alpha Kappa Deltan*, the magazine of the Sociology Honor Society, in 1958 that foretold the problematic effects of the urban renewal going on in Detroit. Blacks, he predicted, would "slip into nearby middle aged neighborhoods. From these neighborhoods many whites have been and are continuing to depart. They are leaving behind many substantial, well-cared for houses." The problem came with the economic disadvantages of the new residents: "Some Negroes as well as whites who cannot afford them are buying them anyway and then quickly forfeiting their land contracts. . . . Sometimes several families buy a home originally built for one family and overcrowd it with two, three, or four families to handle the down payment and monthly installments. Such overcrowding not only accelerates the out movement of the middle class whites that have lived there, it also discourages Negro middle class residents from remaining permanently. (Obviously whites can leave more easily than Negroes penned in.) This kind of housing and economic pressure helps transform these middle aged neighborhoods into the slums of the next ten years."

When he was elected to the council in 1961, Ravitz sought ways to deal with this urban dilemma. He held landlords partially responsible for the problems in the slum areas and proposed that if they would not adequately maintain their properties, the city should confiscate the rents they collected and use the money to make necessary improvements. In the long run, the only reasonable way to solve the larger problem of white flight and the flow of money and a tax base away from the city, he felt, was to develop a metropolitan government and to get the major industries, especially the Big Three automakers, to feel a larger responsibility to Detroit and its social well-being. The landlord bill never passed, the metropolitan government concept never reached fruition, and the Big Three's commitment to the city was uneven and in any case overwhelmed by something else: the decades-long withdrawal of auto factories and jobs to other cities and states and eventually countries.

Patrick, with a law degree from the University of Michigan, had been a pioneer in Detroit politics, the first African American to serve on the council in the twentieth century. Since his election in 1957, he had worked in tandem with Ravitz on issues of economics and race. During the recession that hit Detroit in the late fifties, he helped establish a committee designed to keep working-class Detroiters from losing their homes to repossession. He also pushed for the integration of the police force, supported Commissioner Edwards in his attempts to reform the department, and joined with Mayor Cavanagh in implementing a commuter tax to ease the city's financial difficulties.

To Ravitz and Patrick, their open-housing legislation was more than a matter of urban policy; it was part of the inexorable movement for equality and civil rights. Their proposed ordinance was a tougher local version of what Romney and his two Democratic predecessors had tried to accomplish on the state level. Any person who discriminated in the sale, lease, or rental of housing because of race, color, creed, national origin, or ancestry would be in violation and subject to thirty days in jail or a $100 fine enforced in Traffic and Ordinance Court. The guts of the bill, and by far its most controversial aspect, was that it outlawed discrimination by an individual homeowner, meaning someone wishing to sell a house or rent an apartment could not pick and choose who to sell or rent to on the basis of race. The only exemption would be for a single room in a private dwelling.

Houses divided. No issue more clearly revealed the racial fissures in Detroit. On one side were white homeowner groups who said they were fighting on behalf of individual rights and the sanctity and safety of their neighborhoods. On the other side were African American churches and social groups, white and black religious leaders, and the Detroit Commission on Community Relations, which had been established twenty years earlier, after the 1943 race riots, to try to bridge the racial divide in the city. In August, a few weeks before the March on Washington, the commission had endorsed the Patrick-Ravitz bill by a six-to-one vote, following months and years of compiling incidents of racial discrimination in housing. A recent case involved the travails of Raymond Roberson, who had been trying without success to rent an apartment in the area near Gratiot and Seven Mile Road.

Roberson was black and blind, a piano tuner who worked for Grinnell Brothers out of their branch on Kelly Road. He told the commission that when he arrived in Detroit late in 1962 he contacted forty or so real estate brokers and was told that they would not or could not rent an apartment to blacks. One broker suggested that he look at a flat near Gratiot and Faircrest, which he did on a Sunday, but by the next day he was told that someone else had already put down a deposit. An investigator from the Urban League followed up and learned that when neighbors found out that a black man was looking at the apartment they put pressure on the owner and broker not to rent it to him. In his next effort, after being read advertisements in the newspaper, he started making inquiries over the telephone, describing himself as a blind piano tuner. Only one landlord agreed to meet with him, but when he arrived with his driver and got out of the car, the landlady claimed that she was sick and refused to talk to him, and when he called back the next day she said the apartment was no longer available. One case out of the multitudes—Roberson never found an apartment in the area near where he worked, according to commission documents.

Opponents of the Patrick-Ravitz bill mobilized against it not only by pushing for its defeat but by presenting an alternative bill that would allow them to keep discriminating in the name of a property owner's "freedom from interference." Historian Thomas Sugrue, a leading expert on the dynamics of race in Detroit, noted that at that time "a growing number of white Detroiters believed that open housing advocates were part of a conspiracy that linked together government bureaucrats, civil rights organizations, and liberal religious groups, many influenced by Communism or socialism (terms used interchangeably) who sacrificed white homeowners to their experiments in social engineering for the benefit of 'pressure groups'—repudiating, in the process, property rights and democratic principles." Transcripts of two council hearings on open housing, one held that June, another in mid-September, underscored Sugrue's analysis.

Thomas Poindexter, president of the Greater Homeowners Council, claiming to represent 250,999 voters, said that the legislation was politically motivated and that any member of the council or community relations commission who was also a member of the NAACP had a conflict of interest. There was no need for the Patrick-Ravitz ordinance, he argued, because blacks were well off in Detroit and some of them could "afford better homes than I can buy." Donald Sargent of the National Civic Association said blacks and whites had different "instincts" and that whites would welcome blacks into their neighborhood if they "would observe our marriage customs." Mr. Underwood of the Northeast Council of Homeowners said that a secret government was behind the legislation and that churches that supported it should have to pay taxes. Mr. Dodge of the Wingate Homeowners Association said communists were behind it. Mr. Lutz of the Stoepel Park Civic Association called Patrick's views "slightly subversive." Mr. Christie of the Gratiot-Connors Property Owners Association said the community relations commission was "an integration commission of do-gooders and witch hunters and should be abolished." Mr. Sullivan of the Greater Belmont Civic Association talked about genetics and said open housing was another step toward a classless society. Mrs. Fulks of the Redford Civic Association called it a step toward thought-control socialistic legislation. Another opponent was Orville F. Sherwood of the Michigan Committee for the Protection of Property Rights, who had also been the administrator of the Grosse Pointe point system and a paid organizer for the John Birch Society.

On September 26 Mayor Cavanagh came out in support of the Patrick-Ravitz bill. "To my fellow citizens of Detroit: I have been asked repeatedly to state my position in respect to open occupancy. In order to make my position clear, I have decided to issue this statement: I could have remained silent on this important issue. To do so would have been politically expedient. I cannot in good conscience choose this course. I believe that discrimination is evil. It runs counter to everything that I have been taught about my religious obligations and my obligations to my fellow citizens. The open occupancy ordinance in my judgment is another step along the road to true understanding among Detroiters. Detroit is not and shall not be another Birmingham. Detroit has long been admired throughout the country for its mature race relations. The Detroit Approach substitutes words for bricks, peace for violence, tolerance for bigotry, and understanding for hate."

The next day a letter arrived in his office from W. G. Morneweck, who lived on Fielding Street in northwest Detroit. "One question all of you mayors, councilmen, lawyers, preachers, priests and from Kennedy down how near colored section do you live? When you fellows practice what you preach I will listen and not before. . . . Teach the colored to be like white folks and we will live with them. I worked about 23 years at Fords was foreman and I had colored and white. The time of race riot here two or three of the colored boys come to me and ask me what I thought of it. I told them they will never get along till colored and white are Christian."

Nearly three hundred people crammed into the council chambers to watch the proceedings when the vote was taken on Tuesday, October 8. The bill was defeated seven to two. Patrick and Ravitz were the two in favor.

In response, some disappointed local civil rights activists began spreading leaflets they hoped would reach around the globe. They were upset about the open-housing vote, but their target was not Poindexter and Sherwood and the cluster of homeowner opponents but the establishment, Mayor Cavanagh and Governor Romney and the Detroit Athletic Club big wheels who had been working on a grand scheme to sell Detroit to the world. "America does not deserve the 1968 Olympics," the brochures read. "The Olympic Games represent fair play. . . . Fair play has not become a living part of Detroit and America for all citizens."

Chapter 16

# THE SPIRIT OF DETROIT

**AVERY BRUNDAGE, PRESIDENT** of the International Olympic Committee, was coming to Detroit, and Richard Cross regretted that he would not be there to greet him. Cross, a blue-chip Detroit lawyer who had risen to the top of American Motors, replacing George Romney as chief executive officer when Romney became governor, had to be in California for a speech to western auto dealers on the day Brundage returned to the city of his birth. A few days earlier, from his law office high atop the Penobscot Building overlooking the Detroit River and his downtown domain, Cross had written a letter to the Olympic potentate expressing his hopes for the visit. He addressed Brundage with the familiarity of an old associate, but also in the ingratiating language of a lawyer trying to close a deal, just as a decade earlier he had made his reputation by negotiating the merger of Nash-Kelvinator and the Hudson Motor Car Company into American Motors.

"The days have been so full of action since we left Brazil the first of May that it truly seems only yesterday that we were having the pleasant meals we took together at the Jaragua," Cross began, recalling an Olympic junket that had taken them both to São Paulo earlier in 1963. "Believe me, Avery, the Olympic fervor is profound and at high pitch here in Detroit. After all the years of my involvement since I began to work for Detroit with Fred Matthaei personally nearly 20 years ago, I must confess that I personally have never had my heart so set on our getting the games and I hope you agree that optimism that we will do so is warranted and not misplaced. Everyone here is keenly anticipating your visit on September 10th when there will be an opportunity to show you the many changes in the city and the splendid facilities existing and in prospect."

"In prospect" was a reference to an Olympic stadium on the site of the Michigan State Fairgrounds that had not been built but had been authorized by the state legislature. In the world competition for the 1968 Summer Games, the fact that Detroit alone among the finalists did not yet have an adequate stadium was a possible point of vulnerability, one that Los Angeles had made much out of in its unsuccessful attempt to dislodge Detroit as the U.S. candidate. Cross needed Brundage to understand that the stadium was a reality, even if it did not physically exist, and to vouch for its inevitability he pointed out that Governor Romney had appointed him to the stadium commission overseeing its development. Cross thought of himself as a man of reliability and of Brundage as the epitome of Olympic purity, and the flattery flowed from there to pride in city and country: "I am looking forward to the day when I can stride into the stadium with you and up to the speaker's platform to see you initiate the 1968 Olympiad and receive the signal honors that will be awarded you as a great American in your own country in the city of your birth because of your splendid lifetime contribution in your avocation of amateur sport."

Cross was also deeply involved in Detroit civic affairs, serving on both Governor Romney's state civil rights commission and Mayor Cavanagh's community relations committee, where he supported the open-housing measures and was aware of the racial friction that issue was causing. His letter came several weeks before the Common Council defeated the Patrick-Ravitz open-occupancy bill, but there already had been intimations of trouble ahead no matter which way that vote went. But like Cavanagh in the afterglow of the Walk to Freedom, Cross insisted that Detroit was a model of civil rights, more advanced than other cities. "I also happen to be a member of the Governor's civil rights commission under the new Michigan constitution and while you and I know of many of the difficulties in Chicago, New York, Philadelphia and numerous other communities, I can say to you that we really have a fine, stable community here that is adjusting to the race problems in a very mature way," Cross asserted. Then he closed his case: "I know that everyone on the IOC will be watching you and feeling you out for some sign of approval or disapproval of venue of the games at Detroit. I am sure you will give this approval in view of my assurances as I know that in the past you have entertained some doubts under the existing circumstances as to the ability of Detroit and other American cities to come through in the proper manner." While he had no choice but to be in California that day, Cross said, Brundage could rest assured that "some of our top citizens will be greeting you on the 10th" in Detroit.

Brundage arrived at 10:37 on American Airlines flight 416 from Chicago. Waiting for him were Fred Matthaei Sr., the godfather of Detroit Olympic bids, and Douglas Roby, the Detroiter who held a top spot in the Olympics hierarchy as vice president of the U.S. Olympic Committee and was one of three American voting members on the IOC. The other two U.S. members were Brundage and John Jewett Garland of Los Angeles, a wealthy real estate magnate who had wanted L.A. to get the nomination. It was not without reason that Detroiters wondered whether Garland, the husband of an heir to the *Los Angeles Times* and the son of the man who brought the 1932 Olympics to L.A., would vote for them in the final round. In letters and conversations, he frequently expressed doubts about Detroit's qualifications and chances. In an addendum to a recent note to Brundage, Garland had gossiped sarcastically about something he had heard from an old Detroit car guy while hanging out at the Bohemian Grove, the exclusive California campground retreat of the rich and famous in Northern California. "P.S. While at the Grove I heard K. T. Keller [former chairman of Chrysler] state that he thought the odds were 3 to 1 against Detroit winning the Games of 1968. I was tempted to ask him if he was quoting the odds in the 'book' Roby was making last fall—but refrained." If Garland was no friend of Detroit, the support of Brundage would be even more essential.

First stop on the Detroit tour was Cobo Hall, the modern convention center, where Brundage was ensconced in the back of an electric golf cart and tooted around the vast riverfront facility that would serve as the hub of Olympic activities. Then he was taken to the Detroit Athletic Club for a luncheon with Mayor Cavanagh and Governor Romney and members of the Detroit Olympic Committee. Along with Roby and the Matthaeis, Jr. and Sr., the elite group included Benson and William Clay Ford, younger brothers of HF2; Walker Cisler, chairman of Detroit Edison; Martin S. Hayden, editor of the *Detroit News*; Jack Tompkins, vice president of American Airlines; Thomas B. Adams, president of Campbell-Ewald, the advertising agency for General Motors; the architect Louis Rossetti; and Alfred Glancy Jr., a real estate mogul who brought the Pontchartrain Hotel back to Detroit, had once been part owner of the Empire State Building in Manhattan, and was most proud of his world-class collection of miniature train sets that he brought out for parties at his mansion in Grosse Pointe Shores. Cavanagh opened the luncheon with greetings, praising Brundage as "a builder and a doer" and making a special point of introducing two black officials at the luncheon: Councilman Patrick and Alfred Pelham, the city controller. After lunch Cavanagh led Brundage on a helicopter tour of the city to get a bird's-eye view of the various Olympic sites.

They hovered over Olympia Stadium, the old red barn, where boxing, wrestling, and basketball would be staged. Not a bad name for the site, though the Olympia, home to the Detroit Red Wings, had been around since 1927. Down to the left, near Wayne State University, was the future site of the Olympic Village. Below was the University of Detroit field house, another venue for indoor events, and over there the State Fairground race track, where the 100,000-seat Olympic stadium would rise. Back around toward Lake St. Clair and the Grosse Pointe Yacht Club, site of the sailing; Belle Isle and the Detroit Yacht Club and the calm waters that would serve for rowing; the Brodhead Armory on East Jefferson that was to be home to fencing and weight lifting; and on back to the roof of Cobo Hall. Brundage had to catch a 5:15 flight back to Chicago, and after a quick stop at Detroit Olympic Committee headquarters he rode with the Matthaeis, Roby, and Tompkins from downtown back to the airport.

Tompkins later sent an after-action report to Mayor Cavanagh detailing what he had heard during that ride and while hosting Brundage in the American Airlines Admirals Club lounge as they waited for the flight: "I have been working with Avery over twenty years in the Olympic effort and have never seen him as cordial, friendly and impressed with Detroit's ability to handle the Olympics. He was extremely impressed with the new Spirit of Detroit, the new buildings and changes that are taking place and of course was particularly impressed with Cobo Hall." Tompkins noted that Brundage, usually circumspect, even helped with Detroit's strategy: "He pointed out the advantages that he felt we had and how we might exploit them in our presentation, as well as the disadvantages the U.S. has, mostly political, and suggested ways we might counteract these. To sum up, it was obvious that his visit here was extremely worthwhile and that we were successful in selling him on our sincerity and ability to get the job done. Several times he mentioned how much he appreciated the time you were able to spend with him at the Detroit Athletic Club and in the helicopter. He emphasized that he was very impressed with your enthusiasm, knowledge of the Olympic needs and your desire for the games." Tompkins closed by saying that he and his wife were about to leave on an extensive lobbying tour visiting IOC members in Tokyo, Hong Kong, Bangkok, Delhi, Karachi, Teheran, Beirut, Istanbul, Rome, and Paris, before finally reaching the German resort town of Baden-Baden, where the IOC would make its decision.

The Brundage visit sparked a renewed civic optimism. An oversized hardback book boosting Detroit had been sent out to all members of the IOC and various politicians around the world, including all of Romney's gubernatorial colleagues, and rave reviews were coming back. With a color photograph of the *Spirit of Detroit* sculpture on the cover, the book showed the city at its world-class best: huge crowds goggling at new cars at the 1962 Detroit Auto Show at Cobo Hall; skyscrapers towering over the Detroit River, called "the world's busiest waterway"; molten steel glowing in the Rouge plant; a roll call of world-famous Detroiters, including Henry Ford and Walter Reuther, Chrysler and Dodge, Yamasaki and Saarinen; a ball game at Tiger Stadium; JFK addressing a rally outside the Book Cadillac; couples dining at Mayor Cavanagh's favorite haunt, the London Chop House; models and mannequins on display at the J. L. Hudson Company, the world's tallest department store; students taking art lessons on the floor of the Detroit Institute of Arts; downtown glowing at night with the iconic red beacon defining the forty-seven-story Penobscot Building; and the Detroit Olympic Committee meeting in the City-County Building. Even Detroit's American antagonists were impressed. "If you are as good at being governor as your booklet is in depicting Detroit, you are certainly great," wrote Edmund G. Brown, governor of California. "That is the best book I have ever seen, and you and your people are entitled to a great deal of credit for it."

After a chance airport lounge encounter Romney had with Con Donovan Jr., vice president of a publishing company that owned *Sport* magazine, Donovan visited with Tom Adams, the president of Detroit's Campbell-Ewald advertising agency and a key member of the city's Olympic committee, and afterward *Sport* hit the newsstands with a strong editorial on why such a great sports town deserved the Olympics: "Year in and year out, through good times and not such good times, sports fans turn out in large, enthusiastic numbers to support the Tiger baseball team, the Lion football team, their Red Wing hockey team. . . . People in Detroit and surrounding communities love their sports." The Sunday edition of the *Detroit News* on September 15 ran a special section about "Olympic City," making the case for how and why Detroit would be selected. The next day Cavanagh was at the White House where, at four in the afternoon, President Kennedy signed Joint Resolution 72, expressing Congress's full support for Detroit. Brundage could not attend but sent along a positive note to Pierre Salinger, the president's press secretary: "I have just returned from Detroit, where I met Mayor Cavanagh, Governor Romney and many of the leading citizens of that city who are behind the invitation. . . . We are impressed by the interest of President Kennedy and the administration in the Olympic Movement and I shall see that is reported to the Comité International Olympique at its meeting in Baden-Baden next month." (French was the official language of the IOC, headquartered in Lausanne, Switzerland, and it was common for Brundage, who enjoyed playing the role of globetrotting cosmopolite, to refer to his organization by its French name.)

Of more practical importance to Cavanagh than the congressional resolution of support were two other actions in Washington during that visit. First, Attorney General Robert Kennedy dispatched a letter to IOC headquarters assuring that athletes from every Olympic nation—including some, like East Germany, that were not recognized by the United States—would be allowed entry to compete at the Games. Second, President Kennedy himself took time from his schedule to record a brief film segment the Detroit delegation would include in its Baden-Baden presentation. JFK performed his role flawlessly, though he certainly had other things on his mind. The day before, a bomb planted by members of the United Klans of America exploded under the steps of the 16th Street Baptist Church in Birmingham, a church that had served as a rallying station during the civil rights campaign there the previous spring. The explosion killed four young girls in a group of children who were walking to the basement for a youth sermon. One of the girls, eleven-year-old Denise McNair, was the niece of Detroit resident Matthew Pippins and his wife, who had now left their east side home on St. Aubin and were on their way to Birmingham for the funeral.

Detroit had tried to land the Olympics five times before, but never with the fervor of this effort. Did the Motor City have a legitimate chance, or were its leaders fooling themselves? The breadth of the lobbying campaign reflected their belief that their time was coming at last. Entertaining Brundage in Detroit, Tompkins lobbying around the globe, researchers compiling a dossier on every voting member of the IOC, local television stations staging telethons to raise money to finance the delegation's presentation in Baden-Baden—nothing was left to chance. They even staged a torch relay, an event normally held from the previous Olympic city to the next. This time the torch would be carried from Los Angeles to Detroit, from 1932 to prospective 1968, called the longest relay run in history, some 2,521 miles. With Philip A. Hart, a U.S. senator from Michigan and member of the Detroit Olympic Committee, on hand, the relay began from the steps of Los

Angeles City Hall at eleven on the morning of September 27 when Mayor Sam Yorty handed the two-pound butane-fueled torch to Jim Beatty, world record holder in the two-mile run. The route out of L.A. followed old Route 66 through California, Arizona, New Mexico, Texas, Oklahoma, Missouri, and Illinois up to Chicago, then Route 12 and I-94 through Indiana and Michigan to Detroit, with hundreds of high school and college runners carrying the torch, along with a few wheezing journalists and politicians. The relay went day and night for thirteen days, accompanied by a caravan of six station wagons donated by Ford.

On October 11, the morning the relay reached Detroit, Olympic supporters gathered for a rally outside City Hall in front of the *Spirit of Detroit*, the twenty-six-foot bronze sculpture of a figure sitting cross-legged with arms outstretched receiving emanations from above. Many of the runners from the final day of the race were there. Mayor Cavanagh received the torch from the last runner, two weeks after the race had begun, surrounded by local politicians and members of the Detroit Olympic Committee. "Here before the Spirit of Detroit we witness the true spirit of the Olympic Games and the outstanding cooperation that has always been the hallmark of the American people," Cavanagh said. "More than 300 people, young and old, have carried this torch, which symbolizes the unity of ideals and aspirations of all this nation's people over a long and difficult 2,600 mile path to victory. . . . These Olympic torch bearers have done more than bring the hope and convictions of the nation to this city. They have presented those of us who will go to Baden-Baden with an object lesson and a challenge."

As it happened, there was quite another challenge confronting Cavanagh and his Olympic tribe that morning. About fifty civil rights protesters, equal numbers black and white, attended the rally and booed and jeered and issued catcalls throughout the event. The protesters were expressing their displeasure at the city for the defeat three days earlier of the Patrick-Ravitz open-housing bill. All nine members of the council attended the rally, and the seven who voted against the measure were greeted with boos when their names were announced. So too was Cavanagh, even though he had come out in favor of the bill. Some jeers were heard during the playing of the National Anthem. When the rally was over, the protesters marched in front of City Hall carrying signs conveying the message that a city that denied equal rights did not deserve the Olympics. Cavanagh was outraged by what he considered the rudeness of the protesters in general and their behavior during "The Star-Spangled Banner" in particular. "The booing and catcalling and other disgusting antics during a playing of our National Anthem call for a public apology," he said. "They owe it to the decent citizens of our city. Today's small but frantic group by no means represents the thinking or attitudes of the citizens they presume to represent. The runners of all races and creeds lived, ate, ran, and suffered hardships together. . . . They must have been shocked, as I was, to find at the end of their great endeavor such reprehensible conduct."

Arthur Johnson, executive director of the Detroit chapter of the NAACP, said his organization did not sponsor the protest, although several members participated. "I don't know of any good citizen who would approve booing during the singing of the National Anthem," Johnson said. One of the protesters, David Feinberg, later wrote a letter to Cavanagh explaining his motivations.

Feinberg said he enlisted in the army in 1960 while attending Wayne State and served in the military three years. "One of the many facets of Communism I hate is the way the bosses expect that by giving material benefits to the people under their control the people will not think so much about freedom and equality," he wrote. "Unfortunately, I feel that the people of Detroit have become so excited about the honor and the millions of dollars Detroit would receive from having the Olympics that they have forgotten there are large segments of our population that do not enjoy full equality of opportunity in jobs, education, or housing. It was in this spirit that I demonstrated Friday morning against the bringing of the Olympics to Detroit, even though it would probably be a tremendous economic boost to our city. For how much money are we to accept in order to forget about the Negro and white Americans who died fighting racists in World War II? I love America. I love the principles on which our country was founded. . . . When I returned home Friday afternoon I learned that the Star

Spangled Banner had been drowned out by booing and catcalls. I myself heard no announcement that our National Anthem would be played. I therefore do not actually know whether or not I was booing during its playing. Let me make this quite clear: Had I known that our National Anthem was being played, I would have stood at attention and sang the words."

In an editorial spread across the top of its editorial page, the *Michigan Chronicle* deplored the behavior of the protesters. "Great Negro leaders of the past, from Frederick Douglass to Dr. Martin Luther King, Jr., have been militant yet maintained their honor and dignity in fighting for the honor and dignity of a completely free Negro. However, this fight is reduced to a lower level when our methods become dishonorable and undignified. Because the bigots, the racists, the ignorant and poor whites, the political demagogues resort to such odious, unprincipled behavior, this is no excuse for Negroes to crawl around in the mud with these fools."

Most of the official Detroit party, minus Governor Romney and a few others who would arrive later, left Detroit for Baden-Baden on the Saturday afternoon of October 12, the day after the torch rally. Fred Matthaei Jr. and a vanguard of technicians were already in Germany with three and a half tons of equipment and display materials getting ready for Detroit's presentation to the IOC. Mayor Cavanagh and his wife led the main delegation. At dawn over the Atlantic, they were greeted with news from the Pan Am cockpit that Frankfurt was fogged in and they had been diverted to London. After finding breakfast at the airport, they took off on the same plane but were told that Frankfurt was still closed in and they were flying toward Stuttgart first to get a better look at the weather.

More bad news came during the flight, according to Alfred Glancy, the onetime Empire State Building owner, who kept a journal during the trip: "Jerry Cavanagh mentioned that Dave Diles of WKYZ had announced on the air in Detroit by tape from Paris, where he was en route to Baden-Baden, that one of the Russian delegates had told Diles that Russia was going to vote for Lyon and gave a number of reasons." Lyon, France, was one of the other world finalists, along with Buenos Aires and Mexico City. Cavanagh sought advice on this new problem from Walker Cisler, the Detroit Edison chairman who had been chief of public utilities for the Supreme Allied Expeditionary Force during World War II and had several Soviet contacts. Cavanagh said he would call the White House on Monday to ask for some direct help with the Soviets, and Cisler offered to work his sources as well. But the Soviets were not the only problem, Garland noted. "We also got a report that Doug Roby made the statement that there would only be two of the three American votes cast for Detroit. Garland of Los Angeles will not vote for Detroit. Although they were invited to participate at the send-off of the runners carrying the torch from Los Angeles to Detroit, no one from the L.A. Olympic committee turned up and none of the L.A. Papers carried a line about the run." All of this led Glancy to confess to his journal, "I am getting more pessimistic about our chances."

With the weather at Stuttgart breaking clear, the plane landed there and the delegation arranged to hire cars for the sixty-five-mile journey to Baden-Baden. Glancy rode in a Mercedes with Cisler and Martin Hayden, the *News* editor, who recalled that Stuttgart had been virtually flattened from Allied blockbuster bombs by the end of the war. "The drive to Baden-Baden was pretty . . . Baden-Baden being at the northwest corner of the Black Forest, which covers about 150 miles in this part of Germany running to the Swiss border. Our car, a Mercedes with a diesel engine, being driven by a thwarted race car driver. We did get there safely, although on arrival the driver had no idea where the Waldhotel Der Selighof was. After some delay we found it to be on the outskirts of town, up the side of a mountain, and adjacent to a fine golf course."

Glancy ended up sharing a suite with Hayden that had two bedrooms but only one bath in the smaller bedroom, which he took. "Felt a lot better after the tub—although I was tempted to drop off as it was then 24 actual hours [since leaving Detroit]." Instead he and Hayden took a cab to town, first stopping at the Kurhaus, where the IOC meetings would take place. ("Martin told the cab driver whorehouse, which for a Midwestern German accent was bad enough . . . but made me take another quick look at my friend.") Then they headed off to the hotel where the Soviets were staying because Hayden wanted to interview them; they left when they could not find an interpreter, and went to dinner with Jack Tompkins and his wife, Ginny. The dinner table conversation, mostly about how the Russians might vote, irritated the newsman, so he huffed off to bed, but Glancy stayed up with the Tompkinses, watching them play roulette at the Kurhaus, which doubled as a gambling casino. Ginny, he said, "left a modest amount as her contribution to the prosperity of Baden-Baden."

The next day was all rumors and confusion. Glancy and Hayden went back to the Kurhaus and ran into Fred Matthaei Jr., who expressed displeasure at what he saw as the changing rules of the lobbying game. At first, Matthaei said, all four cities had agreed that they would hold one joint party for the IOC before the vote. "Today we learn that Buenos Aires is giving a cocktail party at noon tomorrow for the IOC and Lyon a big one on Wednesday for everyone but Detroit at noon. Lyon is shipping in its top chef to prepare French cuisine finger food, shipping in 500 bottles of top vintage wines (this may boomerang on them from the Germans who are already raising their eyebrows that 'their food isn't good enough for the G.D. French'). The arrangement committee here set up the times for these parties, there was no time set aside for Detroit in case it wanted to give a party. I have suggested we have a meeting at 6:30 tonight of our entire Delegation to go over these and other points. Jerry Cavanagh just called for the meeting."

The Detroit Olympic Committee staff had taken on the mission of gathering intelligence on the IOC members who came to Baden-Baden. They studied the group by geography and politics. Europe had thirty-four members, of which twenty-seven were characterized as FW (Free World) and seven IC (Iron Curtain). There were also nine from Asia, five from Africa, eight from North and Central America, and three from Australia and New Zealand. Lobbying letters had been prepared for each of them in languages ranging from Icelandic to Hindustani. Their likes and dislikes were reported. (France's Count de Beaumont, the Detroit intelligence gatherers noted, had been a journalist all his life, served as administrator of the Bank of Indo-China, was a member of the Jockey Club, the Explorers Club, and a club called Gentlemen Writers.) Some IOC members appeared susceptible to the high life—accepting gifts, drinks, and women. But the Detroit delegation had been instructed to play it straight. In a letter to Cavanagh a few weeks before they left, Fred Matthaei Sr. had praised the mayor for stating at a strategy meeting that Detroit should be cautious and prudent in its dealings in Baden-Baden. "It would be improper to present hula dances to members of the IOC," Matthaei joked, then added, "It is an extremely critical path we are treading, and we must look at ourselves through their eyes rather than our own. Therefore, I am glad that you made a point of mentioning . . . that our behavior must be above criticism. One's behavior in the church is entirely different than one's behavior in a pub, and actually we will be in church during the week of our presentation. It is indeed nice to know that you will be there to guide the thinking and actions of the other members of the Committee, who in the very exuberance of their eagerness might say or do something which could cost us the Olympics."

The IOC session opened at the Kurhaus on the Wednesday evening of October 16. A little Mozart, some ballet, and the quintessential Brundage speech on the vital importance of amateurism and sportsmanship. "The thing that is not understood is that amateurism is a philosophy of life, a consecration and devotion to the actual task at hand rather than to the payment or to the reward," declared Brundage, a millionaire hotel magnate whose every need in Germany was met by the German hosts, as were his travels throughout his vast Olympic empire. "It is the same devotion that in scholars and scientists has led to the acquisition of knowledge and to the advancement of civilization. It is the same devotion that has actuated the great artists and musicians who have starved in garrets rather than commercialize their work. It is the same devotion that in the great patriotic leaders in all countries has produced all social progress. It is the same devotion that has actuated the unknown sculptors and architects who created the great buildings and cathedrals of the world without even signing their work. It is the same devotion that guided Henry Ford and Thomas Edison to their achievements in the industrial world, which they would have accomplished even if they had never won a fortune."

*Ford. Henry Ford.* The Detroit delegation perked up. Was this a subtle sign from the Olympic leader?

While others gambled in the casino after the banquet, several members of the Detroit delegation went to work in the exhibition hall. The elite group included Martin Hayden, though he was mostly taking notes for a story that appeared in the *News* the next day. By then he had worked out the kinks that had delayed his previous story. First the wire desk at the Kurhaus had held it up for several hours because he had failed to provide telephone numbers, then it was delayed in Frankfurt to determine whether he intended it to go to Detroit, Michigan, or some other Detroit. In his journal, Al Glancy had taken quiet delight in the fulminations of his roommate. But no such worries now; this dispatch made it on time. Detroit bigwigs pulling an all-nighter like fraternity boys finishing a homecoming float. "Detroit may not win the games but it has set a new world's record for the highest paid construction crew in building trades history," Hayden wrote.

> *Until dawn today auto and advertising company heads, a real estate tycoon, utility, public relations and film company executives—were climbing ladders, hanging lights and sawing wood as they raced time to assemble the exhibit supporting their city's bid. A British scribe: "Utterly unbelievable, so totally American." He saw Alfred R. Glancy, onetime half-owner of the Empire State Building . . . on his knees sawing the legs of an exhibit table. His carpenter assistant was Frank Buchanan, Michigan Bell public relations man. Halfway up a wall was Thomas B. Adams, adman, and below him steadying the ladder was Richard Cross, chair of American Motors. Also on duty were Fred Matthaei, retired American Metals Co. president, and his son Fred Jr., known in Detroit less as a furniture mover and more as American Metals vice president. In role reversal they were commanded by four technicians. The four who weeks ago first assembled the Detroit display and then babied it across*

*the ocean to Germany. Lyon used military personnel, Mexico City flew in a team of workmen. At the center of the exhibit, flanked by dramatic photos of Michigan and Detroit athletes in action, is a 12-foot long model of a redesigned Michigan State Fairgrounds with a 110,000 seat stadium. Two normally competitive Detroit architects, Louis Rossetti and Oscar Stonorov, worked together on it.*

They finished the installation at six in the morning, and hours later IOC members and the world press began wandering through the hall to examine the displays of the four finalists. Detroit delegates, including Mayor Cavanagh and Jack Tompkins, took turns manning their exhibit, but the first host was Judge Wade H. McCree, one of two African Americans in the Michigan group along with Councilman Patrick. McCree, an alumnus of Fisk University and Harvard Law School, where he graduated twelfth in his class, had been appointed to the U.S. District Court for Eastern Michigan by President Kennedy in 1961. He was a sophisticated jurist, always courteous but never bullied, who spoke Latin and Greek and was known to recite the *Aeneid* with his law clerks in chambers. Among the leading black figures in Detroit then, McCree stood apart from the political posturing and elbowing, respected by all. He supported the Olympics effort but understood the racial dynamics that took him to Baden-Baden. Cavanagh and Romney and their crew needed him.

The geopolitics of the IOC were changing, slowly but inevitably. Europe remained dominant, with its collection of Olympic barons and lords, but now voters also came from parts of the world that had been shut out for decades and might have questions about the civil rights struggle in the United States and the American commitment to equality. In addition, more athletes of color were participating than ever before. At the 1960 Olympics in Rome, a gold medal had been awarded for the first time to an athlete from sub-Saharan Africa, Abebe Bikila, the great marathoner from Ethiopia. As early as July 1, Governor Romney's legal adviser, Richard C. Van Dusen, acting at the suggestion of Ed Hodges of the Fair Employment

Practices Commission, had sent a letter to Fred Matthaei Sr. urging him to take all of this into account. "In putting together your delegation to attend the IOC meeting . . . it might be wise for you to consider Negro representation," Van Dusen wrote. "Certainly one of the serious problems that any United States city will face in the light of the current racial tensions in this country is to explain that Negro athletes will be welcomed in our country. No one can do that better on behalf of Detroit than a qualified Negro member of your delegation. I recognize this may entail financial problems [underwriting the travel expenses] but I think the idea is worthy of serious consideration."

Matthaei had written back saying that they had tried to get Ralph Bunche, the noted United Nations diplomat, who had spent his early years in Detroit, to narrate a film presentation for them, but that he had to back out because of his UN duties. But they were able to persuade Rafer Johnson, the 1960 decathlon gold medalist, to make a filmed endorsement instead. "In addition to the above, we plan to have at least one Negro in our delegation . . . and the thinking at the present time is that Judge Wade McCree will accompany the mayor." In the end, Patrick came along too, able to separate this task from his disappointment over the defeat of his open-housing bill.

Not long after he arrived in Baden-Baden, Mayor Cavanagh was told by an IOC delegate from the Middle East that he had received a mailing from Detroit undercutting the city's effort. The name on the return address was Lloyd E. Dolby, a Detroit bus driver who had taken to heart the statement by local NAACP leaders that blacks in Detroit should "demonstrate as never before" after the disappointing defeat of the open-housing bill. The envelope he sent to IOC delegates included the "Fair play has not become a living part of Detroit" leaflet, along with a cover letter that read, "This country is not capable of accepting the many colored people from all parts of the world because it has not settled the difference towards the Negro who is struggling to gain freedom. He has been deprived of these rights for over ten decades. Let it be known that on October 8, 1963 the city of Detroit Common Council shamefully defeated an open occupancy ordinance by a 7–2 vote." The message, it turned out, was drafted during a meeting of the NAACP housing committee, which met two days after the council vote and had organized a letter-writing campaign that involved about fifty supporters.

Detroit's best defense was the testimony of Patrick and McCree, who were informed of the letters and prepared to respond. "Wade and I were all over the place," Patrick said later. "We kept a ready ear for any racial overtones." Cavanagh also wrangled a resolution of support from Edward Turner and Arthur Johnson, the local NAACP leaders, who disassociated themselves from the letter-writing campaign and dispatched a telegram to Baden-Baden stating, "Whereas our city fathers and business leaders are in West Germany to present our case, and whereas we recognize the immense benefits to our city if their efforts are successful, now therefore be it resolved that the Detroit branch of the NAACP go on record as applauding their efforts."

In a detailed report of the Baden-Baden adventure that he prepared later, Charles F. Adams, an ad man who helped shape the Detroit presentation, described the competition: "Lyon had a somewhat wandering maze of large blow-ups of the city and facilities. There were some scale models. Buenos Aires had a smaller show with an interesting multiple screen slide presentation. When we saw the finished Mexico City exhibit, however, I believe some of us realized, for the first time, the seriousness with which they were taking their own bid. It was by far the largest and most elaborate. You entered it through a replica of an Aztec ruin. The walls were a network of large color photos of their city and their facilities. And where we were showing scale models of our projected facilities, they were showing actual photographs of their own stadia etc. as they now exist. They had imported their own massive native furniture as a centerpiece so that they might chat comfortably with delegates. And while they might have had fewer people on hand than Detroit, they were all dressed in identical coats, which gave them great vitality."

Yet Detroit came off well, Adams thought. "Our display was excellent. Governor Romney's arrival that afternoon was an electric event and his presence—along with Mayor Cavanagh—gave real stature to our effort. Voting members of the IOC visited throughout the day. Our people performed excellently. They knew our story and told it effectively. Councilman Bill Patrick and Judge Wade McCree represented both their offices and their city with great dignity and effectiveness."

Adams's concerns about Mexico City echoed the feelings of reporters covering the event. A dispatch that morning from Lyall Smith, sports editor of the *Free Press*, said that "Mexico City was scoring heavily" in the discussions among journalists and delegates in Baden-Baden. He quoted Douglas Roby, who told him, "Detroit is definitely not a shoo in. In meetings today I have heard much support for Mexico City. I feel they are our No. 1 threat." Roby told Smith that it might take two or three ballots before the winner was decided. The winner needed thirty votes. Detroit, Roby said, might have about twenty lined up, but that included the wishful thinking that the Soviet Union and other Iron Curtain countries would go Detroit's way. "Rumors making the rounds here . . . put the Russian votes in the corner of virtually every bidding city," Smith reported. A weight-lifting official from Detroit insisted that the Soviets would side with them, but the Mexicans were claiming they had the Russians.

Martin Hayden also sensed Mexico City's rise on the day before the vote, though by his assessment there must have been something unscrupulous about it. He said only a few days earlier Detroit delegates were afraid that by promising competing nations the lowest cost per athlete they might be accused of trying to buy the Games. But now, Hayden wrote, "they woke to the possibility that Mexico City had already made the purchase." Political dopesters, he said, had changed the odds in the four-city race to make it a Mexico City versus Detroit contest. The other contenders were awakening to "the subtleties of the year-long and individualized wooing of fellow IOC delegates by General Jose deJesus Clark, the grand satrap of Mexican athletic affairs. It started last fall when Mexico City staged its Olympic pentathlon and offered free roundtrip tickets to any IOC delegate. Now the word is out that the urbane Gen. Clark, with a key to the Mexico City treasury, stands ready to better the offer—if Mexico City wins, the Games' trips and expenses reportedly will be on the house for each IOC member and any member of his family. Detroit's managers decided not to follow suit. The Mexicans might get away with it, said one. If we try we'll be accused of being rich and ugly Americans trying to buy our way in."

In the *Free Press* that day, Lyall Smith reported, "The only thing that can save Detroit is a driving finish to the wire under the impact of its 45-minute presentation Friday." He quoted Fred Matthaei Sr. saying there was no way Detroit could win on the first ballot: "If we lose this time, this is the end. If we don't get it now, I don't think we would ever have another chance. It would be useless to continue the fight."

One last burst of optimism came Thursday night, when the entire Detroit delegation gathered in the assembly hall for a dress rehearsal of the next morning's official presentation. "Most were seeing it for the first time, and the effect was tremendous," ad man Charles Adams recounted. "It was really a masterpiece. It was technically impressive. It told the story with great excitement and emotion. Matthaei, Cavanagh, and Romney, the three presenters, were superb. And as we prepared to leave the hall to rest up for the big day ahead, word came up from the press room that the betting was two to one for Detroit."

At ten on Friday morning, delegations from the four finalist cities assembled before the IOC members in the Kurhaus. Presentations were made in alphabetical order: Buenos Aires, Detroit, Lyon, Mexico City. "With very little ceremony, Avery Brundage, IOC president, introduced Buenos Aires and told them they had forty-five minutes. What happened then was unsettling, to say the least," Adams reported. "The presentation had not a single visual—and it consisted of three long speeches, each of which had then to be fully translated. It lasted an hour and a half. And it included such sentences as 'A city characterized by a metropolitan character'—'working together, the city has attained a functional homogeneity'—and finally—'the sky is always pure blue.' When it finally ended, the press boxes were half empty. About a third of the IOC delegates had actually left the room. Fully another third was reading the newspaper. One, discouragingly, was observed [reading] the comic section. And that was the atmosphere in which it was announced that Detroit would go on."

Detroit requested five minutes for technical adjustments. It was Old Man Matthaei's tactical move, enough time for him to hustle the wayward IOC delegates back into the room.

*The city asks not what the Olympics can do for Detroit, but rather what can Detroit do to further the Olympic ideal.* Such was the theme, inspired by President Kennedy's inaugural phrase, a variation of which he first delivered in Detroit during the 1960 campaign. *A challenge we fully understand and zealously accept.* Matthaei opened the presentation: "Gentlemen, first, I wish to express the sincere pleasure and appreciation my colleagues and I feel at this opportunity to appear in behalf of our city—Detroit, USA. Detroit has presented its qualifications many times over the past twenty-four years. We are grateful and proud that many of you have urged us to return again to offer the facilities of our city and the warm hospitality of its people. In planning our presentation, we tried to look at Detroit through your eyes. We have tried particularly to answer the important question which I'm sure will guide you in your choice—what can Detroit do to further the Olympic ideal?"

Matthaei then turned it over to Cavanagh, who noted that the people of Detroit were so eager to land the Games that most members of the delegation came to Baden-Baden at their own expense. Then he introduced President Kennedy, who provided Detroit's official invitation by film, calling the meeting "a matter of great international importance," depicting Detroit as "a great sports community in the central United States," and saying that he hoped the IOC delegates would "have the wisdom ascribed to the Olympic Gods in arriving at your very difficult decision." Cavanagh and Romney then took turns boasting about Detroit and describing the facilities and proposed stadium. They spiced their commentary with a widescreen color slide presentation showing the city and the filmed endorsement from Rafer Johnson, who was presented in close-up, sitting informally at a table. Johnson was not only a global star; he was an optimist who looked on the positive side of the civil rights movement. He said he hoped they would choose Detroit not only because of its facilities but "because Detroit has shown that it understands all that the Olympic Games are, and always have been, and always must be. Detroit's understanding of the Olympic ideal is typical of the striving for international and interracial brotherhood that is apparent in so much that is taking place in the United States today."

The presentation was interrupted by applause twelve times. Even some foreign journalists clapped with approval. Watching the scene from above, Adams noted, "When the lights came on, the view from the balcony where I sat was impressive. For a moment, you could hear a pin drop. The press loges were jammed. Every IOC member was in his seat—or should I say, almost literally, on the edge of it. And then a small thunder of applause hit the room." Martin Hayden, working the audience, was told by the German Olympic leader that Detroit's presentation was brilliant. A French delegate said the Americans deserved a gold medal in propaganda. Detroit hosted a luncheon immediately afterward, where Adams and his Motor City colleagues were instructed to do some last-minute selling. "I talked to a rajah, a member of the African contingent, a Norwegian count and the Colombian delegate," Adams recalled. "I also spent ten minutes trying to win the vote of the most distinguished looking guest present—but who, unfortunately, turned out to be the man catering the party. The verdict was unanimous. The presentation had moved them. It was the best presentation they had ever seen. Optimism and friendliness filled the room. We were buoyant."

Lyon took the stage after lunch. The presentation was entirely in French, the first language of the Olympic movement. Adams could not understand much of it, but it seemed to him that "there was much material that seemed extraneous. At one point it showed a Papal procession with about fifty Cardinals filing up an aisle in full raiment. This prompted Judge McCree, who was sitting next to me, to lean over and say, 'I know this is an Olympic film, but I don't recognize the event.'" In the interlude between Lyon and Mexico City, word spread through the room about the letters urging IOC delegates to reject Detroit because of its lack of "fair play" in housing. Cavanagh and the delegation leadership had known about the anti-Detroit campaign for days, but now everyone seemed to know. Adams took it as "discouraging news—and it alloyed our enthusiasm completely."

Then came Mexico City. And more concern, according to Adams. "Without any visuals, but using four well-prepared, obviously competent speakers, they set forth the Mexico City case. One spoke of the city, its history, its abilities and facilities. Another referred to a $2.80 per diem, thereby undercutting Detroit by 20 cents. [Detroit had said it could stage the Olympics at a cost of only $3 per day per athlete.] Then a noted Mexican physician, Dr. Eduardo Hay, presented evidence on Mexico's principal drawback—its altitude. He cited figures to show that Mexico City was below the 3,000 meter level, at which altitude, he stated, physical performance is altered. And then he concluded with this dazzling sentence which I did not write down, but which I cannot forget—'If historians cannot agree on the past, and journalists cannot agree on the present, and scientists cannot agree on the future—how can men of medicine be expected to agree on this small question?' The IOC seemed impressed. The final speaker eloquently reviewed Mexico's history—recounted its place in American and World Civilization—and reminded the delegates that Mexico City represented Latin America, which had never hosted the Olympics. He stated that the selection of Mexico City would best serve the ecumenical purpose of the Olympic movement."

The room was cleared of press for IOC members to ask a few sensitive questions of each city. The Americans were questioned about visas for nations like East Germany and North Korea and about costs per athlete. "Word came out of this the attitude toward Detroit had been friendly and gracious," Adams reported. "Mr. Matthaei seemed filled with confidence. We waited downstairs where one European reporter assured me we were all but in and that he had his Detroit story half written."

There were fifty-eight IOC members present to vote. They deliberated for an hour, and then the chamber doors opened and the results were announced.

Mexico City 30. Detroit 14. Lyon 12. Buenos Aires 2.

Detroit's dream destroyed. Mexico City had won in the first round. One fewer vote and they would have had to go to a second round, where Detroit was expecting to pick up more votes. But the entire Soviet bloc went to Mexico City, and so did a few European nations who had had their fill of Charles de Gaulle. And Detroit got only two of the three U.S. votes. John Jewett Garland was no friend in the end. "The decision hit us like a fist," Adams recounted. "Several Detroiters told me that momentarily they had actually felt physically ill. When I relayed this information to one group in another part of the hall a few minutes later they wouldn't believe me. We were first of all stunned, then confused, then bitter, and finally resigned. A few years earlier, in its bid to win the 1964 Games that went to Tokyo, Detroit spent $20,000 and finished third with nine votes. This time Detroit spent $200,000 and finished second with fourteen votes. All that work, and a net gain of only five votes."

What happened? Some Detroiters believed their city was a victim of its own success. "I really thought we had it," said Doug Roby. "But I am convinced now the members simply do not think the Games should come to the United States even though we haven't had them here since 1932. They think the United States has everything. We are a 'have' nation. This is the era of the 'have nots.'"

Richard Cross, the American Motors executive who had written that solicitous letter to Brundage before his visit to Detroit in September, offered a similar appraisal: "Several IOC committeemen told me that the committee was full of admiration for Detroit and thought our presentation was magnificent. But they also felt that we were such a big, successful city that we did not need the Olympics. Their idea seemed to be that it would be better to send the Games to Mexico City, which has never had a chance in the international spotlight."

In his "Press Box" column in the *Detroit News,* Pete Waldmeir offered another take. He vividly recalled his encounter with a Mexican during that IOC affair in Brazil, the same one where Richard Cross had shared those pleasant meals at the Jaragua with Brundage: "A large Mexican with beady eyes, puffy sockets . . . if you want to know what he looked like ask your nine year old to draw you a picture of Pancho Villa. His name was Gen. Jose deJesus Clark Flores. He had a few comments to make that still hold water on why Mexico City and not Detroit won the Olympics. Where are your facilities? Gen. Clark asked wryly then. Where is your stadium? Do you have a velodrome? Could you hold the Games in your country tomorrow afternoon? We could." Waldmeir said the conversation made him uncomfortable. Clark had all the answers. "I could only say, 'We have plans.'"

Those were not the only reasons Detroit lost. There was also the allure of Mexico City, a cosmopolitan world capital. And in the political sphere, Mexico City, while aligned with the United States, was less beholden to cold war gamesmanship. Some delegates worried that East Germany and North Korea would not be able to get visas, despite Robert Kennedy's assurances. Adams found his way into the meeting room after the vote and was shown papers where "members had actually underscored the phrase in the Attorney General's letter that gave the U.S. an 'out' in issuing the visas."

Did the hometown letter-writing campaign have anything to do with the vote? Members of the delegation insisted that it did not. "The Negroes who think that they had something to do with keeping the Olympics from Detroit are in error and those whites who attribute Detroit's failure to get the Olympics to the letters are also in error," said Judge McCree. "As far as I know, race was never a factor." Councilman Patrick said no one was more upset than he about the failure of the open-housing bill he had sponsored, but the attack on the Olympics seemed misguided. "I guess people have the wrong notions about things," he said. "They are caught in a strategy of chaos. They really feel the way to accomplish things is by creating anarchy. . . . Wade and I were an integral part of everything done over there. We had a very good group of people. All of us worked very well together. If all segments of Detroit could work as well as this group of 50 to 100 persons, I would be very heartened by the prospects of this city."

Counterfactual history deals in speculation and fantasy, and the question it relies on—What if?—is forever unanswerable, but there are times nonetheless when it seems worth asking the *What if?* questions. What if Detroit had been chosen to host the 1968 Olympics? Would it have made any difference in the health of the city? In terms of physical and financial health, the experience of other Olympic cities suggests the answer is probably not in the long run. Some stadia remain, but for the most part Olympic sites turn into eerie athletic ghost villages or disappear altogether in a matter of years or a few decades. The best that can be said of the Olympic Stadium proposed for the Michigan State Fairgrounds is that it might have kept the Lions in Detroit for a time, perhaps preventing the later temporary move to the Pontiac Silverdome in 1975, before Ford Field was built downtown in 2002.

Yet it is within the realm of possibility that the political and corporate team that went to Baden-Baden would have felt a stronger commitment to the city in the sixties with the whole world watching. The expectations would have been greater, with untold ramifications. With the Olympics only a year away, would the riots of 1967 have happened, or happened in the same way, or would the Cavanagh administration have reacted more effectively to prevent or control them? Unanswerable, but worth pondering. And then consider 1968, with the racial dynamics of that year, and the call for a black athlete boycott that almost rocked the Games, and the historic gloved-fist black power salute of sprinters Tommie Smith and John Carlos on the medal stand, and how all of that would have played out had the Olympics not been in Mexico City but in Detroit, a city at the center of the long and complicated story of race in America.

Cavanagh's office had prepared a victory statement that was held for release on October 19 in Detroit. In it he said the Olympics would "place the name Detroit on the lips of every man, woman, and child on this globe." Now, instead, the mayor had to release a statement of loss: "Naturally, we are disappointed at the decision. However, we knew it was a difficult one for the IOC. Detroit accepts this vote in the true sporting tradition and Olympic spirit. We congratulate the committee from Mexico City and their countrymen and want them to know that we will cooperate with them in order that the 1968 Olympic Games will be the best ever staged. The proficient and magnificent effort that went into the Detroit presentation will now be applied to forward other projects which Detroit may be called upon to handle in the future." The mayor sounded a bit less gracious when he arrived in Rome that Sunday night, where he and Mary Helen were looking forward to an audience with Pope Paul. He told the press there that it was obvious that most IOC members had made up their minds even before Baden-Baden and that Detroit was treated unfairly because of anti-American sentiment.

Romney arrived in Detroit that same day. Four hundred people came to the airport to greet the governor and his defeated delegation, Richard Cross and Al Glancy, Martin Hayden, and the Matthaeis and the rest, as they stepped off the Pan Am jet. The Cody High School Band stood below, in what was described as "a dismal drizzle," and played the University of Michigan fight song—"The Victors."

Chapter 17

# SMOKE RINGS

**THE PROSE POEM** was titled "Smoke Rings" and appeared below a sketch of curling cigarette smoke forming the familiar interlocking rings of the Olympic Games. It ran in the October 28, 1963, issue of *Illustrated News*, the Detroit paper affiliated with Reverend Cleage.

*We don't want everything "they" want.*
*But we weren't any more interested in the Olympics than they were in Cynthia Scott.*
*They're trying to act all upset because Negroes mentioned Detroit Race Bias to the Olympic Committee.*
*We didn't know they were ashamed of it.*
*After all, we didn't shoot Cynthia Scott, they did!*

Cleage had made his break from C. L. Franklin by then, moving farther away from his mainstream roots and identifying more as a black revolutionary. Born into the black upper middle class as the son of one of Detroit's first African American doctors, trained with a degree from the Graduate School of Theology at Oberlin College, mentored as a young pastor by Reverend Hood and other moderate Congregationalists and Presbyterians, the fifty-two-year-old Cleage was now on his way to changing his name and denomination; within a few years he would be Jaramogi

Abebe Agyeman, founder and first holy patriarch of the Pan-African Orthodox Christian Church at the Shrine of the Black Madonna, founded on the belief that Jesus was black. The Walk to Freedom was the last time he would participate in an event that included white liberals. He did not want to do it even then, bending only reluctantly at the request of Franklin, but now their alliance was finished, as was his sympathy with any integrationist notions. The dreamy language of Martin Luther King did not suit him, even in its most unflinching denunciations of racism. He stood now with Malcolm X, who was coming to Detroit on November 10 to be the closing speaker at Cleage's Northern Negro Grass Roots Leadership Conference.

There were competing conferences that week. Franklin, trying to keep alive his Detroit Council on Human Rights, sponsored an event downtown, the Negro Summit Leadership Conference, that attracted nearly three thousand people, most of whom came to hear Adam Clayton Powell Jr., the congressman from Harlem who was a frequent visitor to Detroit. Powell's rhetoric was anything but tame. He called for unity among black activists, criticized Mayor Cavanagh for making what he called only token black appointments, and focused on the Cynthia Scott case as an example of police brutality. The crowd to hear Powell made the event seem more of a success than it was. Most black ministers in Detroit declined to promote the rally or have anything more to do with Reverend Franklin, and his attempt to stage a motorized version of the Walk to Freedom—Franklin billed it as a Ride to Freedom—drew barely one hundred cars and drivers. Rather than a rejuvenation of his June glory, this November fizzle marked the end of something. The High Priest of Soul Preaching would not disappear after that, but his days as a leader, or self-styled leader, of civil rights in Detroit were over. A few years earlier Franklin had curtailed his circuit flying out of physical fatigue. Now the mental stress of trying to bridge so many factional divides had worn him out and prompted him to recede again.

The counterconference sponsored by Cleage seized on the "Grass Roots" label after Franklin discouraged radicals from participating. Detroit's grassroots contingent had coalesced around the Cynthia Scott shooting and a philosophy or theology of black liberation. Along with Cleage, its leaders were Grace Lee Boggs and James Boggs, and the Henry brothers, Milton and Richard, who came out of Cleage's church and founded the Group on Advanced Leadership (GOAL) and the Michigan Freedom Now Party. Seeking to build a revolutionary movement in the city, they held organizing and strategy workshops for two days at Mr. Kelley's Lounge and Recreation Center, a popular music hangout often frequented by Motown artists. Workshop sessions were led by the Boggses, Don Freeman of Cleveland, Gloria Richardson of Cambridge, Maryland, and William Worthy of New York. One eventual result was Cleage's decision to run for governor of Michigan on the Freedom Now ticket the following year. The conference was staged at King Solomon Baptist Church, about a half mile from Motown headquarters. Anthony Fierimonte, a young Detroit police officer, had been assigned patrol duties outside the church that day. His orders, he said later, were to place "No Parking" signs in front of the church "and get the hell out of the way" so that members of the intelligence unit could snap photos of Malcolm X and other attendees. Instead, as buses and cars pulled up, Fierimonte started greeting people—"Welcome to Detroit! How are you?"—until two undercover cops grabbed him. "And I sat in the police car and they called me every name in the book. 'You know who this fucker is? You piece of shit!' They were trying to see all the people and get pictures, and I was blocking the view." After five hours of speeches inside King Solomon, the conference concluded with Malcolm X. His speech, among the most significant of his career, was later titled "Message to the Grassroots."

Detroit Red was one of his old nicknames. And Big Red. Red from the tint of his hair, Detroit from his days there in his late twenties. Born in Omaha as Malcolm Little, son of an itinerant preacher active in Marcus Garvey's Universal Negro Improvement Association, Malcolm grew up mostly in Michigan, near East Lansing. After his father was killed by a streetcar and his mother was declared insane and sent off to a mental institution in Kalamazoo, Malcolm eventually left for Massachusetts to live with a sister. He fell into a life of drugs and crime there and in New York and ended up in prison, where he converted to the Nation of Islam, a variant of Islam but one that viewed whites as devils, conceived in Detroit in 1930 by Wallace D. Fard, a mysterious peddler who disappeared four years after arriving in the Motor City, leaving only his religion behind. When Malcolm was released from prison in 1952, he took a bus from Massachusetts to Detroit to live with Wilfred, his oldest brother. He found work first at a furniture store, then at a truck factory, and finally with Ford Motor Company at the Lincoln-Mercury plant, the same assembly line where Berry Gordy Jr. had worked. Wilfred's home was strictly Muslim. He went by the name Wilfred X and was secretary of Temple No. 1 in Detroit, run out of a storefront not far from a hog slaughterhouse. After quitting the auto job, Malcolm X quickly rose up the Nation of Islam hierarchy, and by November 1963, when he returned to Detroit to speak at Reverend Cleage's grassroots conference, he was not only the second most powerful black Muslim behind Elijah Muhammad, who had succeeded Fard and moved the headquarters to Chicago, but also a threat to Muhammad and far more political. His "Message to the Grassroots" was the clearest presentation of his black militant theology, which he connected to revolutionary movements in Africa and Asia, something larger than the American condition.

Five months earlier in Detroit, King had used the geography of American states to evoke his dream; now Malcolm X used it to identify the enemy: "And when you and I here in Detroit and in Michigan and in America who have been awakened today look around us, we too realize here in America we all have a common enemy, whether he's in Georgia or Michigan, whether he's in California or New York. He's the same man: blue eyes and blond hair and pale skin—same man." Where King evoked the dream of the sons of former slaves and former slave owners someday sitting down together, Malcolm X offered a vision of people of color somehow finding unity among themselves: "Argue it out behind closed doors. And then when you come out on the street, you pose a common front, a united front. We need to stop airing our differences in front of the white man. Put the white man out of our meetings, number one, and then sit down and talk shop with each other." There were about twenty or thirty white people sitting in the pews of King Solomon Baptist as Malcolm X spoke. They had been segregated into a separate section.

Not long after expressing his desire for black unity, Malcolm eviscerated King and the leaders of the marches in Detroit (Cleage aside) and Washington. He started by differentiating "house Negroes" and "field Negroes," the terminology of slavery, and placed himself and the black nationalists with the "field Negroes" and King and the integrationists with the "house Negroes." There had never been a successful revolution without bloodshed, he said: "You don't have a peaceful revolution. You don't have a turn-the-other-cheek revolution. There's no such thing as a nonviolent revolution. Only kind of revolution that's nonviolent is the Negro revolution. The only revolution based on loving your enemy is the Negro revolution. The only revolution in which the goal is a desegregated lunch counter, a desegregated park, and a desegregated public toilet, you can sit down next to white folks on the toilet. That's not revolution." He called King a "fallen idol" who "became bankrupt, almost, as a leader," after the Birmingham desegregation campaign, which Malcolm described as a low point in the civil rights movement. When Birmingham failed, the black masses started to take to the streets and talked about marching on Washington. It was then that influential whites started manipulating the movement to take control and stifle a black revolution.

"It was the grass roots out there in the street. Scared the white man to death, scared the white power structure in Washington, D.C., to death. I was there. When they found out that this black steamroller was going to come down on the capital, they called in Wilkins, they called in Randolph, they called in these national Negro leaders that you respect and told them, 'Call it off.' Kennedy said, 'Look, you all letting this thing go too far.' And Old Tom said, 'Boss, I can't stop it, because I didn't start it.' I'm telling you what they said. They said, 'I'm not even in it, much less at the head of it.' They said, 'These Negroes are doing things on their own. They're running ahead of us.' And that old shrewd fox said, 'Well if you all aren't in it, I'll put you in it. I'll put you at the head of it. I'll endorse it. I'll welcome it. I'll help it. I'll join it.'" That is when the Council for United Civil Rights was formed, Malcolm X said, with money from white millionaires and the UAW.

His version of history continued: "Soon as they got the setup organized, the white man made available to them top public relations experts; opened the news media across the country at their disposal; and then they begin to project these Big Six [civil rights leaders] as the leaders of the march. Originally, they weren't even in the march. You was talking this march talk on Hastings Street—is Hastings Street still here?—on Hastings Street. You was talking the march talk on Lenox Avenue. . . . That's where the march talk was being talked. But the white man put the Big Six head of it, made them the march. They became the march. They took it over. And the first move they made after they took it over, they invited Walter Reuther, a white man, they invited a priest, a rabbi, and an old white preacher. Yes, an old white preacher. The same white element that put Kennedy in power—labor, the Catholics, the Jews, and liberal Protestants, the same clique that put Kennedy in power, joined the March on Washington."

This diluted the march: "It's just like when you've got some coffee that's too black, which means it's too strong. What you do? You integrate it with cream; you make it weak. If you pour too much cream in, you won't even know you ever had coffee. It used to be hot, it becomes cool. It used to be strong, it becomes weak. It used to wake you up, now it will put you to sleep. This is what they did with the march on Washington. They joined it. They didn't integrate it; they infiltrated it. They . . . took it over. And as they took it over, it lost its militancy. They ceased to be angry. They ceased to be hot. They ceased to be uncompromising. Why, it even ceased to be a march. It became a picnic, a circus. Nothing but a circus, with clowns and all. You had one right here in Detroit—I saw it on television—with clowns leading it, white clowns and black clowns."

The March on Washington was controlled so tightly, he said, the bosses would not let James Baldwin speak because they feared what he would say. "They controlled it so tight—they told those Negroes what time to hit town, how to come, where to stop, what signs to carry, what song to sing, what speech they could make, and what speech they couldn't make; and then told them to get out of town by sundown. And every one of those Toms was out of town by sundown. Now I know you don't like my saying this. But I can back it up. It was a circus, a performance that beat anything Hollywood could ever do, the performance of the year. Reuther and those other three devils should get an Academy Award for the best actors 'cause they acted like they really loved Negroes and fooled a whole lot of Negroes. And the six Negro leaders should get an award too, for the best supporting cast."

Some of this was irrefutably true; what differed so vastly were interpretations of meaning and motivation. Baldwin did not speak. John Lewis had to tamp down his radical rhetoric. White religious figures joined Reuther in the leadership. Money from white liberals and labor unions shaped the course of the event, including its relocation from the Capitol to the Lincoln Memorial. What motivated all this? Malcolm X would say white manipulation to hold back the black masses. The Kennedys and Reuther would say they were dealing with political reality, doing what it took to keep the civil rights bill alive. In either case, black intellectuals in Detroit understood the impact of Malcolm X's message to the grass roots. In tone and substance it marked a break from the past and laid out a path for the black power movement to follow from then on. Whether or not Malcolm intended it, noted Manning Marable, his biographer, his life was "fundamentally changed" by this address, just as King's had been by his "dream" speech. The content also reinforced whispers already being heard in Detroit and Chicago and New York that Malcolm was breaking away from Elijah Muhammad and his less-confrontational brand of Nation of Islam. The *Michigan Chronicle* hinted at this in the lead of its article on the speech: "Fiery Malcolm X, as of this moment the No. 2 man in the Black Muslim movement, in spite of widespread rumors to the contrary . . ."

Ofield Dukes, who covered the civil rights movement for the *Chronicle*, wrote in that same issue about the power struggles that were dividing the black community in Detroit. He took note of the two competing conferences hosted by Cleage and Franklin and reported that many black leaders refused to attend either of them: "Recent events clearly indicate that the schism between the various segments of Negro leadership is widening. Even the so-called splinter groups are breaking up into factions. Traditional organization is threatened by internal problems and external competition for recognition and position in the leadership hierarchy." The causes were complex, but the vindictiveness and envy were real, Dukes wrote, and served no larger purpose. "Watching this leadership struggle from one end of the social spectrum is the white power structure. And waiting at the other end to contribute to disunity and destruction of responsible Negro leadership is the white subversive element whose aims are to take command and exploit the situation. . . . Class differences in the Negro community also contribute to the murky leadership picture. Most Negro leaders come from the so-called Negro upper class, as reflected in Detroit's NAACP board of directors as well as in the Negro members serving on the local Urban League board. However, it is the lower class Negro stratum that experiences the brunt of racial discrimination and segregation. The noose of prejudice is around the neck of the lower class Negro."

Dukes called the Freedom Now Party an exercise in futility but also had critical words for what he saw as the hypocrisy or timidity of the labor movement. "Reuther was big on the national scene but the Wayne County UAW was not to be seen in the Patrick-Ravitz open housing ordinance," he wrote. This underscored what Dukes saw as a tendency among white liberal labor leaders: "The closer to home a race issue is the less vigorous the union can afford to campaign on its behalf. Labor leaders champion legislation which will have little immediate effect on white workers. But championing an anti-bias housing law is another matter." There was one exception, he pointed out. Reuther's aide Bill Oliver, who had been one of the UAW officials who carried money down to Alabama to bail Martin Luther King out of jail, also testified publicly in Detroit on behalf of the Patrick-Ravitz bill. "Nothing is more frightening than ignorance in action," Oliver had said.

---

One week after the competing conferences of Franklin and Cleage, there was a third major convocation in Detroit. This one had nothing overtly to do with politics or civil rights but attracted more attention in the black community than either of the previous gatherings. For the first time ever, the full collection of Motown artists entertained the hometown audience the same way they had thrilled concertgoers around the country since that October day thirteen months earlier when the first *Motortown Revue* hit the stage of the Howard Theater in Washington.

Little Stevie Wonder, the Miracles, Marvin Gaye, Mary Wells, Kim Weston, Martha and the Vandellas, the Contours, the Marvelettes, the Temptations, comedian and emcee Bill Murry, Choker Campbell and his big band—all on the bill at the grand old Fox Theater on Woodward Avenue for the weekend of November 16 and 17. The second annual nationwide tour had been more difficult than the first, with uneven support and money-handling mistakes along the way, but this homecoming was both a financial boon and a morale boost. The crowd started lining the sidewalk at nine that Saturday morning and filled the theater both days. It was the largest attendance at the movie house in five years, according to William Brown, the Fox's general manager. And much like the Walk to Freedom at the start of the summer, this two-day celebration was staged without incident. A celebrity coffee before the first show attracted not only Little Stevie but also none other than Joe Louis, the Brown Bomber, who came out of Detroit and used to eat those scrambled-eggs-and-steak breakfasts at the now gone Gotham Hotel.

In October 1962, when the *Motortown Revue* headed off on its first tour, Mayor Cavanagh spoke about the economic spirit of the city without mentioning Motown. Now, in a letter to Berry Gordy Jr. welcoming the hometown performances at the Fox, he understood the meaning of the music. "The cast and sponsors of the Motortown Revue are to be congratulated for their part in the revitalization of 'live' musical revues," Cavanagh declared. "It is particularly pleasing that one of the most popular revues to cross the country in the past few years is completely composed of native-born Detroiters. . . . The fine work that these artists have done to make Detroit the national center of the single record business has done much to enhance the reputation of our town."

Smokey and his Miracles closed the last show. "Is everybody ready?" he asked, as the band launched into the first notes of "Mickey's Monkey"—and the place went wild. *A one, a two, a one two three four—Lum de lum de la iiiii.* Everyone up from their seats, dancing and singing along.

## Chapter 18

# FALLEN

**THE FOX THEATER** rocked with Motown stars, and the Flame Show Bar closed in the same week. It could be said that the Flame begat Motown. The Flame is where the Gordy sisters worked the cigarette and photo concessions and introduced their little brother Berry to the managers and artists who helped him get his start in the music industry. It was at the Flame that he first saw Billie Holiday and Dinah Washington and Della Reese and Sam Cooke and Billy Eckstine and Jackie Wilson, and it was from the Flame that he later hired Maurice King and many of the jazz musicians who became Motown's house band, the Funk Brothers. All that left to hazy history now, a jewel of black Detroit gone—like the Gotham Hotel a year earlier. And like the Gotham, "it died without pomp or ceremony, without trumpets . . . or a final requiem," according to a notice in the *Chronicle.*

Some clubs have a deeper meaning. They are not just another venue, but home. The warm colors, the stage above the bar, the rhythm and flow of the place late at night, women dressed to kill and killers dressed to charm, Ziggy Johnson at the microphone, introducing artists and leading the audience in the Soft and the Chick-a-Boom—that was the Flame. *The Hottest Place in Town. The Most Beautiful Black & Tan in the Midwest. Continuous Entertainment. Up to five shows a night. Call the joint at TE2-8714.* Find it at 4264 John R at the corner with Canfield. The lights went on in 1949, followed by fourteen years of lush night colors before the neon drained to empty gray, the site flattened to make way for yet another medical center parking garage. If this decomposition was unavoidable and perhaps even necessary, part of the life processes of a city, that reality made the loss of the Flame no less painful, a void in the culture of Detroit that could not be replicated.

One week later, at 1:39 Eastern Time on the afternoon of November 22, the bells on the long row of teletype machines at the *Detroit News* started clanging. It was rare for any noise to draw extra attention in a chaotic newsroom, but this was different. The bulletin bells kept ringing, all ten at once, incessantly. A group of reporters walked over to the teletype room to see what was up. UPI URGENT—FLASH—KENNEDY SERIOUSLY WOUNDED—PERHAPS FATALLY BY ASSASSINS BULLET.

Aretha Franklin was strolling through the aisles lined with corned beef and salami at the Broadway Market in downtown Detroit. She had returned to her hometown to spend the week before Thanksgiving with Reverend Franklin and other family members. First she noticed people rushing around, huddling, whispering, then she heard radios blaring, and finally the news reached her that the president had been killed. Ziggy Johnson called his mother in Chicago and asked if she had heard the news. "Yes, son, I have my rosary in my hand and we all must pray," she told him. Johnson had a difficult time writing his "Zagging with Ziggy" column that week, his sadness about the demise of the Flame now overwhelmed by his grief for the lost president. Paraphrasing the words that Martin Luther King had used in Detroit and then Washington, he said it was the first time in his memory that there was "someone in the White House who believed solely in merit and not color of skin."

Bob Ankony, the young truant who had witnessed the inferno at the Ford Rotunda, was walking down the sidewalk past the Shirley Manor Apartments near his house on Woodmere at the corner with Sharon. Twice a week he cleaned the incinerators in the building; the tenants knew him. It was Mrs. Douglas, the widow lady who lived in the basement apartment in the southwest corner of the building, who yelled out to him, "Bobby, the president was killed!" His world was too far removed for the news to have much emotional impact, but it did stir his morbid imagination. For a few weeks thereafter, he and a buddy from the Cabot Street gang would reenact the assassination scene in his basement bedroom; Bob would sit on a wooden laundry tub and wave as though he were the president in the open-air limousine, and his friend "would pretend he was the sniper with one of my unloaded rifles." His obsession with guns led Ankony to a connection with Lee Harvey Oswald, who had fired an Italian-made 6.5 mm Carcano rifle that he had purchased from Klein's Sporting Goods in Chicago. Ankony by then had bought a few rifles and pistols from Klein's himself, simply by using their mail-order service and sending along a false note claiming he was eighteen, three years older than his true age.

It was deer hunting season in Michigan, and Raymond Murray, the Detroit cop, was up north that November afternoon deer hunting with four friends between Grayling and Kalkaska off Highway M-72. On the way back to their cabin near Bear Lake, they stopped at a grocery and heard that Kennedy had been shot. By the time they reached the cabin, the president was dead. Murray thought back to the October morning a year earlier when Kennedy had strode right past him, smiling, at the entrance to the Sheraton Cadillac in downtown Detroit, and how it had crossed his mind then that it would be too easy for a sniper to perch on top of a nearby building. *It could have happened right in front of me,* Murray thought.

Berry Gordy was in his office on West Grand Boulevard. As he later related the story, he had just been told about Kennedy's death when the phone rang. It was his assistant Barney Ales warning him that Marvin Gaye, in a foul mood, was headed his way. Gaye had stomped out of the sales department complaining that Motown was not sufficiently pushing "Can I Get a Witness." Now here he was, looming over Gordy's desk. "They're fucking with me, BG," the singer yelled. "I was down in the Sales Department . . . and they're bullshitting, man." He was supposed to get more airplay, Gaye complained, but sales was only pushing Martha and the Vandellas and Smokey and his Miracles. Gordy told Gaye that he was being foolish to yell at the salespeople, who could make or break him. In the process of chastising Gaye, he called him "boy," which only intensified Gaye's tantrum. The confrontation ended with Gordy himself walking out of the room in frustration, yelling, "Don't you realize the president has just been killed?" Little Stevie Wonder, who was at the Michigan School for the Blind that day, went home and sat near the television set with his mother, every report from Dallas reinforcing what one biographer called his "early visions of an American apocalypse."

Out at the Glass House in Dearborn, the news resonated on many levels. Henry Ford II had known JFK socially and politically, and though a lifelong Republican he was moving closer to the Democratic administration as the Detroit auto industry enjoyed its best year ever. Robert S. McNamara, a former president of Ford Motor Company, once one of Ford's Whiz Kids, was serving as Kennedy's secretary of defense. And there was one physical detail to the grisly scene in Dallas that would forever be attached to Ford: Kennedy was riding in a 1961 Lincoln Continental, a four-door convertible manufactured by Ford at its Wixom plant in suburban Detroit and customized in Cincinnati by Hess & Eisenhardt.

The X-100, the Secret Service called the car. Ford leased it to the White House for $500 per year, though its value was more than $200,000. Hydraulic rear seat that could be raised ten inches for better viewing of the president. Removable steel and transparent plastic roof panels. V-8 engine with 350 horsepower. Gold thread hand-embroidered presidential seals in special door pockets. Built-in floodlights. Radiotelephones. Flashing red lights and siren. Auxiliary jump seats for extra passengers. And one feature newly added in 1963: trunk lid grab handles for Secret Service agents. "A big beautiful Lincoln," a Dallas television announcer had declared earlier that day as Jack and Jackie settled in the backseat and the motorcade departed Love Field on its way through the city. Decades later the X-100 would be taken out of storage and put on display at the Henry Ford Museum. Long since analyzed by the Warren Commission and cleansed of scattered brain matter and the gruesomeness of its history, the limousine resided now as another artifact of American mythology not far from the replicas of Thomas Edison's laboratory and Abe Lincoln's law office.

David Laurie, ten years old, was watching a cousin deliver a report on oceanography at the Grosse Pointe University School when word reached the class that President Kennedy had been shot. The private school cut short the school day and sent students home. At the modernist Laurie house on Merriweather Road in Grosse Pointe Farms, David found his father, Bill, head of J. Walter Thompson's Detroit office, lost in front of the television set for most of the weekend. No Saturday morning cartoons, just news about the assassination. David noticed his father was biting his nails, something he did only when he was nervous. David's mother, Thayer, seemed to be getting increasingly irritated. As the unwavering conservative in the family, she disliked the Kennedys, their politics, and their mythology, and thought the drama was being overdone. In some ways Thayer was a right-wing version of Jackie Kennedy, young and beautiful, from the same social milieu. They both had been debutantes in the Newport summer swirl, when Thayer joined her parents, the B. E. Hutchinsons, in their annual pilgrimage to Jamestown, Rhode Island, and Jacqueline Bouvier accompanied her mother and stepfather, Hugh Dudley Auchincloss Jr., to Hammersmith Farm, the summer estate across the bay. But Thayer Hutchinson Laurie had nothing good to say about Jacqueline Bouvier Kennedy, and her attitude in the days following JFK's assassination puzzled her son and remained etched in his memory.

Walter Reuther's daughter, Lisa, was among the students at the Putney School in Vermont who heard the ominous sound of a sledgehammer striking an old train rail, the school's way of announcing an emergency. The news of JFK's death was followed by instructions to carry on as usual. "I couldn't believe it. I had many strong feelings for President Kennedy. I'd met him personally at several UAW conventions and Labor Day celebrations," she wrote later. After finishing her next chore, peeling potatoes, she called her parents in Detroit. Her father's voice "cracked with anger and grief." As distraught as Walter Reuther was, his daughter said, he somehow "helped me regain my hope for the future."

Reuther had been planning to be in Washington early the next week to attend a November 25 state dinner at the White House for Ludwig Erhard, who had recently succeeded Konrad Adenauer as chancellor of West Germany. A telegram reached him early on the morning of November 23: "The President's body will lie in repose in the East Room of the White House Saturday. You are invited to join in paying him respects from 2:30 to 5 p.m.—Robert F. Kennedy."

Ever solicitous in his dealings with President Kennedy, Reuther had been one of the more frequent out-of-town visitors at the White House over the previous three years. A few months earlier, at the request of one of Reuther's longtime aides, the secretary for White House assistant Ken O'Donnell had compiled a list of Reuther's meetings with JFK. Gwen King reported that the list was perhaps not complete, but her best attempt. Not including "large functions, lunches, dinners etc.," Reuther had enjoyed twenty-two meetings with the president "alone or in small groups." More were to follow after the list was put together. Reuther and Kennedy had last met, alone and off the record, on November 6, when Reuther was in town for an executive board meeting of the AFL-CIO's International Affairs Department at the Statler Hilton. Seventeen days later he was back in Washington to pay his final respects.

Reuther was in the habit of writing notes to his files, using the initials WPR to identify himself. That day he wrote, "On Saturday, November 23, following my return from the White House where I reviewed the body of President Kennedy, Hubert Humphrey called to advise me that President Johnson had asked him to contact me and tell me that he, President Johnson, wanted to talk to me at the earliest opportunity and would call me at 4:30 p.m. President Johnson phoned me at the Statler Hilton and his first words were: 'My friend, I need your friendship and support now more than ever.' He advised me he hoped to see me at an early date. About fifteen minutes later, secretary of labor Willard Wirtz called me to advise me that President Johnson had asked him to give me essentially the same message that Hubert Humphrey had given me. I advised Willard Wirtz I had already spoken to the president."

This was quintessential LBJ, networking and lobbying for support in the midst of national mourning, but in Reuther he was dealing with someone who understood the new president's urgency. At the 1960 Democratic convention in Los Angeles, Reuther, skeptical of the Texan's civil rights commitment, had worked to try to keep Johnson off the ticket, and seemed to be angling for the selection himself. But in the years since, Johnson had done much to show that he was committed and ready to apply his immense political skills to the cause in all of its dimensions, economic as well as legal. Eleven months earlier, Detroit's 1963 had begun with a memorable LBJ visit, when he had flown in from Washington to commemorate the hundredth anniversary of the Emancipation Proclamation, placing a plaque at the Second Baptist Church, the oldest black Baptist church in Michigan, whose members had been the first in Detroit to celebrate the emancipation news, a few days late, in 1863. Before delivering a strong civil rights speech at Ford Auditorium, Johnson, with Governor Romney at his side, acknowledged the downtown church's vibrant history, recounted in the plaque that he unveiled. The words, written a century earlier, read in part, "The Negro citizens of Detroit resolved that when in the course of human events there comes a day that is destined to be an everlasting beacon light marking a joyful era in the progress of a nation and the hopes of a people it seems to be fitting the occasion that it should not pass unnoticed by those whose hopes it comes to brighten and to bless."

Over the tumultuous spring and summer of 1963, as the civil rights movement rolled through the South and Congress began to deal with the administration's civil rights legislation, Johnson proved to be a valuable ally inside the White House. And now, in the first hours of his presidency, he was pledging to Reuther that he would see that vision through to completion. "Dear Walter," Johnson wrote a few days later, "I was greatly strengthened by your warm message. I need the support and the help of dedicated, imaginative people like you if the unfinished work is to be carried on, and I find renewed strength in the thought that in the days that lie ahead I can count on you."

With the assassination of President Kennedy, Mayor Cavanagh had lost not only a party leader but an avatar of his beliefs and ambitions. Irish, Catholic, liberal but pragmatic, a handsome man out of a big, handsome family—Kennedy and his clan were everything Cavanagh wanted to be. He did not have the Kennedy fortune or fame, but he saw in the Kennedy family many traits he wished to emulate. Though heavier than JFK and not much of an athlete, he loved to get his picture taken playing touch football with his staff, a scene evoking the Kennedy vigor. There was more than a hint of Hyannis Port modeling in the way he treated his brood of young sons. He paraded them around in ties and sport coats, promised them a reward if they reached twenty-one without drinking or smoking (something he had heard Joseph Kennedy did), and eventually sent them off to prep schools. (Mark, the oldest, went to Georgetown Preparatory School, eight miles from the White House, where his friend down the hall was Robert F. Kennedy Jr.) In the fall of 1963, JFK acolytes were scattered across America, bright and eager politicians who, with a blend of hope and self-delusion, thought they could be some version of him, and Jerome Cavanagh in Detroit was prime among them. On the Monday after the assassination, the mayor led a local memorial service for Kennedy at noon at the Old City Hall. Again there was a Detroit link to events a century earlier.

"On April 15, 1865, seven thousand Detroit citizens gathered here to mourn Abraham Lincoln—victim of an assassin's bullet," Cavanagh said. "Almost a century later, on this same site, we mourn the death of another of freedom's illustrious warriors. The cruel realization of his passing penetrates our unwilling consciousness through the fog of horror and disbelief of these last fateful hours. Though we would have it otherwise, our beloved leader, John Fitzgerald Kennedy, has been torn from our presence and our hearts are pierced. America needs all its strength as it girds to protect our democracy threatened by this foul, this loathsome act. We shall not be found wanting. We shall continue to serve as vigilant watchmen on freedom's ramparts. And we shall bend all our efforts to the end that he shall not have fallen in vain."

A *Michigan Chronicle* editorial linked the Kennedy assassination to what it called "The American Tragedy of 1963," a series of violent events that included the assassination of Medgar Evers in June and the bombing of the 16th Street Baptist Church in Birmingham in September. Rev. C. L. Franklin made a similar connection. There were no indications that race played a direct role in the assassination, but Franklin saw JFK as a victim of the culture of hate that permeated American society. "The sniper did not pull the trigger alone," he said from the pulpit of New Bethel Baptist that Sunday. "Governor Ross Barnett of Mississippi, Governor Wallace of Alabama, General Walker of the White Citizens' Council, and all the forces of hate and evil were as surely in Dallas with the sniper as they were in Jackson, Mississippi, when Medgar Evers was felled."

Malcolm X, a lonely dissenter amid the encomiums to Kennedy, offered a harshly different version of that same concept when asked about the assassination, linking it not only to the American culture of racial violence but the U.S. role in the violent deaths of leaders in Vietnam and the Congo. Kennedy, he said, "never foresaw that the chickens would come home to roost so soon. Being an old farm boy myself, chickens coming home to roost never did make me sad; they always made me glad." The *Chronicle* condemned him for that sharp comment, and so did Elijah Muhammad, whose censure of his disciple demarcated Malcolm's final break with the Nation of Islam. His brother in Detroit, Wilfred X, who had been instrumental in his early understanding of the black Muslim religion, decided to stay with Muhammad.

If there were questions among historians about Kennedy's commitment to the civil rights struggle, there was no doubt about the emotional depth with which Detroit's black churchgoing population reacted to his death. Churches were packed throughout the city that first Sunday after the shooting, reverberating with expressions of respect and grief. Reverend Franklin called Kennedy "the greatest hero of freedom since Lincoln." At the Warren Avenue Baptist Church, several members of the congregation were overtaken with emotion as the choir sang "Is Thine Heart Right with God?" At Northwest Church of God in Christ, children sat somberly with their parents through the service rather than leave for Sunday school classes. At East Grand Boulevard Methodist, Rev. Woodie Wade set aside his prepared sermon to preach extemporaneously to an overflow audience about the meaning of President Kennedy. Macedonia, Calvary, Mt. Calvary, New Harmony, and St. John held a joint memorial for JFK that drew thousands of mourners.

It was noted that Kennedy had appointed eight African Americans, including Wade McCree of Detroit, to the federal bench during his three years in office, while only ten had been appointed by all the presidents before him. He had also brought influential Detroit blacks to Washington during key moments in his career. Damon Keith, William Patrick, and Horace Sheffield had been part of a Detroit delegation that visited JFK at his Georgetown home in June 1960, when he was attempting to solidify black support for his presidential bid. And Keith, John Conyers, and George Crockett were among the 244 lawyers summoned to the East Room at the White House on June 21, 1963, as the administration sought support from the legal community for its civil rights initiatives, a meeting that led to the formation of the Lawyers' Committee for Civil Rights under Law. (At the time, the American Bar Association was divided on the civil rights cause. Its own Committee on Civil Rights and Civil Unrest included several opponents of federal civil rights action. Historian Ann Garity Connell noted that among them were Thomas G. Greaves of Mobile, Alabama, who accused the federal government of encouraging "the colored people" to break the law and battle police, and Rush H. Limbaugh of Cape Girardeau, Missouri, father of a future right-wing radio talk show host, who said that his community "prided itself on the fact that it never allowed a Negro to live in it and no Negro had lived there permanently.")

"We Must Complete JFK's Unfinished Task," blared the banner headline in the last November edition of the *Chronicle*. The subhead, linking the fallen president to King, was "Kennedy Gave Us a Dream." Sheffield, the labor leader, and Keith, the activist lawyer, were among the prominent Detroit blacks who believed LBJ was up to the task of continuing that dream. Like Walter Reuther, they had opposed Kennedy's choice of Johnson as his running mate at the 1960 Democratic convention, but they now believed he had proven himself, as he promised he would do in a meeting with black leaders the day after his nomination. Sheffield said, "All that I have seen since that time indicates that Mr. Johnson meant what he said when he told us the day after his nomination in Los Angeles that if the Negro people just gave him a chance he will do more in the field of civil rights than has been done in the last one hundred years." Keith had met with Johnson "in two or three instances" since he became vice president and found him to be unequivocal in his support of the civil rights bill, "and he was also clear in terms of the essential dignity of man and a man's worth, regardless of race, creed, or color."

Early that Sunday afternoon, Earl Ruby left the dry-cleaning store he owned at the corner of Livernois Avenue and Curtis, not far from the University of Detroit. He was listening to the news on the car radio when he heard that Lee Harvey Oswald had been shot and killed. The assailant was identified as the owner of the Carousel Club in Dallas. It was Jack Ruby, Earl's older brother. The Ruby brothers, whose original surname was Rubenstein, had grown up with eight siblings in the rough-and-tumble of the Maxwell Street neighborhood of Chicago. Jack and Earl were close, Earl would say later, so close that Earl, who moved to Detroit and opened the dry cleaner in 1960, had loaned Jack $16,000 with no expectations of getting the money back—so close that Jack called him from his Dallas jail cell a few hours after his arrest on November 24. Shortly before Earl Ruby died decades later, Jack Lessenberry of the *Toledo Blade* asked him what Jack had said in that call. By then there had been countless theories about Ruby's motives. Voluminous books had been written theorizing about his connections to the Mafia, his dealings with various mobsters who might have ordered JFK's killing, including Detroit-based Teamsters boss Jimmy Hoffa, who had been the criminal target of Bobby Kennedy's Justice Department. The role of Jack Ruby in the Kennedy assassination would take its place in the mythology and mystery of the event, part of the endless debate over who, what, and why. Earl Ruby was in an assisted living center in suburban Detroit when Lessenberry talked to him in 2003. His colorful older brother had been dead for thirty-six years. What did Jack tell him from the jail cell? "Earl, I think we're going to get a lot of good publicity out of this!"

Tony Ripley of the *Detroit News* had been among the journalists in the room when Oswald was shot by Ruby as he was being led out toward the basement garage. The world saw it on live television; Ripley saw it with his own eyes. Ripley seemed to be everywhere that year, a chronicler of

America's unraveling. He had covered the assassination of Medgar Evers, the church bombing in Birmingham, and now the tragedy in Dallas. The day after watching Ruby shoot Oswald at point-blank range, Ripley found his way to Rose Hill Cemetery in Fort Worth to report on Oswald's burial. The only people there were cops and federal agents and Oswald's mother, brother, widow, and two young daughters. No one to carry the casket. As Mike Cochran, the local correspondent for the Associated Press, later recalled, Jerry Flemmons of the *Fort Worth Star-Telegram* turned to him and said, "Cochran, if we're gonna write a story about the burial of Lee Harvey Oswald we're gonna have to bury the sonofabitch ourselves." Ripley joined them. The cheap wooden casket was carried to its grave by a motley crew of newspaper hacks, with Detroit represented. "I was so close to history I could not help but reach out and touch it," Ripley explained a year later in a speech at Michigan State.

George Edwards was in Washington the week of the assassination. On November 21, the morning Kennedy left for Texas, the Detroit police commissioner was on Capitol Hill testifying before the Senate Judiciary Committee as it considered his nomination by the president to serve on the U.S. Court of Appeals for the Sixth Circuit. His days as Detroit's top cop were nearing an end, or so he hoped. Edwards had the support of Michigan's two senators, the chair of the Michigan Bar, the state attorney general, leading African American lawyers led by Damon Keith, and influential Detroit civic leaders, including most of the men who had made Detroit's Olympic case in Baden-Baden, led by Mayor Cavanagh, Councilman William Patrick, Richard Cross, and Martin Hayden and his editorial department at the *Detroit News*. But a counteroffensive against the nomination had taken shape, led by conservative Tennessee lawyers with apparent behind-the-scenes assistance from FBI director J. Edgar Hoover. Tennessee was one of four states in the Sixth Circuit along with Kentucky, Ohio, and Michigan.

Using information supplied by Hoover's agency, the Tennessee opponents reached deep into the past to argue that Edwards was not qualified. They noted that his father, who had been a major influence on him, had been a well-known socialist in Texas, and that Edwards himself during his college years had participated in groups that included communist members and then served as a radical labor organizer, arrested for disturbing the peace during a 1936 autoworkers strike at the Kelsey-Hayes Wheel Company, where he was organizing with Reuther. The *Memphis Commercial Appeal* called him "an unfit man, a sycophant of Walter Reuther." Sheppard Tate, head of the Tennessee Bar, used a more lawyerly vocabulary. Describing the Sixth Circuit as "one of the great courts of the nation," he lamented, "I would not want to see anyone appointed to it who might in any way create a lack of confidence in it."

In the wash of the Kennedy assassination, confirmation hearings seemed beside the point, and it took another three weeks for the Senate to return to the Edwards issue. The Judiciary Committee, with a Democratic majority, approved his confirmation on December 11, despite the opposition of the chairman, James O. Eastland, a conservative segregationist from Mississippi. Soon thereafter the full Senate debated and voted. Hubert Humphrey of Minnesota, who had known Edwards since the late forties when he was mayor of Minneapolis and Edwards was on the Detroit Common Council, stood strongest in support. "If there is any one quality that George Edwards has above all others it is his deep sense of social justice and his sense of fairness," Humphrey said. Those attributes, he added, were apparent in the transformation of the Detroit Police Department under Edwards, which had become a model for the nation.

Edwards was confirmed, and his resignation as police commissioner became effective a week before Christmas. Cavanagh accepted with "great regret" and appointed his chief of staff, Ray Girardin, a former reporter who had once covered the cop beat for the *Detroit Times,* as the new commissioner. Edwards had once explained to an old friend that he had stepped down from the Michigan Supreme Court and taken the police commissioner's position in 1961 with the hope of quelling rising racial tensions in Detroit, "which made many of its leaders feel that they were sitting on a keg of dynamite." He had also hoped to "make the Constitution a living document in one of our great cities." Now, two years later, the experiment was over. He could not know how a race riot four years into the future would obliterate his efforts.

The clubs of Detroit were uncharacteristically quiet in the nights after Kennedy was shot. People still came out, and singers still performed, but the acts were as subdued as the scene at the tables. On Wednesday night, November 27, the eve of his thirty-fourth birthday and the night before Thanksgiving, Berry Gordy celebrated at the 20 Grand with his mother and father, all of his sisters, and Marvin Gaye, the husband of Anna. The featured act that night was Johnny Hartman, a smooth singer with perfect phrasing who earlier that year had recorded an album of jazz ballads with saxophonist John Coltrane. Hartman made his way around the club encouraging others to sing, including at one point a waitress. He eventually handed the microphone to Gaye, who was in exquisite crooning mood and stole the show with "(I'm Afraid) The Masquerade Is Over." Gordy's girlfriend, Margaret Norton, was pregnant that November, and when their son was born four months later he was named Kennedy William Gordy. First name for the fallen president, middle name in honor of William Smokey Robinson.

Gordy had been working that week on a new song to commemorate Kennedy. One day he was writing lyrics in his office with his sister Esther when a visitor was ushered in. It was Lincoln Perry, a black actor better known as Stepin Fetchit. No one could have seemed more out of date in 1963 than Stepin Fetchit, lazy and slow and seemingly discombobulated, unable to do anything right, a black man who played to negative stereotypes and was a hit with certain white audiences. The distance from Stepin Fetchit to Martin Luther King or Malcolm X seemed oceanic. But Perry always insisted that he had been misunderstood. He told Gordy that his character was pimping white audiences just as slaves had once done with their masters, pretending to be incompetent—"puttin' on the old massa"—

as a means of escape. Gordy not only listened; he let his visitor help him with the song. The result was "May What He Lived for Live," sung by the majestic Liz Lands, who with her operatic voice reached F-flat an octave and a half above middle C. The song was meant for JFK but sadly had a revival five years later when Lands sang it at the funeral of Martin Luther King. The writing credits listed Berry Gordy, Esther Edwards, and W. A. Bisson, apparently another pseudonym for Lincoln Perry.

*May what he lived for live*
*May what he lived for live*
*May what he strived for*
*May what he died for live.*

The memorial song's finest moment would come late the following August in Atlantic City, when Joe Lieberman, a young assistant to John M. Bailey, chairman of the Democratic Party, distributed two thousand copies of the record to delegates on the floor of the Democratic National Convention.

In the days after Thanksgiving, when the Detroit Lions and Green Bay Packers played to a 13–13 tie in their traditional holiday game, if someone had walked around Detroit asking citizens if they knew Richard Lane, few would have been able to come up with an answer. But Night Train Lane—that was a different matter. Everyone knew Night Train. Since his trade to the Lions before the 1960 season, Lane had become a Detroit institution, an all-pro defensive back renowned equally for his nose for interceptions and his punishing tackles, especially a stiff-armed clothesline takedown that he used so menacingly the NFL soon made it illegal. Lane, then thirty-five, was at the tail end of a brilliant career that had begun with the Los Angeles Rams in 1952, when he set a rookie record of fourteen interceptions. It was also during that rookie season that he acquired one of the great nicknames in American sporting history. Some thought it was because he was afraid to fly and instead caught trains at night to get from city to city. Others thought it was some evocation of his intensity as a ballplayer, like a locomotive pounding toward the opposition. The most commonly accepted notion was that "Night Train" was coined by Tom Fears, a Rams teammate, who enjoyed music and nicknames in equal measure and often played a recording of "Night Train" in the locker room. However it came to Dick Lane, the nickname fit.

In a town bubbling with talented black musicians and lawyers and preachers, Night Train was one of the precious few star black athletes. The Lions had been among the first NFL teams to bring on black players when they signed Bob Mann and Mel Groomes in 1948. Mann was a brilliant receiver out of the University of Michigan who led the NFL in receiving yardage in 1949 but left the Lions deeply embittered a year later when he was asked to take a pay cut even while two recently drafted and untested rookies were signed for nearly twice as much money. It would take another decade—more than ten years after Jackie Robinson—before the baseball Tigers, owned for decades by Walter Briggs, an auto body magnate and overt racist, signed their first nonwhite player, and that was the Dominican Oswaldo (Ozzie) Virgil, who broke the color barrier when he took the field at Briggs Stadium on June 6, 1958. Virgil at first felt apart from Detroit's black community because he was a black Latino and not an African American. The Tigers were still virtually all white in 1963 but brought up outfielders Gates Brown and Willie Horton before the season was over.

Lane was not just a Hall of Fame–caliber player; he had become a major figure in black Detroit since his arrival three years earlier. He was the proprietor of El Taco, a popular restaurant on Dexter Avenue, where the new chef was Arthur Madison, who had made his reputation cooking for the Ebony Room at the Gotham Hotel. Ads for Dick Night Train Lane's El Taco ran frequently in the *Chronicle*, specializing in fine steaks, shrimp, chops, and whole barbecue chickens. Lane was also a regular on the club scene, hanging out at the Flame Show Bar and other joints with the singers and night owls. And now, since their wedding in July, he was the male half of the most talented couple in town—the husband of Dinah Washington, the great blues singer. They shared a spacious apartment at 4002 W. Buena Vista Street, about a mile from El Taco in northwest Detroit. When Night Train married the Queen of the Blues, he called himself "the lucky seventh."

Dinah Washington had done a lot of living, and a lot of marrying, in her thirty-nine years. He was her seventh husband. "Unforgettable" was her hit tune in 1959, and unforgettable she was, with her diction so clear and direct, her voice so easy, ranging high or low, the touch of Alabama (she lived in Tuscaloosa as a girl) in her effortless notes. She was among the most popular singers of the fifties, though not immune to critics, some of whom would have preferred that she stay pure to the blues and not delve into popular music. She could sing almost anything, and did, from "Smoke Gets in Your Eyes" to "Cry Me a River" to "Is You Is or Is You Ain't My Baby?" but onstage in front of the microphone she could effect an entrancingly personal connection with men in the audience. Night Train Lane had been one of those men.

In early December Dinah returned to Detroit from an out-of-town gig for a weeklong tribute to Night Train built around events raising funds for a scholarship program in his name. She had just made the news again, when a beautician in Las Vegas filed a $70,000 lawsuit against her for critical comments she made about wigs he had prepared for her: between songs, she said, one customer told her that her wig "looked like a rat." While the beautician claimed he had suffered from anxiety because of her comments, Washington told friends in Detroit that she was the one damaged by it all. Now she was happy to be nestled in Detroit with Night Train and looking forward to a holiday break with her family. She had just finished Christmas shopping. She was sick of being on the road, she told James Cleaver, a local photographer, and was eager to settle down in Detroit. Cleaver thought she seemed "full of life, exuberant, displaying her own inimitable brand of humor."

On the Friday night of December 13, while she stayed back at the Buena Vista apartment, Lane drove to Detroit Metropolitan Airport to pick up Washington's two teenage sons from previous marriages, George Jenkins and Robert Grayson, who were coming in from a New England prep school. The couple then spent the night watching television in their pajamas, with the boys in another room, a quiet night for Night Train. Their bags were packed, as they would all leave the next day for Chicago and the

Lions game that Sunday against the first-place Chicago Bears. They fell asleep at about 1 a.m., and at 3:45 Lane awoke to the buzzing of the off-air television set. He found his wife lying on the floor next to the bed, unconscious. Lane called Dr. B. C. Ross, who drove out to the apartment but could do nothing to revive the singer, pronouncing her dead at 4:50 a.m. "She's gone," Lane told her sons, who had awakened and were looking on from the next room. Soon thereafter Detective William Chubb from the Homicide Bureau arrived with two patrolmen. According to the police report, they interviewed Dr. Ross, who said that he believed "the subject had injected an unknown type of pill. There was an unlabeled bottle containing about 50 orange and blue pills on a night stand beside the bed." The pills were sent to the morgue along with her body for an autopsy by the medical examiner. She was found to have barbiturates in her blood, more than double the amount of amobarbital and secobarbital. She had been taking several prescribed drugs to handle her anxiety and try to lose weight. The death was ruled an accidental overdose. *At last I am free,* she had sung, *no I don't hurt anymore.*

The shock of Dinah Washington's death was felt most deeply in Chicago, where her career began, and in Detroit, where it ended prematurely. Berry Gordy had spent many nights listening to her at the Flame Show Bar, entranced by her sultry persona. She was a close friend of C. L. Franklin and a frolicking older sister of sorts for Franklin's singing daughters. One of her last performances in Detroit was at Cobo Hall, in the presence of Martin Luther King, at the rally on June 23 where he delivered his first version of the "dream" speech. Before her body was flown back to Chicago for burial, there was a memorial service at Reverend Franklin's New Bethel Baptist. The church could not hold all of those who wanted to pay respects, and the curbs outside on Linwood and Philadelphia were lined with mourners. Inside the bronze casket, surrounded by a veritable garden of floral arrangements, Washington was dressed in a white mink stole and white gloves, with a diamond tiara on her head and bejeweled slippers on her feet. The High Priest of Soul Preaching handled the sermon, and Ziggy Johnson emceed the entertainment portion of the service. Ziggy too had come from Chicago and was often credited with discovering Washington. He had heard her sing in an amateur contest when she was only fifteen. He watched her leave behind the choir at St. Luke's Baptist Church in Chicago and helped her become the singer for Lionel Hampton's band for eighty-five dollars a week. From then on, she and Ziggy were close. She always called him Ziegfeld. "I just happened to be around when she burst upon the entertainment field," Ziggy said at the memorial service. Detroit was also instrumental in her rise: her first solo performances away from the band were at the Paradise Theater, down the street from the Gotham Hotel. Lovi Mann, the organist at the 20 Grand, who had accompanied her many times there, played the church pipes, softly rendering a medley of her best known songs, and the New Bethel choir featured a soloist whose voice soared and sank and soared again with soulful emotion as Night Train watched, arms folded, eyes dazed, from the front pew.

One last tragedy in the year of the fallen. It was with the resounding gospel incantations of Aretha Franklin that Detroit said good-bye.

Chapter 19

# BIG OLD WATERBOATS

**AT THE DAWN** of his first full year as president, Lyndon Johnson believed that he could use his immense political skill and will to work his way through most problems. When it came to his domestic agenda, his attention often turned to Detroit. The health of its auto industry was essential to the economic well-being of the nation, and the strength of the United Auto Workers union was critical to LBJ in so many ways, both as a base of electoral support and as a progressive lobby for his civil rights agenda. But all of that worked in his favor, he thought, only if there was peace, not overseas but at the negotiating tables of Detroit. Somehow both Henry Ford II and Walter Reuther had to be satisfied. That notion was the backdrop for a recorded conversation about Reuther that Johnson had with Robert McNamara, his secretary of defense, on January 25. Johnson was doing most of the talking that Saturday. McNamara was mostly listening and trying to deflect without sounding too contrary. He knew Reuther in a way the president did not, as an adversary more than an ally. They rose together on opposite sides in the auto world of Detroit after World War II, with McNamara arriving at the Ford Motor Company in 1946 just as Reuther was ascending to the top of the UAW.

McNamara had been one of the young officers out of the U.S. Army Air Force who had applied military planning techniques and statistical analysis to revive Ford with a modernization effort that Norman Strouse witnessed with admiration as the manager of the Detroit branch of J. Walter Thompson. Quiz Kids, they were called at first, with a tone of sarcasm if not derision, for all of the questions they kept asking, but the success of their effort soon enough turned the moniker into Whiz Kids. It was that efficiency in running a massive operation that brought McNamara to Washington to run the Pentagon for JFK, and now for Johnson.

Domestic policy, not defense strategy, was foremost on Johnson's mind in those early days of his presidency. He was determined to finish the work of the Kennedy administration in civil rights and to establish his own, more sweeping economic and social agenda. Since Johnson called Reuther's hotel room in Washington one day after Kennedy's assassination to say that he needed the labor leader's help more than ever, their relationship had only deepened. Reuther yearned to be near the center of power, and Johnson was masterly at the twin arts of flattery and manipulation, making Reuther feel that he was the president's confidant. Two weeks before Christmas, he had given Reuther the title of special ambassador and included him in the U.S. delegation that attended the December 12 independence ceremonies in Nairobi, Kenya. As frequent as Reuther's contact had been with the White House during the Kennedy years, his interactions with Johnson were more intimate. Johnson was incessantly working the Oval Office phone, and Reuther was on the priority list of people on the receiving end. On December 23 Johnson called at 9:18 at night to discuss the civil rights legislation and a tax cut proposal. "We've got to get going on civil rights," Johnson said. Richard Russell, the Democratic senator from Georgia who co-authored the Southern Manifesto, was a main obstacle to the legislation. Johnson told Reuther that Russell was now claiming he could defeat any cloture vote to end a filibuster. "If you fellows can put a little steel in Mansfield's spine . . . that's the only thing that's ever going to best Dick Russell," LBJ advised, referring to Mike Mansfield, the Senate majority leader from Montana.

Before his first State of the Union address on January 8, the president solicited a memo from Reuther on what he should say. The six-page "Economy of Opportunity" plan that Reuther and his aides provided was in some ways a rough blueprint of LBJ's historic address declaring an "unconditional war on poverty in America," calling for the elimination of "not some, but all racial discrimination," and urging the creation of "a high-level commission on automation"—the technological transformation that was high among Reuther's concerns. "If we have the brainpower to invent these machines, we have the brainpower to make certain that they are a boon and not a bane to humanity," Johnson said, echoing a sentiment common in Reuther's own speeches.

Automation, workplace conditions, middle-class wages, job security, meaningful work, and quality of life—those were the central issues for Reuther and his union. His mission involved a difficult balancing act. He had to try to satisfy the immediate complaints and demands of his disparate union constituency, but at the same time he prided himself on looking toward the future to address difficulties he saw headed his way. One problem he foresaw in January 1964 was America's vulnerability in the world car market, and he connected that to other concerns, including displaced workers and the need for smaller cars to counter foreign competition. All of that, along with the demise of Studebaker, was in the background of the conversation between Johnson and McNamara on January 25.

Studebaker's decline was so long and steady that nothing, not even the introduction of the Avanti, a sleek new car the company introduced at the 1962 Detroit Auto Show, could turn it around. With widespread rumors that Studebaker was faltering, its 1964 models, sent to dealers in fall 1963, were virtually ignored by consumers, and the situation collapsed from there. Five days before Christmas, the South Bend plant was shuttered, sending Reuther's UAW members there out into the cold.

At the same time, reports were coming out showing how much the world car market had changed in the fourteen months since that 1962 auto show, when big cars seemed resurgent and Henry Ford II had talked so confidently about Detroit's position against foreign competition. In 1963, for the first time, even as the Big Three were enjoying their best sales year ever, more than half the cars in the world were made outside the United States, with estimates that the gap would only widen year by year from then on. Volkswagen was rising, and even Japan was beginning to stir, both taking hold of the worldwide small car market. Between 375,000 and 400,000 imports were sold in the United States in 1963, and estimates for 1964 were up to a half million. One reason, experts said, was that the compact cars the U.S. automakers started manufacturing in the late fifties in response to an earlier foreign surge were getting so much bigger every year that by now that might as well be classified as midsize vehicles.

Out of these negative developments Reuther saw the possibility of something positive. For fifteen years, since 1949, he had been urging American automakers to adapt to a changing world by making smaller cars. Now he and his aides at the UAW developed a grand scheme to create what he called an "all-American small car." It would require central planning and cooperation between labor and industry and the automakers themselves, concepts that were dear to Reuther, evoking the New Deal and the all-for-one mobilization during the war, but increasingly alien to the impulses of American industry. The car was to be manufactured at the idle plant in South Bend, reemploying laid-off Studebaker workers, and be a joint venture pooling the engineering talents of Ford, GM, and Chrysler. Reuther dug out a quote from Henry Ford II to explain why a joint venture was needed. "Volkswagen sold about two hundred thousand cars last year in this country," Ford had said. "But if we started to compete with it, then General Motors would go in, and probably Chrysler, and by the time we start divvying up what is left in a market of this size, there's nothing there." A joint venture would overcome that problem, Reuther argued. If the Big Three came together in a peacetime version of the Arsenal of Democracy, they could win the economic world war and improve the U.S. balance of payments, which "suffers severely from failure of the nation's automobile industry to produce a small car to compete for the U.S. and world markets." And to save on costs, Reuther argued, the all-American small car could avoid making yearly model changes. He cited a Senate subcommittee estimate from several years earlier claiming that annual model changes added about $200 to the cost of the average car. Volkswagen had already "proved that model changes are not necessary in the small car market."

Any such joint venture would require strong support from the federal government, including an agreement by the Justice Department to suspend antitrust enforcement, which explains how LBJ ended up discussing it with McNamara. It appeared from the conversation that Johnson's interests were not so much in the merits of the small-car proposal as in his desire to keep Reuther mollified—for several reasons. It was not just that Reuther was a key supporter of the president's initiatives; there were raw political calculations involved as well. Labor contracts with the Big Three automakers would be coming up later in the year, just as Johnson was running for election. He did not want to be embarrassed by a massive autoworkers strike that could stall the economy in November. That is where the discussion with McNamara began. One other issue was connected to Johnson's ploy. A year earlier, the European Economic Community had placed a stiff tariff on the import of chickens produced in the United States. In what became known as the Chicken Wars, Johnson retaliated by imposing a 25 percent increase in the tariffs on imported brandy, potato starch, dextrin, and light trucks. The tariff on light trucks was aimed especially at Volkswagen, some of whose vans were classified in that category. It was also aimed at pleasing Reuther, bolstering the U.S. labor force by debilitating foreign competition. Johnson considered this another card in his hand as he tried to pressure Reuther to avoid a future strike.

"He's going to push on [the auto contracts] to the wall and it's going to be murder on us," Johnson said to McNamara. But as a world-class student of human behavior, especially in the political world, LBJ thought he saw a way to placate Reuther. "I think, though, he's vain enough that if we could get some company to . . . put this little car on manufacture it'd be real novel . . . and have the Justice department behave and have it be his idea."

McNamara was nonplussed. What was his boss thinking? Aside from all the ways this idea ran counter to the automakers' free enterprise philosophy, it also seemed naïve, blind to the realities of Detroit. The Big Three would reject the idea outright, McNamara advised, speaking from his experience at Ford, precisely "because it was Reuther who wanted it."

Johnson seemed undeterred. Rather than argue with McNamara, he tried to drag him further into his conniving. The Defense Department could "do a little contract" to help Reuther's plan get off the ground, he said. "You're the biggest users. Why don't you give 'em a contract, instead of running around in these damn big old waterboats you gotta have? Why couldn't you buy a hundred thousand?"

McNamara thoughtfully declined to mention that LBJ enjoyed rides in two of the biggest waterboats around, not only the outsized presidential limousine but a white Lincoln convertible with which he chauffeured guests around his Hill Country ranch in Texas. (JFK too seemed partial to Ford; his favorite was a 1961 Thunderbird convertible, the same cool car that Detroit advertiser Bill Laurie drove.) Small cars were just not right for the Pentagon, McNamara said. The brass needed more room, more comfort. To which Johnson replied, "[Well what about] all those sergeants whirling around in Mercurys, delivering messages for generals?"

Then the subject changed and that was that. Reuther kept pushing his all-American car idea, but it never got anywhere beyond the calculating mind of the president. The auto companies had no more interest in the small car than they did in his suggestion that they lower prices. They would never do that just because Walter Reuther wanted them to. The market would determine what the prices should be, along with the marketers. Reuther nonetheless remained loyal to LBJ; the issues of civil rights, poverty, and federal action to promote social equity were too central to him to be subject to negotiation. He considered himself a social progressive first, a collective bargainer second. But there remained the prospect of labor strikes before the election.

Chapter 20

# UNFINISHED BUSINESS

**OFIELD DUKES OF** the *Michigan Chronicle* started the new year by roaming the streets of Detroit with photographer Jim Cleaver to assess the lives and hopes of those at the bottom. "What does the resident of skid row, the drifter, the wino, the prostitute, the unemployable, the hard pressed escapist have to look forward to in 1964? On what basis do these social lepers, these outcasts of society embrace hope and faith that the wheels of fortune and the laws of destiny will operate in their interest and favor?" The answers Dukes came back with were no surprise.

First stop was a flophouse on Gratiot between St. Antoine and Beaubien, only a block and a half from Detroit Police Department headquarters. It was a bitterly cold night; an arctic air mass had whipped subzero temperatures into Michigan, and the ragged men taking shelter inside looked at the inquisitive intruders with bewilderment, as if any thought beyond the matter of not freezing to death was superfluous. One man said he had been without a job for twelve years, since 1952, when he left Pittsburgh in search of work. Another said he was too old to be concerned with civil rights. A third said he was looking forward to an early spring and the comfort of a jail bed. In the dead of winter, he said, "I could go out on the street and look drunk, even lie on the sidewalk, but police won't arrest me. This is not the season. They don't start picking us up until spring—March, April, and May." Dukes added as a side note that "the man . . . doesn't feel that the

Negro will progress much in 1964." Similar responses came from prostitutes, store owners, and street people up and down Chrysler Drive, an access road paralleling the Chrysler Freeway along what once was Hastings Street. At the bottom, there was not much hope.

That story was published in the first *Chronicle* issue of 1964, an edition brimming with assessments of the year past and predictions for the new one. Rev. C. L. Franklin was named one of eight Ministers of the Year. Mayor Jerome Cavanagh and former police commissioner George Edwards were among the Citizens of the Year. There was a roll call of events connecting Detroit and the national story: The Walk to Freedom. The "Negro Revolt" sweeping the American South. LBJ's visit to Second Baptist to mark the hundredth anniversary of the Emancipation Proclamation. The March on Washington. King's "dream" speech. The police shooting of Cynthia Scott at the corner of John R and Edmond. The drive for federal civil rights legislation. The defeat of an open-housing bill by the Detroit Common Council. The booing of the National Anthem at the Olympics rally in front of the *Spirit of Detroit* sculpture. The political murder of Medgar Evers in Mississippi. The death of four young girls when the Klan bombed the 16th Street Baptist Church in Birmingham. Malcolm X's fiery "Message to the Grassroots" at King Solomon Baptist. The assassination of President Kennedy in Dallas. The overdose death of Dinah Washington. "The year 1963 was the most dramatic, poignant, encouraging, tragic, reactionary, and progressive paradox of any single year that we know in American history," wrote Broadus Nathaniel Butler, a *Chronicle* columnist and administrator at Wayne State University who had served with the Tuskegee airmen in World War II and received a doctorate in philosophy from the University of Michigan. "There have been periods, some long and some short, representing all facets of things that happened in 1963, but no one year to our knowledge encompassed and mirrored—with such complete clarity and depth of meaning—the whole dramatic history of the United States."

Above the Broadus column was an editorial with the headline "1964—A

Year of Unfinished Business." All of that activity in civil rights needed to be met now with legislative achievement, the editors wrote. "The star of the Negro blinking in a murky sky radiates a glimmering ray of hope for 1964. But this hope has to be combined with hard work, determination, and greater unity if the aspirations of the '63 revolt are to be crystallized in '64."

Aside from the glow of the Walk to Freedom, progress in Detroit was modest and subject to contrary interpretations. Despite the defeat of the open-housing bill, Richard Marks, executive director of the Commission on Community Relations, said his agency had recorded sixteen instances where "known Negro families" were living in neighborhoods that formerly had been described as all white—areas west of Schaefer Road on the west side and north of Seven Mile and west of Connor on the east side. But the movement of blacks beyond the de facto confinement of their established territory was met with ever increasing hostility by white neighborhood associations that employed the language, and some of the tactics, of paramilitary organizations, a not so cold racial war that had been intensifying year by year for two decades. As historian Thomas Sugrue noted, these groups referred to "invasions" and "penetrations" and strategies of physical and verbal resistance. "The first black family to cross into the Northeast side neighborhood surrounding Saint Bartholomew's parish in 1963," Sugrue reported, "was greeted with a sign that read 'Get back on the other side of 7 Mile.'"

There were, as always, complicated forces at work when it came to the issue of race in Detroit. At the same time that open-housing advocates were making their irrefutable case and winning in court against a reactionary homeowners' rights ordinance, there came increasing reports of extortion and knifings in Detroit's public schools, including the beating of a teacher at Pershing High. Some law-and-order politicians called for a police crackdown of the sort that took place the year before Cavanagh was elected mayor and Edwards became police commissioner, a policy that was criticized for indiscriminately targeting black citizens. The Urban League, meanwhile, issued a report asserting that racial discrimination persisted within the police department. Despite Edwards's concerted efforts to integrate the department, there were still only forty-four black officers, or 3.25 percent of the force, and they were less likely than their white counterparts to get promotions. Edwards was now on the federal bench, but his allies came to his defense as best they could. They noted that nine blacks were in the latest police academy class, amounting to 7.4 percent of the class, which was an improvement, though modest, and that Patrolman Avery Jackson had been assigned full time to recruit fellow African Americans. It was also pointed out that black officers now worked in all but two of the city's precincts, and that in the Edwards era sixteen were promoted to "preferred" jobs, including a woman officer who became the first black working forensic evidence in the Scientific Bureau.

The career change of William T. Patrick seemed to fall on both sides of the civil rights ledger. When Patrick announced at the end of 1963 that he was resigning as the lone black member of the City Council to take a job with Michigan Bell Telephone, it was seen at once as a blow to the movement and a sign of progress. Some called it the price of integration. Though in a different realm, it could be thought of as part of the same process that saw the demise of the Gotham Hotel and the disappearance of Hastings Street. With his new job as assistant general counsel for the telephone company, Patrick was reaching an executive level few African Americans in Detroit had seen before. Yet with his departure from the council, fears arose that the competition to replace him would further fracture the city's black political community. Horace Sheffield, a leading black labor official in Detroit, said Patrick deserved the accolades, "but for the Negro community to continue to romanticize this situation and ignore the very real political chaos that his withdrawal from council has created is sheer stupidity."

Detroit was 29 percent black then, and council members were elected at large, by the entire voting population, leaving open the possibility that a white candidate might prevail, leaving no African American representation. And fissures were already forming within the black community as various would-be replacements made their ambitions known. Patrick was the rare public figure who could interact comfortably with almost all segments of Detroit society and politics, with the exception of the virulent white neighborhood protectionists and a few black separatists. It was his impressive performance on the Olympic trip to Baden-Baden with the governor and mayor and Detroit business elite that inspired Michigan Bell to recruit him. At the same time, his steadfast sponsorship of open-housing legislation and his role as a black pioneer in city politics solidified his position in the African American community.

"Ah, it's a great life if you happen to be Jerry Cavanagh." Not a bad lead sentence for the mayor of Detroit to read in the *Free Press* as the new year began. There might have been a touch of sarcasm behind Frank Beckman's line—he was, after all, a hard-bitten political reporter—but nothing that followed gave it away. "At age 35, you've got a $25,000 a year job as mayor of Detroit. The politicos see a great future ahead of you. The kids are over the flu and the gorgeous wife isn't so frantic."

Cavanagh had just been named one of the Outstanding Young Men in the nation by the U.S. Junior Chamber of Commerce, a list of rising thirty somethings that also included Birch Bayh, Democratic senator from Indiana; Zbigniew Brzezinski, a professor at Columbia University who specialized in the Soviet sphere of influence; A. Leon Higginbotham of Philadelphia, a black lawyer serving on the Federal Trade Commission; and George Stevens Jr., a documentary filmmaker and producer whose namesake father had directed the movie classic *Giant*. Cavanagh had reached a status where he was wanted on both coasts. The Outstanding Young Men ceremony would take place in Santa Monica, but before leaving for California, the mayor was preparing for a trip to Washington, where he would meet with President Johnson and a select group of mayors to discuss urban issues at the White House. A few years earlier, when LBJ was vice president and Cavanagh was meeting him for the first time at Johnson's office near the Senate chambers in the Capitol, the mayor had the distinct impression that Johnson considered him with caution, if not disdain, as a Kennedy man. "I see you wear those Ivy League shirts," Johnson had said to him then. Describing the scene later, Cavanagh explained, "It was button down. He didn't like it." But everything had changed since then, and now the two men were allies who needed one another.

From the windows of the hideaway annex to his eleventh-floor office, Cavanagh could see south and west toward Cobo Hall and the Ambassador Bridge leading to Canada. When he looked down at the blotter on his desk, he saw a photograph of Louis Miriani, his predecessor. It had been among the detritus left behind during the transition in 1961, and instead of returning it or throwing it out, he decided to put it in a place where he could not help but see it, even though there was no love lost between the two politicians. The photo, he said, served as "a reminder that this too shall pass." But what next? There was talk of challenging George Romney in the next gubernatorial election. One Democrat, Congressman Neil Staebler of Ann Arbor, had entered the race, but Staebler's labor and civil rights credentials were questioned by Walter Reuther and the UAW, who went looking for an alternative. Reuther first approached G. Mennen (Soapy) Williams, the popular former six-term governor who had gone to Washington with JFK's election to serve as assistant secretary of state for African affairs, but when Williams declined Reuther turned to Cavanagh.

Some Michigan political observers said it was a fifty-fifty proposition that Cavanagh would run, even though he had not yet finished his first term as mayor. Beckman described him as "energetic, restless and AMBITIOUS," the capital letters in this case no overstatement, given his overt attempt to model himself after Kennedy. "The job of mayor is very satisfying," Cavanagh said in response to the speculation. "My present inclination is to remain where I am. But one has to consider all things in politics and opportunities as they present themselves."

In his New Year's address for 1964, Cavanagh had echoed the "unfinished business" theme articulated in the *Chronicle*. Nineteen sixty-three was "momentous," he said. "It witnessed economic prosperity for most of the country and looked with special favor on Detroit. The general level of wages and salaries has been improved and unemployment has been reduced. New buildings in Detroit indicate an active past year and bode well for 1964." But there was much still to be done, and Cavanagh was optimistic that it could be done, both in Detroit and nationally under LBJ, who had already defined himself as an activist president. His optimism, Cavanagh said, was "an inherent characteristic of man and his trust in progress." But he added that all of these hopes rested on one condition most of all: a peaceful world. On the same day that he delivered that message, there was a front-page story about two noted West Point graduates who had been wounded in South Vietnam. One was Brig. Gen. Joseph W. Stilwell Jr., the son of a noted World War II commander, and the other was William C. Carpenter, a lieutenant who had been a star college football player, gaining fame as the "lonesome end" on the 1959 Army team. American forces in Vietnam were designated as advisers then, but 163 had already been killed in the developing war.

"I am proud of a young man named Berry Gordy Jr.," Ziggy Johnson wrote in his first "Zagging with Ziggy" column of the new year. "He has given the youth of our town an incentive to strive for unknown goals that can be theirs, once they find something pleasing to the show-going and record listening public."

Motown was entering its sixth year of existence in January 1964. Gordy had closed out the old year with a grand Christmas party at his new showpiece, the Graystone Ballroom. Most Motown accounts, taking their cue from Gordy's own autobiography, *To Be Loved*, placed this Christmas party in December 1962, but that is inaccurate. Gordy did not buy the ballroom until June 1963. The Christmas party in December 1963 was his first at the Graystone. All the Gordys were there: Mom and Pops and sisters Esther, Anna, Gwen, and Loucye, along with brothers Fuller, George, and Robert and their families. So were most of the producers, technicians, writers, salespeople, musicians, and artists in the growing Motown assembly, along with local deejays, emcees, club owners, and friends. "I would be a stupid columnist if I attempted to call the names of all the future stars who were on hand," Ziggy confided. Mohair suits, cocked hats, cocktail dresses, furs—everyone dressed in their finest. Robert Gordy wore a Santa Claus suit and handed out bonus checks. Smokey Robinson played the piano for the crowd, with many of the singers gathered around him, and was given the Motown Spirit Award.

All seemed flush at Motown, just as with the auto industry. But here too 1964 presented itself as the year to deal with things undone.

A few months before his fourteenth birthday, the youngest member of the troupe had dropped the diminutive from his stage name and was now going by Stevie Wonder. His voice was also changing, making it more difficult for him to sing in keys being arranged for him. "Fingertips (Part 2)" had propelled him into stardom and across the ocean. He was in Paris and London over the holiday break, performing in both European capitals and appearing on various television shows. In the middle of the tour, he flew back to New York, missing scheduled stops in West Germany and the Netherlands for what was to be a January 5 appearance on *The Ed Sullivan Show*. It was listed in *TV Guide* and promoted in Detroit, but time ran out and the host was into his weekly end-of-show ritual, a sweeping wave good night, before Stevie could make it onstage. The commitment had been firm since the previous September, but now the Beatles were coming with their British Invasion. They would make their American debut on the show five weeks later, on February 9, while Stevie was still waiting for his chance.

Reflecting the crosscurrents of the times, Gordy had involved his prodigy in a seemingly peculiar back-to-the-future enterprise before the trip overseas. Or maybe it was not so odd, given two of Gordy's proclivities: first, his intention to promote Motown beyond the racial confines of the rhythm and blues market, as the sound of young America; and second, his incipient fascination with Hollywood and the Southern California lifestyle. In the final months of 1963, Gordy had established a small auxiliary operation in Los Angeles. He hired a few writers and producers and scoured the movie culture looking for potential deals and openings for his artists. Along came the producers of *Muscle Beach Party*, an inane movie starring Frankie Avalon and Annette Funicello frolicking and fretting on Malibu Beach. This was the tamest of white teen culture, straight out of the fifties mentality, but there was a supporting role for Stevie Wonder as he joined the beach crowd to lip-synch a song called "Happy Street." The lyrics almost mimicked "Fingertips," which is to say they were barely lyrics at all, mostly encouragements to "clap your hands, stomp your feet, get with the rhythm of happy street."

Even with all of Motown's success, three of its most talented groups still thirsted for their first hit. Gordy was on his way to becoming a wealthy man, his recording company was turning into an international enterprise, the studio on West Grand Boulevard could compete with the best in New York and Los Angeles, and yet this was all without success from the Supremes, the Temptations, and the Four Tops—the very groups that later would define the Motown sound.

In the year of unfinished business, the Temptations were the first to break through, with considerable help from two Miracles. On January 8, a Wednesday afternoon, they went into the studio on West Grand Boulevard and started recording a song that Smokey Robinson and Bobby Rogers, a fellow Miracle, had conceived while out on the road during the second *Motortown Revue* tour. All in the family. Rogers was born on the same day in the same hospital as Robinson. He was not only Smokey's friend, the tenor below Robinson's soprano, but also the cousin of Smokey's wife, Claudette, and husband of one of the Marvelettes, Wanda Young. Of the many talented Detroiters attached to Motown, Rogers ranked among the most underrated, with a natural affinity for writing and choreography. As they rode down the endless highways on tour, he and Smokey would exchange pickup lines and laments and rhymes until they had possible stanzas for a new song. One came up with "You got a smile so bright / you know you coulda been a candle." The other responded with "I'm holding you so tight / You know you coulda been a handle." And eventually they had composed "The Way You Do the Things You Do."

In "the snakepit" studio the day of the recording, Eddie Willis took a Funk Brothers star turn with the urgent syncopation of his joyful guitar chords; Eddie Kendricks, with his signature falsetto, sang lead; and the newest member of the quintet, David Ruffin, melded in with Paul Williams, Otis Williams, and the deep-voiced Melvin Franklin as backup. The talent was all

Temptations, but the words and sound, so simple and clear, were classic Smokey Robinson. "The Way You Do the Things You Do" took its place in the anthology of songs that inspired Bob Dylan to call Smokey "America's greatest living poet." The only problem is that Dylan never actually uttered those words. Al Abrams, a public relations man at Motown, later acknowledged that he concocted the quote after hearing Berry Gordy say Smokey deserved more recognition than he was getting for his songwriting talents. Abrams recalled that he was talking to Al Aronowitz, a music writer close to Dylan, and asked if he could get a quote from Dylan praising Robinson. When Aronowitz wondered what sort of quote he had in mind, Abrams suggested "Smokey Robinson is America's greatest poet." As Abrams recalled the scene, Aronowitz "thought about it for a minute and then said, 'Why bother even telling Bob? That sounds just like something he'd say anyway. Go ahead and do it. If Bob sees it in print, he'll think he said it. He's certainly never going to deny it.'" So Abrams took the quote to Gordy, and from there it went public. "I will admit that I lived in fear every time I heard Dylan was doing a major interview and might say, 'What the fuck? I never said that!'" Abrams recounted. But Aronowitz was right, it never happened, and the Dylan paean to Smokey Robinson found its way into rock and roll mythology.

The Supremes seemed to be everywhere except where they wanted to be, although they were able to escape the frigid Michigan winter for a two-week engagement in Bermuda. Florence Ballard was twenty-one, Mary Wilson and Diana Ross still twenty, but they had been part of the Motown scene so long they were all regarded as adults. They performed each night in a club at the Clayhouse Inn, where the first show started at eleven and the second at one in the morning. Flo raved about Bermuda's pink sand, Mary about the Crystal Cave, and Diana loved the shopping. No sooner had they returned than they joined Ziggy Johnson on an eighty-mile trip from Motown to Jacktown to stage a holiday season concert for inmates at the state prison in Jackson. In sequined dresses and high heels, they danced and sang four songs and inspired the hardened audience to go wild and sing along—four years before Johnny Cash immortalized the penitentiary concert at Folsom Prison.

Gordy had made two decisions in the final quarter of 1963 designed to set the Supremes on a surer course. The first was to name Ross the lead singer instead of rotating that honor among the three depending on the song. The second was to team them up with Motown's hottest songwriting team, Holland-Dozier-Holland, who had written and produced three big hits for Martha and the Vandellas, including that previous summer's blockbuster, "Heat Wave." Could they do the same for the Supremes? An early HDH number for the group, "When the Lovelight Starts Shining through His Eyes," was the first step. Then and forever after, few knew it by its long title but by the infectious, drawn-out, syncopated rhythm: "May—hade me ree—a—lize I should a—pol—o—gize." It eventually reached No. 23 on the *Billboard* 100—better than anything the Supremes had accomplished before, though not enough for stardom.

The alliance with the Holland-Dozier-Holland songwriting team had another matchmaking aspect to it when Brian Holland, who was married, began an affair with Diana Ross. This was nothing new within the Motown culture. Married and single, on the road and at West Grand Boulevard, new sexual partnerships were forming and dissolving month by month, adding to the crackling energy and tension of the scene. Ross was by no means the only one involved, but she was among the more active players. She had already had affairs with several Motown musicians, including most notably Smokey Robinson, and was working on Berry Gordy, who had always been smitten by her. The romance with Brian Holland was brought to an end by his wife, Sharon, after a confrontation one night in February in the Driftwood Lounge at the 20 Grand, which had become the unofficial Motown hangout club. As Mary Wilson and Florence Ballard later told the story, Sharon Holland walked up to the diminutive Ross, loomed over her, started swearing, and shouted, "If you don't stay away from my man, you're a dead woman!" Ross made a fist and stood her ground, until Wilson and Ballard moved in to protect her. "Sharon kept saying she was going to kick Diane's butt"—they always called her by her real first name, never Diana—"and for a few minutes we had to hold her back," Ballard recalled. The affair was said to end that night but might have sparked something else. A few months later the Supremes had their first hit record, and the lyrics were particularly apt. "Baby, baby, where did our love go?" The song's key worked better for Mary. All three Supremes mistakenly complained that it was written for the Marvelettes and they were just getting hashed-over seconds. Flo thought the tune was lame. Diana grudgingly sang it in a lower register. It became their first No. 1 hit. "I've got this burning, burning, yearning feelin' inside me."

Far from the mean streets that Ofield Dukes walked in his canvassing of Detroit's downtrodden, reports were coming one after another about how the Detroit auto companies were prospering. All the predictions and preliminary counts were on target: the Big Three had sold more cars and trucks in 1963 than ever before, were selling even more in the first quarter of the new year, and were reaping the dividends. Ford Motor Company announced that it had just set a net income record for the first quarter of 1964. Chrysler income was up 48 percent from the previous year, and GM topped them both. For those at the top and in the workforce, this seemed like good news all around, but not necessarily for President Johnson. In keeping with his conversation with McNamara about the small-car scheme to placate Reuther, LBJ had spent the early months of 1964 repeating his fear that the heady atmosphere in Detroit might lead to higher car prices and inflationary wage increases. With a season of new cars and the next round of contract negotiations both on the horizon, he was urging management and labor to be mindful of how their actions could spike inflation.

If he understood Johnson's concern, Reuther turned it to his advantage, saying the responsibility rested primarily with the automakers. Following the dictum that the best defense is a strong offense, he made the argument that the car companies were so profitable the burden was theirs, not his. First he went after GM. "General Motors, for example, reported . . . that its profits before taxes for 1963 amounted to a staggering . . . more than $3.3 billion," he wrote in a memo to LBJ. "Not including profits set aside to pay executive bonuses." The company chairman, Frederic G. Donner, made

$1.3 million in salary and bonuses in 1963, and more than fourteen thousand other GM executives shared in bonuses totaling more than $100 million, an unprecedented figure. GM had so much money, Reuther wrote, that "the joke going the rounds in Detroit is that General Motors Corp. is saving up to buy the Federal Government." In fact the automaker, he further argued, made so much money that it could have lowered car prices and raised wages at the same time. "We earnestly hope the industry will reduce its prices, not only because the consumer is entitled to price reductions, but also because lower prices would increase car sales and thus provide more and steadier jobs for our members," Reuther told the president. "Insofar as wages and other economic benefits for auto workers are concerned, you can be assured that the UAW will adhere to its traditional policy and will not press for gains that would create the necessity for price increases."

From late January into March, Reuther refined his goals for the coming negotiations. His top priorities would be working conditions and job creation, he said, but it would be only fair that working men and women enjoyed some of the boom-year profits that were going to the executives. "Only a fool, only an economic moron, would believe that our equity in a year when industry turns out seven million cars is the same as a year when the industry turns out five million," he told one union gathering. "The workers, equity is not a static thing . . . it grows with the stockholders, equity." By the time the UAW gathered in Atlantic City for its annual convention, Reuther, facing pressure from his locals on the issue, added early retirement to his top goals. He continued his assault on the corporate elite, and in his opening speech at the convention turned away from GM and toward Ford and its owner. As delegates cheered wildly, he used as rhetorical fodder a recent speech that Henry Ford II had given in Chicago in which he complained that the failure of profits to keep pace with other economic indicators was a threat to industry growth. In other words, the men at the top needed more. "Now I know he spent a quarter of a million dollars in one coming out party in one night and I know that's costly," Reuther said, referring to an ostentatious debutante party in 1959 for Charlotte, one of his daughters, at the Country Club of Detroit that featured

Frank Sinatra, Gary Cooper, Peter Lawford, and a decorator flown in from Paris who trimmed the chandeliers with exotic fruits. "I know he spent a half million dollars for his newest yacht and maybe he has some other expensive habits. This could be why he has trouble making ends meet. But I want to say this. [Last year] in salary and bonuses and in dividends from Ford stocks—which he did not earn, his great choice was he picked the right grandfather—what did he get? Four million, eight-hundred-ninety-five thousand and seven hundred and ninety nine dollars." It would take an average Ford worker 729 years to earn as much as Henry Ford II earned in one year, Reuther noted. "I say to Henry as an old Ford worker, 'You aren't worth seven hundred and twenty-nine times the people we represent at the bargaining table in this union.'"

Two days later President Johnson spoke at the autoworkers' convention, and while repeating his call for both sides to avoid a settlement that would "undermine the stability of our costs and our prices," he noticeably demurred from placing a ceiling on union demands. To Reuther and other labor leaders, this omission was heartening. That same day LBJ's top economic adviser, Walter W. Heller, left Washington to speak to the Economic Club of Detroit. Would the economy live up to its promise? "The answer for 1964," Heller said, "will in significant measure have a Made in Michigan label."

Paul Riser had been in the same class with Diane Ross at Cass Tech. He did not know her well, but they stood near each other at graduation—sheer alphabetical luck. Like her, he had been hanging out at West Grand Boulevard before he finished high school. He became the kid trombonist in the studio band, an eighteen-year-old playing alongside fellow trombonist George Bohanon and the other Funk Brothers, veteran jazzmen, as ribald as they were talented, there for the money and music and collegiality but not the sorts to genuflect before the Chairman. By the first months of 1964, Riser had worked his way into the regular rotation for session work at least two or three days and nights a week. "Motown was literally a factory then, around the clock," he recalled. The scene was so vivid that Riser could return to the studio fifty years later, long after its useful life but preserved as a museum, and in his mind's eye see each of the Funk Brothers and where they sat and how they laughed and swore and sounded. Bohanon. Earl Van Dyke. Hank Cosby. Benny Benjamin. Chank Willis. Joe Messina, the white brother. James Jamerson. No one crustier than Jamerson, with his stool over there in the corner where he played his Fender precision bass, the master of counterpoint. If Jamerson thought they had it right, he would stomp his foot and stand up and say "That's that," refusing to play any more despite Berry Gordy's instructions to try one more take. It was not just that Jamerson thought the session musicians were not getting paid what they deserved; he also thought too many takes took the spontaneity and soul out of a song.

Riser was awed by Jamerson and the older session men. He had come out of the black apostolic church, his family belonging to the Clinton Street Greater Bethlehem Temple, and was trained as a classical musician at Cass Tech, where they gave out letters for band that were worn on letter sweaters with at least as much pride as a football or basketball letter. What Riser saw and heard inside the Motown studio with the Funk Brothers was thrilling, different from anything he had experienced before. Another classmate at Cass Tech, Dale Warren, who played the cello, had recruited him to Motown even though at the time Riser "hated r & b, hated it, never listened to it." Riser performed well and they kept calling him back until he became an employee. That was part of the Gordy magic that helped make Motown possible. Some might criticize the assembly-line nature of the place and the sound, but there was also a sense of freedom and opportunity and a willingness to try anything, take any talent, however it came in off the street, from the hungry Supremes to the ready-to-type-and-take-messages Martha Reeves to the proper high school trombonist Paul Riser. "How many major companies would accept someone seventeen or eighteen years old? Unheard of," Riser said later. "The opportunity was there. The environment was right . . . the feeling was right. Berry never had a closed shop." Riser could read music, comprehend arrangements, and follow scores faithfully, all of which was impressive if a bit too uptight for his band mates. "What an awakening for me coming there. It was culture shock. The Funk Brothers, I don't have to tell you, they were from the streets, hard core, totally hard core. And I was from a totally different background, spiritual, very straight arrow. No drinking. No carousing." All that quickly changed. "They absolutely did corrupt me," Riser cheerfully recalled. "They taught me everything I know. But it was all fun growing up. And I tell you it was like a rookie going into a football camp. You know how they haze a rookie? I took my discipline from high school . . . into the studio. It didn't quite work. It was like trying to tame a den of untamed lions."

The work at Motown inadvertently changed Riser's life on a summer day in 1963 when he left the studio after a recording session and drove west along the boulevard. Even with Gordy's stingy salaries for the studio musicians, Riser had worked so many sessions by then that he had earned enough money to place a down payment on a new car, and not just any car but a 1963 Buick Riviera, the inaugural model. It was sleek and black. He was nineteen, looking fine, black on black, he would say. At the intersection with Linwood, he turned right, in the direction of C. L. Franklin's church. "And this cute young girl was crossing the street. Sixteen years old. And the rest is history. Two kids and four grandkids. I spotted her. She was going to the store right across the street. I said, 'I will wait and take you home'—a half block! The timing was to the second. . . . When I made that turn off the boulevard going north, there was my future wife going across. She was cute, I had a shiny car—the two came together."

Riser went on the road with Marvin Gaye at the start of 1964. Four days in Cleveland in the dead of winter in a drafty hotel out on Euclid Street with snow blowing in through the windowsill—enough glamorous road work for him. He went back to the studio. By March he was with the session band working on another Smokey Robinson tune written for Mary Wells. "My Guy," it was called. Smokey grew up surrounded by women and was confident he could think like one. In this case he decided to channel Mary Wells and imagine what it would be like for an established star like her to be unyieldingly faithful to a factory worker, maybe at Ford's River Rouge plant. Author David Ritz later memorialized it as "a fluttering study in fidelity." Riser considered Smokey one of three geniuses at Motown, along with Stevie Wonder and Marvin Gaye. Wonder and Gaye shared a creative energy that could be frustrated by the commercial expectations of Berry Gordy, he thought, but Robinson worked right at the Motown sweet spot.

March 13 was one of those long Fridays in the Motown studio. The Funk Brothers were there all day with Smokey and the technicians and their eight-track tapes, working to get the introduction to the song just right. Wells loved the melody and the lyrics from the moment she heard it, and recorded it with a soft, sultry ease, even evoking a bit of Mae West at the end with a stuttering come-on: "There's not a man ta-DAY who could take me away from my guy." Along with Robert White's tripping triplets on the guitar and Earl Van Dyke's churchy chord progressions, a lovely high trombone thread ran through it, drawing on the talented embouchures of Bohanon and Riser, but the introduction seemed off until, very late in the session, with the Funk Brother veterans getting antsy, the trombonists realized that they could mimic an opening riff from "Canadian Sunset," a jazz number from the fifties. A galloping western left-hand rhythm under high trombones sounding a plaintive melodic love call: *Daaaa . . . da-da d-daaa*—C . . . C-A-G-A. And they had it, with a slight revision to avoid copyright suits. "Smokey said, 'Oh, I *like* that.'" So did the public. Before the spring was out, Mary Wells and "My Guy" were at the top of the *Billboard* chart.

"Modest Mary Sinks the Beatles," read the headline in the *Detroit News*. The story noted that she was the first female vocalist "to top the Beatles in record sales since Beatlemania hit America"—with the extra kick that the Beatles themselves sent a telegram to West Grand Boulevard exclaiming, "We like Mary Wells." That represented a thawing in a cold war of words between Detroit and the Fab Four. As the Beatles were landing on American soil on February 7, some students at the University of Detroit started a "Stamp Out the Beatles" campaign. This had more to do with style than sound. It was not to promote Motown over the Brits that these students took up their cause, but more a hirsute dispute, flattops versus flop tops. In any case, when the Beatles were asked about the movement in Detroit, the rejoinder was "We're going to stamp out Detroit." Just looking at the newspapers, it seemed that might happen. There was more coverage in the *Detroit Free Press* and *News* about the Beatles during their first week in the United States than Motown had received over its five-year existence. But in fact, rather than stamp out Detroit, the Beatles more often honored Detroit, covering several Motown songs in their repertoire, beginning with "Money (That's What I Want)," the early Motown hit written by Berry Gordy and Janie Bradford and first sung by Barrett Strong.

For Al Abrams, the Motown publicist, the most important thing about the Mary Wells article in the *Free Press* was simply its existence. "It marked the first time a Motown artist was receiving the kind of attention in one of our two hometown daily newspapers that usually was reserved for sports heroes and movie stars, almost all of whom were white," he noted later. There were two other aspects to the "My Guy" legacy, for better and worse. It was such a success that it inspired Smokey Robinson to write a companion tune for the Temptations that later became their first No. 1 hit and one of the most memorable Motown songs of all time, "My Girl." And it was such a success that Mary Wells and people whispering in her ear thought she should be getting more money and credit, pushing her to break free from Motown and go out on her own, never to shine as bright again. She had only four years at Motown, from 1960 to 1964, and by the end she was being overtaken by the Supremes, who had sung backup on some of her early records. But Mary Wells came first, and her achievements on West Grand lasted. Her voice had a distinct poetry to it, as did her point of view. In a line that Philip Levine, Detroit's poet of the working class, could have used as his own, she once described her young days as the daughter of a cleaning woman by defining misery as "Detroit linoleum in January."

Unfinished business. The Four Tops were still trying to find their place in the Motown firmament during those early months of 1964. Although they were more experienced and polished than most of the other groups at West Grand Boulevard, and as well known locally as any of them, they were the newest group in Berry Gordy's domain and not yet on the national charts. Gordy had spent several years trying to pry them away from Columbia and other recording labels and finally was able to sign them late in 1963 after they came to watch the *Motortown Revue* make its second appearance at the Apollo Theater in Harlem. "We went and saw that and said, Wow, they are good!" recalled Abdul (Duke) Fakir, who sang tenor. "We need to be there."

They were regarded as balladeers, four-part harmonizers, comfortable with a wide range of popular and traditional songs, and Gordy's first notion was to have them cut an album that featured the American songbook. His first love had been jazz, and he saw his fortune at the nexus of soul and rock and roll, but he always had a soft spot for standard melodies and at various times encouraged artists ranging from the Supremes to Marvin Gaye and Stevie Wonder to perform and record songs like Johnny Mercer's "Moon River" and Leonard Bernstein's "Somewhere." The Four Tops seemed to fit that niche better than the others, and they spent their first few months at Motown with producer Mickey Stevenson and the studio musicians recording old standards. But before an album could be completed, Gordy decided that it was not commercial and turned the quartet in another direction. Following the pattern he used for the Supremes, he put them in the hands of Holland-Dozier-Holland and at the same time changed the group dynamics to one lead, in this case the powerfully searing, searching voice of Levi Stubbs, and three backup singers. In most instances—including with the Supremes and Temptations, and to some extent the Marvelettes and Vandellas—this transformation proved successful musically but discombobulating psychologically, creating jealousies and eventual dysfunction. The Four Tops were different, from the beginning.

The soul of the group was the deep friendship of Stubbs and Abdul Fakir, known as Duke. They both came from Detroit's east side, Stubbs from the projects at Six Mile and Fakir in a single-family house farther north near Pershing High. They became so close that before their junior year in high school Duke invited Levi to come live with his family; the basement was cleaned out and they shared it as a bedroom. Both young men had musical backgrounds. Duke's father was an immigrant from the Asian subcontinent, an area that later became part of Bangladesh. He played the sitar and sang on the streets until he had earned enough money to get to London, where he worked as a cook, before finally reaching America. He settled in the north end of Detroit, where he got a job in the Briggs factory making auto body parts and met Duke's mother, the daughter of an African Methodist Episcopal minister who had brought his family up to Detroit from Georgia. Duke grew up in a church resounding with music. He sang in the choirs at church and school until the year he turned ten and his voice changed. "They would not let me in because my voice was in between," Fakir recalled. "It was like I lost a brother or sister I was so hurt. There was music everywhere. When you were walking down the street you could hear beautiful music everywhere you went. There was music in the neighborhood. All the boys were singing. I must have sung in five or six different groups, just messing around until Levi and I became close."

Duke loved sports and excelled at basketball, football, and track at Pershing. Levi might have been an even better athlete, but his lone obsession was music. Fakir recalled seeing him outrun the state champion in the hundred-yard dash and saying, "You're a hell of an athlete," to which Stubbs replied, "Man, all I want to do is sing." The conception of the group that would become the Four Tops began near the end of their high school days with an invitation to a farewell-to-Pershing party thrown by a group of girls who came from black Detroit's high society, upper-middle-class young women who had been debutantes at the annual Cotillion Ball. They were also singers and called their group Scheherazade. The party was invitation-only, and Levi and Duke were invited, mostly because the girls wanted to hear them sing. It was an early variation of the friendly battles of the bands that Berry Gordy later organized at the Graystone Ballroom, in this case Scheherazade versus the boys with no name. To round out a quartet, Stubbs and Fakir recruited two friends, Lawrence Payton and Obie Benson, who attended Northern High, the same school that four years later produced Smokey Robinson. "Just follow me," Levi said to his singing mates when the girls urged them to perform. The result was smooth and harmonic, as though they had rehearsed for weeks—Levi as lead, Duke as first tenor, Lawrence as second tenor, and Obie the baritone-bass.

By that summer they were calling themselves the Four Aims, sporting white wool suits from Hot Sam's, winning amateur shows at the Warfield Theater, and taking bookings at places like Eddie's Lounge in Flint. Duke had earned a basketball scholarship to Central State University, a historically black school in Wilberforce, Ohio, and Obie Benson also had a college scholarship, and their intention was to sing through the summer and then leave for school. "But once we hit that stage, we knew we were not going to college," Fakir recalled. "It was amazing how excited we felt. 'Sh-Boom, Sh-Boom.' 'Sixty Minute Man.' 'Three Coins in a Fountain.' This was something we all loved to do." Renamed the Four Tops, they began a decade-long rise on the show circuit, from the Detroit Auto Show to the Paradise Club up at Idlewild, a black resort in Michigan, to the Flame Show Bar and 20 Grand and Roosevelt in Detroit, to spots in the Catskills, to singing backup for crooner Billy Eckstine on a nationwide tour—and finally, late in 1963, Berry Gordy came calling. "I wanted them bad," he later confided. "I could see how loyal they were to each other, and I knew they would be the same way to me and Motown."

Loyal, but not naïve, not after ten years in the business. Unlike most of Gordy's artists, whose first-ever paycheck came from Motown, the Four Tops knew what a contract looked like. When Gordy handed one to the group, expecting them to sign on the spot, Duke Fakir said he wanted to examine it overnight before signing, even though they had decided ahead of time that they would go with Motown no matter what. When Gordy said he did not like delays and that no one before had ever asked him for time to sleep on it, Fakir studied the contract and said, "I don't see any advance on here." Gordy said he did not give advances, but eventually relented, giving them each a token $100 advance. He also promised to produce hit records and make them stars.

That took longer than expected because of the detour into the unproduced American songbook. Still, they kept busy in the Motown studio, often performing as backup singers for the company's female singers and groups. It did not take long for Fakir to develop a relationship with Mary Wilson of the Supremes. These were the last days of Motown's magical early period, before the debilitating addictions of success and envy and ambition took hold and things and people started to fall apart. "Mary Wilson bought this house and she would have parties and do the cooking and have Marvin Gaye and HDH and Smokey and everyone come over. Ten or twenty people at a time come over," Fakir recalled. "She could cook great, and I was a good bar person and it was such an amazing feeling. You can never capture that in words, just cannot capture it in words, to know how wonderful and full and gratifying and fun it was during those early days."

One night late that spring while the Four Tops were in Detroit playing at the 20 Grand, Brian Holland burst into their dressing room and announced, "Fellows, we got your hit." He was carrying a tape recorder, and when he pushed the Play button they heard a raw instrumental version of a tune on tape with Holland singing the melody live. Motown was operating twenty-two hours a day, and though it was late at night Holland persuaded them to follow him back to West Grand Boulevard so they could start working on the song while the feelings were still fresh. While Brian Holland worked with Duke, Obie, and Lawrence on the background vocals, Eddie Holland took Levi into the control room to perfect the melody. Eddie sang it, over and over, until Levi said he wanted to write it down with his own pen. "Although you're never near / Your voice I often hear." When Levi felt he had the right phrasing, they started to record the first take of "Baby, I Need Your Lovin'," the big hit that Berry Gordy promised and that served as the template for the inimitable sound of the Four Tops for the rest of the sixties decade.

Among the words of wisdom that Gordy's mother, Bertha Fuller Gordy, imparted to her eight children, *What you learn is never wasted* ranked among her favorites. She was a teacher first and always, and a demanding one, from the time her husband met her, when she was instructing third graders in a segregated elementary school in Georgia, through all her years in Detroit as the matriarch of one of the city's most accomplished families. Her second-youngest son spent most of his early years feeling that he was a disappointment to her. She wanted her children to be college graduates; he was a high school dropout. She wanted them to be in professions that she could boast about to her friends. His boxing would not cut it. Working on an assembly line certainly would not. Nor selling jazz records or jotting down songs that popped into his head. But those concerns were long gone. What he had learned as a boxer in terms of competition, what he had learned on the assembly line about how to create a product, what he had learned from his pure love of music—none of it was wasted. It had been Mom Gordy's wordless nod of support that swayed a few of his reluctant siblings to vote to give him the $800 family loan with which he started Motown, and now, with a studio teeming with talented artists, from Stevie Wonder to Marvin Gaye, from Smokey Robinson and the Miracles to Martha and the Vandellas, from the Supremes to the Temptations and the Four Tops, she was so proud of him that she would take friends on tours of the West Grand Boulevard studios, ask various employees to introduce themselves and explain what they did, then proclaim to her guests as they were walking away, "And my son owns it all."

Bertha Gordy had been born in the previous century, in 1899, and in 1964 was turning sixty-five but not slowing down. She was a regular presence at Motown, and also in various social clubs, among them the female auxiliary of the Improved Benevolent and Protective Order of Elks, the African American variation of the all-white club with the same name minus the "Improved," a word that seemed especially apt for Mrs. Gordy's philosophy. The female Elks often held functions at the Graystone Ballroom on Woodward Avenue, now owned by her son, and in honor of Bertha's milestone birthday they joined with Motown to hold a testimonial banquet for her at the Graystone. The men dressed in tuxedos, the women in ball gowns with corsages. All eight of her children and seventeen grandchildren were there. Councilman Mel Ravitz presented her with an honorary resolution from the city of Detroit. Berry Jr., transformed from misfit to family hero, spoke on behalf of her children, delivering tributes and gifts, including one that captured both his rise and the capitalist acuity of the Gordy clan: a long-playing record covered with dollar bills.

---

In the movements of black Detroit, the most common paths traced up and down, north and south. Since the days of the Underground Railroad, through the era of the Great Migration and beyond, Detroit had been one of the pole stars of the industrial North, drawing first runaway slaves, then factory workers and families by the thousands. One and two generations later, many transplanted southerners returned to Georgia and Alabama and Mississippi when they could, enduring the indignities of Jim Crow segregation to reconnect with their roots. Some of them went back precisely because of the South's overt racism—to fight against it. In March 1964 John Conyers Jr. was one of those making the reverse trip.

The Conyers family roots were in Georgia. John Sr. had left Georgia in the early twenties and found work at the Chrysler plant in Detroit, where he was subjected to the northern variation of Jim Crow. He and other painters in the plant were paid less than white painters for the same work, a bitter fact that led him to make a personal complaint to Walter P. Chrysler himself. That started his long career as a union activist, operating on the left wing of the United Auto Workers. His son, a graduate of Northwestern High and a Korean War veteran who worked his way through Wayne State Law School by selling vacuum cleaners to the Gotham Hotel, among other institutions, had taken his father's activism into law and politics. For two years after the 1960 elections, he had worked in the field office of Democratic congressman John D. Dingell Jr. across from the Fisher Y on Dexter Avenue, a mile or so from Motown. During the summer of 1963, after JFK made his nationally televised speech on civil rights, Conyers had been among the Detroiters recruited at a White House conference to help push civil rights legislation and litigation through the Lawyers' Committee for Civil Rights under Law. By the middle of March 1964, he was launching a campaign for an open congressional seat in Detroit adjacent to Dingell's and also volunteering his legal services in the southern struggle.

On March 21 a call came to the Detroit branch of the National Lawyers Guild about a case in Hattiesburg, Mississippi, where a civil rights worker needed legal help. A young worker for the Student Nonviolent Coordinating Committee had been arrested and accused of raping a fifty-eight-year-old African American woman. The young man claimed that he had been framed by local authorities to intimidate the movement. Conyers took the assignment and arrived in Hattiesburg the next day, uncertain whether he would even be allowed to practice in Mississippi, where he did not have a license. He had heard that there were only three black lawyers in the entire state at that time. When he tried to visit his client, the jailers denied him permission; a call to the police chief was needed to secure that most basic legal right. The next day, at a preliminary hearing for the defendant, the courtroom was filled to capacity with white and black onlookers, some from the civil rights movement, some from the community, sitting wherever they could find room. When the prosecutor saw this, he moved "in the name of peace and tranquility" that blacks sit in their own section, still the Jim Crow practice in Mississippi. In response, a bailiff bellowed, "All right, all you niggers, get to your own side!"

Conyers rose to object—to the language and the motion. The judge, according to contemporaneous accounts, apologized only for the language. When officers tried to segregate the courtroom, a few white ministers from the North who were in Mississippi as part of the Freedom Movement refused to budge, prompting the judge to clear the room altogether, defer the hearing, and hold the defendant in jail until the next grand jury was seated. With the case on indefinite hold, Conyers returned to Detroit. Unfinished business. He was preoccupied much of the coming year with his congressional campaign, which he eventually won, taking a seat that he would hold for more than fifty years.

From the South to Detroit while Conyers was still in Mississippi came Martin Luther King Jr. to give a speech at Central Methodist Church at Woodward Avenue and Grand Circus Park. Nine months earlier he had led the triumphant march past that very church on the way down Woodward to Cobo Hall amid the joyful jostling of at least 150,000 people. His host back then, Rev. C. L. Franklin, had largely retreated from the civil rights scene, though not entirely. At a testimonial dinner in his honor in February,

Franklin had announced his intention to stage a Freedom Jubilee at Tiger Stadium in June. No one had heard much about it since. There was no march when King came to town this time, but three thousand listeners filled the church to capacity. Before the address, Ofield Dukes asked King if the assassination of JFK had heightened his own sense of vulnerability. He had a small entourage, but no bodyguard. In cities like Detroit, he said, the police protected him, but they had no interest in doing that when he was in the South. This was one month after Cassius Clay had defeated Sonny Liston in Miami to become the heavyweight champion, stunning most of the sporting world, including the boxing-savvy crowd that watched on closed-circuit TV at the Fox Theater in Detroit. Since then Clay had announced that he had become a follower of Elijah Muhammad and the Nation of Islam. He had taken the temporary name Cassius X on the way to becoming Muhammad Ali. King was not impressed. The black Muslims, he said, were champions of racial segregation, "and that is what we are fighting against." Sounding a theme expounded by many big-city sports columnists, King added, "Perhaps Cassius should spend more time improving his boxing skills and do less talking."

Detroit remained a friendly northern front for King. The politicians, the police, the media were all accommodating. At the start of the year, the *Free Press* had invited him to write a column explaining his goals for 1964 and then turned over much of its Sunday feature section to carry the message. King wrote that the movement of nonviolence was working, that he did not foresee "any widespread turning of the Negro to violence," and that beyond the Negro thrust toward full emancipation he worried about the next step: economic equality. The rise of what he called "monstrous automation" made unskilled and semiskilled black workers especially vulnerable in manufacturing centers like Detroit.

King was followed into Detroit two weeks later by Malcolm X, his intellectual adversary, who had just broken away from Elijah Muhammad and the Nation of Islam, though his brother in the city, Wilfred X, declined to join him in that bold move. Malcolm spoke again at King Solomon Baptist Church, the site of his "Message to the Grassroots," and if anything his words were more explosive. "This is the year of the ballot or the bullet," he said. "We have a younger generation now who don't care about odds. The white man don't have heart. He's brave with tanks and jets and atom bombs, but all a black man has to work out with [is] that blade. On a dark corner, it's even-steven." Betty De Ramus, a local writer, was in the audience that night. She described the speaker as "lean and tall with the stride of a conqueror and a fearless tongue." She thought of Malcolm X as a "master manipulator of emotions" and found that she was arguing with herself as she debated his message. "First aggression, then guilt for not being aggressive sooner, and when it was all over he had you wondering about yourself. He's a man who holds an audience in the palm of his hand." Officers from the Detroit Police Department controlled traffic outside before and after the event. There were no bullets and no blades in dark corners. And nothing was even-steven.

George Edwards, who considered the Walk to Freedom the high point of his tenure as Detroit's police commissioner, had receded from the front lines even farther than Reverend Franklin. He was deciding federal appeals court cases now, not dealing with the racial tensions of Detroit or the insidious doings of the local mob. But there was still unfinished business from 1963 and his days at 1300 Beaubien. On the day that King spoke at Central Methodist, the trial judge in the bribery case against the Party Bus mobster, Tony Giacalone, criticized Edwards for talking so much in the press in the days and weeks after the police made their bust at the Home Juice Company on June 20. Edwards would say later that he knew the judge, John A. Gillis, to be a "freewheeling Irishman" who did not like the police crackdown on the hookers downtown and did not believe the Mafia existed in Detroit.

As it turned out, whatever Gillis believed or disbelieved, he was not the main problem for Edwards and the case against Tony Jack and his boys. The defense lawyers were too good, and the main witness was too weak on the stand. The case turned on a minor issue: where James W. Thomas, the officer who had been wired to take bribes from Giacalone, typed his notes and reports related to the case. When the defense lawyer, Robert Weinberg, questioned Thomas's claim that he had typed the notes only at the precinct office when the notes clearly showed they were the work of two distinct typewriters, Thomas essentially choked and blurted out, "I lied." Where the notes were typed meant very little; Thomas's confession meant everything. Despite the tape-recorded conversations and the solidness of the case, Giacalone was acquitted.

During the heat of the mob investigations in 1963, Edwards had invited Martin Hayden, editor of the *Detroit News*, to lunch at the Detroit Athletic Club and confided that he had written Hayden a letter that was to be opened if anything untoward happened to him. He said he did not think his life was in danger, but this was just in case. "I guarantee you'll have the damndest newspaper story you have ever seen," Edwards said. As it turned out, he survived, and the letter was never opened. Fourteen years later, a box was delivered to the front desk downstairs in the *Detroit News* Building on West Lafayette. It was addressed to Martin Hayden and taken to his wood-paneled office. His secretary opened it, to her horror. Inside was a severed human head. Unfinished business? A classic Mafia move, but the morbid gift-givers remained unidentified, though it was determined that the cadaver head had been lifted from the Wayne County Morgue. When Hayden retired, Pete Waldmeir of the *News* decided to write a column about him. As Waldmeir later recalled, "The interview went along fine until I ran out of questions and finally asked him if finding that head in a box was the strangest thing that ever happened to him in all those years in journalism. 'No,' he responded wryly. 'Having you ask me a dumb question like that is the strangest thing that ever happened to me in all my years in journalism.'"

Chapter 21

# THE MAGIC SKYWAY

**WALTER BUHL FORD** III was the great-grandson of the original Henry Ford. Buhlie, he was called, a nickname that matched his devilish rich-kid personality. His parents had sent him off to the Berkshire School, a coed prep school in western Massachusetts, but he left before graduating and a few years later ended up at Cleary College, a business school in Ypsilanti that had opened a century earlier as the Cleary School of Penmanship. If his uncle, Henry Ford II, was not considered much of a student, the Hotchkiss-to-Yale trajectory of HF2 looked scholarly compared to the academic track of young Buhlie.

At noon on March 7, 1964, a "bleak and cold" Saturday, two branches of the automotive aristocracy of Detroit convened to witness Buhlie's marriage to Barbara Monroe Posselius, whose maternal grandfather had been a vice president of Chrysler Corporation. Bobbi and Buhlie had known each other since their preschool days. They grew up on streets bordering the lush Country Club of Detroit in Grosse Pointe Farms, he on Provençal Road, she on Irvine Lane. She was only eighteen, and he was twenty. The wedding was staged in front of a fireplace in the living room of the rectory at St. Paul on the Lake Catholic Church in Grosse Pointe Farms; the guest list of fifty was limited to relatives and a half dozen of the couple's closest friends.

Buhlie's cousins, Anne and Charlotte, daughters of HF2, came from

New York by private jet in time to attend the rehearsal dinner Friday night at the home of Uncle Benson Ford, and arranged to make their escape back to Manhattan before dusk Saturday after the wedding reception. Their lavish coming-out parties as Detroit debutantes had cost multiple times more than this modest affair, the first Ford wedding of their generation. Now here they came in designer coats and mink hats, accompanied by their father, with whom they were barely on speaking terms since he had separated from their mother, Anne, for la dolce vita with his Italian mistress and soon-to-be second wife, Cristina. The estranged Mrs. Ford was in no mood for a Ford gathering and stayed in New York, preparing for a European trip. As the sisters approached the entrance to the rectory, with the wind lashing off Lake St. Clair, they encountered their father's mother, the elderly Mrs. Edsel Ford, wrapped in a full-length fur coat. "Hello, Granny," they said.

Riddle: What Ford was the direct descendant of the founding Ford but the son of a Ford who had no blood relationship to old Henry? Answer: Buhlie, whose mother, Josephine Clay Ford, known as Dodie, was the granddaughter of Henry Ford and the younger sister of HF2, but who just happened to marry Walter Buhl Ford II, an industrial designer from an investment banking family who was not related but carried the same last name and a wealthy Detroit heritage of his own. On his father's side, Buhlie was the great-great-grandson of a Buhl who was mayor of Detroit in 1848 and related to the Buhls who built the Buhl Building, the downtown skyscraper that housed the Detroit office of J. Walter Thompson, the ad men for Ford. A grandmother on that side, the former Virginia Brush, was the descendant of a Brush who commanded the Michigan Militia during the War of 1812. That is the derivation of Brush Street, which runs north out of downtown between John R and Beaubien. Another Brush married the granddaughter of Gen. Lewis Cass, the first governor of the Michigan Territory. The Cass name is all over Detroit, from Cass Tech, where Motown's Diane Ross and Paul Riser went to high school, to Cass Avenue, which runs parallel with Woodward, one block to the west, and over the years nurtured one of the city's bohemian enclaves.

The wedding was swift and unpretentious. The maid of honor was Barbara's little sister, sixteen-year-old Nancy Posselius, and the best man Buhlie's little brother, fourteen-year-old Alfred Brush Ford. The groom slipped a slight platinum band onto the bride's ring finger at the end of the brief ceremony, and the newlyweds disappeared into the back of a chauffeured maroon Mercury sedan to lead a procession of limousines up to her grandmother's house on Lewiston Road for a champagne reception and luncheon. With the festivities over, Buhlie and Bobbi departed for a three-week honeymoon in Nassau before they were to settle in an Ann Arbor apartment where he would continue his studies at the nearby business school. The wedding was mandatory coverage in the society pages of the *News* and *Free Press,* but its newsworthiness could not match another event that featured Buhlie earlier that same week.

More than seven hundred car dealers from the Midwest were in Detroit for a merchandizing fair at Cobo Hall sponsored by Ford Motor Company. The brainchild of Lee Iacocca at the Ford Division and Bill Laurie and his ad men at J. Walter Thompson, the fair was designed to prepare Ford dealers for the bigger car markets of the future. There were eighteen booths at the fair, each manned by a Ford executive and dealing with a specific aspect of the business, including new models, used cars, trucks, service and parts, and advertising, marketing, and public relations. Ford was in a heady place that month. Its sales for the past year and a half had been at record levels, and it was about to launch a new model it hoped would awe the buying public and overwhelm the competition. "We at Ford Division are taking what we think are some pretty drastic steps to prepare both ourselves and our dealers for these big markets of the future," Iacocca said. This was a not-so-veiled reference to preparations for the car that people had been talking about, but not seeing, most of the new year, the one that was about to start production and would be unveiled in mid-April at the New York World's Fair: the Mustang.

It was never clear whether Buhlie was in on a grander scheme or unwittingly contributed to it in his own carefree way, but here is what happened: Fred Olmsted, who covered the auto industry for the *Free Press,* had been tracking the Mustang's progress week by week, staying in constant touch with his sources at Ford and J. Walter Thompson. At the lunch hour on the Monday before the merchandising fair opened, Olmsted left the *Free Press* Building on West Lafayette, turned north on Washington Boulevard, and was passing an open parking lot near the Sheraton Cadillac when he came across a shiny object that stopped him in his tracks. It was the phantom car he had been waiting to see, and a beauty—a Rangoon red Mustang convertible. Olmsted found a pay phone and called back to his office, "Get a photographer over here quick!" These would be the first public photos of Ford's secret car. Photographer Ray Glonka arrived and started snapping away: side views, grille views, rear views, license plate.

Before writing a story to accompany the pictures of the Mustang convertible in the parking lot, Olmsted contacted a Ford spokesman, who tried but failed to talk him out of running the photos altogether. Maintaining the suspense was Ford's job, not the duty of a newspaper. Working off the fact that the license plate, I 2H36, was visible in one picture, Ford then undertook an investigation of who, among the select number of insiders with access to a Mustang, could have been so foolish as to park it in such a public place. The search led directly to the top. HF2 himself had been tooling around in a Mustang for a few weeks, eschewing his chauffeur to drive from Grosse Pointe Farms to the Glass House in Dearborn. He had been boasting about it to his younger sister, Dodie, who told him she wanted to see what all the excitement was about. So she ended up with the Rangoon red convertible, and when her about-to-be-married rambunctious son asked if he could take it out for a spin, she obliged him. It was Buhlie who took it downtown and steered it into the open parking lot. "It's a hot job," an attendant recalled the young driver telling him. He later told Olmsted that "the engine has a lot of snap."

Olmsted's scoop was the talk of the town and even made the following week's issues of *Time* and *Newsweek*, both of which were already in the process of preparing cover stories on Lee Iacocca and the Mustang. Iacocca would later tell Robert A. Fria, a Mustang expert, that none of this was planned, but "that dirty Walter Buhl Ford just let our secret out of the bag." Whether the whole matter was a setup by Ford or a mistake by Buhlie seemed irrelevant in the end. In a case like that, the truism that all publicity is good publicity certainly applied and was in keeping with a detailed campaign plan. It was an old plan, something that had been in J. Walter Thompson's playbook since it helped introduce the 1948 Fords a generation earlier with "a long, gradual buildup"—drop hints, embargo facts, build excitement with insiders, give the trade journals tantalizing scraps but not too much, let the excitement grow, tease it out month by month. In this latest iteration it would take on mythological proportions as one of the most successful marketing campaigns in U.S. history.

On the morning of March 9, two days after Buhlie's wedding, the first batch of Mustangs to be sold to the public started moving down the line at the Dearborn Assembly Plant at the River Rouge Complex. A line that had been dedicated to Ford Fairlanes was reconfigured to make the Mustangs. The public had been clamoring for the car for three months. They were not taking formal orders yet, but Ford already had the names of twenty-three thousand drivers who visited their local dealers and said they wanted to order the car as soon as possible. Now each car on the line had its own dealer order, with its own specifications and Vehicle Identification Number. The step-by-step assembly began: chassis, paint job, front suspension, body drop down to the main floor for installation of engine and transmission, then fender, grille, wheels, doors, and front bucket seats. In the industry, that first day of production is known as Job One. Iacocca and his entire team were there to witness the Job One they had been anticipating for nearly two years. Don Frey was the idea man who had pushed the car the hardest over that time, though Iacocca hungrily gobbled up most of the credit. Frey, the assistant general manager and chief engineer of Ford Division under Iacocca, had kept at it even when HF2 seemed resistant, and took the heat when the Deuce said it was his ass if the project failed. Job One was his day of affirmation. As he later told the author David Halberstam, "The biggest thrill I've ever had in my life was going to the assembly plant for the first full day of production on the Mustang and seeing Mustangs as far as I could see . . . like a football field filled with Mustangs."

It took some time for the line to reach full speed; 593 Mustangs were produced that first week. At peak production with twelve-hour runs the assembly line would turn out 1,200 cars per day, with a second Mustang assembly going on line in San Jose, California, but even then they would be built at a rate slower than they were being ordered. That too was part of the Mustang tease. In the world of selling things, hype and expectations feed off one another. Customers will wait in line for hours outside a pancake house on a weekend morning if they hear it is the place to be, and they will wait for a car if it is the thing to have. Long before Job One, Ford and its ad agency had skillfully made the Mustang the car to have.

As the manager of J. Walter Thompson's Detroit office, Bill Laurie had driven a Mustang months before Buhlie, or at least an early prototype. On a summer day in 1963, after several Mustang prototypes had been used in research tests with young Detroit couples, Laurie borrowed one for a weekend test drive. As his son David recalled the scene, his father pulled into their driveway on Merriweather Road, collected David and his mother, Thayer, and off they drove across the bridge into Ontario, heading southeast forty-five miles to the tip of Canada's Point Pelee National Park on Lake Erie. "We were in this weird car that no one had ever seen before, and when we parked it a hundred people were coming over and taking photos of it. 'What is it?' 'A Mustang.' No one had ever seen one before."

Truth be told, the car was not Laurie's type—sexy perhaps, but not sophisticated or substantive enough. Still and always he preferred the dark green Thunderbird convertible. Maybe people thought ad men were promoters of style over substance, but that did not mean they had to take home what they were selling, even if there was internal pressure to do so. Memos flowed out of JWT headquarters urging employees to buy the products they advertised, from cars to soap and cigarettes, "as the most significant way we can say to our clients and to our friends that we believe in what we are doing." When Liggett & Myers introduced the new Lark cigarette a year earlier, cartons were made available in the mail room at 420 Lex and an internal memo suggested, "We think you will want to try this new . . . brand. It is, as the package says—Richly Rewarding Yet Uncommonly Smooth." Norman Strouse, the company chairman, would even sign off on personal notes to friends around the country with suggestions that they drive Fords. For Laurie, Thunderbird, yes, Mustang, no. Too much like a middling Falcon in disguise for his taste. It was lower and wider than the Falcon and had a racier look, but many of the underpinnings did in fact come from the Falcon, and so did the engines, either a standard Falcon 170-cubic-inch six-cylinder or a zoomier Falcon 164-horsepower, 260-cubic-inch V-8.

The success of the Mustang to a large extent rested on this paradox: everything about it was geared toward the new, yet very little about it was in fact new. The engines and underpinnings were Falcons; the basic campaign strategy was as old as Ford's relationship with J. Walter Thompson. Was it new that Ford would launch it in spring when all other cars were launched in early fall? Not really. In fact Iacocca had used the same spring launch only two years earlier to introduce the Ford Galaxie 500 XL, a car that had some of the attributes of the later Mustang, a sports coupe with bucket seats and a sharp new interior. Nothing new and yet everything new. The Mustang design looked new, hip, modern, and Ford spent more than $10 million to market it as new. There is always a measure of luck in any commercial success, but usually that luck comes after intense study and practice. The Mustang design evolved from years of practice by Ford's talented designers and intense study on a macro level by Iacocca and the ad men and on a micro level by Ford's research department on what the new generation of drivers wanted in terms of a new car.

From the research department's study of Falcon sales, they determined that customers were requesting more and more options to make the car sportier and more powerful. From their research in Dearborn with young adults brought in to look at prototypes, they determined that a lower price made all the difference in how they viewed the Mustang's practicality. And from their studies of the baby-boom population at large, they realized there was a generational hunger for something iconic that could emblematize freedom and youth. From these studies came the three basic themes of the Mustang campaign: performance, price, and styling.

---

On the first of April, the young men and women who had been hired by Ford Motor Company to work as hosts and hostesses at the Ford pavilion at the New York World's Fair gathered for the first time at the Commodore Hotel at the corner of 42nd and Lexington, a half block from J. Walter Thompson headquarters. They were in their early twenties, most of them, and they arrived nearly two hundred strong from all regions of the country, but a preponderance hailed from the Midwest or the West Coast. Vincent Currie, a student at Wayne State, drove out from Detroit in his little Renault and took lodging at the YMCA until he could find other quarters. Ray Chatelin, another Wayne State student, caught a plane from Detroit and also spent his first nights in the city at the YMCA. Both had seen notices for the job on bulletin boards at school and went through a brief hiring process in Dearborn. It seemed to Chatelin that Ford was looking for "wholesome types" from outside New York. The feeling, he said, was that "New Yorkers were too abrupt and they wanted people who would be a little bit more gentle." The chosen ones spent one day in sessions at the Commodore for orientation and physical exams, then four days of training at the Crystal Ballroom of the Sheraton-Tenney Inn out near LaGuardia Airport in the shadows of the expansive World's Fair grounds.

The Ford pavilion was called the Ford Wonder Rotunda, a name that brings part of our story full circle. The name paid homage to the Ford Rotunda that Alfred Kahn had designed for the Century of Progress exhibition in Chicago in 1934 and that subsequently was moved to Dearborn, where it became one of America's most popular tourist attractions until it burned to the ground on November 9, 1962. Although the New York structure was lightened and brightened with voluminous sheets of glass between curved pylons, while the original was virtually windowless limestone, it nonetheless evoked the old Rotunda in its circular center and overall presentation. John G. Mullaly, the Ford man in charge at the pavilion, had been working on plans for the fair and was on leave from his job as manager of the old Rotunda when it was destroyed by fire. He had viewed the charred remains with Henry Ford II, and though they knew the original would not be rebuilt in Dearborn, the notion of reimagining it in New York in a recognizable if more modern style—what one Ford publicist called "a modern fairyland palace in white"—was already taking hold.

The young hosts and hostesses were to work in various staging areas at the Ford Wonder Rotunda. With its side attachment, a massive rectangular building the size of a football field, the Ford pavilion covered seven acres of the fairgrounds in the Flushing Meadows section of Queens. As Robert Caro reported in *The Power Broker*, his seminal book on Robert Moses, the fair's president and mastermind, Ford and General Motors were granted far more space than other exhibitors because of their cozy relationship with Moses, a planner and proponent of urban highways whose professional interests were inextricably linked to the Detroit auto industry. Inside the Ford pavilion, shiny new Ford cars were on pedestal display, but the wonder around them was mostly the work of Walt Disney. Ford turned to Disney's WED Enterprises to create the amusements. Here was International Gardens, exquisitely detailed miniature reproductions of the landscapes of twelve diverse places in world history, from ancient Rome and medieval Europe to modern Malaysia. There were dioramas of the life and times of Henry Ford, including the Quadricycle that started him on his way. Up there was the Auto Parts Harmonic Orchestra, an automated musical array constructed from car parts. And then the main attraction: the Magic Skyway, Disney's twelve-minute ride from past to future, transporting visitors in custom-fitted Ford-built convertibles, first circling the building to take in a bird's-eye view of the fairgrounds, then slipping into a time tunnel and moving past animatronic displays of volcanoes erupting, dinosaurs lumbering and fighting, prehistoric birds taking wing, cavemen grunting, cooking, and painting, then in and out of another time tunnel to behold the quintessential early-sixties vision of a futuristic space city with sky highways and hovercraft and jagged towers. It was this Magic Skyway that would draw visitors by the hundreds of thousands to Ford's corner of the fair. It was at the Magic Skyway where Ray Chatelin and Vincent Currie and most of their young colleagues would be stationed. And it was on the Magic Skyway that visitors might take their first memorable ride in Ford's exciting new car, the Mustang.

April was a momentous month for Ford, with three dates circled. Moving backward chronologically: April 22 was the official opening day of the World's Fair. April 17 was the official first day the Mustang would go on sale at dealerships around the country. And April 13 was the day Lee Iacocca came to New York to introduce the Mustang to the nation's press. In the middle of all that, the Ford Division chief had scored a public relations coup beyond the greatest expectations of the image-makers at Ford and J. Walter Thompson: he appeared on the cover of both *Time* and *Newsweek*, his portrait alongside pictures of Rangoon red Mustangs, his notoriety now surpassing that of his boss, HF2, whose own appearance at the World's Fair with Walt Disney and Robert Moses would garner far less notice. "Iacocca. Rhymes with Try a Coca," wrote *Time*. The article called him the hottest young man in Detroit and captured him test-driving a different Mustang every morning, racing around Detroit and its suburbs with his "impassive, hawk like face," tapping Ignacio Haya Gold Label cigars into the car's ashtray.

"Good morning, ladies and gentlemen. Welcome to one of the proudest moments of our lives," Iacocca said at his April 13 press conference at the Ford Wonder Rotunda. More than two hundred reporters were in attendance, many of whom had already written extensively about the car-in-the-making since its T-5 mystery days. "We appreciate your coming here to share this moment with us. And we are particularly pleased to have this beautiful setting for one of the most important occasions in Ford Division history." It was so important, Iacocca said, that they arranged to have similar unveilings simultaneously in eleven European capitals in front of a total of two thousand reporters and photographers. The excitement about the Mustang was contagious, he said. People from every state and as far away as Australia had written Ford asking for more information. A high school boy from Louisiana wrote that he was starting a Mustang fan club and predicted the car would be "bigger than Elvis or the Beatles."

Iacocca rolled through the highlights of the car. A completely new series, the fifth in the Ford Division in addition to Ford, Fairlane, Falcon, and Thunderbird. Two-door hardtop and convertible models. Two front bucket seats, bench rear seat. What they claimed was "the longest list of options and accessories ever offered on a new line of cars." And a price so low they would let the world know the basic sticker price down to the last dollar, proclaiming it in all of the advertising: $2,368.

And then there was the marketing campaign devised in conjunction with J. Walter Thompson. The cover stories were part of it, but they came free, along with major stories in all of the auto trade magazines. *Consumer Reports* noted how clean the workmanship was on a car built at such a hurried pace. Jim Wright, technical editor of *Motor Trend,* who had been among a select group of auto writers who test-drove early models of the Mustang, reported that he had no doubt "that this latest personal sporty car from Ford will sell like proverbial hotcakes," though he did feel compelled to point out its Falcon infrastructure. Beyond the free media, Ford became the main sponsor on half-hour shows on all three networks from 9:30 to 10 on Thursday night, April 16, the eve of the first sales, running three-minute commercials simultaneously on *Hazel,* its regularly sponsored show on NBC, and also on *Perry Mason* on CBS and *Jimmy Dean* on ABC. A network monopoly in prime time. The estimate was that 29 million viewers would see it.

That was just the start. Full-color advertisements in *Life, Look,* the *Saturday Evening Post,* and *Reader's Digest.* "Presenting the Unexpected . . . New Ford Mustang! The Mustang has the look, the fire, the flavor of one of the great European road cars. Yet is as American as its name." And there was the price: "$2,368 fob in Detroit . . . and we're not fooling!" And to the left: "Mustang was designed to be designed by you!" Performance. Price. Style. And more blanketing the market: ads in 2,400 newspapers that later studies showed had been noticed by 95 percent of male readers. To saturate the youth market, two hundred of the nation's leading radio disk jockeys were brought to the Dearborn Proving Grounds to test-drive the Mustang and paid to translate their experience into radio commercials, with a bonus on the back end of getting a loaner Mustang when they returned home. Forty-four college newspaper editors were also given Mustang loaners on the condition that they write about the on-campus reaction. In keeping with the Ford dealers merchandise fair held at Cobo Hall the weekend of Buhlie's wedding, dealers across the country received a forty-eight-page confidential plan from J. Walter Thompson showing them how they could tie in with the national advertising and promote the car to the growing youth market on and off campus.

Going young was the key. "This is the car we have designed with young America in mind—for, frankly, we are very much interested in serving young America," Iacocca told the press gathered at the Ford Wonder Rotunda, later adding, "Fortunately, our society is affluent enough to enable young Americans to buy immediately many of the items that it took their parents years to acquire. With the Mustang, we expect to make it easier for them to have the kind of car that will suit their needs, wants, and tastes." Iacocca concluded like the born salesman he was, like *Try a Coca*, like Ed Sullivan introducing the Beatles, or a circus ringmaster presenting the Flying Wallendas. "Ladies and gentlemen—the Mustang!"

And there it was, with the galloping horse insignia. After the presentation, the romancing of the press corps continued with a luncheon at Westchester Country Club and an invitation for writers and photographers to join in a road rally of Mustangs all the way back to Detroit, some 643 miles. It could have been a disaster with breakdowns or accidents along the way, but in keeping with Mustang luck, there were no mishaps.

From that day to the end of April, more than fifty thousand orders were placed with Ford dealers, but that was not enough to meet demand. Most dealers were given original allotments of thirty-five cars but had already sold more than one hundred. Promoted as a car you could design yourself, most buyers were going for the sexiest options. The more powerful V-8 engine was outselling the six-cylinder four to one. Customers wanted the best radios and whitewall tires. A consumer contagion had taken hold. Frank Sinatra ordered one, and so did Debbie Reynolds. Hughson Ford in San Francisco had not seen crowds like this since the introduction of new Fords after the war; people were lining up outside waiting for the doors to open. It was the same all over the country. J. Walter Thompson commissioned a market study that found that Lee Iacocca had hit the sweet spot with the Mustang, marking a complete transformation from the days when Ford sold mostly to older people who lived in rural America. Sixty percent of the buyers had gone to college; 75 percent of them were under forty-five; 70 percent came from homes with more than one car. About 50 percent lived in suburbs and another 25 percent in big cities. And what drew them to the Mustang? Twenty percent said it was price; a similar number said performance. But 80 percent of Mustang buyers said they were taken by its looks.

Two parallel tracks on the Magic Skyway curled around the Ford Wonder Rotunda for 2,300 feet. Ford had prepared sixty cars for each track. After coming off the line in Dearborn, the models had been modified at Carron and Company, a custom plant in nearby Inkster, where they were stripped of engines, transmissions, and radiators, along with fuel tanks and brakes, and fitted with a steering pin that descended from the front chassis and connected to the conveyor belt built into the tracks. Tape players were installed in the trunks, operated by push buttons on the dash, with narration of the Magic Skyway tour provided in several languages. Among the Fairlanes and Thunderbirds and Mercurys, twelve new Mustangs were placed into the Skyway fleet. They were selected from among the 150 Mustangs that had been manufactured months before the official Job One production date. Three were Raven black, three Wimbledon white, three Guardsman blue, and three Rangoon red. It was easy to pick them out from the rest. Ray Chatelin recalled the first time he spotted a Mustang coming around on the track: "I thought it was the most futuristic car I'd ever seen in my life."

In the weeks before the official opening, Chatelin and the other young Wonder Rotunda hosts and hostesses were trained at the site, learning how to monitor and control crowds gliding up the moving ramp to the Magic Skyway entrance on the second level and how to safely usher people into the conveyor cars. Thirty seconds to get everyone in. They were shown panic buttons on the conveyor belt that could be pushed in case of emergency, usually meaning the ride had started while someone was still trying to clamber aboard. They were outfitted in uniforms, the women in white and yellow dresses, the men in black slacks, white shirts, dark ties, and bright yellow blazers. "We looked like giant canaries," Chatelin said.

The World's Fair seemed to them both the center of the world and a giant 646-acre playground. Ford's pavilion was a corner near Grand Central Parkway, between the New Amsterdam Gate and the Peter Stuyvesant Gate. The General Motors exhibit loomed as competition on the other end of the Avenue of Automation. The giant Unisphere globe could be seen in the middle distance across the parkway. There was the Rheingold beer garden and Thai food and Disney fantasy rides. The incessant sound of "It's a Small World" at the Pepsi-Cola pavilion. An animatronic Abe Lincoln at the Illinois pavilion. The world's largest wheel of cheese at the Wisconsin pavilion. Hula dancers in the Hawaii pavilion. Steel bands in the Caribbean pavilion. Flamenco and Gypsy dancers in Spain. Dick Button and his Ice-travaganza. Pavilions for Billy Graham and Christian Scientists and Mormons and the Russian Orthodox Church; for the Boy Scouts and Hollywood and American Indians and Les Poupées de Paris, with hundreds of three-foot-high costumed puppets; for Sudan and Mexico and Berlin and Hong Kong; for Hertz and Avis and Chunky Candy and Parker Pen. The fair was promoted with the theme "Peace Through Understanding," but its essence was corporate salesmanship, and in this realm J. Walter Thompson was at the center of the action, representing not only Ford but ten other corporate pavilions and the World's Fair organization.

It was cold and rainy, the sky a dismal gray, when the gates opened at nine on the morning of April 22, letting in the first of 92,646 opening-day visitors, including President Johnson, who arrived by helicopter and delivered a noonday speech inside the Singer Bowl, filled with a capacity crowd of ten thousand. LBJ spoke of predictions that had been made at the World's Fair in New York a quarter century earlier, in 1939. It was forecast then that people would be able to cross the country by air in less than a day and that American roads would be traversed by 39 million cars. Bold prophecies, he said, but "the reality has far outstripped the vision." Then he made a few bold prophecies of his own: "Peace is not only possible in our generation, I predict that it is coming much earlier." At the next World's Fair, people "will see an America in which no man must be poor," an America "in which no man is handicapped by the color of his skin or the nature of his beliefs," an America "unwilling to accept public deprivation in the midst of private satisfaction." As it turned out, Johnson was just warming up for another speech he was to deliver exactly one month later, after arriving in Detroit and taking another helicopter to another, much larger stadium.

Among the tens of thousands of visitors that day were many hundreds who did not believe America had come close to reaching that vision of a place where no man was handicapped by the color of his skin. Race had been an issue for this World's Fair from its inception, when Adam Clayton Powell Jr., the Harlem congressman, and other black leaders expressed displeasure over the lack of African Americans on the executive staff and a dearth of blacks in the craft unions that constructed the pavilions. Sponsors of the fair had tried in various ways to respond to those concerns, at least superficially, and succeeded to the extent that the *New York Times* at one point ran the headline "Fair a Showcase for Civil Rights." The story pointed out that there were "outgoing, multilingual Negro college students" working at almost all the pavilions (including Ford, where twenty-six of two hundred workers were black). This represented a "conscious effort" to "project an enlightened corporate image to fairgoers."

The presence of black workers at many pavilions did not deter the Congress of Racial Equality, the civil rights group that took the lead in organizing protests in and around opening day. The integration of the fair itself was far less important to CORE than the integration of the institutions represented at the fair. Led by James Farmer, CORE had dedicated itself in 1964 to the idea that the message of the southern revolt against racial inequality was equally important to the North. And there was no larger target to make that case than the World's Fair, which was expected to draw anywhere from 60 to 100 million visitors over its two-year run. Some of the tactics fizzled; some succeeded. The most publicized was a plan to have a few thousand cars driven by civil rights activists purposely stall and block all roads leading to the fair, an idea hatched by the Brooklyn wing of CORE, the most militant in the region. Many mainstream black leaders opposed the "stall-in," adding their voices to those of LBJ and Robert Wagner, New York's mayor, and other white leaders who were still pushing civil rights legislation in Congress. Martin Luther King wrote a long, equivocating letter explaining both his understanding of the anger that fueled the Brooklyn wing and his assessment that the stall-in would be a "tactical error." Farmer himself concluded that it was a mistake and concentrated on other acts of protest and civil disobedience within the fairgrounds.

With the bad weather, the lack of widespread support, and beefed-up squads of patrol cars and tow trucks, the stall-in was poorly executed and barely noticed. But the protests inside were impossible to miss. Chants of "Jim Crow must go!" echoed across the fairgrounds. Farmer and Bayard Rustin, leading a group of a few hundred protesters, white and black, many of them college students, were arrested outside the New York State Pavilion, where they had set up a human barricade. Another group surrounded the Florida pavilion and had a minor scuffle with police. The Louisiana pavilion was another target, but when Farmer and his protesters reached it they discovered that it was not yet open.

At the Ford Wonder Rotunda, the morning hours proceeded without disruption until shortly before noon, when a squad of CORE picketers from the downtown Manhattan branch circled the rear of the building. Within an hour they were inside, staging a sit-down protest in front of the moving ramps leading up to the Magic Skyway. Faced with a variety of choices, none pleasant, Ford officials decided to defuse the confrontation by closing the exhibit altogether at 1 p.m., hoping the protesters eventually would grow bored and leave. Their numbers dwindled to about twenty late in the afternoon but gained strength again after the dinner hour, and by eight that night there were some 120 young men and women participating in the sit-down protest, chanting, "Ford bias must go!" Their stated goals were to force Ford to hire black executives and to divest from South Africa.

The closing of the exhibit infuriated some tourists who spent hours waiting in vain for the Magic Skyway to reopen. By the next day, letters were being sent directly to Henry Ford II at the Glass House in Dearborn. An attorney from Grand Rapids called it a "spineless and disgraceful surrender to lawlessness" and told HF2 that his new 1964 Thunderbird convertible would be his last Ford purchase. A bank executive from Chicago said of the protesters that "it was obvious that the general public resented their presence" and that Ford never should have relented. Eleanor Schilling of Hyde Park, New York, wrote, "Yesterday I viewed the most astonishing situation I have ever witnessed in my life. I saw Ford representatives weak and helpless in the face of a lawless civil rights demonstration at their exhibit at the New York World's Fair." She waited for several hours for the protesters to be ejected, but instead was told that Ford "didn't want to make any trouble." In so doing, "Ford allowed the interests of the general public to be subordinated to this group of unkempt malcontents and their 'angry young men' brothers of the beatnik type. I should like to assure you that Ford's public image suffered considerably in the eyes of virtually all observers." And so the cultural crosscurrents of the sixties whipped around the Ford Wonder Rotunda, with youth "being served" in the name of the Mustang, a market-designed symbol of a certain concept of freedom and individuality, and youth also being disparaged in reaction to a certain style of civic idealism, confrontation, and dissent.

As the Ford vice president for public relations back in Dearborn, Theodore H. Mecke Jr. had his name on the company's letters of response, saying he was writing on behalf of Henry Ford II. He apologized to Mrs. Schilling for having to wait so long at the exhibit without being able to enter. "I should like you to know, however, that the welfare of our visitors was our primary concern. As reluctant as we were to inconvenience guests by closing the exhibit, we thought it better to do so than to subject them to the risk of violence and possible physical harm that might have resulted if we had sought to have the demonstrators removed." It was a one-day protest, not to be repeated, Mecke said, and fair organizers in any case promised more security in the future.

Through that first week and beyond, Ford had to deal with more mundane eruptions of discontent at the Magic Skyway. The lines were too long.

The cars were too small. The technology was too iffy. Robert Ferguson of Woodmere, New York, complained in a letter to Ford, "After an interminable, uncomfortable wait on line, a hustling gang of overeager juveniles literally pushed my wife, my 18-year-old daughter and myself into the rear seat of a small convertible. My ankle was badly twisted in the melee and the car ride was by all odds the most uncomfortable I ever had." To make matters worse, the push-button narration got stuck on the German version and "none of the occupants understood a word. . . . I can't understand what kind of idiot decided that the commentary should be in German instead of English." Mecke responded as best he could, inviting the Ferguson family back for a free ride and explaining the push-button narration options. Gene Fernett from Cocoa Beach, Florida, wrote that the exhibit was better than GM's but too slow because "the convertibles did not handle enough people and made it crowded and slow. . . . I saw dozens of persons turn away in anger when they saw how few persons could move through the ride at a time." Ralph T. Schrenkeisen from Garden City, New York, informed Ford that he and his wife "spent a lovely day at the Fair . . . marred only by our visit to Ford. It took us two hours standing in line before we could get in a car, at which time we didn't care what kind it was, and were too tired to fully appreciate the splendid exhibit." Again Mecke tried to explain the problem. The ride was designed to handle 3,600 people an hour, but they "were not reaching that figure because some families refused to ride with strangers." He welcomed any and all suggestions on how to shorten the wait.

Even in a fabricated fairyland palace, the real world intruded with the imperfections of man and machine. It would be easier to fix the Magic Skyway ride in the Ford Wonder Rotunda than to repair the wounds of racial segregation. As Martha Reeves and the Vandellas would soon sing on a hit record and in a Motown music video in which they danced and skipped their way down a Mustang assembly line at Ford's Dearborn plant, "Nowhere to run, baby, nowhere to hide."

Chapter 22

# UPWARD TO THE GREAT SOCIETY

**ON THE FOURTEENTH** of April, the day after Iacocca's unveiling of the Mustang at the Ford Wonder Rotunda, the news made its way from the White House to Mayor Cavanagh's office in Detroit: LBJ was coming to town, or at least to Metropolitan Airport. He would arrive on the morning of May 22 on his way to Ann Arbor, where he was to deliver the commencement address at the University of Michigan. With about five weeks to prepare, Cavanagh and his aides were instructed to make sure the welcoming party at the airport met the president's expectations. This was an election year, Johnson was running, and Detroit was important to him for many reasons. As the capital of the automobile industry and the center of the progressive labor movement, it was critical to the economic well-being of the nation and the political well-being of the man in the Oval Office. Detroit was also where JFK had started his campaign in 1960 with his invocation of a New Frontier, and LBJ wanted to match or surpass that with a grand inspirational slogan of his own.

As the weeks went by, the instructions sharpened. The airport rally should have the feel of a spontaneous outpouring of affection for the president, not an overt political event for a candidate. The crowd needed to be large, in the tens of thousands, enough to signal the inevitability of his triumph in November, and it should be composed of more than the usual Democratic partisans. As Cavanagh later recalled in an oral history conducted for the LBJ Library, Johnson wanted "some prominent businessmen, Republicans or at least non-Democrats, as most of them were, to serve on the welcoming committee." As part of that effort, Cavanagh called a Ford vice president who also presided over the Detroit Regional Chamber of Commerce and asked if he would serve. Sorry, came the reply, the Ford man would be out of town that day. "But shortly after I spoke with him I received a call back from him, saying that he again apologized that he couldn't make it but he'd like to recommend a substitute," Cavanagh said later. "I said, 'Fine. Who is that?' He said, 'Henry Ford himself would like to serve.'" HF2 on a welcoming committee with Walter Reuther and August Scholle, president of the Michigan AFL-CIO—that sounded like something that might slake the unquenchable thirst of the president.

The genesis of the visit went back to the previous July, when Kennedy was still alive. Roger Lowenstein, a student leader at the University of Michigan, wrote a letter to Harlan Hatcher, the school's president, suggesting that they invite JFK to be the commencement speaker the following spring. Many students at Michigan felt a special bond with the young president. It was on their campus that he had first articulated his idea for what would become the Peace Corps, and over the years the Wolverines had supplied a generous number of Peace Corps volunteers. When university officials broached the idea with the Kennedy White House, the answer came back that the president was interested but his schedule could not be fixed that far in advance. One month later, Kennedy was assassinated. Michigan eventually asked President Johnson, who accepted on the condition that they move up the commencement from Saturday to Friday morning to accommodate his schedule.

In the hour or so before Air Force One touched down that morning of May 22, there already had been a day's worth of politicking at the airport. When Cavanagh got there, he discovered that his staff had placed Governor Romney three positions back in the receiving line, behind the mayor himself, and Romney was fuming about this slight. He was, after all, the highest-ranking official in Michigan; he deserved to be at the foot of the stairs when LBJ deplaned. Cavanagh quickly acquiesced to the governor's demand. In the months since they had bonded in bipartisanship over Detroit's ultimately unsuccessful bid to win the 1968 Summer Olympics, both Cavanagh and Romney had flirted with greater political ambitions that placed them in partisan conflict.

Cavanagh had started the year by entertaining the idea of running for governor, or at least not discouraging stories and conversations speculating that he might challenge Romney. The notion never went further than talk, and Cavanagh soon set his sights on becoming the nation's leading urban spokesman during an era when the focus in Washington was turning to big cities and their problems and possibilities. Whatever policies the Johnson administration had in mind, Cavanagh wanted Detroit to be a laboratory for their implementation. Neil Staebler, the congressman from Ann Arbor, had emerged as the Democratic challenger to Romney, despite doubts about him expressed by labor and civil rights leaders in Michigan, which meant that Romney started the campaign year as a heavy favorite for reelection. But, like Cavanagh, the governor also had considered moving his show to a larger stage. Barry Goldwater, the conservative Republican senator from Arizona, had visited Michigan at the start of his presidential primary campaign in early January, stating at a rally in Grand Rapids, "Americans didn't want a choice between Tweedledee and Tweedledum." That same day Romney, who disagreed sharply with Goldwater on civil rights, was in Washington telling a National Press Club audience that Goldwater was taking the party in a losing direction. "A party representing one or a few narrow interests cannot indefinitely survive in this country," he said. When a reporter followed with a logical question—Was he an active candidate for president, and if not, would he consider being one if there was a public demand for him?—Romney responded "No" to the first part and "Possibly" to the second, explaining that "to do anything else would be sheer effrontery and refusal to accept my duty." The reaction back in Michigan was mostly confusion, forcing Romney to hold another press conference to try to explain himself, which by most accounts he failed to do.

Whatever his intentions, his immediate future was essentially decided for him by Martin Hayden, the influential editor of the *Detroit News*, who wrote a strongly worded editorial on the subject. The headline was "Romney in GOP Race? Count us Out!" Hayden exploded the myth that Romney was merely waiting for the people to beg him to run for president, labeling it a classic political ploy. "That's the standard form for presidential race entry, and no one using it in the past ever has waited for a draft," Hayden wrote. The *News* had endorsed Romney for governor and had supported and praised his work in Lansing. "But if Governor Romney places his obligations to the people who elected him here second to what he may believe is his obligation to make himself available as a candidate for the Republican nomination this year, the *News* will not support him in that contest." The *News* was the foundation upon which Republican candidates built their campaigns in Michigan, and without that home-state base, Romney retreated quietly back to state matters, which included wanting to be in on the action when the president of the United States came calling.

The twenty-four-member welcoming committee gathered in the American Airlines maintenance hangar awaiting Johnson's arrival. "We had set some coffee and doughnuts up for these men and women, and a number of reporters were mingling through the crowd," Cavanagh recalled. Those were the days before the press corps was herded into pens and treated like children at the zoo. *(You can look when we tell you to, but don't get too close.)* Frank Beckman of the *Free Press* came across Henry Ford II and found him not only surprisingly approachable but with something newsworthy to say. This was no day for Ford to be grouchy. He was living free and easy, his company was making record profits, and the Mustang was the hottest car in America.

"Mr. Ford, what is your opinion of President Johnson?" Beckman asked.

"I think he's terrific," HF2 responded.

"Do you think he will be reelected?"

"There's no question about it."

"Will you support him?"

"Yes."

"Have you ever voted for a Democratic presidential candidate?"

"He'll be the first I've ever voted for."

"Regardless of whom the Republicans put up?"

"Regardless."

"How do you view the way he's handling his job?"

"He's doing an excellent job as president. I've heard him say many times that he's for all the people in the country—for business, labor, and the general public. I agree with what he says."

Ford also told the *Free Press* that he had known LBJ since the Texan was the Senate majority leader but had been to the White House only once in the six months that Johnson had been president. He said he thought of himself as an independent, not a Republican. A check of records indicated to Beckman that indeed HF2 and his brothers, Benson and William Clay, had made significant campaign contributions to both Democrats and Republicans since 1962.

In Washington, Johnson was awakened that morning at seven by a call from the White House operator. He was served breakfast in bed before meeting with aides Bill Moyers, Jack Valenti, Walter Jenkins, and Dick Goodwin, who had been the main speechwriter for the commencement address. As Goodwin later recalled, Johnson reviewed the speech at his Oval Office desk, scratched in a few changes with his pencil, and without looking up said, "It ought to do just fine, boys. Just what I told you." Then he turned to Valenti: "What time's that plane leave? And why are we always running out of Fresca?" Johnson departed the South Grounds of the White House at 8:57 for the thirteen-minute helicopter ride to Andrews Air Force Base, where a contingent of state congressional members and administration officials with Michigan ties waited to hitch rides home, a delegation that included both senators, thirteen House members, one former governor, and two assistant cabinet secretaries. Air Force One touched down in Detroit at 9:11, according to the White House Daily Diary.

Behind the airport fence, a crowd had been building since sunup. The Detroit Police Department Band was there, and the Detroit Fire Department Band, and the Redford High School Band, all entertaining a throng now estimated at thirty thousand. The silver-and-blue 707 "glinted in the bright sun as it landed and taxied," Beckman and his colleague, Barbara Stanton, wrote later of the scene. "The ramp was placed, the door opened, and the shout went up THERE HE IS" as the combined bands played "Hail to the Chief." Waiting in line below were Governor Romney, Mayor Cavanagh, labor leaders Reuther and Scholle, and the talkative Henry Ford II, along with John Leary, a vice president at Chrysler; Walker Cisler, president of Detroit Edison (and one of Cavanagh's colleagues during the Olympic effort in Baden-Baden); J. Arthur Mullen, vice president of the Detroit Region Chamber of Commerce; Horace Sheffield of the Trade Union Leadership Council; and other leaders from business, labor, and academia—the sort of mix the president wanted.

This was LBJ's first appearance in Michigan as president. He seemed spry, buoyant, in good humor. He asked Romney and Cavanagh to stand next to him and get proper introductions. He went through the list of politicians who flew out from Washington with him. Then he addressed the crowd: "I want you to know that there is nothing that restores a president's soul more than a warm Detroit greeting." So what if his staff had virtually demanded such a showing? "I want to thank each of you so very, very much for coming out here this morning. My first thought is to sing an old song, 'Will You Love Me in November as You Do in May?'" The election was never far from his mind.

But he had come to Michigan to say something larger. This is where he would present his vision of the societal good that a powerful and committed federal government could achieve, and though he would deliver that speech twenty-eight miles away, in Ann Arbor, no place seemed more important to his mission than Detroit, a great city that honored labor, built cars, made music, promoted civil rights, and helped lift working people into the middle class. "This city and its people are the herald of hope in America," he said. "Prosperity in America must begin here in Detroit. You folks in Detroit put American citizens on wheels; you have the American economy on the move. Unemployment in Detroit is down, profits are up, wages are good, and there is no problem too tough or too challenging for us to solve."

This was Walter Reuther's kind of talk, and in other circumstances he might have been arm in arm with the president, but instead he was lingering in the shadows. He had been criticizing HF2 harshly in recent speeches, their symbiotic relationship as friendly adversaries now decidedly in nemesis mode as contract talks approached later in the year. There were complicated and competing factors at work here: pragmatism versus idealism, conflict versus cooperation, the narrow interests of collective bargaining versus the broad interests of progressive government. Johnson had been urging Reuther to tamp down both his rhetoric and his demands in the larger interests of helping the president maneuver his way through the election year and implement the policies that he and Reuther equally believed in. And here was Henry Ford II, embracing that same president, an unprecedented moment that demanded that Reuther recede. LBJ even scratched him from his airport speech, choosing instead another labor leader, the state AFL-CIO president, to make a point about his new coalition. "My cup runneth over here when men come here to greet me like Gus Scholle and Henry Ford," Johnson said. "When the president has Gus and Henry by his side, the sky is the limit. And the sky is bright today."

At 9:55, at the end of a short whirl over from the airport in Detroit, four identical helicopters landed on an opening to the east of Michigan Stadium, carrying the president and his entourage. Valenti walked behind his boss, carrying notes and a copy of the speech. A radiant spring day, the blue sky high and bright, the heat of the sun beaming down. Waiting inside the stadium was the largest crowd ever to attend a university commencement address, or so it was called. Somewhere between seventy thousand and ninety thousand people. Faculty members often shun commencement ceremonies, but this time more showed up than ever, along with almost all of the 4,943 graduating seniors. President Hatcher greeted Johnson near the landing area and ushered him into a trailer next to the Yost Field House, where he donned his black gown with three velvet bands ringing the sleeves and prepared for the processional through the gates and on toward the extensive speaker's platform at the north end of the stadium. The massive bowl was filled except for the end zone, behind the platform, closed off on orders of the Secret Service. A roar went up when the president came into view. His speech was fed into a teleprompter, ready for delivery after all degrees had been conferred en masse, ending with the honorary Doctor of Civil Law degree for Lyndon Baines Johnson.

Nine paragraphs into his speech, after pleasantries and jokes, LBJ issued the clarion call of his presidency. "Your imagination, your initiative, and your indignation," he told the graduates, "will determine whether we build a society where progress is the servant of our needs, or a society where old values and new visions are buried under unbridled growth. For in your time we have the opportunity to move not only toward the rich society and the powerful society, but upward to the Great Society."

*The Great Society.* The phrase was not yet well known, nor was it new. Adam Smith, the eighteenth-century philosopher and political economist, had used it in his writings. Walter Lippmann, the most influential columnist of the mid-twentieth century, took it down a notch but discussed the meaning of a Good Society. More recently a British journalist and author named Barbara Ward, who had frequented LBJ's White House, wrote about a Great Society in a book Johnson read at night, *The Rich Nations and the Poor Nations.* The president himself had tried it out once before, at a fund-raising dinner a month earlier at the Conrad Hilton Hotel in Chicago. Now it would be attached to this commencement address and live on, for better and worse, for decades thereafter. Mostly it would be connected to poverty programs Johnson tried to implement over the next five years, and sometimes would be referred to with disparagement, sarcasm, or wistfulness to signify good intentions gone awry, as a symbol of hopes and dreams dashed by big-government excesses and LBJ's inability to create something great at home at the same time that he was waging war overseas. But to listen again to Johnson delivering it on that spring morning, to read the words anew—even knowing all that was to come after—is to appreciate that it was meant to convey something deeper, a spiritual rising.

What did Johnson's Great Society require? Abundance, liberty, an end to poverty and racial injustice, the opportunity for every child to have a good education—but more than that. His Great Society was "a place where the city of man serves not only the needs of the body and the demands of commerce but the desire for beauty and the hunger for community," "a place that honors creation for its own sake and for what it adds to the understanding of the race . . . a place where men are more concerned with the quality of their goals than the quantity of their goods," "a place where the meaning of our lives matches the marvelous products of our labor." Beauty, community, creativity, quality, meaning—this was moving past Kennedy's New Frontier into ethereal realms of personal fulfillment usually considered beyond the reach of politics.

Johnson also imagined what the world would be like fifty years into the future, in the year 2014. "Many of you will live to see that day," he told the students, predicting that four fifths of all Americans by then would live in urban areas, that the urban population would double, that the size of cities would double, and that there would need to be a commitment to "rebuild the entire urban United States." He quoted from Aristotle—"Men come together in cities in order to live, but they remain together in order to live the good life"—and said it was becoming increasingly difficult "to live the good life in American cities today. The catalog of ills is long: there is decay of the centers and despoiling of the suburbs. There is not enough housing for our people or transportation for our traffic. Open land is vanishing and old landmarks are violated. Worst of all, expansion is eroding the precious and time honored values of community with neighbors and communion with nature. The loss of these values breeds loneliness and boredom and indifference. Our society will never be great until our cities are great."

Only an hour earlier, at the airport, he had called Detroit "the herald of hope." Now, in his litany of urban ills, he could have been describing a decaying Detroit of the future.

The twenty-minute speech was interrupted by applause fourteen times. When he talked about bringing "an end to poverty and racial injustice," Paul Julius Alexander, a noted classics professor and refugee from Nazi Germany, appeared to be the first to clap, initiating a ripple of applause that increased in intensity as it moved through the stadium. Johnson's first mention of the Great Society was met with silence. Gene Roberts, who had spent much of the previous half year covering the Kennedy assassination and its aftermath, was in the stadium for the *Free Press*. It was six months to the day since Kennedy had been killed. There are times when reporters for various reasons miss the immortal rhetoric of history as it is being made. At the last historic address, Martin Luther King's "I Have a Dream" speech the previous August, the hometown *Washington Post* failed to get that phrase into its main story. This time Roberts nailed it as he outlined the speech Johnson delivered in "his familiar molasses drawl." In the lead paragraph of the story Roberts would write after the event, he noted that Johnson "tossed a new phrase—the Great Society—into the nation's political vocabulary." An editorial writer for the *Free Press* set about defining what that foretold. He concluded that LBJ had "adopted wholeheartedly the liberalism" of JFK. "The accent will continue to be on big government, with Washington taking the leadership in the attacks on poverty, pollution, and poor education." Some of Johnson's ideas for the Great Society "frighten more than inspire," the editorial concluded. But "it was a beautiful day, and a fine commencement address."

As the commencement ceremony drew to a close, the Michigan band played "The Yellow and Blue," the school's alma mater, and the massive crowd, warmed by the late morning sun, sat in silence while a lone bugle call pierced the moment. Taps and reveille. End and beginning.

Johnson and the platform guests led the procession out of the stadium and back to the trailer where he would shed the black robe and freshen up. Walter Reuther was waiting for him outside the trailer. Reuther had not been onstage, but he had witnessed the speech. Johnson's vision was his vision. The support of his union, and Reuther's own unequivocal voice, were essential to the civil rights legislation that was moving through Congress at long last and would finally be enacted in July. Reuther, like Johnson, believed deeply in the vital role of government in improving the lives of the people. He was working on his own version of a similar oration, one that championed the role of government. He wanted to "destroy the myth" that the government that governs least governs best. He believed that big government was a product of twentieth-century life, just as Ford Motor Company was a product of twentieth-century technology, and that government's bigness was in accord with the magnitude of the problems that needed to be solved. According to the White House Daily Diary, Reuther and LBJ "spoke for a few minutes" before the presidential entourage boarded the helicopters for the return to the Detroit airport.

Mayor Cavanagh had missed the speech, staying in Detroit, but was at the airport when Johnson returned from Ann Arbor. He was booked as a guest on the flight back to Washington to attend that night's White House Correspondents Dinner. LBJ, he said, looked "extremely hot and sort of rumpled when he came back to the airport." But what a day this had been. The largest commencement ceremony in history. A new slogan for his administration. The fervent crowds at the airport. An endorsement from Henry Ford II.

It all looked so promising, Mayor Cavanagh remarked to LBJ as Air Force One lifted above Detroit. The reference was to political prospects, but the context was larger. In the urban landscape below them stood Henry Ford II's Glass House and Walter Reuther's Solidarity House and Diego Rivera's muscular *Detroit Industry* murals and the River Rouge complex churning out alluring new Mustangs. Receding into the distance were Berry Gordy's recording studios, where Motown was rollicking as Hitsville USA, and the wide lanes of Woodward Avenue flowing south past the Graystone Ballroom and the Fox Theater and on toward Cobo Hall, where Martin Luther King first dreamed his dream at the water's edge as barges freighted with iron ore and automobiles budged up and down America's busiest working river.

Herald of hope? President Johnson said they would just have to wait and see.

Epilogue

# NOW AND THEN

**WHILE RESEARCHING THIS** book, my wife and I often stayed at the Inn on Ferry Street, a hostelry located on a quiet block within easy walking distance of the Detroit Institute of Arts, the Detroit Historical Museum, the Detroit Public Library, and the Walter P. Reuther Library on Labor and Urban Affairs. The inn comprises three old brick manses and a carriage house, all restored to early twentieth-century comfort—a hint of resurrection in a city of decay. Some guests at the inn were tourists who came to admire the world-class paintings at the art museum, but others were there to take in the decomposition of a city in the same way they might view the remains of an ancient civilization. Detroit might prefer it otherwise, but one of the ways it stayed in the public eye was through photographs and videos that came to be known by the hideous phrase "ruin porn."

Detroit is vibrantly alive in some places, despite wide swaths of emptiness and despair and foreclosed homes. Beautiful things can grow in forgotten places when no one is looking, and that is happening to some extent in Detroit. The downtown and parts of midtown and other nearby neighborhoods are being reconfigured and repopulated not just by developers and entrepreneurs betting on a comeback, but by artists, poets, musicians, activists, foodies, and techies, mostly young people of all races who see the desolate urban landscape as a haven for freedom and opportunity.

There were mornings nonetheless when I could walk across eight lanes of Woodward Avenue at the corner with East Kirby, on my way from the inn to the Reuther Library, and not see a car within hailing distance driving in either direction along the city's main thoroughfare. It felt as though I could safely read *War and Peace* while crossing, confident that I would not get hit. And there were chilly nights when we sat nearly alone in a cinematic French bistro across the street from the art museum, enjoying tomato soup and grilled cheese sandwiches while listening to a talented classical guitarist, and wondered what had happened to everyone. What the Wayne State sociologists had predicted in 1963 had proven only too accurate. They calculated that the population of Detroit would drop from 1.7 million to 1.2 million in that decade, and continue dropping for the foreseeable future. By 2014 it was down to about 688,000. Maybe that was rock bottom.

One day I went driving up Woodward, took a left at West Grand Boulevard, and rode past the Fisher Building and Ford Hospital and the Motown Museum until I reached the triangle with Grand River and Dexter, where I turned north on Dexter and went searching for landmarks in the northwest Detroit neighborhoods of my earliest childhood. The Fisher Y, where I learned to swim, a six-year-old shivering naked in a cold pool with other little boys, was at that corner. It was boarded up, but I could see "YMCA" etched into the cornice above the front door. The flat on Dexter where my family lived for a few years was now an empty lot in an area where it seemed as though two of every five houses were gone or fire-charred or abandoned; the house we moved to next, farther north and west on Cortland Street, seemed occupied but in a state of disrepair. Will the Detroit recovery, when and if it comes, include the people of these lost and forgotten quarters? Can it be called a recovery if they are left behind? On another trip I explored the neighborhood with Tom Stanton, a writer and professor at the University of Detroit Mercy, and we drove farther into the back streets in search of Winterhalter School, where I had attended first grade. The building was still there on Broadstreet, but the school had changed. It was a charter school now, going by the name Hope Academy.

It was a summer day, the school year done, but a security guard in the parking lot said we might find the principal inside. Her name was Vaneda Fox Sanders. She was a product of the Detroit public schools who graduated from Cass Tech, received a graduate degree from Wayne State, and eventually settled in the east side neighborhood of Indian Village. Her academy was named Hope for a reason. From kindergarten through eighth grade, it taught nearly eight hundred children, who came from all quarters of the city. Ten percent of the parents were categorized as transient or homeless. Ninety-five percent of the students were on free or reduced meal plans. "This is the new wing," she said, leading me on a tour of the school. The new wing was built in the 1960s. Talk about feeling old; that was *after* my time there, in 1955 and 1956. "Could we see the old wing?" I asked. The old wing was built in the twenties. As we walked down a hallway from new to old, I was overwhelmed by sensory perceptions long buried and seemingly forgotten. It was the woodwork, so solid and thick and blackish-brown, that got me, the windowsills, the trim, the benches at the stairwell landings—the sight of them incited a rush of memories, not as poetic as Proust's taste of the madeleine cake, and not easily defined as sweet or sour, good or bad, but dizzyingly powerful. Detroit has that effect on me. Fox Sanders came out of a family of nine children, and of the six still alive, she was the only one who stayed in Detroit. At family reunions, her siblings would ask, "When are you leaving?" Never, she would say. She had no desire to leave.

What happened in Detroit after this story ends is mostly a litany of dissolution and leave-taking. Rev. C. L. Franklin was shot by armed intruders at his home on La Salle Boulevard in northwest Detroit an hour after midnight on the Sunday morning of June 10, 1979, and fell into a five-year coma, dying in 1984. The memorial service at New Bethel Baptist for Aretha Franklin's father, organizer of the Walk to Freedom, went on for much of a day. Twenty-three preachers from Detroit and other cities delivered tributes, along with Coretta Scott King and Jesse Jackson, and the Staples Singers performed with two full church choirs.

John White died in prison two years after his Gotham Hotel was raided and razed.

Walter Reuther and his wife, May, were killed in a crash in 1970 as the pilot of their small plane attempted to land in bad weather near Black Lake, Michigan. It was believed the altimeter had malfunctioned. One of the most influential Americans of the twentieth century, a pragmatic idealist who, from his base in Detroit, had been instrumental in enlarging the nation's middle class, was gone at age sixty-three, his autoworkers union already in a long, slow decline from its peak of power. There were strikes against the automakers in the fall of 1964, but not serious enough to jeopardize the election of Lyndon Baines Johnson over Barry Goldwater. The civil rights push of the previous summer resulted in nation-changing legislation, first the 1964 Civil Rights Act and then the 1965 Voting Rights Act, and Detroit—with the financial and lobbying support of Reuther's UAW along with the city's strong African American community—played some small but vital role in the creation of both. After Martin Luther King was assassinated in 1968, it was John Conyers, a Detroit congressman, who led the long and eventually successful effort to make his birthday a national holiday, with essential help from Stevie Wonder. By then, many disaffected white union members from the Detroit suburbs had turned away from Reuther's progressive ideals to vote for George Wallace and later Ronald Reagan.

Jerome Cavanagh became a pivotal voice for the cities of America during the early years of the Johnson administration, in 1966 becoming the first mayor to serve simultaneously as president of the U.S. Conference of Mayors and of the National League of Cities. But his life and career disintegrated the following year. His wife, feeling emotionally abandoned, booted him out of the house and filed for divorce—so much for the all-American, Kennedyesque family. Then his city went up in flames. During five days in July 1967, after a police raid of an after-hours joint known in the vernacular as a "blind pig," Detroit was devastated by a race riot, or rebellion, depending on one's perspective. The spasm of civil disorder resulted in forty-three deaths (thirty-three black, ten white victims),

483 fires, widespread looting, and more than seven thousand arrests. Cavanagh was criticized for the city's slow response. Three years into an attempted transformation of Detroit through Model Cities and War on Poverty programs, this marked a low point in the aspirations upward to a Great Society as well as the end of an era of racial progress that Cavanagh and George Edwards, his first police commissioner, had hoped would make Detroit a haven of tolerance and equality. It also halted Cavanagh's political ascent, the once-promising career of a JFK acolyte left smoldering in the ruins. He died in 1979 of a heart attack, long out of politics.

After avoiding conviction on the police bribery charge in 1963, Tony Giacalone, the Detroit mobster pursued so vigorously by Commissioner Edwards, was convicted of income tax fraud in 1976 and served ten years in prison. Of greater national interest was Tony Jack's role in the disappearance of Teamsters boss Jimmy Hoffa, who was last seen on July 30, 1975, in the parking lot of the Machus Red Fox restaurant in Bloomfield Township outside Detroit. Hoffa had gone to the restaurant for a meeting with two mobsters. One was Tony Provenzano, a Teamster boss in northern New Jersey; the other was Giacalone.

After winning reelection to a third term in 1966, George Romney became an early favorite for the Republican presidential nomination in 1968 but hurt himself with a series of missteps, including a statement upon returning from South Vietnam that he had "just had the biggest brainwashing anyone could get" from the American military. Far more than that, he found his moderate brand of Republicanism increasingly out of favor in the GOP and finished fifth in the nomination contest won by Richard Nixon. He was appointed secretary of housing and urban development under Nixon and continued pushing civil rights issues, including programs intended to desegregate housing in the suburbs, a concept that was nowhere more unpopular than in the communities outside Detroit and that also further isolated him from the conservative movement within his own party.

Henry Ford II's second marriage, to Maria Cristina Vettore Austin, lasted fifteen years. Near the end of that tumultuous relationship, the Deuce uttered the famous last words that defined his personal life. "Never complain, never explain," he said after being arrested for driving while intoxicated in the company of Kathleen DuRoss, his mistress (and next wife). Ford and the flamboyant Cristina divorced in 1980. His professional relationship with Lee Iacocca did not last as long as that marriage. He fired Iacocca in 1978, explaining, "Sometimes you just don't like somebody." HF2 died of pneumonia at age seventy in 1987 at Ford Hospital. He and his occasionally friendly nemesis, Reuther, were both awarded the Presidential Medal of Freedom—Ford by LBJ and Reuther, posthumously, by President Clinton three decades later.

The Mustang, after a remarkable early burst as a driving and marketing phenomenon, a sexy and stylish symbol of the sixties, grew fat and heavy and out of favor by the early seventies. Though it staged several comebacks and celebrated its fiftieth anniversary in 2014, it could never duplicate that first golden era. Much the same could be said for all of the Detroit auto industry.

The buildings designed by Albert Kahn still stood a half century later. Except, that is, for the Ford Rotunda, which burned to the ground, and the Hotel Gotham, which was axed by officers in the gambling raid and then leveled for urban renewal. The massive River Rouge Complex in Dearborn had been automated and reconfigured, its workforce trimmed since its heyday, with many of the manufacturing tasks once undertaken there spread to plants across the country. But Kahn's designs remained as symbols of Ford Motor Company's might. The General Motors Building, Kahn's neoclassical fifteen-story colossus on West Grand Boulevard, no longer served as headquarters for GM; it became known as Cadillac Place and housed a few dozen agencies of the state of Michigan. GM relocated to the high-rise Renaissance Center down on the Detroit River. The Detroit Athletic Club on Madison Avenue and Detroit Police Headquarters at 1300 Beaubien were largely unchanged, outside and in, with the exception that both fortresses were now fully integrated.

Three blocks apart on West Lafayette, the newspaper buildings Kahn designed for the *Detroit News* and *Free Press* were still there, but not serving the same purpose. The *Free Press* cleared out of its plant in the late 1980s to move in with the *News*, and both announced plans to leave the *News* Building, an aging architectural jewel, for another space several blocks away—struggling newspapers adjusting to a changing culture, just as they had a half century earlier. In fact Frank Beckman's report on Henry Ford II's endorsement and Gene Roberts's dispatch from Ann Arbor would not have had an audience if LBJ had delivered his Great Society speech seven weeks later. Newspapers were in turmoil then too, as back shops rebelled against automation and work conditions, and on July 13, 1964, Pressmen's Local 13 went out on strike against both Detroit papers and did not return until shortly before Thanksgiving.

The Fox Theater, restored to gilded glory in the late eighties, held its place along Woodward Avenue, marking a fifty-year continuum from the sellout crowds that came to see Motown artists perform there to the Chrysler commercial featuring Eminem and a black gospel choir. But the Graystone Ballroom, where Motown once staged vibrant battles of the bands, is long gone—one small loss in the larger departure of Motown. In 1967, the year of the riot, Berry Gordy uprooted from the houses on West Grand and moved the operation to the Donovan Building, closer to downtown at 2457 Woodward. That address had an unlikely reverberation in our story. Robert Ankony, the truant and future cop and PhD who witnessed the burning of the Ford Rotunda, lived at 2457 Woodmere in southwest Detroit. Woodward, Woodmere—same numbers. Mail intended for Motown often ended up in his parents' mailbox, and Ankony remembered how his father "would get angry and throw it away, swearing."

By 1972 Gordy had abandoned Detroit altogether, moving Motown body if not soul to Los Angeles, where it waxed and waned for decades but was never the same, even as Michael Jackson from the Jackson 5 burst into global stardom, Diana Ross became a movie star and diva, and Smokey Robinson and Stevie Wonder burnished their reputations as musical marvels. Gordy, fit and trim in his eighties, was living in a mansion high above Bel Air when I interviewed him for this book. Marvin Gaye, the third of the Motown geniuses, was dead, shot by his father. Also gone were Mary Wells, four of the five original Temptations, one of the Supremes, and three of the

Four Tops. Most of the groups had been torn asunder by ambition, drugs, or dissension, their lead singers eager to break out as solo acts and new group members coming and going. Only the Four Tops stayed together—one for all, all for one—until Lawrence Payton and then Obie Benson and then Levi Stubbs died, leaving Duke Fakir behind. They had kept their base in Detroit after most everyone else left, their cohesion a point of pride and a reflection of the confidence and humility of Levi Stubbs. Over the years, Fakir pointed out, there were a few dozen Temptations, but, while they were all alive, "there were only *four* Tops."

Mom and Pops and the rest of the Gordy family followed Berry out to Los Angeles, all except his big sister Esther Gordy Edwards. She had been the keeper of the castle, taking photos, gathering documents, storing memorabilia and records. For many years after her brother left, she noticed that people still made pilgrimages to the old brick houses on West Grand Boulevard, where it all began in 1959, and it was her idea to transform that location into the Motown Museum. "Berry, I think we made history and don't even know it," she once explained to her brother. The museum opened in 1985 and has survived through the decades, modest but lively and informative, and the people keep coming. Esther died in 2011 at age ninety-one, and Motown's stars descended on Detroit again to pay homage. Stevie Wonder, who called her his second mother, gave a musical tribute, and her brother Berry and Smokey Robinson offered reflections, along with her stepson, Harry T. Edwards, a federal judge in Washington. By the time I visited the museum it was being run by Esther's granddaughter, Robin Terry, and Allen Rawls, a Detroit native and music lover who had attended Winterhalter, my elementary school. The tour led down to Studio A, where the Funk Brothers played, and it was noted that the piano in the room, for decades out of tune, had been restored as a gift from one museum visitor who had found early inspiration in Motown, Sir Paul McCartney.

There was a world map on one wall with push pins designating the homes of visitors. They came from Vietnam, Jakarta, New Zealand, Mongolia, Greenland, Iceland, Ethiopia, Madagascar, everywhere. On one of my days there, I encountered a delegation of South Africans dancing and singing and posing for pictures on the front walk. Another day it was a busload of Japanese tourists who were awestruck at the site of Tamla-Motown, as they called it in their country. Motown was and is a global language. In the winter of 2014, at the same time that *Motown the Musical* was running on Broadway, I went to see Martha Reeves when she and the Vandellas appeared in Washington. It had been fifty-two years since the first *Motortown Revue* rolled out of Detroit to introduce the music of Motown to the nation. The first stop then—during that frightening week of the Cuban Missile Crisis—had been the Howard Theater, only a few miles from the White House, and now the Vandellas were back on that same stage. Martha Reeves was in her early seventies, but her voice had the familiar joyful kick, and in her long, shimmering silver dress and high heels she could still outdance anyone in the room, or in the streets. *Don't forget the Motor City.* And here came the heat wave and the quicksand and we all had nowhere to run and nowhere to hide and we came and got those memories. What lasts? What did Detroit give America? You could hear the answer in every song.

## CONNECTIONS

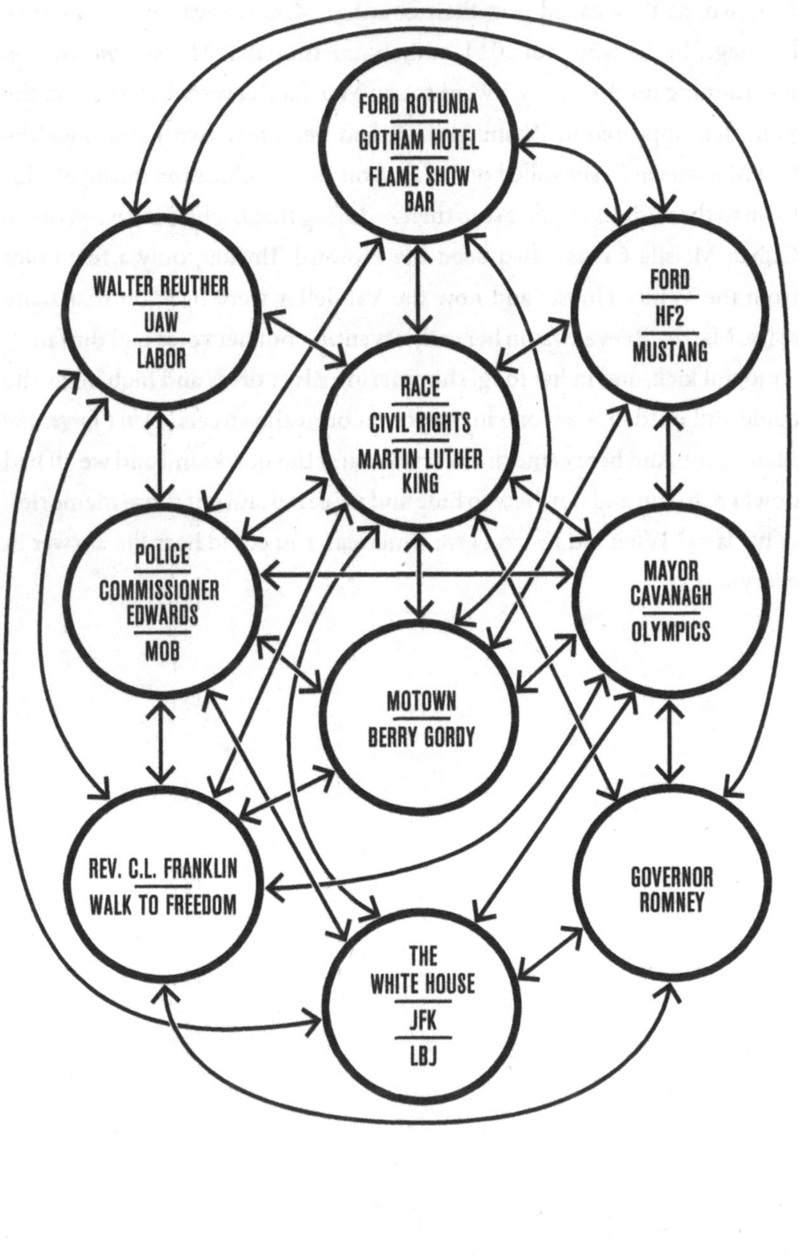

# TIME LINE

## 1962

| | |
|---|---|
| **October 7** | President Kennedy campaigns in Detroit in off-year elections. |
| **October 20** | Detroit Auto Show opens, unveiling 1963 cars that sold more than any in history to that point. |
| **October 22** | LBJ, scheduled to appear at the auto show, cancels his trip at last minute because of the unfolding Cuban Missile Crisis. |
| **October 23** | Motown artists leave Detroit on nationwide *Motortown Revue*. First stop is Howard Theater in Washington. |
| **November 6** | George Romney, former president of American Motors and a moderate, pro–civil rights Republican, is elected governor of Michigan. |
| **November 9** | Ford Rotunda burns to the ground on the same day federal agents and Detroit police, under orders by Police Commissioner George Edwards, raid the gambling operation at the Gotham Hotel. |
| **Mid-November** | J. Walter Thompson advertising agency establishes a secret room known as the Tomb at its Buhl Building offices in Detroit to work on schemes to market a new Ford car that will become the Mustang. |
| **November 20** | Motown roadie Eddie McFarland is killed and trip manager Beans Bowles is severely injured in a traffic accident in Florida during *Motortown Revue* tour. |
| **December 31** | Motown artists Mary Wells, the Miracles, Little Stevie Wonder, Marvin Gaye, and the Marvelettes return to Detroit and perform at Michigan State Fairgrounds. |

## 1963

**January 1** In his New Year's Day message, Mayor Jerome Cavanagh declares 1962 "the year of Detroit's rebirth" and promises the momentum will be carried into 1963.

**January 5** Police Commissioner Edwards breaks the story linking Detroit Lions football star Alex Karras and a few teammates to the Party Bus and local mobsters Tony and Vito Giacalone.

**January 6** LBJ visits Detroit to mark the hundredth anniversary of the Emancipation Proclamation.

**January 11** *Life* magazine runs a feature spread on the auto boom, "Glow from Detroit."

**Mid-January** Ford Division general manager Lee Iacocca guides J. Walter Thompson executives into a top-security styling room in Dearborn to show them a model of what eventually will be named the Mustang. At this early stage they start working on a marketing campaign calling the model a Torino.

**February 15** Detroit Olympic Committee mobilizes to hold off an attempt by Los Angeles to strip Detroit of its nomination as the U.S. candidate for the 1968 Summer Olympics.

**February 20** A report released by sociologists at Wayne State University predicts that Detroit will lose one quarter of its 1960 population by the end of the decade. The report finds that productive taxpayers are leaving the city, "leaving behind the nonproductive."

**February 22** Motown releases "Come and Get These Memories" by Martha and the Vandellas, a song that captures the Motown sound.

**March 17** Rev. C. L. Franklin, Aretha's father, moves his New Bethel Baptist Church congregation to new quarters on Linwood Avenue, ending the wandering that began with urban renewal demolition of the old church on Hastings Street.

**March 19** U.S. Olympic Committee turns back L.A.'s attempt to preempt Detroit and reaffirms its support of Detroit's bid for the 1968 Summer Olympics.

**April 20** Martin Luther King is released from Birmingham jail after protests there. From Detroit, Walter Reuther and the United Auto Workers provide much of the money to win the release of King and his supporters.

**May 17** Reverend Franklin and others form the Detroit Council for Human Rights and begin planning a rally in support of Martin Luther King and the southern civil rights movement.

**June 11** The Kennedy administration confronts George Wallace, governor of Alabama, at the schoolhouse door and forces the integration of the University of Alabama. That night JFK delivers a nationally televised speech unveiling his civil rights legislation. Hours later Medgar Evers, NAACP field secretary in Mississippi, is assassinated.

**June 22** Reuther joins King and other civil rights leaders at a meeting in the Oval Office with JFK regarding plans for protest marches that summer. That same day, back in Detroit, Police Commissioner Edwards announces the arrest of mobster Tony Giacalone on bribery charges.

**June 23** King, Reverend Franklin, Mayor Cavanagh, and Walter Reuther lead a Walk to Freedom with more than 100,000 citizens down Woodward Avenue to Cobo Hall, where King delivers a version of the "I Have a Dream" speech that will become famous two months later.

**June 29** Governor Romney, who missed the Walk to Freedom because as a Mormon he does not work on Sundays, joins an open-housing protest march in Grosse Pointe, the elite suburb east of the city.

**July 5** Detroit prostitute Cynthia Scott, known as St. Cynthia, is shot and killed by Detroit police early in the morning near the corner of John R and Brush, setting off a hot summer of protest over police treatment of black citizens and undermining Commissioner Edwards's two-year effort to improve relations between his department and the African American community.

**August 2** Work crews haul debris from the site where the Gotham Hotel has just been demolished. John White, the owner, is on his way to prison on gambling charges.

**August 5** Berry Gordy concludes contract negotiations with Martin Luther King and the Southern Christian Leadership Conference for permission to sell an album recording of his speech in Detroit.

**August 28** King delivers his "I Have a Dream" speech at the end of the March on Washington. Reuther also speaks at the historic rally. Berry Gordy, realizing the Washington version has overtaken the Detroit version of King's speech, begins the process of turning it into an album.

**September 10** International Olympic Committee president Avery Brundage comes to Detroit, the city of his birth, and is courted by Detroit officials seeking 1968 Summer Games.

**October 8** Detroit Common Council defeats open-housing legislation.

**October 13** The Olympic torch arrives in Detroit after being carried by a relay of runners 2,600 miles from Los Angeles. Protesters angry at the defeat of open-housing legislation boo during the playing of the National Anthem at the arrival ceremony.

**October 16** Mayor Cavanagh and Governor Romney lead Detroit delegation to Baden-Baden, the resort town in West Germany where the IOC is meeting to select a site for the 1968 Olympics. They learn that IOC delegates have been sent letters from Detroit saying the city should not be picked because it did not play fair on open housing.

**October 18** IOC awards the 1968 Olympics to Mexico City. Detroit, once optimistic of winning, finishes a distant second.

**November 10** Malcolm X delivers his "Message to the Grassroots" at King Solomon Baptist Church in Detroit, criticizing King and other mainstream civil rights leaders. During the same week C. L. Franklin stages a Negro Summit Leadership Conference that is shunned by most of Detroit's black Baptist preachers.

**November 16** Motown presents its full *Motortown Revue* to sellout crowds at the Fox Theater, with Smokey Robinson and the Miracles closing each show with a raucous version of "Mickey's Monkey." That same week, the Flame Show Bar, Detroit's premier black music club, closes after being targeted for demolition in the name of urban renewal.

**November 22** President Kennedy is assassinated in Dallas.

**November 24** President Johnson calls Walter Reuther, who is in Washington for the funeral, at his Washington hotel room and says he needs his help.

**December 11** Former police commissioner Edwards is confirmed by the U.S. Senate for a seat on the federal bench.

**December 13** Blues singer Dinah Washington, wife of Lions defensive back Night Train Lane, dies of an overdose of pills at their Detroit home. Aretha Franklin sings at her memorial service at New Bethel Baptist.

## 1964

**January** Mayor Cavanagh is named one of the Outstanding Young Men in America by the U.S. Junior Chamber of Commerce. Talk begins that he might challenge Romney and run for governor. Romney, meanwhile, says he would consider seeking the Republican presidential nomination if people want him and that the policies of candidate Barry Goldwater would prove a long-term disaster for the party.

**March 5** Walter Buhl Ford III, nephew of Henry Ford II, drives a red Mustang convertible into downtown Detroit a month before the car is to be unveiled. Photos are published in the *Free Press*. Assembly-line production of Mustangs at Dearborn plant begins the following week.

**March 13** Motown's Mary Wells records "My Guy," written by Smokey Robinson, that takes her to the top of the charts, displacing the Beatles from the No. 1 position.

**April 13** Lee Iacocca unveils the Mustang at a press conference in the Ford Wonder Rotunda at the New York World's Fair, launching one of biggest marketing campaigns in history.

**April 17** The Mustang goes on sale across the country, setting sales records.

**April 22** New York World's Fair officially opens. Civil rights demonstrators attend fair, and a sit-down protest at the Ford pavilion prompts closing of the Magic Skyway ride.

**May 22** LBJ lands in Detroit, met by Mayor Cavanagh, George Romney, and Henry Ford II, who endorses him. After declaring the city "the herald of hope," the president travels to nearby Ann Arbor to deliver his "Great Society" speech at the University of Michigan commencement.

# NOTES

The narrative of this book was constructed from more than 120 interviews in Detroit, Los Angeles, Nashville, and Washington, D.C., and documents from the following archival sources:

Benson Ford Research Center, Dearborn, Michigan (BFRC)
Boston University, Howard Gotlieb Archival Research Center (BU)
Detroit Historical Museum (DHM)
Detroit Institute of Arts (DIA)
*Detroit News* Library (DN)
Detroit Public Library, Burton Historical Collection (BHC)
Detroit Public Library, E. Azalia Hackley Collection (EAH)
Duke University, Hartman Center for Sales, Advertising and Marketing History (HC)
John F. Kennedy Presidential Library, Boston (JFKL)
LA84 Foundation Library, Los Angeles (LA84)
LBJ Presidential Library, Austin, Texas (LBJL)
Library of Congress (LC)
Motown Museum (MM)
University of Michigan, Bentley Historical Library
Walter P. Reuther Library of Labor and Urban Affairs, Detroit

## Chapter1: Gone

1 The ninth of November: "Pleasant, Fair, Warmer," *Detroit News,* Nov. 9–10, 1962; "When Flames Consumed a Christmas Fantasy," *Detroit News,* June 12,

1996; *Detroit Free Press*, Nov. 9–10, 1962; Associated Press, Nov. 10, 1962; interview, Robert Ankony, Dec. 2013.

2 The Ford Rotunda was circular: Michigan in Pictures, Dec. 12, 2009; Ford Rotunda, File 1, BFRC; "Ford Rotunda, Glory and Tragedy," Automotive Mileposts, online.

2 Ankony . . . was fourteen in November 1962: Interviews, Robert Ankony, Dec. 2013, May 2014. Ankony said he started going downtown by himself when he was nine or ten. He would either walk or take the Baker bus and transfer to the Woodward bus north if he wanted to go to the Detroit Public Library or Detroit Institute of Arts.

4 Ankony's parents were Lebanese and French: Interview, Ankony. His grandparents on his mother's side moved from Lebanon to a small Arabic enclave in Hull, Quebec, at the turn of the century. His father's family came directly to Dearborn. His father was Muslim, his mother Presbyterian. "My mother was a great cook, and she cooked all the Arabic meals as well as pork. The names of Arabic meals are about the only words I know in Arabic as my mother was a proud American and would only speak Arabic with our aunts and uncles."

5 Roof repairmen since midmorning: Description of Rotunda fire drawn from AP, "Ford Rotunda, Big Draw for Tourists," Burns, Nov. 10, 1962; "Ford Rotunda, Glory and Tragedy," Automotive Mileposts, online; "Sift Mystery of Rotunda Fire," *Detroit News*, Nov. 10, 1962; "Rotunda Destroyed by $16-Million Fire," *Detroit Free Press*, Nov. 10, 1962; "Fire Had Too Big a Start for Dearborn Department," *Detroit Free Press*, Nov. 11, 1962; follow-up stories in *News* and *Free Press*, Nov. 11–20; Ford Rotunda file, BFRC; interview, Ankony.

7 The rest of Detroit was mourning: "Tears for the Rotunda," Mark Beltaire, the Town Crier, *Detroit Free Press*, Nov. 10, 1962. "How many will remember that in the 30s Fred Waring and the Lane Sisters played three shows a day as the Rotunda became more firmly implanted in the public mind?" Beltaire wrote.

9 The phone call finally came: Description of George Edwards's actions on the day of the Gotham Hotel raid from unpublished manuscript of Edwards autobiography, George Edwards Collection, Series III, Personal Papers 1961–63, Box 68, Reuther Library.

10 In its headline of the raid: "T-Men Hit Gotham Hotel Like Raging Football Team," *Michigan Chronicle*, Nov. 17, 1962.

10 To walk into the Gotham: Depiction of Gotham Hotel drawn from interviews, John Conyers Jr., David Williams, Berry Gordy, Nicholas Hood; also Borden, *Detroit's Paradise Valley*, 25–67.

12 Martin Luther King Jr. stayed at the Gotham: MLK Archive, BU, letters between King and White, Sept. 25, 1959. In his return letter, White told King that he had also placed copies of the book at the Phyllis Wheatley Home for Aged Women in Detroit.

13 And now here came those police: Drawn from accounts in *Detroit News*, Nov. 10–11, 1962; *Detroit Free Press*, Nov. 10–11, 1962; *Michigan Chronicle*, Nov. 17, 1962; and unpublished Edwards autobiography; also Stolberg, *Bridging the River of Hatred.*

## Chapter 2: Ask Not

17 Raymond Murray was stationed at the west entrance: Interview, Raymond Murray, November 2013. When Murray arrived at the DPD in 1962, he said, "Most of the veteran officers were World War II vets, and they emphasized safety above everything else they would teach you. I was trained by guys who were tail gunners on bombers, guys who parachuted into France during the Normandy invasion, and guys who fought at Iwo Jima, Bougainville, and Saipan. . . . I was enchanted by their stories."

17 With its 1,200 rooms: Ibbotson, *Detroit's Historic Hotels and Restaurants*, 48–49.

18 He had arrived the night before: Details of JFK's campaign visit drawn from *Detroit News*, Oct. 8, 1962; *Detroit Free Press*, Oct. 8, 1962; *Washington Post*, Oct. 8, 1962; *New York Times*, Oct. 8, 1962; interviews, Mark Cavanagh, Jack Casey, Raymond Murray.

21 Raymond Brennan, an engineer: JFK letter to Brennan, White House Central Subject Files, Box 979, JFKL.

22 Kennedy was much in demand: Detroit Auto Show papers, Box 7, File 8, BFRC. President Eisenhower had attended the show and spoke at Cobo Hall in 1960; Henry Ford Name File, JFKL.

23 In a telegram earlier that year: Letter to Charlotte Ford, Henry Ford Name File, JFKL. Telegram delivered April 3 1962: "% Henry Ford, Club 2, 2 West 52nd Street, New York City."

## Chapter 3: The Show

25 The Motor City had an intoxicating buzz: Szudarek, *The First Century of the Detroit Auto Show*, 179–181; Detroit Auto Show file, BFRC; *Detroit Free Press*, Oct. 18–19, 1962; *Detroit News*, Oct. 17–20, 1962.

27 Charlotte Ford later called her parents' relationship: Transcript of Charlotte Ford interview with David Halberstam, The Reckoning file, BU.

27 Anne was a patron of the arts: *Bulletin of the Detroit Institute of Arts*, 42, no. 3, Spring 1963.

28 He sounded just like LBJ: Transcript of Cal Beauregard interview with Halberstam, The Reckoning file, BU.

29 "We will re-live in Asia": HF2 press conference at AMA Inc. press luncheon, Oct. 19, 1962, File 9, Detroit Auto Show, BFRC.

31 Saturday it rained in Detroit: Description of auto show drawn from *Detroit News*, Oct. 20–28, 1962; *Detroit Free Press*, Oct. 20–28, 1962; Szudarek, *The First Century of the Detroit Auto Show*; Detroit Auto Show file 9, BFRC.

33 African Americans in Detroit were as attached: *Michigan Chronicle*, Oct. 20, 1962. Statistics also showed that Cadillac and Thunderbird were more popular proportionately among blacks than whites.

34 As Davis described it: Davis, *One Man's Way*, 20–24. One day, Davis said, he overheard a white salesman on the telephone say to a customer, "What color do you want? Black? We have them—black as a nigger's heel."

36 "President Has Cold, Halts Trip": *Washington Post*, Sunday, Oct. 21 1962; also Oct. 21 editions of *New York Times*, *Detroit News*, *Detroit Free Press*.

37 Once the big wheels: *Detroit Free Press*, Oct. 23, 1963.

38 Reuther was JFK's most frequent: Reuther Name file, White House Central Subject Files, Box 979, JFKL.

38 Mayor Cavanagh had prepared: Cavanagh Papers, Box 52, Reuther Library; also *Detroit Free Press*, Oct. 23, 1962.

## Chapter 4: West Grand Boulevard

42 Mrs. Edwards, her young charges: Interviews, Berry Gordy Jr., Allen Rawls, Robin Terry, Martha Reeves.

42 Roberta Wright, her close friend: Interview, Roberta Wright. Mrs. Wright was a spry nonagenarian when interviewed at the Charles Wright Museum of African American History in Detroit, founded by her late husband.

43 Their day of departure: *Washington Post*, Oct. 24, 1962; also *New York Times*, *Detroit News*, *Detroit Free Press*, Oct. 23–24, 1962; interviews, Berry Gordy Jr., Katherine Anderson Schaffner.

45 Soon after arriving in Detroit, Berry Sr.: Account of Gordy family drawn from interviews Berry Gordy Jr., Roberta Wright, Robin Terry, Harry T. Edwards; Gordy, *To Be Loved*.

45 The rats part was real: Interview, Berry Gordy Jr., Dec. 4, 2013. Gordy was inter-

viewed in the pool house of his elegant but not ostentatious mansion high in the Bel Air hills of Los Angeles.

49 Grinnell's was not just the dominant: Interviews, Dan Aldridge, David Williams, Berry Gordy Jr., Juan Carlos Hearn; also Dan Austin of HistoricDetroit.org on Grinnell Brothers Music House.

50 The Gordy family was among Detroit's piano multitudes: *Color*, June 1949. The subhead was "The Famous Gordys of Detroit Have What It Takes."

51 His sequence on the line: Interview, Berry Gordy Jr.

52 After the war, the jazz clubs: Drawn from Bjorn and Gallert, *Before Motown: A History of Jazz in Detroit*; Boland and Bond, *The Birth of the Detroit Sound*. Also Borden, *Detroit's Paradise Valley* "Found Michigan: Legends of Detroit Jazz," by Lars Bjorn, professor of sociology at University of Michigan, Dearborn.

53 In the fire song of Detroit: Interviews, Berry Gordy Jr., Dan Aldridge, John Conyers Jr., Paul Riser, David Williams; Borden, *Detroit's Paradise Valley*; Boland and Bond, *The Birth of the Detroit Sound*.

55 The loan that helped fund Motown: Loan document at Motown Museum; interview, Berry Gordy Jr.

56 The First Five, they called themselves: Interview, Janie Bradford. Bradford moved to Los Angeles with the Motown operation and still lives there. Through the years she has evolved into a version of Esther Edwards on the West Coast, a keeper of the Motown castle.

57 West Grand was the place to be: the *Hitsville Platter*, internal Motown newspaper. "It's What's in the Groove That Counts." Under the headline "Short Cut," one brief began, "Leave it to Smokey to find the means to the end."

59 When Harry was not in Ann Arbor: Interview, Hon. Harry T. Edwards. Judge Edwards was interviewed in his chambers at the U.S. Courthouse on Constitution Avenue in Washington. He had very little contact with his father, he said, until he was graduating from Cornell and deciding where to go to law school. "We then were somehow in touch when one of my mentors at Cornell suggested I ought to think about the University of Michigan. And [his father] said, 'Yeah, it's a great school, you really ought to come out.' I think we both saw it as a way we could get together and really know each other. . . . I really had no connection to Detroit then. I did not know my stepmother then. I did not know the Gordy family. That was my way in."

59 The decision to send Motown artists: Description of Motortown Revue drawn from interviews, Berry Gordy Jr., Martha Reeves, Janie Bradford, Katherine Anderson Schaffner; Gordy, *To Be Loved*; Love and Brown, *Blind Faith*; Ribowsky,

*Signed, Sealed and Delivered*; Robinson and Ritz, *Smokey: Inside My Life*; Whitall, *Women of Motown*.

64 Twenty years later these points of tension: *Michigan Chronicle*, Oct. 20, 1962; Sugrue, *The Origins of the Urban Crisis*.

64 The theaters where they performed were segregated: Interviews, Martha Reeves, Katherine Anderson Schaffner, Berry Gordy Jr.; Ribowsky, *Signed, Sealed and Delivered*; Posner, *Motown*; Whitall, *Women of Motown*.

66 Eleven days later: Interviews, Martha Reeves, Katherine Anderson Schaffner; *Michigan Chronicle*, Dec. 8, 1962. The *Chronicle* article ran more than two weeks after the accident. As far as could be determined, neither the *Free Press* nor the *News* covered the accident.

67 Smokey returned to the *Revue*: Robinson and Ritz, *Smokey: The Inside Story*.

68 "First of all, we grew up in Detroit": Account of when Smokey Robinson first encountered Ray Charles drawn from oral history of William "Smokey" Robinson conducted by Steve Rowland, Columbia University Libraries, Center for Oral Histories, June 3, 2008. "I think that the Miracles and I came in, fortunately, on the last legs of vaudeville, because we used to do shows and they were actually variety shows," Robinson said. "You know, when you go and see a concert nowadays, normally you're going to see either a band that's popular or some singers who are popular, and that's all you're going to see."

70 The temperatures in New York City: Interviews, Berry Gordy Jr., Martha Reeves, Katherine Anderson Schaffner; *Motortown Revue*, Vol. 1, *Recorded Live at the Apollo*.

70 In his last *Michigan Chronicle* column: *Michigan Chronicle*, Dec. 29, 1962. Ziggy had been talking to Aretha's manager, Ted White, whom she had just secretly married.

### Chapter 5: Party Bus

73 Here was the Lindell: Description drawn from photograph of Jimmy Butsicaris standing outside the old Lindell at Cass and Bagley, Reuther Library collection; "Amid Newfound Glory, Echoes of Old Detroit," *New York Times*, Oct. 8, 2012; "Lindell Hotel Bar, 1963, The Way It Was," *Hour Detroit*, March 2013.

74 the bar was attracting agents from the Federal Bureau of Investigation: *Detroit News*, Jan. 6, 1963; *Detroit Free Press*, Jan. 6–7 1963; Edwards unpublished autobiography, Reuther Library, Edwards Papers.

74 The Party Bus was the movable feast: Account of the Party Bus drawn from Edwards unpublished autobiography, Reuther Library; Stolberg, *Bridging the*

*River of Hatred; Detroit Free Press,* Jan. 9–10, 1963. One article described Lions "who lived in the openhanded, boozerunning world of Detroit gamblers."

77 He had arrived in Detroit in 1936: John Herling Archive, Reuther Library. Edwards wrote many letters to his friend Jack Herling, and also sent along speeches he had delivered. He said he took his first auto job for thirty-seven and a half cents an hour. George Edwards Archive, Reuther Library; Edwards unpublished autobiography, Reuther Library; Stolberg, *Bridging the River of Hate.*

77 They had ordered chop suey dinners: *Detroit News* Archive, six articles, April 1938.

78 The day after receiving the report: Account of how Detroit police dealt with mob connections to the Lions, and the commissioner's fears that something might happen to him, drawn from Edwards unpublished autobiography; *Detroit News* and *Detroit Free Press,* Dec. 25–Jan. 11, 1963; Stolberg, *Bridging the River of Hatred.*

## Chapter 6: Glow

85 When it came to his wardrobe: Drawn from interviews, Mark Cavanagh, Maurice Kelman, Bernie Klein, Bob Toohey, John P. Casey. Mark is Jerome Cavanagh's older son. The others worked in his administration.

86 "He was charming": Interview, Bob Toohey.

86 It was in that frame of mind: Cavanagh Papers, Boxes 103, 104, Reuther Library.

87 The political conventions seemed out of reach: Interview, John P. Casey.

87 Detroit seemed to have much going for it: Depiction of first meeting of Detroit Olympic Committee drawn from Cavanagh Papers, Boxes 103, 104, Reuther Library; Romney Papers, Box 34, Bentley Historical Library, University of Michigan; Brundage Papers, LA84; interview, John P. Casey; *Detroit News* and *Detroit Free Press,* Feb. 15–17, 1963.

89 Wayne State University's Institute for Regional and Urban Studies: "The Population Revolution in Detroit," Wayne State University, Feb. 1963; *Detroit Free Press,* Feb. 21, 1963.

92 Detroit dying and thriving at the same time. *Detroit Free Press,* Jan. 1, 1963.

93 Cavanagh's own momentum came to a sudden stop: Cavanagh Papers, Box 52, Reuther Library; *Detroit News* and *Detroit Free Press,* Jan. 2, 1963.

93 *Life* magazine hit the newsstands: *Life,* Jan. 11, 1963. The magazine cost twenty cents. More than half the full-page advertisements in the eighty-four-page issue were for automobiles, some shown in photographs, others in sensual night-lit full-color illustrations. In a sixties variation of "the rich get richer," the Imperial

ad for Chrysler was titled "A provocative challenge to directors of America's major corporations" and began, "In the next few days, you and the executive officers of your firm will be invited to accept new Imperials for personal comparison with your present cars."

95 Found on Road Dead: Interview, George Largay.

96 Detroit aglow and modern: Hill and Gallagher, *The American Institute of Architects Guide to Detroit Architecture.*

96 Over on East Grand, the House of Diggs: *Michigan Chronicle,* Nov. 3, 1962 and Jan. 25, 1963.

97 In the months since Berry Gordy Jr.: Interview, Berry Gordy; Gordy, *To Be Loved*; "Gordy Captures Record Awards," *Michigan Chronicle,* Feb. 2, 1963. "Since he turned out hits for Jackie Wilson when Wilson was starting his drive to fame seven years ago, Gordy is rated one of the nation's most prolific composers and since that time has over two dozen hits to his credit."

98 "Come and Get These Memories": Interviews, Martha Reeves, Janie Bradford, Berry Gordy Jr.; *The Complete Motown Singles,* Vol. 3, 1963. The excellent liner notes in this set were written by Craig Werner.

100 the music teachers and programs in the Detroit schools: Interviews, Martha Reeves, Paul Riser, David Williams, Berry Gordy Jr., Dan Aldridge, Allen Rawls.

103 "I walked up to the lobby": Interview, Martha Reeves.

104 The song's live premiere: *The Hitsville Platter,* Vol. 1, Motown file, EAH.

104 Los Angeles was the common enemy: Account of Detroit's victory over Los Angeles drawn from Cavanagh Papers, Box 103, 104, Reuther Library; Romney Papers, Bentley Historical Library, University of Michigan; Brundage Papers, LA84; *Los Angeles Times,* March 1–20, 1963, *Detroit News* and *Detroit Free Press,* March 1–20, 1963.

## Chapter 7: Motor City Mad Men

107 Four agency men from J. Walter Thompson: Colin Dawkins Papers, Box 9, J. Walter Thompson collection, HO.

107 J. Walter Thompson was one year short of its hundredth: *JWT News,* Dec. 4, 1964, Norman H. Strouse Papers, Box 1, J. Walter Thompson collection, HC.

108 Strouse brought vast experience dealing with Ford: Norman H. Strouse Papers, Box 1, J. Walter Thompson collection, HC

109 In developing its advertising plan for Ford: Norman H. Strouse Papers, Box 21, J. Walter Thompson collection, HC.

110 As the secret meeting in Dearborn: Colin Dawkins Papers, Box 9, J. Walter Thompson collection, HC.

111 The Detroit offices of J. Walter Thompson: Norman H. Strouse Papers, Box 1–3, J. Walter Thompson collection, HC.

112 This was William D. Laurie: Account of Bill Laurie at work and home drawn from Box MN1, J. Walter Thompson collection, Box MN1, HC; Norman H. Strouse papers, Box 1, J. Walter Thompson collection, HC; and interview, son David Laurie.

117 The forward planners had set up shop: Colin Dawkins Papers, Box 9, J. Walter Thompson collection, HC.

118 After a few false starts: Oral histories, Donald Frey, Henry Ford II, John Najjar, BFRC; Colin Dawkins Papers, Box 9, J. Walter Thompson collection, HC; Fria, *Mustang Genesis*; Clor, *The Mustang Dynasty*; Iacocca and Novak, *Iacocca: An Autobiography.*

## Chapter 8: The Pitch of His Hum

121 For the flock of New Bethel Baptist: *Michigan Chronicle*, March 1963.

122 C. L. Franklin, who had just turned forty-eight: Depiction of Rev. C. L. Franklin drawn from interviews, Nicholas Hood, Ronald Scott, Wendell Anthony, Dan Aldridge; transcript of oral history interview with Erma Franklin conducted by Nicholas Salvatore, Franklin collection, Bentley Historical Library; Salvatore, *Singing in a Strange Land*; Franklin, *Give Me This Mountain*; Ritz, *Respect.*

124 The interplay of story and storyteller: John R. Bryant theology thesis, Franklin Papers, Bentley Historical Library.

126 The makings of a united front: "Declaration of Detroit," Detroit NAACP, Box 24, Reuther Library; City of Detroit Inter-office Correspondence, to R. V. Marks, from J. C. Coles, May 22, 1963, Detroit Commission on Community Relations, Box 19, Reuther Library.

129 Franklin's preemptive bid: Detroit NAACP, Box 24, Reuther Library; "NAACP Opens Drive for 50,000 Members: A Gala Evening," *Michigan Chronicle*, April 4, 1963; "Call for 100,000 to Greet Dr. King," *Michigan Chronicle*, May 25, 1963; Salvatore, *Singing in a Strange Land.*

130 Johnson had been friends with King: Arthur L. Johnson oral history interview, Salvatore, Franklin Papers, Bentley Historical Library; Johnson, *Race and Remembrance.*

130 And once Cleage heard about attempts to constrain him: Albert B. Cleage Pa-

pers, Box 1, Bentley Historical Library; "Rev. Cleage, Zuber Blasts 'Old' Leaders," *Michigan Chronicle*, June 1, 1963.

131 As the contretemps continued: City of Detroit Inter-office Correspondence, Box 19, Reuther Library; "Franklin Denies Blast of Leaders," *Michigan Chronicle*, June 8, 1963; Salvatore, *Singing in a Strange Land*; Johnson, *Race and Remembrance*.

133 Then there was the sensitive matter of Walter Reuther: Oral history interviews, Horace Sheffield, Buddy Battle, Reuther Library; Marc Stepp interview, Franklin Papers, Bentley Historical Library; Salvatore, *Singing in a Strange Land*.

## Chapter 9: An Important Man

135 Walter Reuther spent much of his time: Reuther depiction drawn from Reuther Papers, Boxes 536, 577, 599, Reuther Library; and two first-rate books, Lichtenstein, *The Most Dangerous Man in Detroit*; Boyle, *The UAW and the Heyday of American Liberalism*.

137 Reuther's relationship with JFK: Reuther Papers, Box 367, Reuther Library; Reuther Name File, White House Central Subject File 979, JFKL.

139 Attorney General Robert Kennedy called Reuther: Boyle, *UAW and the Heyday of American Liberalism*; Lichtenstein, *The Most Dangerous Man in Detroit*.

140 Months after Birmingham, Reuther asked for: Reuther Papers, Box 577, File 14, Reuther Library.

141 That same day, thousands of miles away: Cavanagh Papers, Box 112, Reuther Library; transcript, JFK speech at Honolulu, June 9, 1963; JFK Library.

141 Two days later, on June 11: *New York Times*, June 12, 1963; *Washington Post*, June 12, 1963; Daily Diary of JFK, June 11, 1963, POF Box 44, JFKL.

142 For Reuther, the Evers assassination: Depiction of 1948 Reuther assassination attempt drawn from Frank Cormier Papers, JFKL; Dickmeyer, *Putting the World Together*; Lichtenstein, *The Most Dangerous Man in Detroit*; Reuther testimony before National Labor Relations Board trial examiner John T. Lindsay.

144 Eleven years later, after Reuther survived: Reuther Papers, Box 157, File 8, Security for Walter Reuther, Reuther Library.

145 The question was not power itself: Reuther Papers, Box 552, Reuther Library. "There is a tendency within the camp of unreconstructed conservatism to view democracy as a completed conquest, rather than as a continuing campaign," Reuther said. "There is too much complacency over past accomplishment, not enough awareness of present and emerging problems; too many Americans take refuge in a timid conformity which prevents our coming to grips with the

over-riding need to renew our basic principles in terms relevant to our time. We desperately need to see our society as it has become; to distinguish, in terms used by President Kennedy in his Yale address, between Myth and Reality."

146 Civil rights was not a new issue for Reuther: *Detroit News*, April 12, 1943.

146 "The cry for freedom": Reuther Papers, Box 536, Folder 12, Reuther Library.

147 As his brother Victor later recounted: Boyle, *The UAW and the Heyday of American Liberalism*; Frank Cormier Papers, JFKL.

147 On the Thursday evening of June 20: Jerome Cavanagh Papers, Box 112, Reuther Library. Among those in attendance was Mrs. Margaret Edwards, the wife of Police Commissioner George Edwards, representing the Episcopal Society for Cultural and Racial Unity.

148 Reuther was back in Washington: Depiction of June 22 meeting in Oval Office drawn from Lee C. White file POF 97, JFKL; Branch, *Parting the Waters*; Lichtenstein, *The Most Dangerous Man in Detroit*; Reuther diary, Reuther Library.

150 Mayor Cavanagh had returned from Hawaii: *Detroit News*, June 22, 1963; *Detroit Free Press*, June 22, 1963.

## Chapter 10: Home Juice

153 the gambling raid at the Gotham Hotel: John Herling Papers, Reuther Library; George Edwards unpublished autobiography, Edwards Papers, Reuther Library.

154 a classic underworld conversation: *Detroit Free Press*, June 23, 1963.

156 Giacalone lived in a redbrick palace: Depiction drawn from "Tony Giacalone Rules with Regal Flair," *Detroit Free Press*, Jan. 12, 1969; *Detroit Free Press*, Sept. 2, 1963; *Detroit News*, June 21, 1963; Stolberg, *Bridging the River of Hatred*.

157 Douglas was game: Transcript, Advisory Council of Judge's Speech, May 1963, John Herling Papers, Reuther Library.

158 "Well, you know what I mean": Stolberg, *Bridging the River of Hatred*.

159 In that speech Edwards also recalled how his father's last case: George Edwards Collection, Box 112, Reuther Library; Edwards unpublished autobiography, Reuther Library.

## Chapter 11: Eight Lanes Down Woodward

160 Police Commissioner Edwards went to the airport: Account of events at airport and hotel drawn from Edwards collection, Series III, Reuther Library; *Detroit Free Press*, June 24, 1963; *Detroit News*, June 24, 1963; Edwards unpublished biography, Edwards collection, Reuther Library.

164 Some people started singing "God Bless America": Account of the march down Woodward drawn from interviews, Nicholas Hood, Booker Moten, Ron Scott, Wendell Anthony, Hildy Best; Cavanagh Papers, Box 112, Reuther Library; Reuther Papers, Reuther Library; Detroit Commission on Community Relations, Box 12, Reuther Library; Detroit NAACP Papers, Box 24, Reuther Library; *Detroit News*, June 24, 1963; *Detroit Free Press*, June 24, 1963; *Michigan Chronicle*, June 29, 1963; transcript, Arthur Johnson oral history interview, Salvatore box, Bentley Historical Library; Johnson, *Race and Remembrance*; Stolberg, *Bridging the River of Hatred*.

### Chapter 12: Detroit Dreamed First

177 With every seat occupied: Account of events at Cobo Hall leading up to MLK's speech drawn from Detroit NAACP papers, Box 24, Official Program, Detroit Council for Human Rights, and Box 6 correspondence, Reuther Library; *Illustrated News* (undated); interviews, Nicholas Hood, Ron Scott, Booker Moten, Berry Gordy Jr., John Conyers Jr., Duke Faker; *Detroit News*, June 24, 1963; *Detroit Free Press*, June 24, 1963; *Michigan Chronicle*, June 29, 1963; Dickmeyer, *Putting the World Together*; Branch, *Parting the Waters*; Johnson, *Race and Remembrance*.

180 The call-and-response had begun: Recording of MLK's speech, "The Great March to Freedom, Rev. Martin Luther King Speaks," *Detroit Press*, June 23, 1963, Motown Record Corp., produced by Berry Gordy—juxtaposed with transcript of King's "I Have a Dream" speech, March on Washington, August 28, 1963; account of politics behind Washington speech from Jack Conway oral history, JFKL; Branch, P*arting the Waters*; Lichtenstein, *The Most Dangerous Man in Detroit*; Boyle, *The UAW and the Heyday of American Liberalism*.

187 Four days after the Walk to Freedom: Cavanagh Papers, Box 112, Reuther Library. Another sadly typical letter came from R. L. Garver: "Dear Mayor, I sure hope you won enough NAACP supporters to insure your reelection next time you are up. You sure lost a lot of white votes and some colored. I'm a 'damnyankee' but a staunch believer in segregation. . . . I know some mighty fine people in the colored race but not a one was present or took part in this day's folly. In fact they say it's only the colored and white trash that will have anything to do with it."

## Chapter 13: Heat Wave

189 The gray terra-cotta structure: *Michigan Chronicle*, July 6, 1963; HistoricDetroit .org, Dan Austin; "Woodward: Avenue of Escape," *Detroit News*, March 27, 2007; Whitall, *Women of Motown.*

190 "It was the most beautiful ballroom": Interview, Berry Gordy Jr.

191 The wonder of this record began: Interviews, Berry Gordy Jr., Paul Riser; Ribowsky, *Signed, Sealed and Delivered*, 86–90; *The Complete Motown Singles*, Vol. 3, 1963.

195 The structure of activities on West Grand Boulevard: Interviews, Berry Gordy Jr., Martha Reeves, Ed Wolfrum, Paul Riser, Janie Bradford; *Hitsville Platter*, Vol. 1, Detroit Public Library; Robinson and Ritz, *Smokey: Inside My Life.*

197 It propelled Martha and the Vandellas: Interviews, Martha Reeves, Berry Gordy Jr., Paul Riser; *The Complete Motown Singles*, Vol. 3, 1963.

197 At three on the morning of July 5: Account of Cynthia Scott shooting and responses of police and community drawn from *Detroit News* and *Detroit Free Press* coverage all of July; Edwards unpublished autobiography; *Michigan Chronicle*, July 20, 1963; Stolberg, *Bridging the River of Hatred*; Cleage's *Illustrated News*, n.d., summer 1963; interviews, former DPD officers John Tsampikou, Anthony Fierimonte, David Wright.

202 "As one who bears both the physical and psychological effects: Cavanagh papers, Box 112, Reuther Library, letter to Commissioner George Edwards, 1300 Beaubien, Detroit, Mich., from SCLC, Martin Luther King, 334 Auburn Ave NE Atlanta 3, Georgia, June 27, 1963. "Let me also thank you for the services of Lieutenant Harge," King wrote. "I was tremendously impressed with him. He represents the highest and best that can be found in a police officer."

## Chapter 14: The Vast Magnitude

205 . . . a fleet of sedans double-parked outside: Interview transcripts of David Lawrence, Holmes Brown, Halberstam Papers, BU.

206 On the second to last day of July: Cavanagh Papers, Box 98, Reuther Library, Files 27, 28.

208 This was the infected heart: Account of Henry Ford and anti-Semitism drawn from "The International Jew," *Dearborn Independent*, Vol. 2–4 (1920); Gelderman, *Henry Ford: The Wayward Capitalist*; Collier and Horowitz, *The Fords: An American Dynasty*; *New York Times*, Sept. 5, 1927; Logsdon, *Power, Ignorance and Anti-Semitism: Henry Ford and His War on Jews.*

210 "I started right out to change that": Henry Ford II oral history interviews with David Lewis, Apr. 14, 1980, Apr. 16, 1985, BFRC.

212 It was under Reuther and Henry Ford II: Lichtenstein, *The Most Dangerous Man in Detroit.*

213 One day in mid-July 1963: *Detroit News* archive, July 1963.

214 "We used to remark lightly": David W. Burke oral history interview by Sheldon Stern, Apr. 17, 1979, JFKL.

215 A stump speech that he delivered: Reuther Papers, Box 552, 599, Reuther Library.

216 "Three young men in dirty work clothes": Philip Levine, "Salt and Oil."

216 Steelworkers with fifteen years seniority: *Detroit News,* June 23, 1963. Asher Lauren, the newspaper's labor writer, wrote a column headlined "UAW Eyes Steel's 13-Week Vacations."

217 After arriving at Ford Motor Company: Iacocca and Novak, *Iacocca: An Autobiography*; Henry Ford II oral history interview with David Lewis, BFRC.

218 His philosophy was encapsulated in a speech: Lee A. Iacocca, "The Four Freedoms of Advertising," Conference Luncheon, October 26, 1965, Plaza Hotel, New York, Box FM 30, J. Walter Thompson Archive, HC.

218 "To fire up the enthusiasm": The Mustang story memo, Franklyn R. Thomas, JWT vice president, Colin Dawkins Papers, Box 9, J. Walter Thompson Archive, HC.

221 There is a story told by Walter Murphy: *Ward's Auto World,* May 1966.

221 "Frey, I'm tired of your fucking car: Oral history interview with Donald Frey, BFRC; Clor, *The Mustang Dynasty.*

### Chapter 15: Houses Divided

223 George Romney, hair slicked back: AP, June 29, 1963. The story ran across the country, including in Birmingham, Alabama, prompting hate mail.

224 The Grosse Pointe point system persisted: Sidney Fine, "Michigan and Housing Discrimination 1949–1968," *Michigan Historical Review,* Fall 1977; "Grosse Pointe Residents Condemn Anti-Jewish 'Point System,'" Jewish Telegraphic Agency, June 21, 1960.

224 As historian Geoffrey Kabaservice: Author of the insightful *Rule and Ruin: The Downfall of Moderation and the Destruction of the Republican Party.*

225 A memo from Charles M. Tucker: Romney Papers, Box 220, Bentley Historical Library. Among those Tucker singled out for replacement were Broadus N. Butler, the Wayne State professor and *Michigan Chronicle* columnist who had been a member of the Michigan Cultural Commission. The memo said Butler at-

tacked Romney and "should be replaced at all costs if possible. Repeat should be replaced." Minister Charles W. Butler, not related, was also targeted for replacement, with the memo noting that he "was one of sponsors of Rev. Martin Luther King to help get out Negro vote."

225 His first public appearance as governor: *Detroit News*, Jan. 4, 1963, *Detroit Free Press*, Jan. 4, 1963.

226 When President Kennedy delivered: Romney Papers, Box 29, Bentley Historical Library. Romney received a note back from White House aide Lee C. White saying "We appreciate receiving your support."

226 One of his early correspondents was E. V. Hogge: Romney Papers Box 29, Bentley Historical Library.

229 Now came reports that police: *Michigan Chronicle*, August 10, 1963. The article concluded, "The activity at the corner Monday was labeled abominable by citizens who called the *Chronicle*."

229 The larger purpose of the meeting: Detroit Commission on Community Relations, Box 19, Reuther Library.

230 A *Michigan Chronicle* reporter covering the convention: *Michigan Chronicle*, July 13, 1963.

232 Almost beyond dispute was the rising talent: *Michigan Chronicle*, August 31, 1963.

232 In the days and weeks after the Walk to Freedom: Account of Berry Gordy dealing with SCLC regarding MLK recording drawn from MLK Papers, BU, Box 79, folder 6; King Center Digital Library, MLK Library, Atlanta.

235 Reuther and the UAW played a more central role: Account of Reuther before and during March on Washington drawn from Reuther Papers, Box 577, Files 13–14, Reuther Library; Boyle, *The UAW and the Heyday of the American Liberalism*; Branch, *Parting the Waters*; Lichtenstein, *The Most Dangerous Man in Detroit*.

238 It did not take Berry Gordy long: MLK Papers, BU, Box 79.

240 The two local politicians, one white, one black: Common Council Papers, Box 79, file 15, Cavanagh Papers, Reuther Library; Open Housing, Box 112, File 24, Reuther Library; Community Relations File, Box 5, Reuther Library; Ravitz Papers, Reuther Library.

243 Roberson was black and blind: Open Housing, Box 112, File 28, Reuther Library, Report of Community Relations Commission from Field Division, to Richard V. Marks, Subject: Attempt of Raymond Roberson to rent an apartment in Seven-Mile Gratiot area.

243 Opponents of the Patrick-Ravitz bill: Open Housing, Box 112, File 24, Cavanagh Papers, Reuther Library. Cavanagh received a letter of support from Abraham F. Citron, Michigan Area director of the American Jewish Committee, who closed by writing, "More and more people are catching on to the idea that housing discrimination is only for the bigots, the brokers, the Birminghamers, and the birds."

245 "America does not deserve": Leaflet, Olympic File, Box 103, Cavanagh Papers, Reuther Library.

## Chapter 16: The Spirit of Detroit

247 Avery Brundage, president: Brundage file, LA84. August 28, 1963, to Mr. Avery Brundage, LaSalle Hotel, 10 North LaSalle Street, Chicago, Illinois. Cross's lawyerly buttering up included lines such as "From our long friendship, which I cherish"; Olympics, Box 103, Cavanagh Papers, Reuther Library.

249 Brundage arrived at 10:37: Olympics, Box 103, Cavanagh Papers, Reuther Library; Brundage file, LA84.

249 First stop on the Detroit tour: Account of Brundage in Detroit drawn from Brundage schedule, Detroit Olympic Committee, 322 Veterans Memorial Bldg., Sept. 6, 1963, LA84; Memo from Jack Tompkins, Brundage Papers, LA84.

251 An oversized hardback book: Jack Casey personal collection.

251 "I have just returned from Detroit": Brundage Papers, LA84.

253 This time the torch would be carried: Cavanagh Papers, Box 79, File 20, Olympics, press releases, Detroit Olympic Committee, Reuther Library. Contact was Cavanagh's press secretary, Jim Trainor. See also Brundage Papers, LA84.

254 On October 11, the morning the relay: Account of controversy involving Olympics rally drawn from Olympics, Box 79, Cavanagh Papers, Reuther Library; Romney Papers, Box 34, Bentley Historical Library; *Detroit News,* Oct. 14, 1963; *Detroit Free Press,* Oct. 14, 1963; *Michigan Chronicle,* Oct. 19, 1963.

256 Most of the official Detroit party: Account of the Detroit delegation in Baden-Baden drawn from Travel diary of Alfred R. Glancy, Charles F. Adams speech before Adcraft Club after the Baden-Baden loss, Box 103, Cavanagh Papers, Reuther Library; *Detroit News,* Oct. 12–23, 1963; *Detroit Free Press,* Oct. 12–23, 1963; Brundage Papers, LA84.

## Chapter 17: Smoke Rings

273 We don't want everything: *Illustrated News,* Oct. 28, 1963.

274 He called for unity among black activists: *Michigan Chronicle,* Nov. 16, 1963.

275 Detroit Red was one of his old nicknames: Malcolm X and Haley, *The Autobiography of Malcolm X*; Marable, *Malcolm X: A Life of Reinvention.*

276 "And when you and I here in Detroit": Transcript, "Message to the Grassroots," Nov. 10, 1963.

279 Ofield Dukes, who covered: *Michigan Chronicle,* Nov. 16, 1963.

281 The crowd started lining the sidewalk: *The Motortown Revue,* Motown Record Corp., 1964, produced by Wm. Stevenson, liner notes by Ronald Miller; *Michigan Chronicle,* Nov. 23, 1963; interviews, Martha Reeves, Janie Bradford.

## Chapter 18: Fallen

283 "it died without pomp or ceremony": *Michigan Chronicle,* Nov. 23, 1963.

284 Aretha Franklin was strolling: Franklin and Ritz, *Aretha: From these Roots.*

284 "Yes, son, I have my rosary": *Michigan Chronicle,* Nov. 30, 1963.

284 "Bobby, the president was killed!": Interview, Robert Ankony.

285 It was deer hunting season: Interview, Raymond Murray.

285 Berry Gordy was in his office: Interview, Berry Gordy Jr.; Gordy, *To Be Loved.*

286 Out at the Glass House: Details of presidential limousine from Henry Ford Museum, Dearborn, where the vehicle remains on display.

286 David Laurie, ten years old: Interview, David Laurie.

287 Walter Reuther's daughter: Dickmeyer, *Putting the World Together.*

287 Reuther had been planning to be in Washington: Account of Reuther in days after JFK assassination drawn from Reuther Papers, Box 368, Reuther Library.

289 Before delivering a strong civil rights speech: *Detroit News,* Jan. 5–6, 1963.

290 There was more than a hint of Hyannis Port: Interviews, Mark Cavanagh, Bob Toohey; Cavanagh Papers, Boxes 103, 104, Reuther Library.

290 "The American Tragedy of 1963": *Michigan Chronicle,* Nov. 30, 1963.

293 Early that Sunday afternoon, Earl Ruby: Jack Lessenberry, *Toledo Blade,* Sept. 28, 2003.

294 The day after watching Ruby shoot Oswald: *Detroit News,* Nov. 26, 1963.

294 George Edwards was in Washington: George Edwards unpublished autobiography, Edwards Papers, Reuther Library; Stolberg, *Bridging the River of Hatred; Detroit News,* Nov. 21–22, 1963.

296 The clubs of Detroit were uncharacteristically quiet: *Michigan Chronicle,* Nov. 30, 1963; interview, Berry Gordy Jr.

297 But Night Train Lane—that was a different matter: Doug Warren, "Black, White and Red All Over," Nov. 27, 2012; Dick "Night Train" Lane Official site; Dan

Holmes, "Clearing Up Some Confusion about 'Night Train' Lane and His Nickname," DetroitAthletic.com, Jan. 8, 2012; Neft, *The Football Encyclopedia.*

299 In early December Dinah returned: To Chief of Detectives, Death of Dinah Washington Lane, 37 N, 4002 Buena Vista, phone 933-1908 (married), DPD; *Michigan Chronicle,* Jan. 4, 1964.

### Chapter 19: Big Old Waterboats

303 Johnson was doing most of the talking: Transcript of LBJ conversation with McNamara, Jan. 25, 1964, Beschloss, from *Taking Charge: The Johnson White House Tapes, 1963–64.*

304 "We've got to get going on civil rights": Transcript of LBJ conversation with Reuther, Dec. 23, 1963, in Beschloss, *Taking Charge.*

304 Before his first State of the Union: Lichtenstein, T*he Most Dangerous Man in Detroit.*

306 Out of these negative developments: Depiction of UAW proposal for joint small-car operation drawn from Reuther Papers, Box 368, Reuther Library: "Proposal to Reduce Balance of Payments and to Provide Employment for Displaced Studebaker Workers by Production of an All-American Car."

### Chapter 20: Unfinished Business

310 That story was published in the first: *Michigan Chronicle,* Jan. 5, 1964.

313 "Ah, it's a great life": *Detroit Free Press,* Jan. 11, 1964.

314 In his New Year's address: *Detroit Free Press,* Jan. 1, 1964.

315 "I would be a stupid columnist": *Michigan Chronicle,* Dec. 29, 1963.

316 A few months before his fourteenth birthday: *Michigan Chronicle,* Jan. 11, 1964; Ribowsky, *Signed, Sealed and Delivered*; "Happy Street" lyrics: "Everybody come on yeah yeah clap your hands / ah hah yeah / Everybody come on yeah yeah clap your hands / Come on and clap your hands / Stomp your feet / Get with the rhythm of happy street / 'Cause that's my street, happy street."

317 In the year of unfinished business: *The Complete Motown Singles,* Vol. 4, 1964.

318 Dylan never actually uttered: Abrams, *Hype and Soul.*

318 The Supremes seemed to be everywhere: *Michigan Chronicle,* Jan. 11, 1964; interviews, Berry Gordy Jr., Janie Bradford; Ribowsky, *The Supremes.*

320 If he understood Johnson's concern: Reuther Papers, Box 368, Reuther Library; *Detroit Free Press,* Jan. 23, 1964. Gene Roberts Jr. covered UAW meeting in Chicago for the *Free Press.*

322 Two days later President Johnson: *Detroit Free Press,* March 23, 1964; *Detroit News,* March 23, 1964.

322 Paul Riser had been in the same class: Interview, Paul Riser. In later years with Motown, Riser emerged as an accomplished producer, creating, among other classics, Jimmy Ruffin's "What Becomes of the Brokenhearted?"

325 "Modest Mary Sinks the Beatles": Abrams, *Hype and Soul; Detroit News,* March 12, 1964; Christopher Petkanas, *T Magazine,* Nov. 23, 2010.

327 They were regarded as balladeers: Account of Four Tops drawn from interviews, Abdul (Duke) Fakir, Berry Gordy Jr., Dan Aldridge; *Four Tops Biography,* Rock and Roll Hall of Fame and Museum; *Beat Instrumental,* May 1970.

330 Among the words of wisdom: Interview, Berry Gordy Jr.; Michigan Chronicle, April 23, 1964.

332 The Conyers family roots: Interview, John Conyers Jr.; *Michigan Chronicle,* March 20, 1964.

335 He was deciding federal appeals court cases now: Stolberg, *Bridging the River of Hatred.*

336 When Hayden retired: Correspondence with Pete Waldmeir, former *Detroit News* columnist.

## Chapter 21: The Magic Skyway

337 At noon on March 7: *Detroit News,* March 8, 1964; *Detroit Free Press,* March 8–9, 1964.

339 Fred Olmsted, who covered the auto industry: *Detroit Free Press,* March 3, 1964. The story ran without Olmsted's byline in the B section above Mark Beltaire's "The Town Crier" column.

341 On the morning of March 9: *Detroit News,* March 10–April 20, 1964; Fria, *Mustang Genesis.*

342 As the manager of J. Walter Thompson's: Interview, David Laurie; J. Walter Thompson Papers, Box 2 cl, Duke University, HC.

344 They were in their early twenties: Interviews, Ray Chatelin, Jim Hartnett, Vincent Currie.

344 The name paid homage to the Ford Rotunda: *Official Guide,* New York World's Fair; *Ford Motor Company Guide to the New York World's Fair,* BFRC.

346 April was a momentous month: *Detroit News,* April 1–20, 1964; *Detroit Free Press,* April 1–20, 1964; *Time,* April 17, 1964; *Newsweek,* April 20, 1964; Iacocca and Novak, *Iacocca: An Autobiography*; Fria, *Mustang Genesis.*

348 Going young was the key: Remarks by L. A. Iacocca, Mustang National News

Conference, New York, April 13, 1964, Editorial Services Dept., Public Relations Staff, Central Office Building, Ford Motor Company.

348 A consumer contagion had taken hold: Colin Dawkins Papers, Box 9, J. Walter Thompson archive, Duke University, HC.

349 Two parallel tracks on the Magic Skyway: *Extravaganza of Fun*, Ford Motor Company brochure on Magic Skyway, Ford Motor Company; Samuel, *The End of Innocence.*

349 In the weeks before the official opening: Interviews, Ray Chatelin, Jim Hartnett, Vincent Currie.

350 It was cold and rainy: *New York Times*, April 23, 1964; *Detroit Free Press*, April 23, 1964; Samuel, *The End of Innocence*; Lyndon B. Johnson Remarks at the Opening of the New York World's Fair, The American Presidency Project, UC–Santa Barbara.

351 The integration of the fair itself: Account of protests on first day of World's Fair drawn from *Detroit Free Press*, April 23, 1964; *Detroit News*, April 23, 1964; *New York Times*, April 23, 1964; Samuel, *The End of Innocence*; *The New Yorker*, May 2, 1964; an excellent narrative by Tamar Jacoby; Someone Else's House: *America's Unfinished Struggle for Integration*, chapter 1; Brian J. Purnell, "Drive Awhile for Freedom: Brooklyn CORE and the 1964 World's Fair Stall-In," NYU; interviews, Vincent Currie, Jim Hartnett, Ray Chatelin.

352 The closing of the exhibit infuriated: Ford Motor Company, New York World's Fair, Box 14, File 1m, BFRC.

## Chapter 22: Upward to the Great Society

355 With about five weeks to prepare: Jerome P. Cavanagh oral history, LBJL, digital transcript.

356 The genesis of the visit: "The Anatomy of a Speech: Lyndon Johnson's Great Society Address," Michigan Historical Collections, Bulletin No. 28, Dec. 1978.

356 When Cavanagh got there: Jerome P. Cavanagh oral history, LBJL, digital transcript.

358 "Romney in GOP Race?": *Detroit News*, editorial, Jan. 8, 1964.

358 "Mr. Ford, what is your opinion": *Detroit Free Press*, May 23, 1964. The story was stripped across the top of the front page: "'I'll Vote for Johnson,' Says Henry Ford."

359 In Washington, Johnson was awakened: White House Daily Diary, May 22, 1964.

359 Behind the airport fence: *Detroit Free Press*, May 23, 1964; "The Anatomy of a

Speech"; Remarks upon Arrival at Metropolitan Airport in Detroit, May 22, 1964, Public Papers of the Presidents, Lyndon B. Johnson.

361 At 9:55, at the end: White House Daily Diary; *Detroit Free Press,* May 23, 1964; "The Anatomy of a Speech."

362 Nine paragraphs into his speech: Transcript from Public Papers of the Presidents of the United States, Lyndon B. Johnson, 1963–1964, Book I, 704–707.

364 As the commencement ceremony drew to a close: *Detroit Free Press,* May 23, 1964; "The Anatomy of a Speech"; White House Daily Diary, May 22, 1964.

365 It all looked so promising: Jerome P. Cavanagh oral history, LBJL, digital transcript. That Sunday, May 24, the *Free Press* ran an editorial about the "Great Society" speech that mixed praise with concern: "Mr. Johnson has adopted whole heartedly the liberalism of his predecessor. The accent will continue to be on big government, with Washington taking the leadership in the attacks on poverty, pollution, and poor education, if not doing the whole job. . . . Some of the ideas for the Great Society frighten more than inspire . . . but it was a beautiful day, and a fine commencement address."

# SELECTED BIBLIOGRAPHY

Abrams, Al. *Hype and Soul.* Lilleshall, Shropshire, U.K.: Templestreet, 2011.

Babson, Steve. *Working Detroit.* New York: Adama Books, 1984.

Barnard, John. *Walter Reuther and the Rise of the Auto Workers.* Boston: Little, Brown, 1983.

Benjaminson, Peter. *Mary Wells.* Chicago: Chicago Review Press, 2011.

Beschloss, Michael, *Taking Charge: The Johnson White House Tapes.* New York: Simon & Schuster, 1998.

Bjorn, Lars, and Jim Gallert. *Before Motown: A History of Jazz in Detroit.* Ann Arbor: University of Michigan Press, 2001.

Boland, S. R., and Marilyn Bond. *The Birth of the Detroit Sound.* Charleston, S.C.: Arcadia, 2002.

Borden, Ernest H. *Detroit's Paradise Valley.* Charleston, S.C.: Arcadia, 2003.

Boyle, Kevin. *The UAW and the Heyday of American Liberalism.* Ithaca, N.Y.: Cornell University Press, 1995.

Branch, Taylor. *Parting the Waters: America in the King years.* New York: Simon & Schuster, 1988.

Brinkley, Douglas. *Wheels for the World: Henry Ford, His Company, and a Century of Progress.* New York: Viking, 2003.

Bucci, Federico. *Albert Kahn: Architect of Ford.* Princeton, N.J.: Princeton Architectural Press, 2002.

Clor, John M. *The Mustang Dynasty.* San Francisco: Chronicle Books, 2007.

Collier, Peter and Horowitz. *The Fords.* New York: Summit Books, 1982.

Connell, Ann Garity. *The Lawyers' Committee for Civil Rights Under Law.* Chicago: LC-CRUL, 2003.

Davis, Ed. *One Man's Way.* Detroit: Edward Davis, 1979.

Dickmeyer, Elizabeth Reuther. *Putting the World Together.* Lake Orion, Mich.: Living Force, 2004.

Early, Gerald. *One Nation Under a Groove.* Hopewell, N.J.: Echo Press, 1995.

Eugenides, Jeffrey. *Middlesex*. New York: Farrar, Straus & Giroux, 2002.

Franklin, Aretha, and David Ritz. *Aretha: From These Roots*. New York: Villard, 1999.

Franklin, C. L. *Give Me This Mountain: Selected Sermons*. Urbana: University of Illinois Press, 1989.

Fria, Robert A. *Mustang Genesis*. Jefferson, N.C.: McFarland, 2010.

Garofalo, Reebee. *Rockin' Out*. Boston: Allyn & Bacon, 1997.

Gavrilovich, Peter, and Bill McGraw, *The Detroit Almanac*. Detroit: *Detroit Free Press*, 2001.

George, Nelson. *Where Did Our Love Go?* New York: St. Martin's Press, 1985.

Goldstein, Laurence, ed. "Detroit: An American City." Special Issue of *Michigan Quarterly Review*. Spring 1986.

Goodwin, Richard N. *Remembering America*. Boston: Little, Brown, 1988.

Gordy, Berry. *To Be Loved*. New York: Warner Books, 1994.

Gould, Jean, and Lorena Hickok. *Walter Reuther: Labor's Rugged Individualist*. New York: Dodd, Mead, 1972.

Halberstam, David. *The Reckoning*. New York: William Morrow, 1986.

Hall, Peter. *Cities in Civilization*. London: Weidenfeld & Nicolson, 1998.

Heilbut, Anthony. *The Fan Who Knew Too Much*. New York: Knopf, 2012.

Hill, Eric J., and John Gallagher. *The American Institute of Architects Guide to Detroit Architecture*. Detroit: Wayne State University Press, 2003.

Iacocca, Lee, and William Novak. *Iacocca: An Autobiography*. New York: Bantam Books, 1984.

Ibbotson, Patricia. *Detroit's Historic Hotels and Restaurants*. Charleston, S.C.: Arcadia, 2007.

Ingrassia, Paul, and Joseph B. White. *Comeback: The Fall and Rise of the American Automobile Industry*. New York: Simon & Schuster, 1994.

Jarvis, Donna. *Detroit Police Department*. Charleston, S.C.: Arcadia, 2008.

Johnson, Arthur L. *Race and Remembrance*. Detroit: Wayne State University Press, 2008.

Kabaservice, Geoffrey. *Rule and Ruin: The Downfall of Moderation and Destruction of the Republican Party*. New York: Oxford University Press, 2012.

Latzman Moon, Elaine. *Untold Tales, Unsung Heroes*. Detroit: Wayne State University Press, 1994.

Leithauser, Brad. *The Art Student's War*. New York: Knopf, 2009.

Lichtenstein, Nelson. *The Most Dangerous Man in Detroit*. New York: Basic Books, 1995.

Love, Dennis, and Stacy Brown. *Blind Faith*. New York: Simon & Schuster, 2002.

Malcolm X and Alex Haley. *The Autobiography of Malcolm X*. London: Penguin Books, 1965.

Marable, Manning. *Malcolm X: A Life of Reinvention*. New York: Penguin Books, 2011.

Martelle, Scott. *Detroit (A Biography)*. Chicago: Chicago Review Press, 2012.

Morgan, Robin, and Ariel Leve. *1963: The Year of Revolution*. New York: It Books, 2013.

Posner, Gerald. *Motown*. New York: Random House, 2002.

Reuther, Victor G. *The Brothers Reuther*. Boston: Houghton Mifflin, 1976.

Reuther, Walter P. *Selected Papers*. New York: Macmillan, 1961.

Ribowsky, Mark. *Signed, Sealed, and Delivered*. Hoboken, N.J.: John Wiley, 2010.

———. *The Supremes*. Cambridge, Mass.: Da Capo Press, 2009.

Ritz, David. *Respect: The Life of Aretha Franklin*. New York: Little, Brown, 2014.

Robinson, Smokey, with David Ritz. *Smokey: Inside My Life*. New York: McGraw-Hill, 1989.

Ryan, Jack. *Recollections: The Detroit Years*. Whitmore Lake, Toronto: Glendower Media, 2012.

Salvatore, Nick. *Singing in a Strange Land*. New York: Little, Brown, 2005.

Samuel, Lawrence R. *The End of Innocence: The 1964–65 New York World's Fair*. Syracuse: Syracuse University Press, 2007.

Smith, Suzanne E. *Dancing in the Street*. Cambridge, Mass.: Harvard University Press, 1999.

Stolberg, Mary M. *Bridging the River of Hatred*. Detroit: Wayne State University Press, 1998.

Sugrue, Thomas J. *The Origins of the Urban Crisis*. Princeton, N.J.: Princeton University Press, 1996.

Szudarek, Robert. *The First Century of the Detroit Auto Show*. Troy, Mich.: Society of Automotive Engineers, 1999.

Tyler, R. L. *Walter Reuther*. Grand Rapids, Mich.: William B. Eerdmans, 1973.

Voyles, Ken, and Mary Rodrique. *The Detroit Athletic Club*. Charleston, S.C.: History Press, 2012.

Waller, Don. *The Motown Story*. New York: Charles Scribner's Sons, 1985.

Ward, Brian. *Just My Soul Responding*. Berkeley: University of California Press, 1998.

Whitall, Susan. *Women of Motown*. New York: Avon Books, 1998.

Widick, J. J. *Detroit: City of Race and Class Violence*. Detroit: Wayne State University Press, 1972.

# ACKNOWLEDGMENTS

**DURING MY LIFE** and writing career I have been lucky to work with many great editors. The first were my mother and father, Elliott and Mary Maraniss. Then came Dick Harwood at the *Trenton Times*; Len Downie, Bob Woodward, and Bob Kaiser at the *Washington Post*; and Alice Mayhew at Simon & Schuster. Another editor who influenced my life died at age ninety-three the same week I finished the manuscript of this book. There will never be another Ben Bradlee, not even close. His search for truth, unafraid yet joyful, is something I will not forget. A few months earlier, after the paper I love was acquired by an outsider, Don Graham moved his offices from the *Post* Building on 15th Street and his niece left as the *Post*'s publisher, ending the era of the family newspaper. I worked my entire adult life for the Grahams and consider Don Graham the greatest boss ever. I cannot thank him enough for all the support and advice he provided over many decades. Whatever happens with the *Post*, good or bad, it will never be the same.

All of our friends in Madison and Washington and far-flung places once again provided a wonderful support system for Linda and me during the years I worked on this latest writing obsession. This is the eleventh book for which Alice has been my editor and Rafe Sagalyn my agent, and I could not ask for a finer tandem. Thanks to everyone else at Simon & Schuster and the *Washington Post*, my inspiring and embracing home courts, and to my new pals and colleagues at Vanderbilt University.

My time in Detroit doing research was made more productive and meaningful with the help of Jon Wolman, editor of the *Detroit News*, an old Madison buddy and fellow second-generation journalist. I'm also grateful to Detroiters Tom Stanton of the University of Detroit, Mercy; Allen Rawls and Robin Terry at the Motown Museum; Mike Smith and Mary Wallace at the Reuther Library; Romie Minor at the Detroit Public Library; and Danielle Kaltz at the *Detroit News* library; as well as Bob Ankony, Mark Cavanagh, Bob Toohey, Matt Lee, Maurice Kelman, Jack Casey, and the friendly staff at the Inn on Ferry Street. My way into the world of Motown was eased with the gracious assistance of Harry T. Edwards, chief judge emeritus on the U.S. Court of Appeals for the D.C. Circuit, who happens to be the stepson of the late Esther Gordy Edwards, older sister of Berry Gordy. My path into the subculture of Detroit law enforcement was paved by Ron Fournier, a fellow Washington political journalist who grew up in Detroit, the proud son of a DPD cop. Fournier and Wolman were also generous enough to serve as early readers of the manuscript. I am indebted to the archivists at the Benson Ford Research Center and the Bentley Historical Library in nearby Dearborn and Ann Arbor.

I rank librarians and archivists near the top with nurses and teachers in my personal hierarchy of Good Samaritans. Along with those mentioned from Detroit, I am also grateful to the staffs at the John F. Kennedy Presidential Library, the Boston University Howard Gotlieb Archival Research Center, the Duke University Hartman Center for Sales, Advertising, and Marketing History, the University of Wisconsin Library, and the LA84 Foundation. In the year before her death, Jean Halberstam, widow of David Halberstam, one of my writing heroes, eagerly allowed me access to his papers at Boston University, including raw notes he accumulated for *The Reckoning*, his powerful book on the Detroit auto industry of a later period. A special thanks to Gabrielle Banks, John Pulice, John U. Bacon, and Andy Cohn for at various times helping me accumulate and sift through thousands of documents, and to Sheila Weller for sending me one.

My main editor always, along with being researcher, photographer, videographer, publicist, and friend-maker, is my wife, Linda, who was with me every step of the way with this book as with all the others before it. From Green Bay to Rome, from Nairobi to San Juan, from Ho Chi Minh City to Detroit, she has made wherever we are feel like home. She loves

Motown as much as I do and never complained about the rollicking sounds pounding full blast out of my office as I wrote. *My Girl,* always. Andrew and Alison with Eliza and Charlie in Nashville; Sarah and Tom with Heidi and Ava in Lawrenceville, New Jersey—this is the family that makes every day worthwhile, the human miracle that somehow arose from those summer nights in 1949 when Linda and I came into the world. I don't know if it's true or not, but I like to believe the story that my dad took my older brother and sister to a Tigers game at Briggs Stadium the day I was born, once in a great city, in Detroit.

# INDEX

# PHOTO CREDITS

© H. Armstrong Roberts/Classicstock: 1

Courtesy of the *Detroit News*: 2, 4, 5, 8, 15, 17, 20, 21, 22, 23, 24, 30, 33

Courtesy of the Ankony family album: 3

Courtesy of the Walter P. Reuther Library, Archives of Labor and Urban Affairs, Wayne State University: 6, 26, 27, 28, 29

Courtesy of the Tony Spina Collection, Walter P. Reuther Library, Archives of Labor and Urban Affairs, Wayne State University: 10, 14, 25, 34

Courtesy of the Detroit Public Library: 7, 16, 18, 19

Courtesy of the Cavanagh family album: 9

Courtesy of the Associated Press: 11

Courtesy of the *Washington Post*: 12, 13

Courtesy of the Laurie family album: 31

Courtesy of the Benson Ford archive: 32

# ABOUT THE AUTHOR

David Maraniss is an associate editor at the *Washington Post* and the author of six critically acclaimed best-selling books about history, politics, and sports. Among the most honored writers and journalists of his generation, Maraniss won the 1993 Pulitzer Prize for National Reporting for his reportage on Bill Clinton, was part of a *Post* team that won the 2008 Pulitzer Prize for coverage of the Virginia Tech tragedy, and has been a Pulitzer finalist twice more for his journalism and once in history for *They Marched into Sunlight.* A fellow of the Society of American Historians, Maraniss was born in Detroit and grew up in Madison, Wisconsin. He lives in Washington, D.C., and Madison with his wife, Linda. They have two grown children and four grandchildren.

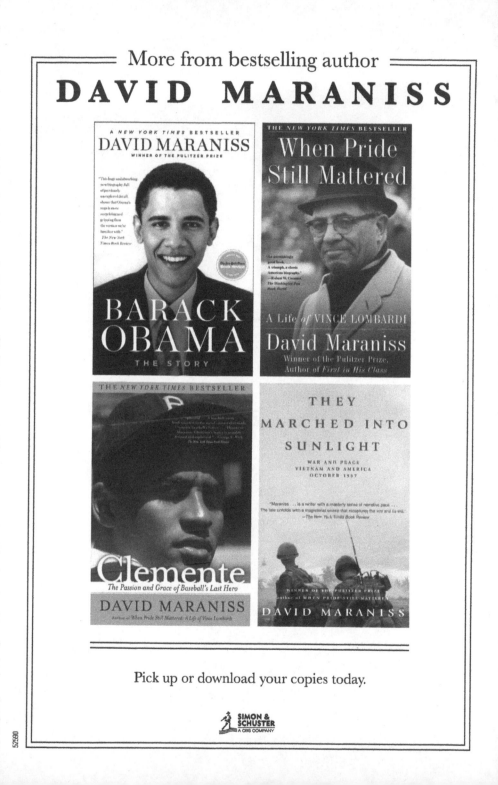